Babylon Girls

BABYLON GIRLS

GIRLS

BLACK WOMEN PERFORMERS

AND THE

SHAPING OF THE MODERN

JAYNA BROWN

DUKE UNIVERSITY PRESS

DURHAM AND LONDON 2008

© 2008 Duke University Press
All rights reserved.
Printed in the
United States of America
on acid-free paper ∞

Designed by Jennifer Hill
Typeset in Warnock Pro
by Tseng Information Systems, Inc.

Library of Congress
Cataloging-in-Publication Data
appear on the last printed
page of this book.

TO TYSON, SIMONE, AND HAZEL

⟶ CONTENTS ⟶

Matt
17 Highgate #10
Boston, MA
02134

Preparation for this book began while I was on my junior year abroad at the University of Sheffield. I was passionately awakened when the young lecturer Tim Armstrong introduced me to Marxist and feminist theory. That was part of my development; the other source of my inspiration came at night, boogying in the dance clubs of Sheffield, the private dj parties held in the basement of the housing estates, and the Hacienda in Manchester. The worlds I lived in didn't mingle, but my work comes out of where they met. Returning to California the next year, I took courses with Angela Davis in the women's studies department at San Francisco State University. Davis was beginning to write about blues women, and in a class called "Wild Women in the Whirlwind" she introduced me to the work of Hazel Carby. That was it. I knew I had found my way. One of the most important moments of my life was a few years later: when working with Hazel Carby as a graduate student at Yale University, I had the honor of introducing Professors Davis and Carby at the Women Defending Our Name conference in 1993. I thank them both for demonstrating to me what an active intellectual commitment to social change can look like.

I have many people to thank for helping me to make this book happen. I am grateful to Paul Gilroy for his intellectual breadth and generosity, his creativity, and his bibliographic knowledge. As my principal advisors at Yale, Professors Carby and Gilroy gave me continued guidance and friendship. Joseph Roach and Michael Denning read this work in dissertation form and gave me excellent criticism. Candace Allen, St. Clair Bourne, David Krasner, and Michelle Wallace kindly shared the results of their archival research with me. Daphne Brooks and Sherrie Tucker were keenly attentive and insightful as my readers at Duke University Press. My editors Ken Wissoker and Courtney Berger have been fantastic to work with. Many thanks also to Jennifer Brody, Harry Elam, Sharon Holland, Matthew Jacobson, Emory Elliott, Jean-Christophe Agnew, Toby Miller, and Deborah Rosenfelt for their professional support.

I wouldn't have been able to write this book if it were not for the financial generosity of the Ford Foundation, which awarded me grants for my dissertation and postdoctoral work. The Ford Foundation has consistently offered substantive support for academics of color, and as a result has made possible at least a generation of excellent scholarship. I thank the Rockefeller Foundation for awarding me a postdoctoral fellowship, and the Stanford Humanities Center for hosting me in my fellowship year.

Many archivists helped me immeasurably in locating hard to find materials: Dan Morgenstern and Tad Herschorn at the Institute for Jazz Studies, Jeremy De Graw at Lincoln Center, New York Public Library, James Hatch and Camille Billops, and archivists at the Schomburg Center for Research in Black Culture, the Beinecke Library, the British Library, the Theatre Museum in London, and Getty Images. The archivists at the Jazzarkiv in Stockholm went out of their way in translating articles for me, and the private collectors in Sweden, including Ellis Igneby, were of particular assistance. Moa Matthis and Lena Ahlin translated materials from Danish and Swedish. I have lasting memories of the time I spent with Moa in Sweden, including our talk for the Young Socialists in Barnens Ö; we ate steaming sausages from a huge pot and I was given a case of knackerbröd in thanks.

I am lucky to share a kind friendship with Martin Summers. Over the years Martin made me dinner, lent me money, and spent many fun holidays with me. Karl Mundt laughed with me when I was glum. Lori Brooks and I wrote and graded papers together, and she very patiently taught me how to drive. At the University of Oregon Shari Huhndorf gave me crucial support as my department chair and as my friend. Tavia Nyong'o has been an invaluable friend and co-conspirator. Thank you all for sustaining me.

From Yale and beyond I thank Leigh Raiford, Rebecca Schreiber, Alyosha Goldstein, Eric Wright, Ivy Wilson, Anthony Foy, Jennifer Greeson, and Issa Diabate; at the University of Oregon, Lynn Fujiwara, Jeff Ostler, and Peggy Pascoe; at the University of California, Riverside, Dylan Rodriguez, Jodi Kim, Vorris Nunley, Scott Brooks, Anthea Kraut, Priya Srinivasan, and Melissa Blanco. I thank the members of the SoCal women of color writing group, and folks from the Black Performance Theory group. I give additional thanks to Martin Summers, Tavia Nyong'o, Dylan Rodriguez, Shari Huhndorf, and Jodi Kim for reading parts or all of this book in manuscript form.

My friends are my family, and I thank Katherine Mraz, Olga Montes, Kristin Bebelaar, Nkemdilim Ndefo, Astrud Castillo, Natalie Drillings, Michael Franti, Lulu Hagen, Kenly Warren, Elspeth McDougall, and Annabella Lwin. Big love to my long-time loyal sistren in the UK: Loo Howe, Claudine Eccleston, Kumari Salgado, and Julie Stewart. You have looked after me during some very trying times. I thank my sister Geneva Biggers, Tyson Stockton, Simone Biggers, Margaret, Frank, and Yvonne Thibodeau, my brothers Joel and Michael McKelvey, and their families for the unconditional love they continue to give me. And I thank Alan Karme for his irreverence, Cheryl Feldmann for her no-nonsense, Peter and Rufus for languorous afternoons in Elysian Park, and, last but not least, little Roxy.

BLMC   British Library, Music Collection

BR   Billy Rose Theatre Collection, New York Public Library

DC   Dance Collection, Billy Rose Theatre Collection,
New York Public Library

HAJC   Helen Armistead Johnson Collection, Schomburg Center
for Research in Black Culture, New York Public Library

IJS   Institute for Jazz Studies, Dana Library, Rutgers University,
Newark, New Jersey

JHCB   The James Hatch-Camille Billops Collection, New York City

JWJ   James Weldon Johnson Collection, Beinecke Rare Book and
Manuscript Library, Yale University

LC   Lincoln Center for the Performing Arts,
New York Public Library

KB   Kungligen Biblioteket, Stockholm

MC   Music Collection, Billy Rose Theatre Collection,
New York Public Library

NYPL   New York Public Library

SCB   Schomburg Center for Research in Black Culture,
New York Public Library

SNT   Scrapbooks of the Negro in the Theatre,
James Weldon Johnson Collection, Beinecke Rare Book
and Manuscript Library, Yale University

SVJD   Svenskt Visarkiv, Jazz Division, Stockholm

TML   London Theatre Museum Library

WNP   British Library, Westminster Branch, Newspapers
and Periodicals

This book is a cultural history of African American performance in the first half of the twentieth century. It charts an early genealogy of black female performance, with my central subjects women of the variety stage: the lesser-known performers Belle Davis, Stella Wiley, Ida Forsyne, and Valaida Snow; the better-known artists Ada Overton Walker, Josephine Baker, and Florence Mills; and two generations of black chorus line dancers, many of whom remain nameless. This is also a book about the ways ideas of the raced body were performed, navigated, and challenged. It is about the history of female minstrelsy and other forms of race mimicry, particularly early twentieth-century uses of black dance vocabularies, for performing race had everything to do with articulating the modern world. The book is about bodies and is shaped by territories, as the raced and gendered politics of space—the plantation, the stage, the street, the cabaret—organize my arguments throughout the book.

Like its topics, this book is unruly and willfully disobedient at times. The chapters do not offer linear, complete, and seamless biographies of their subjects. This book is not a "recovery" history; though it has a similar inclination, it is not designed to fill the gaps left in masculinist and/or white womanist theories. I hope to leave enough provoked and unanswered that further work gets done on performance, dance, and racialized bodies in resistance to oppressive social regimes.

My analysis is framed by four eras, or areas, of performance. The first, the focus of my first two chapters, is the small black children performers who toured Britain at the end of the nineteenth century and the beginning of the twentieth. In small troupes led by women singers, picaninny choruses signified the complex racial and sexual politics of plantation slavery and colonialism as well as the connections between these and other systems of labor and social oppression. The second era is opened by *The Creole Show* (1890). Staged in a period of U.S. imperial and industrial triumph, it was the first variety show to cast a large number of black women. Its satire linked the cultural economies of racialized sexual oppression at home to eroticized imperial conquest. The third era is opened in 1913 by *Darktown Follies*, which heralded the beginning of Harlem as a black cultural and social capital. Ethel Williams, the "little girl at the end of the chorus line" in this show, trained the Ziegfeld girls as well as Irene Castle: I show how the meanings of the black woman's body in motion were central to the anxieties and hopes imbedded in white ideas of the modern city space as well as in the politics of black cultural self-representation. As Harlem became a black cultural capital, the landmark black musical *Shuffle Along* (1921) marked the symbolic, if not actual, invasion of what had become known as the Great White Way. *Shuffle Along*, and the shows that followed in its wake, mark the fourth era, as these shows also cast famous chorus lines of actresses, comediennes, and female musicians, choreographers, and singers. I contextualize the female casts in relation to literature and drama, European primitivisms and colonialism. This book is designed to unsettle assumptions about black cultural production; it reperiodizes how we think about black migration and self-fashioning (New York City in 1910; popular song and dance as well as literature). In the contexts of anti-slavery activism, U.S. and European imperial conquest, and urban development, this book resituates black transnationalism to include the Pacific as well as the Atlantic, Denmark as well as Paris. By focusing historically on black women performers and analytically on constructions of raced femininity, *Babylon Girls* demands that we ask new questions about cultures of the modern, and it unsettles the raced and gendered concepts used to legitimate these cultural and political terrains—the relationships between public and private, foreign and domestic, work and play, national belonging and citizenship, and writing and the expressive arts.

Since I began work on this project a true flowering of scholarship has appeared on performance theory, theater history, and dance.[1] Expressive cultural forms are now beginning to receive true critical attention in current interdisciplinary dialogues on performance, race, space, gender, and the body. This book hopes to contribute to these dialogues, offering a number of interventions. I challenge the male bias shaping earlier works on blackface minstrelsy and the formation of popular culture. Too often the creation of vernacular forms has been traced, and only considered legitimate, when produced from affairs between men.[2]

This masculinism is a problem and its consequences are grave, as it shapes the very fields we work within and questions we ask. In works of revisionist history and cultural theory the model figures of black diasporic creation are most often men: seventeenth- and eighteenth-century black male slaves, sailors, and rebels; nineteenth-century black nationalists and missionaries; twentieth-century expatriates and intellectuals. This does not mean historical accounts of women will not be there, but the terms of their presence will be shaped by the underlying assumption that men shape history. By considering how black women dancers, singers, and musicians worked and played on the trans-urban popular stages, this study challenges the tendency within studies of vernacular culture and its circulation to trace itself solely along the routes of male labor.

Looking to what these studies exorcise, this book poses some conceptual categories for understanding what I call racial mimicry. This refers to forms of race delineation, with and without cork, as enacted by white women. It includes the seventy or so years of women performing in blackface as Topsies; "shimmy" dancing of the 1910s; and the Charleston craze of the 1920s. Popular urban stages were key sites where changing notions of the self were given shape. "New women" embraced black expressive forms, adopting racialized gestural vocabularies to shape and redefine their own bodies as modern. Yet black women performers are seldom recognized as agents of these new physical vocabularies. I am critical of such gender studies that assume universal white subjecthood, and I argue throughout for a more supple language to discuss "cross-racial exchange" and racial borrowings between women performers.

I have shied away from writing a book that focuses solely on the long and fascinating history of white women in blackface. I have instead attempted to provide a more integrated study in which racialized subjects, black men and women, are part of the discussion of how and where race is performed and constructed. To focus solely on white uses of race is to reproduce what I am critical of here, which is a politics of power and access often underplayed in studies of white investments in black culture. How white womanhood is produced through these investments is part of the complex story I think through here, but I argue that to focus on white women performers would be to, yet again, evacuate the black body, to divorce ideas of blackness and their currency from those bodies and souls that lived as racialized subjects. Instead I struggle with the difficult connections between acts of race and lived race, which I believe should not be pulled apart in the service of providing a smooth, linear story.

I also question the ways official histories of jazz are constructed by distancing themselves from black women artists. Music developed in the spaces where black women often worked and played—brothels, jooks, parlor recitals, house parties—and jazz came from these spaces as much as it did from the all-male company of the military band. I am interested in the messy worlds of the cabaret, the nightclub, the variety stage, and the dance competition. These are places where dance, song, and improvisational comedy all together made "jass." And in these spaces music was always produced in conjunction with movement; it was connected to bodies. Canonizing male jazz instrumentalism required that it be extracted from, divorced from, this heterogeneous, sweating world.

THE BLACK VARIETY STAGE

Of these spaces I focus on the variety stage because I find it a fabulously raucous public sphere. In contrast with "legitimate" drama, which depended on continuous narrative and/or thematically controlled material, black revues were only loosely organized; acts often changing nightly. Emerging out of the minstrel era, these shows were made up of a rollicking number of skits, songs, sketches, and specialty acts. The revue's fluid structure allowed for quick-fire changes, impromptu additions, and spontaneous creative embellishments. Nancy Nenno writes, "Variety sketches worked more under the theory of montage, thus affirming the fragmented, stepped up pace of urban life."[3] The librettos of the early musical comedies were thinly plotted conceits designed to showcase the talented dancing and singing of the casts.

Most of the performers I look at were excluded from the white vaudeville circuits, and so throughout I refer to the stages where these black artists appeared as variety stages. Cultural forms traveled in and between the streets, the club and cabaret, the stage. Artistic expressions are developed in motion; they have no single originating site. I understand the urban variety stages as marking a crucial moment in the development of modern identities and pleasures. They were key sites at which black female urban presence was articulated and expressed, and they were important nodal points in the circulation of expressive forms. It is tempting to legitimate dance and theatrical practices at their most recognizable moments, as they appear on the variety stage or on film, but accepting their ephemerality requires that we resist thinking of the variety or "legitimate" stage as the place these forms needed to pass through in order to earn legitimacy. *Then how do we give them legitimacy?*

As many performance scholars affirm, performance is particularly slippery; shows and performance moments are never the same twice, and they are impossible to catch in words. Live performances are notoriously difficult to evaluate critically in terms of delivery or content.[4] Haunting any study of popular stage performance is the question of how to assess the critical faculties of artistic expression and the boundaries of those faculties. What can be considered artistic agency? What kinds of processes are inherent to the form itself? And what happens in spite of both? It is easier at certain moments to trust that the artists were explicitly engaged in acts of resistance and social criticism. At others, particularly when working with variety stage performance, for which "texts" vaporize instantly, it is impossible to prove in which directions the artists may have gestured. But some aspects of the revue form encourage a space of dialogic interchange and public critique. The fluid structure and mutability of the variety stage acts rejected the monologic narratives of the dramatic play. Different acts could break off from various shows, and re-form in other venues. Constant improvisation, versioning, and multi-signification were possible in this space.

Variety stage shows were comedies, and for later generations of black artists they became the signature for racist humiliation and self-denigration. What I emphasize in this study is that black laughter is a powerful form of criticism.[5] Black farce and satire, often smuggled in behind the wide white mouth, shine light on the fissures in hegemonic claims, revealing the ways hierarchies breed their own instabilities.

We are also freed up here by considering that acts signify on multiple levels to different audiences at the same time. The format of the variety revue poses particular opportunities to explore the malleable strategies developed by black performance women. Playing in the field of racialized fantasies was the "guileful ruse" of the black variety performer, and her stock and trade.[6] Black women stage performers negotiated the currencies that their bodies commanded on the world markets. Their artistic efforts were multi-signifying practices of dissemblance. Their performances must be understood as a "double operation," exploiting the spurious racialisms of their time as well as enabling a space for satirical comment on the absurdity of such depictions.[7]

I consider the question of audience as an indicator of artistic evaluation a bit differently here than do others. Black artists, performing in a culture of surveillance, always anticipate a white audience. Black artistry, forced to glance in many directions as it moves, is always already preparing for the eyes of white spectators. But that is not all the black artists prepare for. While the white gaze is always incorporated on some level and in some way, the scope, range, and rhythm of their artistry is not limited to the expectations of white spectatorship.

I suggest we allow these artists an interiority, to understand their agency as possible *through* their state of always looking at the self "as if through the eyes of others." The complex expressivities of black bodies in motion exist in and of and for themselves. Black artists looked at each other, performed for each other, and were looking at themselves always in the many mirrors they dressed themselves in. They looked with glee at their ingenious forms of bodily malapropism and disguise.

On the variety stage, racial and sexual inscriptions on the individual and social body were permeable. The core of the variety show was an ability to transmute the self. The variety of acts and their rapid procession acknowledged the often violent, often coercive process by which race, gender, and class were assigned. The swirl of racial and sexual signs on the stage was a dialogue on social-sexual taboos and the "open secret" of their transgression.[8] Legal and extralegal boundaries between categories could never be completely free of ambivalence; the variety stage was a designated site at which the porousness of the self, the way lines were already blurred, could be acknowledged and played upon. On the black variety stage, racial authenticity and gendered imitation, natural proclivity and skillful artifice frequently interchanged and remained ambiguous.

INTRODUCTION

I am not particularly interested in searching for racially authentic art forms. I argue instead that popular expressive forms resist purity. Expressive forms are inherently promiscuous, absorbing everything in their wake. They are contaminated from the minute they hit the air, and they refuse to be contained. With regard to dance and other expressive forms, gazing backward for originary moments of inception is a misguided project; with gestural vocabularies there are no beginnings, only continuations. As W. T. Lhamon states, gesture can never be owned, only exchanged.[9] But I do take seriously the ways in which expressive forms remain inflected by history, the way they carefully carry remembrances of past forms and fold them into the present. Exchange is not a word I take lightly, and this study interrogates the politics of gestural exchange, arguing that the politics were primarily shaped by the exploitative conditions under which black artists lived, even if at certain moments they reached toward affirming racial parity.

By looking at the ways work and play were blurred for black artists, this study contends that black women reclaimed their bodies *in*, as well as *from*, the world of work. The limited opportunities the so-called legitimate economies offered working-class black women impressed them into lives of service, menial and manual. Working black women's bodies were defined by their worth as exploitable labor. The very act of making money through the beauty, grace, and comedy of their bodies' talents reframed what could be produced by physical effort, by sweat and disciplined tenacity. Such production cannot be recovered as moments of pure resistance to oppression, but rather as a complex of often-times bald commercialism and a resilient striving for the body's creative autonomy. Their acts formed a complex offering to the various kinds of audiences they performed for. For European audiences and white audiences in the United States they offered nostalgic evocations of agrarian innocence, reassuring examples of a happy rural folk, and titillating forms of imagined contact with women from the colonies. For urban and rural African American audiences they brought forms of sly self-recognition and urban chic. Hovering throughout this study is the trope of the black female performer transforming herself in her place of work. Dancers such as Ida Forsyne recuperated the creative disobedience of the figure of the dancing Topsy as she frolicked before the glass in her mistress's best Canton shawl. Ethel Waters recalled that while she worked as a chambermaid, she would strut through the rooms of the apartments she was cleaning as the actress

1 Chorus girls from *Shuffle Along*. Billy T. Rose Theatre Collection, New York Public Library for the Performing Arts, Astor, Lenox, and Tilden Foundations.

she would become. These black women performers ragged the rhythms of work time into the ineffable qualities that give their signature to both the Jazz Age and the Swing Era (see fig. 1).

Troubling these pages is just how the creative artistry of a nation's most beleaguered and disenfranchised citizens came to represent that nation's most prized claims to freedom, equality, and opportunity. This contradiction forces us out of a search for national essences.

A SALTWATER VOYAGE

"Darktown is Desolate" reads an unidentified newspaper article from April 24, 1904. "High-toned Colored Folk of Williams and Walker Go Abroad, Sixty fun-makers sail on *Aurania*. Salt Tears shed at pier before the Elite of 'Coons' set out on salt water voyage." The performers setting a course for England that day in April were the second cast of Bert Williams's, George Walker's, and Ada Walker's successful play, *In Dahomey*, which had run from May until December of 1903 in London's Shaftesbury Theatre. Yet the reporter marvels, describing the travelers as "one of the strangest cargoes that America ever exported to England":

> When the steamship *Aurania* left port yesterday she carried one of the strangest cargoes that America ever exported to England. Bert Williams, George Walker and sixty other ebony funmakers were aboard, destined for London, where they expect to carry all before them as they did during their successful engagement in this city. The scenes at the dock were ludicrous to the extreme. For almost everyone in the company a salt water voyage was a distinct novelty, and each had prepared for it in a different way.[10]

This report's insistence that such a saltwater voyage was a "distinct novelty" to the members of this strange cargo is a complete fiction. In fact for many on board (they did not travel in the cargo hold on this journey) it was a return trip to Britain with the Williams and Walker Company. For others it was one in a series of journeys between the United States and Europe, before and after the run of *In Dahomey*. For some of the "ebony funmakers" this trip was a first run with the Williams and Walker Company, but those among them who hadn't yet been abroad had spent many years touring throughout the United States and had no doubt heard of other performers' experiences overseas.

It is not surprising that the report denies black people any mobility, except as exported commodity. There is much at stake in suppressing the ways African American expressive practices and cultural and political forms are constituted out of the geo-histories of movement. To acknowledge black people in voluntary transit runs the risk of affirming black people as world historical agents, rather than as a timeless people inextricably tied to the land and to a timeless past. To acknowledge even their status as traveling performers would be to acknowledge, at least partially, the threat of black dispersal. From the earliest moments of black people's dislocation throughout the diaspora, their expressive forms have circulated out of the ambivalent terms of "belonging," that is as *to* and not *in*, Europe and the Americas.

The anthropologist James Clifford insists that African American cultures are still in some ways exceptional to other cultures of the black diaspora. "They are not transnational or diasporic in the same way, or to the same degree," he writes.[11] "The specific experiences of plantation slavery, emancipation, South-North mobility, urbanization and race/ethnic relations have a regional, and indeed a national, focus that cannot be subsumed by an Atlanticist map/history of crossings."[12] With this assertion Clifford denies, in a manner inconsistent with his usual attentiveness, black transnational affiliations that may not show up on his definitional radar. His conditional naturalization of "nation" ignores the multi-focused movement of black people's conscious travel as well as the ripples of ideas and expressive art forms they created. I argue here that African American cultures, in historically specific ways, draw multiple lines of affiliation and are perhaps less circumscribed by national boundaries than Clifford implies. The lives of African Americans, and especially of African American performers, were inherently itinerant, as they often situated themselves as both of and in between nations, races, and civilizations.

Women, according to Clifford, are also "exceptions" to existing paradigms of travel and mobility, here a paradigm that assumes its normative subject to be the white bourgeois male traveler.[13] I agree as he suggests that "we need to know a great deal more about how women have traveled and currently travel, in different traditions and histories."[14] And here I do not mean white women; one of the reasons black female mobility has remained so invisible is that the normative category "women" continues to be rendered in white. In order to open up the cultural-historical record, we must not only consider how black women traveled, but recognize their modern presence in such a way that the rules that circumscribe them as "exceptions" are forced to change.

This study takes journeying black women not as exceptions, but as critical modern subjects, citizens of the world. Working black women could not always access pen and paper as did the white male explorers and adventurers whose exploits have become foundational histories. Nor have they been granted the kind of historical publicity garnered by black male artists and activists. But a number of narratives do exist that tell of black women's voyages. Most of these remain understudied, or at least not considered for what they say about movement and mobility. Nancy Prince wrote her narrative in 1853 not as a slave narrative but as a travelogue. Prince describes, with the "authority of cultural experience," the nine years she spent living in St. Petersburg, Russia with her husband, Nero Prince, who was an attendant to the czar.[15] She quite consciously writes in the style of contemporaneous travel books. But her narrative is shaped by several additional forms of itinerancy: the forced restlessness of poverty, transoceanic movement of labor, a missionary calling, and the continual possibility of re-enslavement.[16] Another understudied travel narrative is that of the free-born Jamaican Mary Seacole. Racism also informs her movement. Trained as a nurse, Seacole first sets up shop in Panama. She is then turned away when she attempts to volunteer with Florence Nightingale and her nurses during the Crimean War. Not to be discouraged, Seacole travels by herself to the Crimea. Seacole offers her report from the field: her experiences ministering to the British troops during the war; and her years as a "doctor" in the Panama region, fighting malaria and poverty-related diseases.[17] Her medical reports from the field are aware of themselves as an encroachment on white professional privilege. The Crimea and Panama are isthmuses, both strategically situated geographically at international crossroads, and at the time of Seacole's travels both were undergoing volatile historical transformation. I suspect that Seacole's choice to work in these precarious regions was not simply about demonstrating her devotion to the British crown, although she argues throughout the book for a proper pension on the grounds that she deserves recognition for her faithful service. Instead her motivation may have been her own adventurousness, her joy at being betwixt and between and beholden to no one.

Another tale that should be considered for the ways it is informed by movement and travel is Harriet Jacob's *Incidents in the Life of a Slave Girl*, now one of the most often read black fugitive slave narratives thanks to dedicated feminist recovery work. This text is shaped by explicitly gendered tropes of immobility and mobility. In her harrowing account, Jacobs contrasts the soul-confining institution of sexual concubinage, the seven years of torturous physical confinement in the crawlspace of an attic, with her escape and exile to London. Even after she is "safe" she seems unable to shed her restlessness, and she neither mothers well nor marries.[18]

The working woman Juanita Harrison fulfilled her goal to travel around the world; between 1926 and 1935 she lived in twenty-two countries in Asia and Europe, and she titles the narrative of her remarkable travels *My Great Wide Beautiful World*.[19] She traveled solo, staying at YMCAS and small boarding houses in Edinburgh, Palestine, Egypt, Istanbul, Bombay; when she needed money she would pick up work as a domestic or ladies' maid. Harrison prided herself on being a "true Rover," with a latitude between worlds no middle-class man or woman could enjoy (126). She gloats often over her mobility—as she swims in the Dead Sea and sleeps outside under the stars in Belgium—continually contrasting her own freedom of movement and unfettered exploration with the class and caste confinement she sees the upper- and middle-class women of various countries experience. "I have learned that the high castes would like very much to walk and save their Rickshaus fare like I do but of course their caste won't allow it," she writes from India. "I enjoy teaseing the Girls and ask if they Wish to be free like me to go out in the street at any hour . . . now they wish to be like me" (101). She describes the many pleasurable chance meetings, intellectual exchanges, and friendships she enjoys in her travels, and she pointedly emphasizes the moments of mutual recognition between herself and other working women around the world.

It is the feeling of being "betwixt and between" that she enjoys, and she likens her own protean abilities to slip between worlds with ease to work on the stage. "I like being in a country and yet feel I am of another at the same time," she writes (27). To be between states and cultures is the aim of her journeys. "11:30 pm. In route to Calcutta," she writes. "A Burma Lady said to me at Darjeeling you are just betwixt and between. One minute you have a fine time with the lowest caste next minute with the highest Hindoo. One minute you wear a blue suit next minute a dress of 2 cent a yard crape then a little velvet dress with diamond earrings how can we tell" (141). Harrison, like a true stage performer, gleefully employs costumes. On route to Bombay, she writes, "In my red shawl and black veil on my head no one would think I had seen Broadway" (112). For her such abilities are a crafty navigation, as she is traveling with little money or protection of any kind. "I am willing to be what ever I can get the best treatments at being," she writes. "I am the poorest girl that ever traveled alone. I have a very Oriental looking scarf I ware most of the time on my head everyone think I am Arabian but are puzzled to see me with such a short french dress and the first thing they ask my friend If I am Arabian then when I ware my little French cap they take me for Jewish," she writes from Jerusalem (75).

Harrison concludes her travels in Hawaii. With the proceeds from her narrative, published in the *Atlantic Monthly*, she purchases a seafront lot in Waikiki and has a seven by seven foot tent built for her. For a dollar, she has a hard floor built inside, "good and light so I can carry it on my head when I want to move," she writes (317).

The women performers in this study were all quite familiar with the politics of costuming, as well as with frequent saltwater voyages. A longer history of black women's travel literature would include those I have mentioned as well as the narratives left by black women performers, such as the memoirs of Laura Bowman. With her husband and friends, Bowman was a member of both the first and second casts of *In Dahomey*. Her trip to Britain in 1904 was a return journey. Bowman and her husband were not aboard the *Aurania*; they sailed on a small Cunard Line vessel named the *Anchoria*, bringing seventy-two replacement cast members with them. They sailed into Glasgow; Bowman vividly describes the journey up the Clyde River to her amanuensis. "I knew all the ways and customs now . . . I'll tell the truth. I was more excited than I had been on our first trip. Perhaps it was because I knew more what to expect," she states.[20]

Movements and migrations, forced and/or voluntary, structure African American cultural expression and historical narrative. The specific histories of their oppression, their resistance, their music, words, and songs have traveled, with or without them, around the world and have been a part of shaping what diaspora has meant to black peoples. I prefer another suggestion from Clifford, that these "practices of displacement might emerge as *constitutive* of cultural meanings rather than as their simple transfer or extension."[21] This suggestion opens up our understandings of black culture in a mobile context.

THE BLACK BODY IN MOTION

As it developed around the concept of mobility, *Babylon Girls* became very much a study of black vernacular dance (see fig. 2). Dance as a topical field has been theoretically underdeveloped until fairly recently because vernacular dance has been dismissed as subordinate to music, or at best an accompaniment to it, although many musicians have acknowledged dance as co-constitutive. As well as being elided from studies of music, dance gets lost from those analyses of cultural production that are based in semiotic models. Studies that prioritize aural vocabularies or literature miss what is important about "bodies in motion."

The body has been the subject of theoretical scrutiny for the ways in

2   Josephine Baker. Postcard. Beinecke Rare Book and Manuscript Library, Yale University.

which it is marked by categories of identity formation. But with a herme-
neutic model these bodies are understood as two dimensional, still, non-
moving. "Critical work on the body is focused more on representations of
the body and/or discursive policing than with its actions/ movements as
a 'text' themselves," the dance theorist Jane Desmond explains. "The aca-
demies' aversion to the material body, as well as the fictive separation of
mental and physical production has rendered humanities scholarship that
investigates the mute dancing body nearly invisible."[22] I add to Desmond's
salient critique that the many works that do consider dance and women
remain anemic on race and black dancers. They either focus on the histories of ballet and modern dance, the "classic" European stage dance forms,
rather than the social dance forms from which they were derived, or on
the social activities of white, working-class women, with black dance and
other so-called primitive dances furnishing only sometimes inspirational
illustrations of folk technique.

Recognizing artistic tenets and agency in black music and song, a number of scholars have established that there are always multiple meanings encoded in these forms. Claims to freedom and calls for social revolution, spiritual love, and fleshly bliss are layered within them. But it is only recently that scholars have begun to recognize dance as also layered and multiply coded. It seems to me that the body is a fundamental location to look for forms of response to regimes that are, in the first instance, based on very fleshly practices of violence and physical coercion.

Different sites of dance production, the where and the when, inform the meaning of the movements, but I argue emphatically that black movement is always multiply signifying. This means that the same dance phrase can be read differently by different people, depending on the place and the time. It also means that there is never a clear-cut teleological relation between the composition of an audience and the meaning of a particular performance.

My interest is in black popular and social dances for the ways they resist containment but hold history. They continually change, as people respond to new environments. At the same time as dances work to record and share experience, they also are ephemerally about the moment they come out of. Studies of dance have focused on the ways practices from Africa are retained in modern forms. But I argue that there are no pure, authentic, recoverable moments of a time-free Africanicity capable of restoring the body (solo, collective) to wholeness. Nor is there a single identifiable point of a dance's origins. Dance is a means for communication, forming new communities, remembering, and cultivating cultures. But as well as considering what it preserves, recovers, and retains, I am interested in what it picks up along the way. Popular dance offers wonderful heterogeneity and contradiction. Forms can be immediately commercialized, yet they are incapable of being owned. They are by definition public and collective, yet they can also be intensely private, articulations of a bodily interiority.

My study is based in the premise that working understandings of the social and individual body, formed in response to previous historical moments, can never be restored. What was spoken with the flesh was sometimes nostalgia for what had been lost but was not a fantasy of return. Instead, the protean resilience of black vernacular dance composition was formed out of the modern conditions of disorientation, dislocation, and alienation. Yet contingent moments of communality were continually being created. Analyzing such performance moments recognizes the fluidity of communal formation as its main contingency, that the processes by which community could be created demand a complex of unities.

In this study I explore the ways in which the most profane of black dance forms—those dances developed between the street, the club, and the popular stage—offer a particular perspective on modernity and the formation of urban cultures. A resituated examination of the dance practices developed between black people as they moved restlessly through the modernizing urban spaces reveals the multi-timed terrains out of and inside of which these modern black subjects formed themselves. For black people, dancing was an analogous creative response to shared and individual experiences of dislocation and relocation, itinerancy, and the fraught negotiations of claiming a geographical space to call home.

The experiences of race and place in the modernizing world were sensorial phenomena, negotiated by bodies in motion. In the age of electricity and machines, the human body in its various motor capacities became the form through which the modern was designed. Dance was the lexicon reflecting the dialectic process of modern transformation: the modern body continually reinventing itself, in and against its environment, at the same time as the environment made its claims upon the body. The capitalist innovations of Taylor and Ford were based on specific strategies for the use of the workers' bodies, concerned with training the workers' hands, feet, and eyes to a mechanized efficiency. In dances of the modern age, "The body is rethought as an assemblage of parts. . . . The movements most expressive of modernity incarnate fragmentation, repetition and velocity into the human figure, but the figure is only a synecdoche, a part for the whole."[23] Modern bodies in motion were fragmentary, the new ground from which they sprang a shifting terrain.

The fragmentation of the body occurs as a trope for the experience of modernity, and it was articulated in many forms of popular dance throughout the early twentieth century. The trope houses the relationship between the potentially lethal and potentially freeing effects of progress on the human spirit and body. The emergence of the chorus girl formations embodied this dialectic between industrial capitalism's disciplinary claims on the (white) body's time and energies and the potential freedom and pleasures technological innovation was making possible in the urban environment. As explored in chapter 5, black expressive forms, miscoded as signatures for a timed and timeless past and separated from actual black subjects, were used as the source by which the modern (white) body could re-member itself.

In exploring the multi-timed prerogative of black expressions, I consider black performance women in a critique of modernity. As Kevin Mumford's analysis of the historical records kept on urban prostitution attests, African American women were rarely seen at all in relation to the development of urban cultures.[24] Not seen, yet forced to view herself "as if from the eyes of others," black women experienced a double consciousness that is a salient place from which to intervene on this critical absence.[25] Yet their bodies and beings have been traversed, surveilled, excluded, and claimed in multiple ways, from many directions. The theoretical framework of double consciousness may prove insufficient to account for black women's relationship to racial and national belonging. Black women have had to create forms of consciousness and resistance against a plethora of strategies that have barred them from inclusion in both dominant and resistant collective political-cultural bodies.

Taking to the stage was to embrace this condition of complete spectacularization. Considering the African American woman performer, working in and between cities and nations, invites the appropriation of the Benjaminian concept of the person in the street whose perception is formed by "glances in all directions."[26] This concept is key here and recurs throughout the chapters. The artists' talent was her agile ability to navigate between and manipulate discursive terrains. Engaged in multiple directional strategies of perception, working within the hall of mirrors, the black female *flâneur* occupied a privileged vantage point from which to view the world. As she is gazed upon, she also gazes back, and it is her body that questions.[27]

"LITTLE BLACK ME":
THE TOURING PICANINNY CHORUSES

getting af ams
Natl
exposure

"WE SAW MORE OF BRITAIN
THAN MOST BRITONS"

On June 5, 1901, the S.S. *St. Paul* sailed out of New York
Harbor bound for Southampton, England. On board
was Belle Davis, a young mezzo-soprano from the black
variety stage, who was booked on a tour of Britain's Empire music
hall theaters. The twenty-seven-year-old singer was already a veteran of the stage, beginning her career in 1890 as one of the illus-
trious teenaged chorus girls in the Chicago revue *The Creole Show*.
This was also not her first overseas tour; she had gone to Britain in
1897 with the revue *Oriental America*, one of several shows that
was staged after *The Creole Show*'s success. But this was her first
trip touring the overseas circuits with her own specialty act. Like
other chanteuse, Davis was now accompanied by her very own
"picaninny chorus." On board with her that day were two boys—
seven-year-old Fernandes "Sonny" Jones and nine-year-old Irving
"Sneeze" Williams—traveling with Davis as the core members of
her troupe (see fig. 3). Their first booking was a North London
music hall; Davis, billed as "America's Greatest Coon Cantatrice
of the Century," was to be "assisted by her two Picaninny Actors."[1]
Over the next few years Belle Davis and Her Picaninnies worked
on the Empire circuit of music halls. Davis, Sonny, and Sneeze
were to "[see] more of Britain than most Britons" as they traveled
throughout England, Scotland, Wales, and Ireland.[2]

With other black acts, Belle Davis and Her Picaninnies also
entertained audiences in continental Europe. They toured Britain

3 "Miss Belle Davis and Her Pickchicks," Fernandes "Sonny" Jones and Irving "Sneeze" Williams, from *Variety Theatre*, circa 1905. Rainer Lotz collection. Used with permission.

during the fall and winter seasons and then spent the summers performing in various European cities, including Paris, Vienna, Prague, Berlin, St. Petersburg, and Copenhagen. Black specialty acts packed European and British music halls over the turn of the century, but the act of Davis, Jones, and Williams was among the most successful. In January 1902, they recorded for Gramaphone Records in London, and in 1906 they appeared in a short film in Paris. Black variety acts, particularly dance, remained in demand. Davis continued to tour variety circuits throughout the Austro-Hungarian Empire, Germany, Russia, and the Netherlands with various casts of children until 1917, years after Sonny and Sneeze had left the troupe. Neither Davis nor the boys returned to the United States on a permanent basis. Through the Great War and after, they remained in Europe with many other African American performers. In the 1920s they were based in Paris, there to greet a second generation of black performers to the overseas city circuits.

This book begins with a chapter that considers the histories of picaninny choruses, singer-led troupes of black children performers in Britain and Europe during the 1900s and 1910s. Most of the artists in this book began performing as small children, dancing and singing with touring companies, shows, and choruses, traveling the informal circuits of tent shows and fairs in the United States and then popular stages abroad. These children were talented dancers and developed dance techniques that would influence later dance phraseologies of eccentric, tap, and chorus line dancing. "The Charleston originated with the Picaninnies," Florence Mills states, who herself began performing at three years old.[3] Their antics gave us the convention of the "mischievous girl at the end of the line," of particular importance for this study of black women variety performers, as this is a convention later given signature by the (teenaged) performers Ethel Williams and then Josephine Baker.

Casts of African American children performers grew up on trains and boats, in cafes, clubs, and performance halls, receiving their artistic training from more seasoned performers. Their experiences were not mediated by the institution of family in the sense that we think of it; their time and training were not regulated by the school, church, or factory bell. The boundaries of nation did not contain them, as their transcontinental worldviews were formed within a loose circuitry of linked cities; London, Vienna, and St. Petersburg were as familiar to them as were Chicago and New York. These troupes were enthusiastically received by a number of audiences, composed of different class compositions. They danced something for everyone: working-class audiences in northern England, royalty in London, a growing class of the bourgeoisie in Prague. The acts of these small *flâneurs* presaged the trans-urban movement of later African American performers between cities in Europe and America.

To understand the cultural meaning of their acts, this chapter goes back in time, to a much earlier period of antebellum slavery. It reads their acts in relation to the circulating discourses of plantation slavery, civic freedom, and the laboring black body, and it argues that these earlier discourses profoundly shaped their significance, as well as their performance strategies. The children, as well as the young women who led the troupes, were working in and against a circulating commerce of black iconography, spun out of nineteenth-century discourses on race and black subjecthood in the United States, Great Britain, and Europe. Debates, assertions, and appeals of anti- and pro-slavery literature shaped these ideas. Competing claims about race were negotiated in and between these discourses, such as the educability and physiology of the Negro and the consequences of miscegenation. Christian missionary doctrine and treatises of natural science also informed common-sense notions on the constitution of raced bodies, which I focus on in chapter 2. Aided by new technologies of manufacture and transportation, these debates and discussions had been relayed with remarkable immediacy into popular culture.

This chapter is about how the picaninny choruses figured in relation to ideas of blackness and the laboring body circulating in slave-owning and then imperial Britain and Europe. Dialogues fostered between these earlier black anti-slavery activists, whose lectures were well attended and whose narratives were read vociferously, and organized labor in the United Kingdom informed the reception of the later picaninny performances in the cities and small towns of working-class England. The figure of the child had a specific resonance. Parallels were drawn by labor, in conversation with the black activists, between chattel and wage slavery, and particularly between the condition of the laboring child of Victorian industrial England and the slave child of the New World. That these parallels were drawn is important in our understanding of the black performers who toured later, as it keeps the black actors from being understood simply as icons, produced and controlled by the paternalism of the major abolitionist movement. Their presence was dialogic, invoking the complex conversations mentioned above.

Thinking about what these acts may have meant to audiences in Poland, Germany, and the Austro-Hungarian Empire, I suggest that the European currency of the black children performers was shaped first by racializing narratives from U.S. slavery and British colonization, but also in relation to specific sociopolitical conflicts and struggles in the regions of Europe where they were invited to perform. The reception of the artists and their creative choices were informed by the shifting class formations and ideological evocation of the folk in early European nationalist movements.

The dancer Ida Forsyne went to Britain with a picaninny troupe called the Tennessee Students, led by Abbie Mitchell. Forsyne did a star turn as "Topsy" in London and Budapest and then toured Eastern Europe for nine years from her base in St. Petersburg (see fig. 4). Her versions of both the cakewalk and the Cossaski gave audiences a symbol for Western imperial wealth and so-called democratic freedoms, but also referenced the growing uses of the folk in Europe, accompanying the relaxation of the feudal system and the rise of the nation-state. Serfs were emancipated in 1863,

4 Ida Forsyne as Topsy. Postcard sent from Budapest, 1914. Institute for Jazz Studies.

two years before the emancipation of slaves in the United States. Mid-century, Russian activists had drawn comparisons between the systems of serfdom and slavery in their arguments against systems of unfree labor. The cultures of those closest to the land took on new meanings in this moment, representing the people of the nation. These folk cultures, though, could also come to represent nostalgia for past hierarchical stabilities and an (imagined) pre-industrial peace. It is ironic that the most unfree populations from the center of the free world, black Americans, should come to represent the promises of the Enlightenment come to fruition. This is an irony that threads throughout this book.

PLANTATION TIME *New Orleans*

The term picaninny comes from *picayune*, a coin of small value circulating in the United States during the 1800s. The derivation of the term picaninny signals the interchangeability between the black child bodies and the small bits of money required for their acquisition. Not always purchased but often "made" on the plantation, they embodied the very public marketplace politics of sexualized subjection at the heart of the domestic sphere. Slave children were living currency. The picaninny was a key symbol of the conflation of sex and commerce, which defined the peculiar institution.

On the plantation, the domestic sphere of the home was fused with large-scale commercial concern. As Hortense Spillers eloquently points out, the private (home) and the public (marketplace) were "useless distinction[s]":

> Deeply embedded . . . in the heart of social arrangements, the "peculiar institution" elaborated "home and marketplace" as a useless distinction since, at any moment, and certainly 1850—the year of the Fugitive—the slave was as much property of the collusive state as he or she was the personal property of the slaveholder. We could say that slavery was, at once, the most public private institution *and* the ground for the institution's most terrifying intimacies, because fathers *could* and *did* sell their sons and daughters, under the allowance of *law* and the flag of a new nation, "conceived in liberty," and all the rest of it.[4]

U.S. plantation slavery disrupted communities and severed family ties, at the same time that it staged itself as a family romance. But in this system of "terrifying intimacies," master and slave relationships were figured as those of parent and child, as well as owner and saleable property. "The Children must be particularly attended to," a plantation record reads, "for rearing them is not only a duty, but also the most profitable part of plantation business."[5] The children, as the most private and miraculous expressions of family life, were the products of the most cruelly public of marketplace rituals. The figure of the picaninny symbolizes the convergence of the domestic and commercial at the heart of the American racial drama.

Perhaps the most apt imprint of the "terrifying conflation of sex and commerce," the slave plantation and the intimate histories it contains, sits on the back of the nickel, the modern picayune. Thomas Jefferson's massive slave plantation, Monticello, is engraved on the back of every five-cent piece, the small change that still circulates through millions of daily monetary transactions. Monticello is celebrated as a feat of architectural genius and serves as a symbol of colonial American nation building—practical, utilitarian, sensible, democratic. Jefferson himself designed Monticello and worked on it for over fifty years. His engineering and aesthetic innovations are said to "produce domestic democracy"; for instance, Monticello's biographer claims Jefferson's "simple stairway . . . demands [that] the meeting of those who are equal before the law be conducted on an egalitarian surface, level ground."[6] His claim, that the architecture demands a leveling of social hierarchy, is an obscenely absurd one considering that it was slaves who staffed the household. Like the dumbwaiters and the kitchen below level, the stairwells were designed for the discrete passage of unpaid labor. Monticello's ingenuity for hiding the slaves who lived within it is literally part of the blueprint of American architectural history. Notable also is Jefferson's bedchamber, which is fitted with a closed alcove for the bed itself, and with a stairwell leading to it. The movements of Sally Hemings through this "domestic democracy," as her mother had moved through her own master's plantation house, are the ghostlike imprints on the historical record, remaining profoundly unrecognized.

I think it useful to include Jefferson's plantation compound as a form of captivity equivalent to the camp, the prison, and the reservation. Including the "southern household" as a public space whose business was a traffic in "bare life" expands and decentralizes our concept of what constitutes "exemplary places of modern biopolitics."[7] Love was work in this model site of domestic democracy; and bodies for sale were created there, in its most private alcoves. It deserves emphasis that Jefferson's case was a well-known and often-used argument of both the abolitionists and black anti-slavery activists.

The family was the central trope and problematic in sentimental fictions, and the southern cotton plantation, as a peculiarly American "family," became the prime site at which the racio-sexual drama of chattel slavery unfolded. At the center was the capering black slave child, a key product of this drama. The mischievous and often unruly "picaninnies," grown on the plantation, would become long-standing stock characters of the popular press, the minstrel stage, and the music score.

Mid-century, ideas of the black child and the childlike races from abolitionist, Christian, and scientific discourses shaped the course and tactics of much sentimental fiction. Picaninnies were an integral part of the domestic space of the (imaginary) southern plantation. Unlike the primitive races Europeans were subduing in far away places, African Americans were internal colonial subjects, not only geographically, in the public spheres of nation and colony, but also within the "private" sphere of the home and family. Picaninny performers did not begin in *Uncle Tom's Cabin*, but they are markedly present in Harriet Beecher Stowe's text. The novel is opened by the forced cavorting of a small black child, Little Harry. In his act, prompted by his master in the interest of a sale, the popular stage is conflated with the auction block.

The fantasy of the plantation returns again and again in popular cultural forms well into the twentieth century. It does so because histories of plantation slavery (particularly large cotton plantations in the South) form the key topos in the nation's dialectic of racial formation. The staged plantation was a prime site of return. Traveling shows were often referred to as "plant shows," and, as I explore in chapter 4, the fictive plantation was the setting for inner-city spectacles at the turn of the century. Black dancers competed in huge Cakewalk Jubilees in New York City's Madison Square Garden, with black sporting celebrities such as Jack Johnson officiating at the proceedings. A stranger event was a summer-long plantation recreation called *Black America*, which was staged over the summer of 1894 in a Brooklyn city park. We begin and will return to the strange space of the plantation, but we will not remain there. Instead I will incorporate these returns into the larger questions of race and place which run throughout this book.

Not all literary renderings of black children were situated on the plantation, but most were associated with the beleaguered black laboring body, with dance, and with the stage. Herman Melville introduced his character Pippin, or Pip, in *Moby Dick*, published in 1851, the same year as *Uncle Tom's Cabin*. Pip is "the little Negro" among a fantastic collection of sailors from around the world working aboard the *Pequod*. He is introduced during a midnight frolic among the sailors on deck during the night watch; the frolic is part minstrel breakdown and part Shakespearian blank verse. "French Sailor: 'Hist, boys, let's have a jig or two before we ride to anchor . . . what say ye? . . . stand by all legs! Pip! Little Pip! hurrah with your tambourine!'"[8] The scene of music-making and tomfoolery between the sailors runs as a segment from a play within the larger novel. The jigging diminutive Pip participates in the seamen's breakdown on tambourine, dancing along with other sailors as they engage in racial punnery. The scene ends with an equally punning soliloquy from Pip. "Oh, thou big white God aloft there somewhere in yon darkness," he concludes his speech, "have mercy on this small black boy down here; preserve him from all men who have no bowels to feel fear!"[9]

Poor Pip is cast away at sea. Although he is eventually brought back in, Pip goes mad. His "brilliant" mind cannot find its way back to his body and he wanders the ship, looking for himself. Pip's fate is a poignant dramatization of the effects of severe alienation accompanying forms of unfree labor. "The sea had jeeringly kept his finite body up, but drowned the infinite of his soul."[10] In his final soliloquy Pip calls out to himself, "Pip! Pip! Ding, dong, ding! Who's seen Pip?" His demise is to remain profoundly dislocated as he imagines himself in the third person, from a distance; part dead and part alive, his "drowned bones now show white, for all the blackness of his living skin."[11]

Mid-nineteenth-century literary renderings of black dance are also situated in the city. The English writer Charles Dickens saw William Henry Lane, who was also known as "Juba," dance while visiting New York City in 1842. His depiction of Juba, in his travel journal *American Notes*, is an often-quoted passage, one of the most vital literary glimpses we have on black dance.[12] Dickens describes the impression Juba's dancing made on him:

> Single shuffle, double shuffle, cut and cross-cut; snapping his fingers, rolling his eyes, turning in his knees, presenting the backs of his legs in front,

spinning about on his toes and heels like nothing but the man's fingers on the tambourine; dancing with two left legs, two right legs, two wooden legs, two wire legs, two spring legs—all sorts of legs and no legs—what is this to him? And in what walk of life, or dance of life, does man ever get such stimulating applause as thunders about him, when, having danced his partner off her feet and himself too, he finishes by leaping gloriously on the bar counter, and calling for something to drink, with the chuckle of a million counterfeit Jim Crows, in one inimitable sound![13]

This enlivened performance takes place during Dickens's guided journey through the notorious Five Points district of Lower Manhattan, which he undertakes escorted by two policemen. The district is a center of "vice and misery" (138). Sinking into the muck and mire, his journey is a descent into the underground subliminal spaces of the city. His description of this squalid environment is like those found in his tales of urban poverty in Britain, but with important differences. Here, the residents are "Negroes," and his description of their living quarters is clearly evocative of a hold in a slave ship.

Ascend these pitch-dark stairs, heedful of a false footing on the trembling boards, and grope your way with me into this wolfish den, where neither ray of light nor breath of air, appears to come. A negro lad, startled from his sleep by the officer's voice . . . officiously bestirs himself to light a candle. . . . The match flickers . . . and shows great mounds of dusty rags upon the ground; then dies away and leaves a denser darkness . . . mounds of rags are seen to be astir, and rise slowly up, and the floor is covered with heaps of negro women . . . their white teeth chattering, and their bright eyes glistening and winking on all sides with surprise and fear, like the countless repetition of one astonished African face in some strange mirror. (137)

Everywhere are "cramped hutches" full of Negroes, who "crawl as if half-awakened . . . as if . . . every obscene grave were giving up its dead" (137–38).

Dickens then descends a dank set of stairs and enters a pub called the Almack. Like the hull of another ship, this den is one of the "underground chambers where they dance and game; the walls bedecked with ships, and forts, and flags, and American Eagles out of number." Dickens is greeted by the swirl of dancing black bodies in a "'regular breakdown.'" It is here that Dickens gives his awestruck illustration of the skillful Juba. Dickens is especially sensitive to the power of black expressive form, and his description makes palpable a moment of individual black male artistry and captures what it is that makes the dance transformative. With "all sorts of legs and no legs" at all, a black dancer articulated the torture of confinement and disfigurement and simultaneously embodied the pulse of freedom, evoked in moments in which the limbs twist and spin free of their irons. To the strum of the banjo and rhythm of the tambourine, a lone black dancer articulated the black body's experience of slavery, urban poverty, and creative resilience.

This passage is quite rightly a common reference point in theoretical discussions of black dance. But what drops out from these analyses is that Dickens's evening entertainment was not just the solo act of one man, not just the celebration of individual artistry. The evening was a social event in which a number of dancers participated. It was a moment of collective black performance, a "regular breakdown," within the "assembly room of the Five Points Fashionables." The Almack is presided over by a "buxom fat mulatto woman with sparkling eyes" and a landlord "attired in a smart blue jacket, like a ship's steward." A "corpulent black fiddler" and a tambourine player strike up a "lively measure," as "five or six couple [sic] come upon the floor," including "two young mulatto girls, with large, drooping eyes . . . who are shy, or feign to be, as if they had never danced before" (138). The meaning of this performance moment that Dickens so powerfully responds to is one shaped by men and women, reclaiming their bodies together.

It is important to notice that Dickens dramatizes this space with dancing women. It is also important that he emphatically condemns the "police discipline of the town" for unjustly incarcerating these women in "indecent and disgusting dungeons. . . . He has had five and twenty young women locked up in this very cell at one time, and you'd hardly realize what faces there were among 'em." (139). Dickens's critique is a rare account, literary or otherwise, in which black women are explicitly recognized as members of the urban poor, criminalized and unjustly punished by the penal system. Black women are elided from the landscape in the later work of social reformers and sociologists in New York City.

Dickens evokes the narrative conventions of abolitionist appeal and working-class activism. He also describes his exploration of this environment as would an adventurer in a new land. Descriptions of natives, and particularly native women, engaged in rituals of dance had become an expected feature of the travelogue. When Dickens wrote *American Notes*, the genre of European travel writing, in which established authors and authorities recorded their observations in foreign lands and colonies, was at its peak. The precedence for such ethnographic observation of dancing women was recorded in 1784 by Captain James Cook in *Voyages to the Pacific Ocean*.[14] The famous opening to David Livingstone's *Travels and Research* is also framed by dancing: "What do you dance?" an (anonymous) African asks Livingstone at their first encounter. This format became a convention, carried on in future travel accounts through which Europe created its maps.

Dickens was not the first nor was he the last Brit to offer his observations of New World slavery and U.S. racism. So had Francis Trollope in her travelogue, *Domestic Manners of the Americans*, which was published in 1827, preceding Dickens's by fifteen years; I will discuss Trollope's visit and impressions of U.S. racial politics later in the chapter. British traveler's accounts, as well as fugitive slave narratives and anti-slavery fiction, shaped the expectations of British audiences for the black performances at the turn of the century, such as those of Davis and Mitchell and their picaninny choruses, but they also informed black performers' choices about what to stage and how to stage it in Britain.

The troupes were still in demand a half-century later, well after slavery's official end. By the turn of the century the figure of the capering black child had taken on new meanings, the picaninny icon was revived and figured into new accounts. During this period of intense British empire building as well as European and American colonial expansion, the picaninny was no longer a slave but was rearticulated as a colonial subject. In Britain narratives surrounding the child from the system of plantation slavery were folded in with ideas of childlike races from colonies in Africa, parceled out in Berlin in 1885, as well as those in Britain's India and the Caribbean. This served a vital purpose in supporting Britain's idea of itself as a stabilizing and beneficent force in the lands over which it ruled. Chattel slavery was the terrible institution the British had long ago abolished, and tales of the sublime suffering of its victims could be safely rendered as stagings of the past. The presence of African American performers was proof of British beneficence, as the nation had even given asylum to the fugitives of the savage system. One reason black acts were so popular among white audiences is that they gave body to these remembrances. This served to obscure and distract from the bloody reality of colonial rule "far away" in Africa, India, and the Caribbean. The staged caperings of children reminded the British that they bore a burden of responsibility to their colonial subjects. These acts also represented for urban audiences the fruits of industrial and colonial enterprise; the triumph of British industriousness had made a delectable, delightful selection of entertainments available to everyone at the heart of empire.

"TAKE YOUR MONEY AND SEE THE WORLD!"

African American popular performance was not just a recent import from the new continent when Belle Davis and Her Picaninnies first appeared in Britain, Austro-Hungary, and Russia. The reception of these performers was informed by the earlier presence of both African Americans and various peoples from the African continent in these territories.[15] In the 1700s, Negro servants were a voguish addition to the courts in Russia, Sweden, and Denmark, as well as to the homes of aristocratic and well-to-do families in Britain.[16] In the 1820s the freeborn Nancy Prince accompanied her husband to St. Petersburg, where he worked as a servant in the palace of the czar.[17] African American performers also toured Britain and Russia in the 1800s. William Henry Lane (Juba) traveled to Britain in 1848 with a minstrel troupe and settled there.[18] From New York City's black repertory ensemble of the African Grove Theatre, seventeen-year-old Ira Aldridge migrated to Britain in 1824 or 1825. Touring Europe and Russia, Aldridge was the first actor to bring Shakespeare to the Russian provinces. Like Lane, he settled and died in Britain.[19]

The later African American child performers whom I focus on here, such as those who accompanied Belle Davis to Europe, were the second and third generations out of U.S. chattel slavery. They were from families struggling to survive the violent and reactionary political climate of the post-Reconstruction South. The dancer Ida Forsyne's grandmother had been a slave in Kentucky, and the family had migrated to the Chicago area some time before Ida was born in 1883. Some children, like Ida, began singing and dancing in front of the general store and on street corners, hustling for change.[20] "I was picking up pennies dancing in front of the candy store when I was ten," she recalls.[21] "[Before] I started traveling, I was dancing all around the streets for money all the time, begging and hustling. Later on I danced for money. They asked me to dance, I said, 'How much you goin' give me?' I was a real born hustler!'"[22] Ida's first act on the road was at the Chicago World's Fair in 1893. Accompanied by a "little dark boy," she danced the cakewalk on the Fair's Midway Plaisance.[23] Ida, along with many other child performers, traveled long distances, supporting themselves on the road with impromptu performances. In 1897 when Ida was fourteen, she hit the road performing in a tab show, a variety show of performers each with a specialty act, called *The Black Bostonians*. Ida sang a "coon song," "My Hannah Lady," and did a "Buck Dance." When the show went broke in Butte, Montana, Ida and a five-year-old boy earned money singing on the train ride home. "There was a young boy in the show and I took his hat and my hat and went through the coaches singing 'On the Banks of the Wabash,' and collected money," Ida recalls. "I didn't write and tell my mother I was stranded. I was having a ball." Ida's mother gave her consent for her tours and Ida helped the family out financially with her earnings. "My mother was very understanding. She let me go on these tours. She was in [domestic] service, and my father had left her when I was two years old," Ida remembers.[24] "I had a real good mother. I came home from dancing and gave her some money. She would say go ahead, and I would leave, when I was a little girl."[25] For Ida and other performing children, the lines between work and play were blurred. But Ida proudly emphasizes that the fruits of her labor (the small coins she earned in exchange for her dances) were her own.

The dancer Louis Douglas also started performing as a young boy. Douglas joined Belle Davis and her picaninnies on their later tours and would go on to become an important choreographer and prominent presence on the European variety stage circuits. Douglas's mother had wanted him to be a missionary and carry the Christian faith to Africa. But his father was a vaudeville performer with a juggling act as his specialty. "I have [sic] spent my early childhood helping my father in his theatre work," says Douglas in 1931 in a newspaper interview, while performing in Cairo, Egypt with his own company. "He had a stunning act juggling plates . . . I was his understudy . . . my task was to hand my father the plates."[26] At the age of eleven, Douglas joined a picaninny troupe headed for Britain. On May 11, 1903, the troupe landed in Liverpool, having been booked for its first shows as the Georgia Picaninnies. This troupe was large, with

"LITTLE BLACK ME"

5 Louis Douglas and Sonny Jones, Paris, 1923. Rainer Lotz collection. Used with permission.

twelve performers, and toured Europe until 1912. Sometime in 1904 or 1905, Douglas left the Georgia Picaninnies. He joined Belle Davis, Sonny, and Sneeze and stayed with them until 1908, when he left their company to start his own (see fig. 5).[27]

Many black performers cut their teeth dancing and singing as young members of established black touring companies. One such troupe, Black Patti's Troubadours, led by the black opera singer Madame Sissieretta Jones, toured for twenty years, from 1896 to 1916. The large company served as a crucial training ground for two generations of black performers. The composer Eubie Blake, who had lived near Madame Sissieretta in Baltimore, began his career with the Troubadours.[28] Ida Forsyne joined with Black Patti's Troubadours in 1898 and stayed with them until 1903, touring San Francisco and New York. "I learned many different dance steps," Ida remembers. "There were twenty-six people in the show and I was the only young girl."[29] In Black Patti's revue of 1901, entitled *Darktown Frolics*, Ida was billed as "Slewfoot Sal, the Tiger Lily."[30] Recalling her act, Ida explains: "For my specialty I pushed a baby carriage across the stage and sang a lullaby, "*You're Just a Little Nigger But You're Mine All Mine.* . . . No one thought of objecting in those days."[31] In 1903 Ida Forsyne joined with another troupe, led by the singer Abbie Mitchell, and went to Britain. Abbie Mitchell and Her Tennessee Students would tour Europe and Britain until the second decade of the century; all of them knew each other, and most worked together at some point. "So many real coons figure in the current programme at the Palace Theatre that one is almost tempted to describe it as an 'All-Black Bill,'" reads a review of Belle Davis and Her Picaninnies from January 1906.[32] Mitchell's and Davis's troupes appeared on the same bill at the Palace Theatre in London, a variety house on Shaftesbury Avenue, from the second half of December 1905 through the first half of January 1906. In the mid-1900s the Palace Theatre had black revues on its bill almost every week.[33] The composer and lyricist duo of Bob Cole and J. Rosamond Johnson frequently performed there between 1904 and 1907. The cakewalking couple Dora Dean and Charles Johnson—reviewed as the "King and Queen of Coon Swelldom"[34]—also appeared on the Palace show bill throughout 1906.

From her first appearance in London in December 1905, Ida Forsyne's quirky antics distinguished her in the cast of the Tennessee Students. Tiny, dark, and quick-footed, clad in a bandana and a gingham dress, Forsyne was identified with the capering picaninny character Topsy, a central figure in the many stage adaptations of *Uncle Tom's Cabin* that had toured England. Under her full-page photograph on the cover of *The Sketch* on December 20, 1905, Forsyne is described as "the coloured dancer who has made such a 'hit' at the Palace." The caption goes on to say that "Topsy's dancing in the 'Tennessee Students' turn at the Palace has aroused considerable interest and enthusiasm, and is perhaps the best example of negro dancing ever seen in this country. Topsy is 'called' half-a-dozen times each evening" (see fig. 6).[35] From then on, Forsyne was booked as "Topsy" in London. A picture of Forsyne from a Palace Theatre playbill appeared on the sides of buses, as well as in the front and back pages of magazines.[36] Because in 1905 the buses servicing London were motorized for the first time, the figure of the picaninny literally circulated throughout the modernizing metropole.

After one of their appearances at the Palace Theatre in London in January 1905, a review described Belle Davis's trio of children (most likely Sonny, Sneeze, and Louis Douglas) as the "quaintest and cleverest picaninnies imaginable . . . just the sort of little nigger boy you find in children's picture books." The popular means through which the figure of the child circulated informed each other. The review continues: "The ebony youngsters appear to enjoy the show just as much as kind friends in front and rouse the usually undemonstrative Palace audience to much enthusiasm."[37] The trope of mutual enjoyment between the ebony youngsters

The Sketch

No. 493.—Vol. LII.   WEDNESDAY, DECEMBER 20, 1905.   SIXPENCE

THE COLOURED DANCER WHO HAS MADE SUCH A "HIT" AT THE PALACE:
TOPSY, OF MISS ASH MITCHELL'S "TENNESSEE STUDENTS."

6   Ida Forsyne at the Palace
    Theatre, London, 1905.

[handwritten margin notes: Still today. How is Hollywood still racist when Denzel + Halle have Oscars?]

[handwritten margin notes: How is the country racist when B. O. is president]

and their kind friends suggests that discourses of paternalist abolitionist rhetoric were still useful in the post-slavery era. Such discourses masked both the truths of black colonial subjugation, away in distant lands, and Britain's dependency on extracted black labor for its own economic dominance. In the popular imagination, the presence of African Americans served to graft utopic myths of pastoral innocence over the bloody exploitation of land and labor. The ritual interactions between the black performers and their white audiences in the metropole were performed moments of "proof" that civilization's promises—freedom, brotherhood, and equality—had been realized. Carefully contained in the sphere of stage and gallery, these interactions were a therapeutic parallel to the violent and coercive performances of racial "exchange" taking place in the peripheries of empire.

The presence of children, capering across the stage to accompany their mistress, evoked the trope of family—the family of man, headed by the white patriarch, the plantation as family, the family as made sacred in the Victorian era. For these child dancers, family meant the performing troupe or show they toured with. The Whitman Sisters, for example, organized their troupe as a family concern. Starting as child jubilee singers in their father's church in Atlanta, Georgia, the four sisters—Mabel, Alberta, Essie, and Alice—toured stateside variety circuits into the 1930s.[38] The Whitman Sisters' troupe was known for its large cast of children performers, who were coached by the iron-fisted Mabel. "If there were any mother's child with ability and we had them, they would be great," Essie recalls.[39] "May really took care of the young girls," remembers Catherine Basie, who toured with them in the 1910s. "Any mother could tell you that if the young girls were with the Whitman Sisters they were safe."[40] Part of the Whitman Sisters' strategy was to pitch the children performers to their audiences as "friendless and homeless orphans . . . they had picked up in their travels," although this was far from the truth.[41] Aaron Palmer joined the troupe as a picaninny dancer in 1910. "I was working in Atlanta with two other kids," Palmer remembers. "[The Whitman Sisters] came through and saw our act. They followed us around trying to find out where we were from and they finally went to our home town, Charleston, and got permission from our parents to let us join their show. A little after we joined, Sister May took out her pick show called *Mabel Whitman and the Dixie Boys*. We toured all over, even Germany and Australia, and the other sisters just stayed home and lived off the money we made."[42] The troupe's youngest sister, Alice, married Aaron Palmer in 1919. Their son, Albert "Pops" Palmer, was hoofing with his parents' troupe at the age of four (see fig. 7).

The Whitman Sisters worked primarily in the southern United States. But from about 1903 up until World War I many black variety entertainers formed loosely webbed communities in Europe and American with London, New York, and St. Petersburg as primary cities. When not working together, performers such as Belle Davis and Abbie Mitchell kept track of each other's movements and often organized their tours so as to appear in the same town, at the same venue, or on the same bill with a different act.

Between 1904 and 1909, St. Petersburg was a center for black performers. Ida Forsyne, her cousin Ollie Bourgoyne, and the ex-*Creole Show* chorus girl Mattie Wilkes were some of the earliest performers to base themselves there. By 1907, Forsyne was touring her solo dance act throughout Russia and Austria. Bringing the cakewalk with her from

7   Albert "Pops" Palmer.

America, she soon incorporated Russian dances into her act and became known for her version of the Cossack dance. Settling in St. Petersburg, Ida Forsyne toured Europe for nine years. "Everywhere I went I was lauded. I was paid good money and I had a ball. Everything I ever wanted I've had it," Forsyne recalls. "I bought it with my good money in Europe . . . I enjoyed every minute." Forsyne welcomed fellow performers coming to Russia in the years that followed. "In Russia, everybody used to stay while we were there," she remembers:

Colored Americans all came over to Europe, if they had their own money in my day. They came with husbands, or they had an act or something. They just flooded the place. We was all friendly. We'd have them for breakfast, [we'd say] "come on! I'll cook you some neckbones and beans!" so they'd feel at home. I tell everybody, take your money and go see something and learn something about the world![43]

Laura Bowman met Forsyne while performing in Odessa with her husband, Pete Hampton, and the two other members of their troupe, the Darktown Entertainers. "I was so glad Ida was working in the same town. I would have company and someone to run around with," Bowman remembers.[44] The troupe joined Forsyne in Russia, and Bowman and Forsyne would become lifelong friends.

Laura Bowman's memoirs of traveling and performing with her husband, friends, and fellow artists are an example of black performers claiming a transnational sense of themselves. The ability to travel, and to resettle, was a powerful act of self-possession. As the ex-slave Felix Haywood put it, "Just like that we was free . . . nobody took our homes away, but right off colored folks started on the move. They seemed to want to get closer to freedom, so they'd know what it was like, like it was a place or city."[45] As I will explore further in this book, movement, in and of itself, should be understood as part of a complex, multi-noded, conceptualization of home. What I hope to show is that there is a dialogic relationship between gesture and place in the kinetic vocabularies of black dance, as suggested here by the nomadic, expressive artistry of African American dancers. In the next section I consider the children dancers, including Ida Forsyne and Louis Douglas, as artists of their multi-sited modern moment.

Black acts in Europe and Russia were also understood in relation to local political and social climates. In post-1848 Europe, the rising tide of nationalist movements and localized class struggles ushered in the end of monarchial rule and the rise of the urban bourgeoisie, as well as the shift away from agrarian to industrial economies.[46] Ideas of the folk took on new importance in relation to national identity. The presence of black acts such as Belle Davis and Her Picaninnies in Europe provided a condensation point for ideas of the emancipatory potential of folk culture. The presence of ex-slaves from the plantations, "the people of the soil" from the New World, served to carry and contain the anxieties created by these huge shifts and mediated several sets of relationships, especially those between peasant and landlord, aristocrat and burgher.

The prominent artistic presence of African Americans in *fin-de-siècle* St. Petersburg was informed by perceptions of Western raciologies, as well as by Russia's history of serfdom and emancipation—Russian imaginings about their own peoples tied to the land.[47] While Ira Aldrige was touring in Russia, Russians were comparing American slavery with their own system of feudalism, and Western abolitionist protest with their own movement for the emancipation of the serfs. Russian progressives used *Uncle Tom's Cabin*, which was translated into Russian in 1853, in support of the emancipation of Russian serfs.[48]

European newspaper and trade paper reviews tried to capture the effects of the picaninnies' dancing. These reviews struggle to capture the eccentric quality of the black children's performances, which seem to be made up of contradictory, clashing elements. As well as carrying a folk connotation, the black children brought earlier associations of aristocratic ostentation. Described as "baroque," and "grotesque," the picaninnies carried the idea of decadence and excess, and of the strange and foreign. *Contradictions!*

Performing in Dusseldorf in September 1904, Belle Davis's picaninnies were described as "three very agile Negro boys," performing "strange and grotesque nigger songs and dances . . . arranged to Anglo-American tastes."[49] German and Eastern European reviewers regularly mentioned the contrast between the lightness of Belle Davis's skin and the ebony hue of her pupils, although the nature (or artifice) of Davis's race differs from report to report. "A strange turn are the grotesque Nigger dancers, with their white sovereign, la Belle Davis," a review in the German paper *Das Organ* reads, missing the finer points of the U.S. politics of racial classification.[50] In March 1904, Belle Davis, Sonny, Sneeze, and the newly joined Louis Douglas appeared in Vienna, the *fin-de-siècle* capital of culture, at the Orpheum Theatre. The three dancing boys were described as "very young lads of astonishing suppleness and comic power," and the smallest boy as particularly adroit at "artful jumps, enforced gestures, and incredible distortions of the face."[51] Of their appearance at the Circus Busch in Berlin, September 1906, one German review acknowledges their dancing as technically perfect. The review describes their movements as demonstrations of "fabulous agility and astonishing suppleness"; at the same time, however, they are also "anything but graceful" and "become more and more strange."[52] *Because they couldn't give a 100% review*

Reading these reviews suggests that the children's acts can be understood in relation to other modern forms of art. The rigorous physical phrasing of the children's dancing bodies was a fragmentary and improvisatory pastiche. Their acts embodied the immediacy of perceptual experience that hallmarks modernity, their mercurial (anti)language of the body expressing the fleeting, dislocated climate of life. In this way one can think of the "scraps of songs and dances" offered up by Davis and her pupils as very much like the *feuilleton* of the Viennese newspapers, and like the works of the impressionists living in Vienna in the 1900s. As early *flâneurs*, the travels and artistry of African American children performers recorded and commented upon the development of the city. Through their gestural phrases, the children interpreted changing perceptions of time and space, and the spectacle of technological advance.

Away from home and living on the road in adoptive family situations, these children were working/playing in a kind of exposed contact with the world. They mediated this experience through their fantastical bodily inflections. "I copied everything, I was a real copycat!" remembers the dancer Ida Forsyne.[53] What the children saw and learned about the world in their travels they copied in their dances, spelled out with their bodies. Every surrounding influence was subject to their exceptional abilities of perception through which they grabbed hold of the world through its likeness.[54] Mimicry is thought of as the natural ability of children. But we need to understand the children's physical phrasing not as natural reactive instinct but as skilled response in the guise of effortless spontaneity. Spontaneity and improvisation in themselves form a complex interpretive strategy. The children were quintessential eccentric dancers, with their acts becoming "more and more strange" over the course of their turns. European critical reviews stress the contrast and combination of the elegant and the grotesque in the act. Belle's tightly bound hourglass figure, swathed in glittering gowns, was surrounded by her tiny tumbling keeps. It was as if the children, with their "fabulous suppleness," embodied a strange and unknowable, mutative place.

Stage conventions changed in the second decade of the century, and the dance reviews at the Palace and other English music halls began to include chorus lines of young women as a regular feature. Audiences had begun to respond to their synchronous routines, their "machinelike uniformity in performance."[55] In this new era of precision dancing, the picaninnies' improvisatory technique and eccentric interpretive strategies were disturbing to audiences and seen as "lacking any method or order." To one English reviewer in 1917, their dances were uncontainable "odds and ends of tumbling," a seemingly "go-as-you-please rehearsal," lacking any narrative continuity: "Belle Davis and her Cracker Jacks is just a scramble. No one seems to have any method or order in this act—we get broken scraps of songs, bits of dances, odds and ends of tumbling. It is like a go-as-you-please rehearsal. And I don't care much for the exploitation of the mediocre and dubious eccentricities of niggers anyway."[56] Despite the Fordist turn, the "dubious eccentricities" of the children dancers would still

Other

capture European audiences well into the 1920s. Belle Davis continued to tour throughout Europe with her children. The reporter Norris Smith regularly sent news to the *Chicago Defender* of the movement of black artists throughout Europe. "Belle Davis and Crackerjacks have been in London, oh so long! Her act like gin, improves with age," writes Smith in 1916.[57]

Once past puberty, many of the dancers who had worked with Belle Davis stayed in Europe and continued performing. Sonny and Sneeze based themselves in Paris and later formed a jazz band called the International Five. Louis Douglas is one of the most important artists to have remained in Europe. His choreography influenced many and hallmarked an era. During World War I Douglas continued touring the musical hall circuits in Eastern Europe.[58] Douglas stayed in Britain through the war and in 1918 he married Marion Cook, the daughter of Abbie Mitchell and the composer Will Marion Cook, who were also living in Europe. Douglas, Mitchell, and Cook settled in Europe, though they would travel between Europe and New York to stage shows. In the early 1920s Douglas worked again with Sonny and became the in-house choreographer at the Casino de Paris. In 1924, after being contacted about an exciting new show being planned for a Paris opening, Douglas returned to New York to help in the stateside arrangements for *La Revue Nègre*, for which he provided staging and choreography. Douglas continued producing shows in Europe through the 1930s. As he worked with almost all of the women in this study—from Ida Forsyne to Valaida Snow—his story will thread throughout this book.

A BLIGHTING BONDAGE: OR BLACK ACTIVISTS, FACTORY CHILDREN, AND THE LANCASHIRE MILLS

As were other black shows and acts that toured the circuits of the Empire circuit of British music halls over the turn of the century, the picaninny choruses were popular with working-class audiences. The children toured widely throughout northern England and Scotland, appearing in cities including Manchester, Liverpool, Newcastle, Hull, and Glasgow. To understand why picaninny acts were so popular and still retain such iconographic power, we must think back to the comparisons drawn between the institutions of wage slavery and chattel slavery in the conversations between British labor activists, black activists, and fugitives of the slave system living in Britain. Sometimes interconnections between the systems of unfree labor were acknowledged. As activists of the Free Soil movement eloquently emphasized, the cotton grown and picked by slaves in the southern United States was the same cotton spun and carded in the Lancashire textile mills. Comparisons were also drawn, particularly in British fiction, between children who were exploited by the factory system and children who suffered under the system of plantation slavery. Often the plight of the factory children was dramatized by being likened to slavery. Descriptions of working conditions depict the children, sometimes chained to the machines, with their young bodies twisted and abused by the heavy machinery. As I suggest, the appeal of the scampering, resilient black children on stage was perhaps that it brought an imagined health to the bodies of the factory children. To stretch Siegfried Kracauer's famous analogy, the hands of the factory children corresponded with the legs of the black children dancers.[59]

The number of black Americans visiting Britain was at its highest between 1848 and 1854. Many were fundraising: Alexander Crummell was raising money for his church, James W. C. Pennington to pay his debts, and Josiah Henson for the Dawn Institute, his community of former slaves in Canada. Others escaped to Britain after the U.S. Congress passed the Fugitive Slave Law in 1851. Appearances by William Wells Brown and Ellen and William Craft in 1851 and 1852 actually reactivated dormant anti-slavery societies in England and Scotland.[60] Fugitive slaves and black activists in the United Kingdom themselves formed a society centered in London, which they named the American Fugitive Slaves in the British Metropolis.[61] Slave narratives and speeches published by the fugitives of the slave system and black anti-slavery activists, including those by Ellen and William Craft, Frederick Douglass, James W. C. Pennington, William Wells Brown, and Josiah Henson, were widely read across Britain and had all been translated into French and German. It is important to remember that it was the *already circulating* autobiographies of the survivors that set the stage for the successful reception of Harriet Beecher Stowe's *Uncle Tom's Cabin*, and that many of the novel's characters were created out of these autobiographies.

In Britain, labor struggles regularly used the language of slavery. Marcus Cunliffe writes that "the slavery comparison, whether meant literally or figuratively, became a standard feature of reformist and radical analysis."[62] Some people provided analysis of the conditions and causes for mutual suffering and oppression. In 1853, the economist Henry Carey had connected the condition of "slavery—helpless, impoverished labor—around the globe, from country to country and colony to colony."[63]

The presence of black activists in Britain was not synonymous with that of established abolitionist movements, and their presence was felt differently. Labor in Britain was frustrated with the primarily middle-class leadership of the organized abolitionist societies. The middle classes, they criticized, were all too eager to take up noble causes abroad while remaining apathetic to the political situations at home. But labor activists also protested the support given to the organized abolition movement by members of the aristocracy and landed gentry, including Prince Albert and the duke of Sussex. Working-class activists were suspicious of the British Antislavery Society's agenda. They argued that the charity of the aristocracy, the church, and the wealthy manufacturers was calculated to draw attention away from oppressive regimes at home. When Harriet Beecher Stowe visited the United Kingdom, she stayed with wealthy families of the land-owning class, notably the duchess of Sutherland. The duchess was lambasted regularly in the literature and speeches of labor activists, as she was held responsible for dispossessing hundreds of Scottish crofters from their lands.[64]

In the 1830s black activists and fugitive slaves had toured with organized anti-slavery societies, but after 1840 they more often traveled and lectured as independent agents and by the invitation of ad hoc anti-slavery organizers. They met a quite different reception. As they toured the small mining and milling towns, "free exchange was made between working class audiences and black abolitionists." They were often mutually supportive, despite the differences in agenda and method. For labor activists in Britain the black fugitives "symbolized successful resistance to oppression. While the analogy of slavery was employed by British labor to condemn the excesses of industrialism, it also provided a useful mechanism for comparing and attacking both systems"[65] But relationships between organized labor and the visiting black Americans, although they could be forged, were not automatically of identification and alliance. Black anti-slavery activists, while they strategized for broad-based support, were less eager to accept slavery as a metaphor for all oppressive systems. Douglass

still criticized today

and others stressed that there were fundamental differences between the two systems, as chattel slavery was a total state of unfreedom.[66]

In other instances, class bias would shape black speakers' positions. Wells Brown stressed that aid need not go to all of Britain's poor but only to the respectable poor, the hard working and the sober, as intemperance was so often the cause of poverty. At other times fugitives and former slaves, as they considered the sources of their financial support (particularly when it came to the purchasing of their freedom, one issue of division with Garrison and his followers), would exercise necessary diplomacy with members of the moneyed classes and in doing so frustrate labor spokesmen.

Some white Britons argued that the conditions under chattel slavery were much better than for the laboring classes, as masters retained an interest in their slaves' health. "I would sooner see the children of my love born to the heritage of southern slavery, than to see them subjected to the blighting bondage of the poor English operative's life," wrote C. Edwards Lester in 1841.[67] The narratives and other writings of fugitive slaves were very popular among the working classes. *Uncle Tom's Cabin* was a fictionalized compilation of these previously circulating narratives. Stowe developed her central and soon-to-be ubiquitous figure, Uncle Tom, out of the published narrative of Josiah Henson. The heroic escaped slave George Harris was based on the recollections of the former slave Lewis Clarke, as "related personally to the author," and also on his published narrative. Stowe had an instant readership for her novel because it featured characters based on public personas with which readers were already familiar.

Stowe's other characters were based in slaves' experiences as recorded by abolitionists. She stated that she based the iconographic figure of the suffering slave mother, Eliza, on a "beautiful Quadroon" whom she spotted in a Kentucky church, although by the time of the novel's publication a number of women's slave narratives had been circulating for some time, notably the narrative of the West Indian slave Mary Prince published in 1831. Firsthand accounts of slave women were available in Theodore Dwight Weld's *American Slavery as It Is*. Within a year of the novel's release, Stowe offered up her sources in *A Key to Uncle Tom's Cabin*, which, as the subtitled information promises, "*Presents the Original Facts and Documents Upon Which This Story Is Founded, Together with Corroborative Statements Verifying the Truth of the Work.*"

The reception of *Uncle Tom's Cabin* increased interest in the previously circulating fugitive slave narratives. William Wells Brown toured Britain in the months before Stowe's visit, his lecture titled "American Slavery and *Uncle Tom's Cabin*," and "hundreds attended to hear the fugitive confirm Stowe's claims."[68] It was usually the case that the word of some respectable member of the abolitionist community established the truth of the slave narrative's claims. But here the published words and voices of former slaves were what legitimated Stowe's story. The presence of black performers in the 1900s was partly understood through these earlier histories. What is established here is that later performers were not symbols of abolitionist commitment, nor simply references to what were by then stock characters from Stowe's novel. They referenced the historical presence of black fugitives in dialogue with a British working class.

The black children performers were working/playing during a critical period in the history of childhood. The moral sanctity of the family was one of the defining tenets of the Victorian era; that slavery was a moral violation of the family was a key abolitionist argument. The presence of slave children naturally dramatized this point in Stowe's novel. With the cult of true womanhood came ideas of the sacredness of the child. A child was the embodiment of innocence and purity and was especially vulnerable to the vagaries of the corrupting world outside of the home, as were white women. Born free, children had the right to a period of life free from work and designated for intellectual, moral, and spiritual instruction. Motherhood was a sacred duty; as "God's reasoning moral creatures," women were to watch over and instruct the children.[69] These mid-century ideas would develop further over the turn of the century.

A broad ideal, in actuality this familial configuration indicated middle-class privilege. Children of the "lower orders" were expected to work. There was organized resistance to the use of children's labor; however, most child labor laws focused on reform rather than on complete eradication of child labor. Total eradication was often in conflict with the self-interest of capital, a system that exploited the cheap labor provided by many little hands, but was also resisted by the working families who depended on the contribution of their children's income to survive.[70]

As the Industrial Revolution transformed the countryside, working-class children became an integral part of the industrial wage labor system. In the emerging industrial cities, children became the victims of long hours and terrible conditions in the factories. Malnutrition and exhaustion led to horrific plagues of tuberculosis, diseases such as rickets, and muscular deformities. After the mechanization of textile factories and mills in northern England, children were "harnessed to power-driven machinery" to clean the machines without stopping production. Children were mangled, dismembered, and killed as they were dragged into the machines' moving parts.[71]

Oh no!

In Britain, appeals for the protection of working children under industrial capitalism drew parallels between their plight and that of slave children.[72] In the mid-nineteenth century, while working-class English children suffered from the unchecked powers of industrial labor, African American children were born into lives of oppressive indenture, as the products of a transnational slave economy. The slaveholder Thomas Jefferson wrote: "A child raised every 2. [*sic*] years is of more profit than the crop of the best laboring man. . . . It is not their labor, but their increase which is the first consideration with us."[73] The president's comments on how to run a tobacco plantation most efficiently clearly accounts for slave children, however begat, as investments for future adult labor. Slavery became a powerful metaphor that was used to dramatize the condition of indentured children.

The figure of the child chimney sweep dramatized the pathos of child indenture. As a writer for the *Sheffield and Rotterdam Independent* reasoned, no one could be shocked by American slavery yet ignore the suffering of "hundreds of ulcerated, crippled, *little black-looking*, half-naked, shivering chimney sweeps, who were sold by their parents and attired in that full sable undress in which they are sent out by 4 o'clock through the snow to be employed in tasks more horrible, maiming, demoralizing, and destructive than ever America enforced on even adult slaves" (my italics).[74] The figure of the "black-looking" chimney sweep child "in full sable undress" embodied the comparison and became a common figure in children's literature, like the main character Tom in Charles Kingsley's *Waterbabies*, which was published in 1863. Tom's coal-blackened body is a sign of abjection, abuse, and abandonment under wage labor, and his death is a release from bondage.

Works of protest fiction, like Frances Trollope's novel *Michael Armstrong*, would also dramatize the suffering of factory children by using the analogy of black children under the system of chattel slavery. Trollope *mère* describes the children of the factory as they "dragged their attenuated limbs along . . . driven to and fro, till their little limbs bend under them—hour after hour, day after day—the repose of a moment to be purchased only by yielding their tender bodies to the fist, the heel, or the strap of the overlooker!"[75]

Child labor laws were still at issue over the turn of the century. In January 1904, while Belle Davis and Her Picaninnies were in Britain, Parliament passed the Employment of Children's Act, restricting the hours a child could work. This bill had a direct effect on the many children working on the variety stages, with their parents or in separate acts, and the place of children on the variety stages was hotly defended in the trade press.[76] Most likely, Belle Davis and her band were issued foreign work permits, as they kept working after the law was passed, performing for mostly working-class audiences in the industrial towns of northern England.

Many former slaves recount in their narratives a golden period of their childhood, before the age of six or seven, which was free from toil and when they were free to play with the sons and daughters of the plantation owner. The authors' strategy was to affirm the idea of natural equality, evoking the principle of universal brotherhood in the argument against slavery. Many of them actually were brothers or sisters, by blood as well as principle, of the white children they were playing with. Abolitionists repeatedly played on this irony by referring to Thomas Jefferson's own children, his plantation progeny born unfree and unequal. Despite the slave narratives' claims to a period of innocent and unmolested childhood, children were put to work on the plantations in the southern states, as caregivers for the younger children and in "trash gangs" with the elderly and pregnant women.[77] "Work, work, work was scarcely more the order of the day than of the night," wrote Frederick Douglass.[78] Post-emancipation was not much better for the small charges, as the child labor laws in the United States were not enforced when it came to protecting them. By the 1890s, following Ida B. Wells's anti-lynching campaign tours across Britain, British audiences were aware that, although formal slavery had been eradicated, conditions had worsened for African Americans.

As I explore in the next chapter, by the time Belle Davis and Her Picaninnies were performing in Britain, the figures of the picaninnies also invoked the recent growth of the colonies and the subjects of the master-servant laws in the West Indies, India, and Africa. But it was the figure of the child slave, stilled in time and iconized, that audiences associated most closely with contemporary children laboring in England's mills and factories. The figure was a timeless signature of resilience and a seeming ability to survive "even the toughest blows." This association would resonate in how audiences enjoyed the capering, hyperbolic routines of black child dancers. I argue that the body in motion was a privileged site of resilient response to oppressive regimes, and that black children gave English audiences an imagined response to the pained bodies of unfree children working in the textile mills and factories of industrial England. Their supple wriggling forms offered a staged restorative to the beleaguered bodies of the laboring children.

There are limits to how we interpret moments of cross-identification between the working classes and black exiles. The therapeutic restorative offered by the shows was also based in a primitivist folk nostalgia. Black children of the soil, naturally free and closer to nature, gave body to the fantasy of English agrarian pastoralism, a pre-industrial life before land enclosures. The evocation of a stilled figure from the U.S. plantation also helped to obscure the subjects of British exploitation of labor elsewhere in the colonies.

Black children were considered to embody metonymically the condition of the lesser races, locked in a perpetual state of childlike simplicity, prone to excess, always emotional and immediate in their responses. Their "natural" behavior was irrepressible physical and vocal expression. Part of how the children performers were understood also was shaped through scientific discourses on race, which were filtered into popular thought. Racial differences were more than skin deep; they were located in the Negro's physiognomy. Pro-slavery advocates in particular kept a tenacious hold on biological difference, searching for physiological ways to account for blacks' inferiority. According to the pro-slavery Samuel Cartwright, as an expert physician he had proven through legitimate medical research that "the negro's respiratory system was under the same physiological laws as an infant child of the white race, and liked warm, wet air."[79] Yet these beliefs were not simply the pathologies of a few racists. Many of those who considered themselves the closest friend to the Negro carried ideas of the race's need for careful tutelage and guidance. The idea of human equality would be put to the test in the education of black people.

White person in charge! But a nble one/Gentle woman.

Debates about universal education help us to further contextualize the convention of the picaninny chorus. The figure of the white teacher and her eager black pupils was a standard configuration in popular abolitionist and feminist literature and children's primers. In the United States after the Civil War, it was familiar practice for white women songstresses to take picaninny choruses with them on tour throughout the states. The children were often booked as the pupils of the singer-instructor, and the singer's role in relation to her picaninnies was that of the motherly schoolmistress. The light operas sung by the chanteuse were accompanied in the choral segments by her band of merry black children, and interspersed with their spontaneous eruptions of frenetic dance. The troupes of performing children evoked earlier debates about the education, or the educability, of the black race. This format held currency for audiences well into the next century. Variety stage performers and singers were expected to bring a troupe of children with them.[80]

Multiple layers of meaning were attached to the figure of the white singer and the black children in her tutelage. The white woman as the pillar of piety stood as a metonymic signifier for the moral (though perhaps not ethical) well-being of the national body. Her patient guidance stood as an example of white women's sacred responsibility to the lesser races. As references to the history of white women educators tutoring the illiterate ex-slaves in the South, these acts staged the post-emancipation narrative of northern philanthropic goodwill and worked as a metaphor for national reunification.

The fight to end slavery nurtured a broad spectrum of radical thought. Before the abolition of the slave trade, antislavery activism schooled a generation of idealists—utopians and free thinkers, as well as feminist and Christian reformers—all with freedom and emancipation on their minds. They planned and established ideal communities, many of which, as early as 1829, began with the express purpose of preparing the slaves for their freedom. The radical Scotswoman Fanny Wright, a friend to Frances Trollope, traveled from Britain to establish Nashoba in Tennessee as such a community. With three of her children, Trollope traveled to America with Wright to observe and help the utopian community. "This question

carried over into the houses of the ...

of the mental equality, or inequality between us, and the Negro race, is one of great interest, and has certainly never been fairly tried; and I expect for my children and myself both pleasure and information from visiting her establishment, and watching the success of her experiment," Trollope wrote.[81] Facing terrible conditions, Trollope soon left with her children. The state of Tennessee forced Wright to shut down the community; Wright bought the slaves their freedom and sent them to Haiti.[82]

After emancipation, northern middle-class American women would travel south and set up schools for the former slaves. "When emancipation came to the Negroes, there arose in the northern part of the United States an almost divine sentiment among the noblest, purest and best white women of the North who felt called to a mission to educate and Christianize the millions of Southern ex-slaves," Ida B. Wells wrote in her anti-lynching pamphlet *A Red Record*. Wells's description is laden with irony, as she is well aware of the maternalistic and self-congratulatory selflessness of the martyrs from the North. Yet she is careful to let her words also compliment, aware as she is of the ambiguities; after all, she did not want to alienate the very audience that could be marshaled to speak out against lynching.[83]

The figure of the white teacher and her eager black pupils was a standard configuration in popular abolitionist and feminist literature and children's primers. In the United States after the Civil War, it was familiar practice for white women songstresses to take picaninny choruses with them on tour throughout the states. The children were often booked as the pupils of the singer-instructor, and the singer's role in relation to her picaninnies was as motherly schoolmistress. This format held currency for U.S. audiences well into the next century. From the 1910s into the 1930s, white female singers working the American variety and vaudeville circuits, such as Mayme Remington, Eva Tanguay, and Sophie Tucker, brought picaninny choruses with them as insurance of a well-received show.[84]

Multiple layers of meaning were attached to the figure of the white singer and the black children in her tutelage. The white woman's place as the pillar of piety stood as metonymic signifier for the moral (though perhaps not ethical) well-being of the national body. Her patient guidance stood as an example of white women's sacred responsibility to the lesser races. As references to the history of white women educators tutoring the illiterate ex-slaves in the South, these acts staged the post-emancipation narrative of northern philanthropic goodwill and worked as a metaphor for national reunification. The common practice of white women taking picaninny choruses with them on the road was also informed by the ways sexual relationships had been shaped by marketplace demands in the United States. Slavery blurred the lines between sexual consent and coercion. There were to be official and unofficial versions of family, those practices that would be recognized and recorded by history and those that would be denied on paper. In these forms of popular performance, earlier understandings of such official and unofficial worlds were carried forward into the choreographies of contact and proximity between the races in the post-reconstruction era.

Beginning in the 1890s, black dancers and coon shouters such as Belle Davis, Dora Dean, and the Whitman Sisters took children out on the road as well. Dora Dean, like Belle Davis, was a former chorus girl from *The Creole Show*. Dean took on the picaninny chorus format in the 1910s after her split with her dance partner, Charles Johnson. "At last, a pick [*sic*] act without a white woman for the feature," a review reads. "With three girls and as many boys, Dora Dean and Company make a fast going aggregation. . . . The boys' dancing at the finish leaves a fine impression. The acts are dressed well, the girls make a number of changes while the boys look very nifty in dark green coats and flannel trousers and later in evening dress."[85] Led by the light-skinned chanteuses, the irrepressible presence of the picaninnies demonstrated the "open secret" of the transgression of anti-miscegenation laws.[86] As the capering picaninnies interacted with their singing mother/teacher, their bodily inflections re-membered the spectrum of sexual servitudes at the heart of chattel slavery. The near whiteness of the chanteuses glowed in stark contrast to their jet-black keeps. All one had to do was look to see that somebody (or bodies), at some point in time, had "jumped the fence." Sexual access was a tenet of white mastery, and these shows referenced on stage the coercive breeding policies, as well as the ambiguous conceptions of unfree consent, by which these children were not born but "just grew."

Despite the supposed lightheartedness of the music hall show, much was not humorous in these acts. As well as referencing the intimate business of slavery and post-slavery oppression, these acts informed, and were informed by, a range of politics. The business of dance was a synechdotal antidote to the pain and suffering of generations of children who worked in the factories or in the fields and yards of sharecroppers. The conversation between anti-slavery fugitives and English factory workers, and the relationship between slavery and wage labor were animated by the figures of the dancing children. Part of this I argue was restorative, the recognition and reclamation of rightly moving limbs. Part of it was also part of a very familiar kind of racism, the audience expecting the childlike races to love nothing better than to entertain.

There is more work to be done on the extensive Eastern European tours of these acts. There I suggest the children embodied a wide range of politics: they referenced feudalism and anti-feudalist movements, and the increasing importance of a folk to the ideological projects of the nation-state. From the earth, made to labor, and also rising up against oppression, black performers were references to such folk. But here they also evoked the memory of the aristocratic families and their fashionable house servants, small children brought from Africa, bought to do light service in the house. These children were sometimes educated as "experiments," designed to test the concept of human equality. As in the case of Badin, they were sometimes not educated, but allowed free run of the place to assess Rousseau's theories of humankind's right to be free held. Arriving as Anglo-American acts to Europe, the children and their mistresses took with them specific iconographies from the American colonies and English West Indies, both of which bore histories and policies about racial admixture and its relationship to national/racial/familial belonging. When the mistress was a light-skinned, young songstress, the act also referenced the practice of the fancy trade, centered where the Americas met the Caribbean Islands.

THE INSTITUTION OF CONCUBINAGE

Frances Trollope hated America and gave a relentless critique of U.S. cruelty and hypocrisy in her travelogue. "It is impossible for any mind of common honesty not to be revolted by the contradictions in their principles and practice. . . . You will see them with one hand hoisting the cap of liberty, and with the other flogging their slaves," she writes.[87] She was particularly outspoken about the system of concubinage she observed in New Orleans, noting that the practice formed a social infrastructure. She described two sets of people: the Creole families, "chiefly planters and merchants . . . very grand and aristocratic," and the "excluded but amiable Quadroons. . . . The acknowledged daughters of wealthy American or Creole fathers . . . are not admitted . . . into the society of the Creole families of Louisiana. . . . They cannot marry. . . . Unfortunately they perpetually become the objects of choice and affection."[88] Such sexual service shaped generations of black women's families, and their children were often both property and progeny of their masters.

British and American literature that featured mulatto, quadroon, and octoroon concubines shaped the way the picaninny acts, led by light-skinned black women, were understood. But it was also the slave narratives of black women who had lived as sexual servants that informed these acts. These accounts were live, working documents, as many times the authors were fugitives and in very real danger. Harriet Jacob wrote her narrative, *Incidents in the Life of a Slave Girl*, in 1861, as a fugitive in Britain. Resisting her master's sexual demands, she describes living for seven years in an attic crawlspace of a shed in her grandmother's house. Through her "loophole of retreat," Jacobs renders her bodily experience in relation to the "architectonics" of the southern household, the soul- and body-crippling domestic and commercial space. Jacob's five by six by eight box is in her grandmother's attic, but even this freewoman's house is territory easily permeated by the "peculiar institution." After Jacobs makes her escape, walking and standing upright are difficult and are accompanied by pain for many weeks.[89]

Raising funds to purchase her mother from slavery, the former concubine Louisa Picquet told her tale to the Methodist minister Hiram Mattison in 1860. Picquet's and Mattison's narrative describes the system as at once familial—when one concubine dies, the master takes her sister—and also commercial, with the owner/father buying his own children at auction.

But the language of Mattison's appeal against the practice hinges black women's sexual servitude, imperial conquest, and the delectations of leisure travel, all with a slight drool. "There is not a family mentioned, from first to last," he writes, "that does not reek of fornication and adultery. It turns up as naturally, and is mentioned with as little specialty, as walrus beef in the narrative of the Arctic Expedition, or macaroni in a tour of Italy."[90] This piece of literature reveals sexual servitude as not a rare occurrence, nor only the experience of a few privileged women. Concubinage was an institution that figured centrally in the nation's economy. Picquet's narrative, spoken by Mattison, raises the specter of the unverifiable, the unreliable, the contaminated.[91] Is what she says "true?" How do we "tell?" Indeed, the art of "telling"—telling one's parentage, telling on those who were your parents, being able to tell just who a slave resembled—was the lexicon of such family dramas. The shows and acts staged by the black performers played with and upon these politics of authenticity and artifice.

Fanny Trollope continues her impressions of the southern United States by commenting on Thomas Jefferson and his slave family at Monticello as a perfect demonstration of slave women's sexual concubinage as a generational and familial story. Sally Hemings was both family and property to Jefferson. She was Martha Jefferson's half-sister, one of ten children by Martha's father John Wayles and his slave concubine Betty Hemings, inherited by Thomas Jefferson the year that Sally was born.[92] Sally Hemings's duties as chambermaid, in the main house of the five thousand acre tobacco plantation, situate a politics of sexual labor at the center of the national stage. Jefferson's case was commonplace in 1830s anti-slavery arguments.[93] "'All men are created free and equal' . . . this false and futile axiom which has done . . . and will do so much harm to this fine country, came from Jefferson; and truly his life was a glorious commentary upon it," wrote Trollope, her caustic sarcasm well placed.[94]

Trollope criticizes American boorishness and barbarism but ignores British slavery and colonial exploitation. In considering the enthusiastic reception of the picaninny choruses in Britain, we need to remember that the icon of the black child circulated transnationally, and that black people were doing "plantation time" throughout the Atlantic world. Although *Uncle Tom's Cabin* came to represent a distinctly "American" ethos and problematic, U.S. plantation lore and British and European colonial lore were already wedded in the book. In popular understanding, reflected in Stowe's novel, the southern states were the tropical regions of the United States. To Miss Ophelia, her trip to New Orleans "seemed . . . most equal to going to the Sandwich Islands, or anywhere among the heathen."[95] Topsy, capering about the plantation mistress's bed chamber, draped in her mistress's best Canton shawl, is as much a figure from a British colony as she is a product of American racism.

After the abolition of the slave trade, the picaninny grew even more to represent all the "childlike races" of the colonies. Popular iconography, especially in children's literature, blended plantation myths of the black child with colonial imaginings. In Frances Upton's *Gollywog* series, begun in Britain in 1895 with *The Story of Two Dutch Dolls*, and in Helen Bannerman's *Little Black Sambo*, written from her husband's colonial post in India in 1899, plantation fictions from the United States were linked to and overlapped with European and British imperial fictions. These fictions informed the picaninny shows at London's Palace Theatre in 1905, and Ida Forsyne's star turn as Topsy in particular.

Still known today, Butter Song of the South

LETTING THE FLESH FLY:
TOPSY, TIME, TORTURE, AND
TRANSFIGURATION

"DOING" TOPSY

I n the winter of 1905, Abbie Mitchell and Her Tennessee Students performed at the Palace Theatre in London to an enraptured audience. The show's "culminating triumph" was "the *pas seul* done by a little negro girl, whose wild and rapid gyrations send the house into ecstasies." This "little girl" was a five-foot one-inch, twenty-three-year-old dancer named Ida Forsyne, whose Topsy antics turned out the house.

An energetic chorus of working-class teenaged girls from the north of England accompanied Forsyne for the finale. These girls were trained to be chorus girls at the residential schools of the former cotton manufacturer and amateur dramatist John Tiller, who then hired them out to the Palace. They were energetic, "almost exuberant," as *The Era* notes. Legs flew, and sequins and feathers filled the air as "shoes and headgear . . . detached in the wild frenzy of their evolutions."[1] Forsyne's rendering of Topsy's unruly presence gave the young women of the chorus license to "raise Cain."

This chapter takes Topsy in two directions: first, considering Topsy as a female minstrel role I discuss the strange choreographies of female race delineation on the urban stage. Second, in the context of black re-versionings of the iconic figure I read Topsy as a trope for black female expressive resilience. In this second section I take up questions of the black(ened) body, of how meanings of race are produced and fought over, arguing that this process must be understood as fundamentally both corporeal and relational. Black expressive forms are a strategic way to think through the theoretical problems we face when weighing the relationship between discourse, inscription, and the black body's agency.

In the first part of the chapter I trace Topsy's iconographic power as a role developed exclusively by and for white women in the more than fifty years of stage and screen productions of *Uncle Tom's Cabin*. The white woman performer in blackface, and in childface, enacted the contradictory claims of white female matronage and entitlement. I lay out some ways to think about these politics of feminized racial enactment, a dynamic that rearticulates in later historical moments and which I address in subsequent chapters.

Resisting the masculinist blind of minstrelsy studies, we find that female minstrelsy has its own history, shaped by notions of the black female body's abilities, availability, and utility. In the mid-nineteenth century, "female minstrelsy" was an official stage circuit term. It evolved into and was renamed "burlesque" in the 1880s but carried forward the practices of racial mimicry from earlier stage conventions. Early burlesque was female-dominated popular stage work that was often satirical and always about dance, presaging the later chorus line dancers.

To make sense of various moments and instances of racial transmutation, which still operate today in popular cultural forms, I begin in the mid-1800s, with the graphic depictions of female slave suffering that traveled the abolitionist circuits, appealing to female abolitionist sensibilities. Female abolitionist appeals were empathic, imploring women to feel slave suffering in their own bodies as a way to engage their moral commitment. I argue that within this imagined process of absorption, the female body is thought to naturally yield to the sublime suffering of the slave women. This process then forms the basis, the (il)logic behind the practice of female race mimicry. I suggest that this process of sensate absorption underlies later instances of white women's racially imitative strategies evolving in the 1910s and 1920s.

Topsy manifested in a number of places and ways. I contend that the subject positioning of the actor in the mask has everything to do with the ways the act plays out and can be read. Black women's performances of Topsy carried different meanings than white women's versions. In the second half of the chapter I argue that they create a version recoverable as a symbol for black female unruliness. The disruptive creativity of the black female child, transforming herself in the place of work, resonated in the performance strategies of black women singers, musicians, and especially dancers into the twentieth century.

Considering the heavily scarred, mischievous, and misbehaving Topsy as a figure from which to analyze the wider meanings of black dance, I focus this second section on the body. I first examine the influence of race science on popular ideas of black female subjecthood. I begin by looking at how stories proliferating out of plantation lore melted together European colonial fictions with U.S. antebellum plantation nostalgia. I then look at how scientific rhetoric shaped popular ideas of black bodies and their abilities, and how Christian rhetoric joined with it in forming discourses of the constitution of the Negro. Out of these discourses came weird laws of contact and gruesome forms of intimacy: missionary codes of discipline, laws of racial segregation and anti-miscegenation, and those rituals of pain and torture developed to control the unfree body. Physical rituals of discipline and control were used to consolidate the power of chattel slavery. These carnal practices were given names, and as I point out they formed a lexicon. Descriptions of these named rituals were powerfully evoked in struggles against the bloody regime by black activist testimony and in abolitionist writings. We should think of this strategy as not simply a lower form of appeal because it is "sensational," but instead understand it as powerful and effective because it *was* sensational, about the flesh, based in a language of the senses. My argument rests on the premise that discourses attending systems of oppression, although they speak for and help perpetuate these systems, only work in relation to actual flesh and bone. These systems needed moving bodies, their economies first and foremost depend on muscle and sinew. I argue that it is moving black bodies that are the logical and primary medium for contrary acts of resilience, that they are literally alive in complex response to these systems.

The body in motion moves to rhythmic timed pulses. I consider the relationship of the raced body to discourses of time. According to popular ethnographic science, lesser races were governed by a simpler concept of time. I argue instead that black expressivity was formed in a complex web of time registers. Creative and improvisatory moments of bodily inflection were multi-zoned comments on geographical "origin." The centrality of dance in black culture, then, must be understood as much more than a cultural retention of (timeless ahistorical) African practices. They were formed as articulations of diasporic movement, of technologies of time and displacement. Whirling, twisting, and refusing to behave, Topsy "rags" the master's time; her movements prove that a body is never fully containable.

TALKING THE BODY

The question of how to "talk" about bodily reception and response poses tenacious conundrums. Do we assume that the body can be read and defined completely as a discursive field? Is it always the word made flesh? Can we talk about physical expression as outside of language? Current critical work on the body addresses these questions. In her book *Volatile Bodies*, Elizabeth Grosz summarizes four lines of investigation. One line of thought considers the body as it is rendered through discourses of the natural and biological sciences. Understanding how race was constructed through these cruelly imaginative discourses helps dispel the concept of race as a matter of skin tone alone, or as a subset of caste relations in the United States. The second line of thought outlined by Grosz considers the body as a "vessel," which has two interpretations. On the one hand, this vessel can be occupied by "an animating, willful subjectivity"; on the other hand, it can be thought of as a "passive . . . object over which struggles between the 'inhabitant' and others/exploiters may be possible." The latter, that the body is a contested site, is the most common definition used in discussions of the body as a traversed discursive terrain. By this definition the body is like an "instrument . . . it requires discipline and training . . . subduing and occupation."[2]

Grosz introduces a third and related line taken by theorists. This line of thinking understands the body as a "signifying medium, a vehicle of expression . . . a two-way conduit: on one hand it is a circuit for the transmission of information from outside the organism, conveyed through the sensory apparatus; on the other hand . . . a vehicle for the expression of otherwise sealed and self contained, incommunicable psyche." While this model suggests the body as more than a vessel, the body is still a medium, channeling energies from "elsewhere."[3]

Grosz's fourth conceptual point is the most productive, for it allows for right-sized renderings of resistance to seemingly hermetic systems of discursive control. Grosz explains that we can think of the body as a "productive and creative body which cannot be definitely known since it is not identical with itself across time. The body does not have a 'truth' or a 'true nature' since it is a process and its meaning and capacities will vary according to its context."[4] The crucial difference in this analysis is that it understands the body as always grounded in its historical context, as produced from and producing in specific historical conjunctures, as constantly moving and changing meaning. This helps a great deal in counteracting static, or normative, concepts of the body. It also avoids the tendency in resistance theories to search for an authentic true body, which can be recovered or restored.

Scholars working on race, performance, and the body are thinking through these problems and attempting to conceptualize the black (or racialized) body as active, signifying. "The body might be a blunt field of matter, inscribed and reinscribed, but does not the body signify in specific historical and cultural ways?" asks E. Patrick Johnson. With the impetus to theorize the body, an important shift, as Johnson states, is "to not only describe the ways it is brought into being . . . but what it does once it is constituted and the relationship between it and the other bodies around it."[5] I would add that the body is never finally constituted, like a sealed envelope, but is continually a contested field and an instrument of contestation and question. Johnson's last point, however, that power is generated *relationally*, is particularly important to hold onto. Power is performed between bodies and groups of bodies, and, as I emphasize here, it is quite visceral.

I share the concern that we think about the body not as a *tabula rasa*, as a passive or powerless terrain upon which dominant ideologies etch their claims indelibly. Thinking about the body in motion, and about bodies in relation to each other helps us to unthink this rigid version of the individual body as produced discursively. Discursive claims compete, conflict, and are never complete. Racialized bodies wriggle through, around, with, and against these claims.

In some of the work being done on the body there is a concentration on legal and literary discourse, and the visceral, the blood and guts of race and racisms, gets lost. Race and racist regimes are made by and out of flesh—muscle and ligament, blood and bone. Rituals of violence and torture were constitutive acts in themselves, not simply supporting or buttressing litigation. As long as bodies move, constitutive claims can never rest; they have to be repeated and intensified. Nineteenth- and twentieth-century racisms were spectacularly gruesome. Saidiya Hartman and others protest the use of the graphic and numerous accounts given by former slaves and slave owners by abolitionists and activists as a lurid strategy, appealing to people's base sensationalism. My point is that oppositional strategy is by necessity sensational, that is, of the body. The slavery regime was written in the language of the body. It was designed as spectacle. Rituals of control were choreographed for audiences and audience participation.

This is not to deny or elide the myriad extra-bodily forms through which racist hegemonies maintain control. Nor do I mean to be reductive, denying the complex relation between the physical and the discursive. But I do mean to underscore that it was and is bodies that racist regimes need. Techniques of terror, force, and coercion are devised to insure control of bodies. Furthermore, violence or its threat always shadow other forms. I do not argue that there is some discrete, boundaried space that the belea-guered self can access, outside the reach of dominant claims. I am also not arguing that all black acts are thoroughly resistant. But I am suggesting that the body is never an empty vessel, or completely open to being named and claimed in toto.

While "doing Topsy," as Forsyne put it, at the Alhambra Theatre in 1906, a chorus line of ballet dancers, in blackface, accompanied her. "They paid white girls extra to brown up and work behind me," Forsyne recalls. For this turn, Forsyne performed her "sack dance." Carried onstage in a potato sack, she emerged limb by limb, then danced wildly until a shot rang out and she fell to the floor. "I was doing Topsy in a potato bag," For-syne explains. "A stage hand brought me out . . . I'd eventually come out of this sack and I'd start running around like a wild woman. [My] costume was a bag and it had straw on it. I'd look here and there and then there [would] be a shot, and I [would] fall down and roll over and over and up— that was the dance."[6] This second performance moment from Forsyne's stage appearance as Topsy opens up to the larger question of what meth-ods we can develop for talking about black dance and gestural technique as responses to the ritual violence of racist regimes. In the language of variety melodrama, her breathtaking act references the historical memory of living as a commodity, as well as the black child's familiar proximity to violence, cruelty, and death.

This dance's description suggests how tenaciously terror and pleasure were linked when it came to the spectacle of black bodies dancing.[7] But there is an interesting discrepancy between the version of Forsyne's description as published by Marshall Stearns and Jean Stearns in their seminal study *Jazz Dance* and the version from the transcriptions of Forsyne's interview. While Forsyne remembers herself at the end of the dance rolling "over and over and *up*," the published version reads that she "rolls over and over *dead*."[8] Neither version can be marked as the "truth" and both versions make sense. The staged sublimity of black human suffering had long been firmly nestled in popular imagination. So had the fantasy of black subjects' inhuman ability to survive bondage, poverty, and peonage. These qualities were linked together and animated in the figure of Topsy. The discrepancy between the descriptions suggests that there is the potential in popular performance for layered meanings, for multiple signification. The version of the dance from the transcription (over and over and up) suggests a much more complex metaphorical response to terror and violence. To wriggle out of a sack, to be shot, and to rise up is the drama of ever-present danger to life and limb; these actions also suggest that death (social, bloody, or otherwise) may be (and had been) tricked, dodged, wiggled out of.

The arts of the body, particularly vernacular dance and song, are key responses to the rituals of violence "marking" and "claiming" black people's bodies. Through the metronomic wielding of the whip, slavery had indelibly marked its disciplinary claims on Topsy's small body, leaving its history inscribed on her back in calloused welts. I argue that, through the protean suppleness of her performance, a version of Topsy can be read as transfiguring reiterative rituals of inflicted pain.

A FEARFUL PROGENY

A large number of black children frisked and frolicked throughout the pages of Stowe's *Uncle Tom's Cabin* and onto the popular stage. When Topsy is introduced, she is added to what is already a physical cacophony of small black children, "mopping and mowing and grinning between the railings, and tumbling over the kitchen floor," exhibiting a ubiquitous and disruptive physicality, calling for vigilant discipline and guidance.[9] They refused to behave, defying all order necessary to the smooth running of a "home." These children were not born out of Stowe's book. The icon of the picaninny was already a familiar figure in popular imaginings of the U.S. South.

Stowe's novel is a pastiche of numerous sources. Reflecting its influences, the text acted as a condensation point; in turn versions and echoes from this text proliferated, affecting the developing genre of children's literature, the minstrel, and variety stages. Plays based on *Uncle Tom's Cabin* became fixtures in the United States, Britain, and Europe.

Stowe's book is intensely theatrical, its melodramatic immediacy marking it as a central text in popular culture's transition to visual mediums. "Stowe's relation to the minstrel show was an intervention that went both ways," as minstrel stage conventions influenced Stowe's fiction as much as her fiction would then influence the popular stage.[10] Stowe's novel was immediately followed by a myriad of popular stage versions. The decades-long phenomena of *Uncle Tom's Cabin* plays congealed the tradition of plantation nostalgia, of "take me backs" and plantation fiction. George Aiken's dramatization of Stowe's novel was the longest running and the most popular stage version. This was a family business, as were most of the Tom companies that followed. Aiken wrote the play in 1852 for the Howard family—his cousin Caroline Howard, her husband George Cunnabell Howard, and their small daughter Cordelia—who ran a small stock company with whom Aiken worked and traveled.[11] The traveling *Uncle Tom's Cabin* shows across the United States were family affairs, either literally or scripted, and the role of Topsy was played by the mother figure of the troupe.

Momentously received abroad, Stowe's novel was quickly translated into a number of languages and distributed widely throughout Europe. Just as quickly hundreds of dramatic adaptations were staged across Europe. "Tom Shows" became a transnational cultural institution; just months following the novel's publication, staged versions ran simultaneously in New York, London, France, and Germany. Small acting troupes, called Tommers, toured the United States and England for the next fifty or so years. Almost all of the productions were musicals, featuring the melodramas of Tom's Christian suffering and Eva's death, and the farcical antics of the mischievous Topsy.

It wasn't until after emancipation in the United States that black performers began appearing in these shows. In the mid-1870s, during the second wave of the *Uncle Tom* craze, black specialty acts were added to the bill. Troupes of African American jubilee singers began accompanying Tom shows on tour. After about 1880, black women performers began to appear more frequently in these specialty acts. "Colored women had always been barred from minstrel shows but this play opened the way for them," recalls the performer Thomas Fletcher.[12] In one version playing in the English provinces a "ballet of negro girls" was added. "They dress entirely in black and send the audience home feeling as though they had attended a funeral."[13]

In the 1890s white actors in blackface were still the only performers in the principal roles. Topsy and Uncle Tom were played by whites in burnt cork and black actors were only permitted to play the dancing and singing "slaves on the plantation."[14] That black actors were not permitted to play themselves in an anti-slavery narrative is an absurdity that will last throughout this book. Considering their long exclusion, the appearance of black actors in the principal roles has a historical dimension and a trajectory that cannot be subsumed into the history of the white-cast Tom shows.

Black performers had more willing audiences in England, who had grown tired of the white blackface dramatis personae and were eager to see a cast of "real American freed slaves" play "themselves."[15] The veteran black performer Sam Lucas was among the first black performers to play the role of Uncle Tom, with Charles Frohman's company in 1878.[16] Lucas also appeared in a version of the play put together in 1880 by the Hyers Sisters, an African American singing duo. This version had a black and white cast, in which "whites [played] in white roles and blacks in black roles."[17] Lucas was also the first black actor to appear as Uncle Tom on film, in 1914. It wasn't until this period that any black women began to appear as Topsy in versions of the Tom Shows, though this was most likely infrequent.[18]

In Britain an explosion of Uncle Tom ephemera accompanied the novel and stage versions. In Britain the "Tomist phenomenon" included children's literature—primers, catechisms, storybooks—as well as songs, board games, dolls, and even Uncle Tom's Cabin wallpaper. Images of black children featured prominently in the growing toy industry, with Topsy's place most prominent.[19] This is a moment to consider the centrality of race in the formation of western ideologies of childhood and popular child culture.

The figure of Topsy circulated not only as an orphaned child from North America's plantations but also as a figure of English and European colonial subjecthood. "As for depictions of the black child," writes Harry Birdoff, "English audiences had seen but one type, the little page from India who officiates as trainbearer to Lady Teazle—and that was exactly the way the Adelphi, the theatre Royal Manchester and other playhouses presented Topsy."[20] But such colonial versions of Topsy were not actually that far from the figure as she appears in Stowe's novel. As well as a product of the system of U.S. chattel slavery, she is drawn in Stowe's novel to represent the childlike races of Africa and India, the uneducated natives to be tamed and trained by Christian charity. The picaninny was a lasting figure for the primitive; the project of civilizing Topsy was a metaphor for colonial missionary programs and their paternalist agendas. Topsy is framed and developed in the novel as a heathen, a native in need of the Christian missionary's ministrations. "It is in the context of established and indeed strengthening links of abolitionism with missionary activity that *Uncle Tom's Cabin* became a classic instructional text," writes Marcus Wood. "In the illustrated children's versions it became almost a new missionary bible, but the original novel certainly encouraged such a reading—in many ways the book increasingly becomes a missionary tract."[21] This was part of the reason why the English responded so readily to the character.

With the advent of colonial regimes replacing the formal system of slave labor, the racist infantilization of black people, from several sites on the map of Western empire, were represented in the figure of the black child. A political cartoon from the *Punch* issue of April 21, 1894 is titled "The Black Baby." It features Uganda as an orphaned baby, left at the doorstep of Britain. In the cartoon Mr. Bull leans over: "What! Another? I suppose I must take it in!!!" he exclaims.[22] African nations are figured as helpless infant burdens, thrust, unsolicited, on the good will of British officials. Empire becomes the result of fatherly, absent-minded benevolence. In 1895 Florence Upton and her mother Bertha authored and illustrated a children's story called *The Adventures of Two Dutch Dolls and a Golliwogg*, featuring a black-faced, wide-eyed doll. This figure was a combination of images of the picaninny associated with the fictional U.S. plantation as well as with British colonial lore. The Uptons wrote twelve more *Golliwogg* books, until 1909. The iconographic power of these fictional characters had an incredible longevity, reoccurring well into the twentieth century. Golliwoggs appeared in early issues of Enid Blyton's *Noddy* series, although they were replaced in later editions. Blyton's 1944 title, *The Three Golliwogs* (named Golly, Woggy, and Nigger) has fallen out of print.[23] Yet golliwoggs can still be found as a range of stuffed dolls and, until 2001, appeared on the jars of jam bottled by the British company Robertson's. Strangely enough, the golliwogg has become a focal point for a particular brand of British nationalist nostalgia. Defending the memory of a proud British empire, proponents pledge to fight to "save our gollywogs" from rampant anti-race censors.[24] "Gollies" are drawn as a grafted combination of human and animal. On a promotional website for Australian tourism, golliwoggs are referred to as having become an "endangered species" after the 1980s. "Whether it was climate, or their habitat, they were becoming very scarce."[25] Such language evokes the history of Britain, and her representatives in the commonwealths, as one of loving caretakers. Such nostalgia blames meddlesome multicultural politics for the loss of correct forms of recognition and appreciation between the races.

Another colonialist children's classic sprang from the picaninny convention. In 1899 Helen Bannerman, the Scottish wife of a British army surgeon stationed in Madras wrote *Little Black Sambo*. Raised in several British colonies, Helen Bannerman herself would live for thirty years in India. The story goes that Bannerman wrote the tale to amuse her children on long train rides in the hot months when they traveled from Madras to the cooler mountain regions.

In her illustrations Helen Bannerman renders Sambo quite dark, small, and slim, a composite of colonial subjects. He is at once sub-Saharan African, South Indian, and the scampering picaninny of U.S. southern plantation fiction. The story of the small boy outwitting a group of hungry tigers ends with a feast of pancakes made by his mother. The narrative of Bannerman's story is clearly influenced by the continued commodification of U.S. plantation nostalgia, specifically the introduction of Aunt Jemima pancake flour at the Columbian Exposition in 1893, advertised by Nancy Green's performance as a 'mammy.'

While the Golliwogg figure remained a British icon with little currency in the United States, versions of Bannerman's *Little Black Sambo* would cross the Atlantic. A number of children's books featuring the character of Little Black Sambo were published after 1920 in the United States, as the story was refitted for a new era of plantation and colonial nostalgia. Joining a plethora of picaninny figures, including Farina, Stymie, and

8 Little Black Sambo,
   Helen Bannerman.

Buckwheat from *Our Gang*, re-versions of *Little Black Sambo* authored by Americans would appear in children's books, cartoons, and films in the 1920s, 1930s, and 1940s.

Topsy, then, birthed generations of black children characters. Some were gendered male, as in versions of Little Black Sambo, some had male and female versions, as is the case with the Upton and Blyton Golliwoggs. Some versions were rendered ambiguously when it came to gender, as in the early versions of the character Farina in *Our Gang*. Whatever the gender of the picaninny figures that followed her, Topsy herself, as a little girl, emerges from the novel to be one of the most resonant characters in popular stage versions.

Stowe fabricated the figure of Topsy, W. T. Lhamon suggests, from the minstrel stage. We can see the influence of the popular minstrel stage when Topsy is introduced as a "funny specimen in the Jim Crow line," whose first order from her new owners St. Claire and Miss Ophelia is to dance. "The thing struck up, in a clear shrill voice, an odd negro melody, to which she kept time with her hands and feet, spinning round, clapping her hands, knocking her knees together, in a wild, fantastic sort of time, and producing in her throat all those odd guttural sounds which distinguish the native music of her race."[26] Lhamon situates Stowe's Topsy in relation to white men in blackface on the mid-century stage. "Topsy's steam whistle imitation is one indication of her indebtedness to the minstrel stage. . . . Another indication is her 'wild' syncopated time," he writes. "A third is her body-warping, which Stowe might have lifted from any of the grape-vine twisted figures spelling out the titles on minstrel show posters. Any of these signs would have pointed contemporary readers to Topsy as a wench figure from the minstrel show."[27] Lhamon rightly acknowledges the fluidity of forms and figures, the porousness of cross-pollinating popular forms. But his analysis does not account for why Topsy was, from the beginning of her stage life, a role developed and delineated exclusively by white adult women, and not a role developed for, or by, male minstrel cross-dressers.

Studies of vernacular culture and minstrelsy, such as Eric Lott's *Love and Theft*, develop and innovate within masculinist conceptual frameworks. In doing so they exclude the histories of women working in blackface and most importantly the theoretical implications of these histories.

Topsy was not a cipher of identification for the rebellious spirit of white working-class men. Topsy was from the very beginning rendered by white women. She was not a wench role, but a *female* blackface role. "For white actresses, Topsy was the most promising role in the 'Tom circuit,'" writes Judith Williams. Topsy "became a testing ground for young actresses to prove their mettle."[28] In full burnt cork and wooly wig, Mrs. Caroline Howard was the first Topsy, and she would play this blackface role for thirty-five years, until her retirement in 1887. "Mrs. Howard's dancing as Topsy was the precursor of a school of Topsies doing 'breakdowns,'" writes Harry Birdoff.[29] Other white female Topsy performers, such as Charlotte Crabtree, followed, blacking up and singing Howard's signature song, "I'se So Wicked," for their acts. Generations of white female blackface delineators continued the practice as literal Topsies but also in other racial guises on the popular stage.

With the advent of film, screen versions of *Uncle Tom's Cabin* were soon to follow. At least seven versions of *Uncle Tom's Cabin* were made between 1903 and 1927. The films followed the staged plays, with white actors in the principal roles. In each of the film versions Topsy was a blackface role played by an adult white woman.[30] Universal Studios' *Uncle Tom's Cabin*, produced in 1927, was long and lavish. The actress Mona Ray offers a hyperbolically and painfully self-humiliating version of Topsy.

Also in 1927 United Artists produced a film called *Topsy and Eva*, which had been designed around the long-standing vaudeville act of the Duncan Sisters, Rosetta and Vivian (see fig. 9). The film starred the black actor Noble Johnson as Uncle Tom. Rosetta Duncan, in full cork, wig, and whitened lips, became perhaps the most famous Topsy and would spend her entire career playing Topsy to her sister Vivian's Little Eva. Rosetta "played Topsy so entertainingly that for many she personified the role" (see fig. 10). The Duncan sisters' stage act opened four years before the film was made, in 1923 in San Francisco. The plot drew only loosely on the novel; Rosetta's and Vivian's farcical slapstick and vaudeville songs, such as "Sweet Onion Time," were the focus of their stage versions. The chorus line was intimately associated with blackface female roles. When the show moved to Chicago, they were joined by none other than a chorus of the London Palace Girls, dressed as picaninnies and with blackened-up skin (see fig. 11).[31]

Following the movement of female minstrelsy into burlesque, techniques of racial mimicry enacted by women proliferated on the popular stage. In the 1890s white stage women would become "coon shouters," and through the 1910s and 1920s vaudeville comediennes including Sophie Tucker and Fanny Brice would work in blackface. Even when not in literal blackface, staged delineations were imitations of the idea of the black working female body—active, agile, licentious, ingenious. In their shimmering blonde wigs, Eva Tanguay, Mae West, and Gilda Gray fantasized black female bodily techniques in their versions of the shimmy, which they had seen black women dance on the TOBA circuit. Racial mimicry was not exclusively a working-class phenomenon. As the dance scholars Jane Desmond and Amy Koritz have discussed, early modern dancers such as Ruth St. Denis regularly "went native," darkening their skin; Orientalist eroticisms and colonialist fantasies intertwined with those from North America.[32] But literally rendered Topsies did not disappear; besides Rosetta Duncan's frequent stage revivals, the figure would appear on film as late as 1938, when Judy Garland blacked up and donned the gingham dress for a musical sequence in the film *Everybody Sing*. This film was directed by her husband, keeping it, again, a family affair.

In *The World's Greatest Hit*, Harry Birdoff includes a photo of the Tom Show performer Charlotte Crabtree tippling on a fence in blackface, pigtails, and ragged dress. What are we to do with this strange image of a

9 Rosetta and Vivian Duncan. Image from *Uncle Tom's Cabin and American Culture*. Used with permission of John Sullivan.

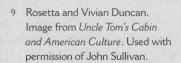

10 Rosetta Duncan, from the film *Topsy and Eva*. Image from *Uncle Tom's Cabin and American Culture*. Used with permission of John Sullivan.

11 Rosetta Duncan and black-faced chorus girls, Gaiety Theatre, London, November 1928. Image from *Uncle Tom's Cabin and American Culture*. Used with permission of John Sullivan.

grown white woman made up in the guise of a small black slave-child? Long-standing identifications suggest themselves as explanations. Lottie Crabtree, with her mischievous grin, reminds us of the equation in medical science, politics, and philosophy between women and children. Like children, women were imagined as susceptible to outside stimuli, easily impressionable, emotionally immediate. Both were prone to misbehavior, both were in need of guidance and discipline. But the appeal of such acts of mimicry rests on more than just the imagined affinity between women and children. First, this particular child was not quite human, not quite tamable; she was a little demon. Second, she was also a possession, property, without the right to inhabit her own body on her own terms.

In this blackface act, the adult woman's body is transmogrified into the body of a prepubescent girl. On the one hand, playing a misbehaving and rebellious female picaninny represented a therapeutic opportunity for white women, providing access to realms of prepubescent expressive freedoms womanhood was otherwise constructed against. On the other hand, as the role was developed for and consistently played by the mother of the Tommer troupe, the process suggests itself as a response to the sublimation of female sexual maturity and desire in the Victorian bourgeois gender ideal. Disavowed or made diminutive, forced back into a child's body, female sexual maturity returns in the form of the grotesque, the monstrous, the heathenous.

The act can be thought of as a working-class response to this normative model of womanhood, a playful refusal to behave. But such mischievous disruption is held in carefully contained moments of transgression. It should not be construed as an act of alliance with unfree black female subjects. On the contrary, it stabilizes the difference between them. Female minstrel acts were performances of white women's proprietary access to the black female body, as surrogate, as servant, as always already available for use. The mimetic act gave symbolic license to the forms of racialized and gendered oppressions under which black women and girls labored.

Black children were also unfree subjects, produced in bondage. The act of performing as the black child staged a resolve to the ambiguity between the "owned" and the "free" female body. Were white women "free"? Created equal? Did they have the right, as the black children did not, to shape the terms of their own bodily inhabitance? On the one hand, the white woman could perform an affiliation with the black child, both being in some sense property. On the other hand, her act affirmed the profound difference between the forms of ownership binding them. (As she was inhuman, and chattel herself, what could Topsy inherit?) The ability to inhabit both meanings pivots on the performance as overdetermined as an act of power, that is, as an enactment of access to the services of the black body.

Many cultural critiques seek to recoup some egalitarian affirmation in moments of racial mimicry. I cannot share their hope. As Saidiya Hartman asserts, "The seeming transgressions of the color line and the identification forged with the blackface mask through aversion and/or desire ultimately served only to reinforce relations of mastery and servitude."[33] Some versions of the role of Topsy offered a form of populist critique, and Tommers regularly toured farming regions in the Midwest. But populism does not infer egalitarianism. The use of the *idea* of black suffering, an icon for all types of suffering, does not imply active alliance with black people or their continued struggles for space and resources.

The dangerously unequal politics of "contact" are at the heart of how racial mimicry works. The historical availability of black bodies, as commodities, allows for a sense of entitlement to these bodies' abilities and efforts. This extends into the cultural imagination as access to sets of (often contradictory) imagined properties associated with blackness—spiritual, sexual, obedient, rebellious, strong, weak. This sense of entitlement is affirmed and strengthened by the performance.

The boundaries separating owned from free black bodies, however, had to be heatedly defended, and needed constant reinforcement, as these bodies were under constant challenge from the owned black female bodies themselves. Black women understood these acts, after all, as false intimacies designed to maintain a white female subject category. They were imagined resolutions to white anxieties, and did not amount to a natural reach for universal suffrage.

The politics of this enacted access in female blackface have a history in the evocation of female slave suffering found in nineteenth-century abolitionist appeals. Like her male counterpart, the icon of the suffering female supplicant crying "Aren't I Your Sister?" was stereotyped into a design used for tokens and stationery. The impassioned abolitionist poet and essayist Elizabeth Chandler rendered the supplicant figure with words, beseeching women to the anti-slavery cause with her article "Mental

Metempsychosis" in 1831. This was the same year that the narrative of the escaped slave Mary Prince was published in Britain. Prince's story was a graphic and gory account of a variety of tortures. Like Prince's rendering, Chandler's appeal was particularly bloody and fleshly. She appealed to women in sensorial terms. Addressing other Christian ladies, Chandler "urged them to try to identify with the enslaved," to feel what they had felt. Free white women were urged to "Let the fetter be with its bearing weight upon their wrists, as they are driven off like cattle to the market, and the successive strokes of the keen thong fall upon their shoulders till the flesh rises to long welts beneath it, and the spouting blood follows every blow."[34] The appeal to feel is a call to a visceral reaction before it is a call for emotional response. In this process of mental metempsychosis, then, a woman was to invite the suffering soul of the (dead) slave woman, and her painful physical memory, to pass into her own body. This spiritual appeal is thoroughly sensate and was meant to activate and intensify her Christian sensitivities, to make her feel as she felt in her faith the ecstasy of Christ's suffering, a shiver through her body as she ate his flesh and drank his blood.

Empathic access to black bodily memory is made possible in conjunction with the history of how these bodies were understood as commodity. The body becomes the medium for the *one-way* transmission of empathic appeal. The process is based on the concept of contact, but it requires, oddly enough, no actual physical touch of any kind with living slave bodies. The empathic appeal is pornographic in its urge; in the language of eroticized violence, white women were encouraged to "feel successive strokes of the keen thong." This is an encoded reference to the sexual violations black female slaves routinely suffered. But there is a more disturbing type of participatory voyeurism here, a devouring intimacy that I am loath to call love.

Thinking of imitative techniques on stage, this process of empathic access can be called absorption, suggested by the spread of cork on the skin as it seeps into the dermis. The concept of absorption is a useful one, which we will revisit in subsequent chapters. This absorption is both more than skin deep and nothing but; it is a symbolic and temporary indulgence. This process, I argue, forms the epistemic foundation for the dramatic economy of female minstrelsy and future forms of racial delineation.

White women's acts of racial delineation, in cork and out of it, do not close off the range of motion shaping the meanings of the black female body. Other possibilities are held captive under the skin and under the skirt. But I add that to critique the power relations of white female minstrelsy we do not have to reinscribe the idea of a "real" black subject or "real" set of black female cultural practices. Nor does this critique rely on stable definitions of whiteness; minstrelsy actually helps produce and stabilize these definitions and to resolve any conflicts around access to the privileges the category implied. However, I insist that the meanings of racial delineation change in relation to the historico-political subject positioning of the actor. Blackface roles resonate differently when practiced by black women. Blackface, performed by black women, operated on alternate tonal registers than that of the "real" delineators such as Mrs. Howard and Charlotte Crabtree, whose acts were always overdetermined by the politics of proprietary power.

Black women's acts were capable of multiple articulations, coded struttings within the terms of bondage. As a purely comedic figure, this Topsy is potentially subversive. I want to reclaim a trope of black female performance, hidden in the skirts of blackface nostalgia, masculinist revision, and the forgetfulness of black communal shame.

As I stated above, this subversive quality is not equally present in manifestations of Topsy across the board. A type of transgression is available on the white female minstrel stage, a conditioned rebellion against the proscriptions of white female duty. But the transgressiveness is not the same as identification with racialized subjects themselves. The role always signifies ownership of the black female body. But when rendered by racialized subjects, performances of Topsy potentially bring alive a sense of the ability of farce to disrobe authority. Her self-denigrating antics are executed with a sly grin, suggesting the defiance behind them. As a nonperson, as a manufactured product (raised in the pen) she steals and lies, disobeys orders with impunity. The system has created its own problems: how can property steal? How can an immoral heathen, not knowing the value of truth, be held accountable for lying? These trespasses in fact reveal the arbitrary lines drawn in law between truth and deception, theft and purchase, for, as the abolitionists argued, owning a person was a criminal act.

Topsy was the one supporting character that grew up in the plays from a comedic character into a larger role. Ultimately the narrative contains her; at Eva's death she is tamed by Christian forbearance and beneficence. But it is the Topsy *before* her salvation that remains in our cultural memory. Topsy's penitent tears cannot wash away the effect of her earlier glee-filled miscreant paganism. Perhaps this is why mid-century Tommers kept the role out of the hands of black performers. They might have run away with it.

For a black cultural elite centered in Harlem in the 1920s, black farce did not suggest social critique but rather the "pernicious influence" of blackface minstrelsy. This was understandably so in many ways; it took until 1923 for any black legitimate drama to make it to Broadway (the triple bill of black-authored *A Chip Woman's Fortune*, Oscar Wilde's *Salome*, and Shakespeare's *Comedy of Errors*) and that same year the Duncan sisters' *Topsy and Eva* act opened as a huge success, with the supporting chorus of Palace Girls in blackface. According to Montgomery Gregory's cultural assessment in *The New Negro*, black actors who worked in the mediums of "grotesque comedy . . . farce, mimicry and sheer burlesque" were participating in their own debasement, reproducing white racisms.[35]

Black cultural arbiters Alaine Locke and others repeatedly cautioned against the deleterious effects of comedy, popular music, and dance. For the producers of the Negro Renaissance, variety hall specialty acts, blues, and jazz were forms governed by base sentiment and filled with vulgar expression, and they obstructed the world's view of the Negro's true abilities. Black artistic philanthropists needed to guard against these forms as they helped Negro art rise up and reach for the light of serious endeavor. These base forms were at best untutored folk tradition, needing to be guided in the proper channels. Intra-race class conflict over artistic representation was not new. A self-consciously black elite had long been urging the race to bring forth its best and finest, warning against the corrupting vulgarities promoted in burlesque halls, jook joints, clubs, and cabarets.

Equally, poking fun at high-toned colored folk and their elitist pretensions had long been a convention on the black comedic stage and was taken up by the comedic artists in the 1910s and 1920s. Early Williams and Walker shows included such compositions as "The Leader of the Colored Aristocracy," and "She's Getting More Like White Folks Everyday," satires of the well-heeled dilettantes from elite black communities in Washington, D.C. and New York. The primary function for such low farce was as a critique of intra-racial class hierarchies; the use of laughter was a social leveler.[36]

For many of the New Negro intelligentsia, however, Topsy was the quintessential symbol of black artistic denigration and humiliation. Topsy's "baneful influence" continued to stymie serious black drama. So writes Montgomery Gregory, an English professor at Howard and a graduate of Harvard, in his essay "The Drama of Negro Life," which the editor Alain Locke included in the anthology *The New Negro*. "Although *Uncle Tom's Cabin* passed into obscurity, 'Topsy' survived," Gregory writes. "She was blissfully ignorant of any ancestors, but she has given us a fearful progeny." He continued:

> With her, popular dramatic interest in the Negro changed from a serious moralistic drama to the comic phase. We cannot say that as yet the public taste has generally recovered from this descent from sentimentalism to grotesque comedy, and from that in turn to farce, mimicry and sheer burlesque. The earliest expression of Topsy's baneful influence is to be found in the minstrels . . . these comedians, made up into grotesque caricatures of the Negro race, fixed in the public taste a dramatic stereotype of the race that has been almost fatal to a sincere and authentic Negro drama.[37]

As the Duncan sisters' *Topsy and Eva* act was in its second successful year, most likely the image of Rosetta Duncan's by then ubiquitous blackfaced and white-mouthed Topsy sat forefront in Gregory's mind. He did concede that a few great actors (he names Bert Williams and Florence Mills) were able to rise above their tainted material and develop their talent. But for the most part the "unfortunate minstrel inheritance" found in musical comedies, had, in his assessment, "been responsible for a fearful misrepresentation of Negro life."[38] Black farce, mimicry, and burlesque became the "fearful progeny" of Topsy, folded into a shameful past that was best forgotten. The well-founded nervous desire for "sincere and authentic Negro drama" did much to cast an earlier era of black stage history into darkness.

In her analysis, the critic Saidiya Hartman interprets Topsy as a symbol of low farce, contrasting and heightening the melodramatic dignity of Uncle Tom. "Blows caused the virtuous black body of melodrama to be esteemed," but "humiliated the grotesque body of minstrelsy. Uncle Tom's tribulations were tempered by the slaps and punches delivered to Topsy."[39]

But what makes farce funny is the ability of its figures to take the slaps and punches, to fall from the fist but still get up again, bruised and bleeding yet all the while slyly glancing up and around, in multiple directions. Topsy taunts her owners to inflict punishment from which she then refuses to suffer. As Bakhtin asserts, in its true form farce is layered, dialogic. The figure cannot be slapped down, but keeps rising up, keeps refusing to obey, keeps offering pun and quip.

There was power in the tactics of farcical disobedience developed by early black children performers. Looking at the character of Topsy in light of the histories of black children dancers, a version of Topsy can be understood as a way to read a quality of defiant and disruptive resilience in black expressive acts. Topsy is inured to pain and proudly so; in her defiance she refuses humiliation. She seems to erupt upon the scene as from some unearthly place; as I shall explore she exists seemingly outside the bounds of chronological time. The twisting body of the dancing girl is a reclaimable trope of black expressive transfiguration.

DOING SCIENCE, OR "THE DISEASE CALLED 'RASCALITY'"

Popular notions of racial essence and typology were developed and circulated widely in the nineteenth century. Theories of race as debated in the natural sciences did not have to travel very far to reach the realm of the popular. "Racialism was a cultural as much as a scientific idea," writes Robert Young. "Racial theory was always fundamentally populist in tone."[40] In being pitched to the popular, these theories were, from their inception, decidedly spectacular. Racial theories circulated regularly in the popular press and through a visual language of photographs and etchings. Lectures were a common form of delivery, but they were only part of the performance. Embodiments and bodily differences were enacted through particularly grisly and carnal stagings. Body parts were dissected in hospital theaters; live specimens, skeletons, and preserved organs were displayed at fairs, museums, and zoos. The Scotsman Robert Knox procured recently murdered bodies for the good of science. Samuel Morton, the Philadelphia physician, craniologist, and founding member of the American School of Ethnography, boasted the world's largest collection of skulls.

Comparative anatomy proved that it was the physiognomy of the primitives that distinguished them from the civilized, the external features indicating, as phrenology argued, the internal temperament and workings of the nervous system and brain. The work of the American School of Ethnography, led by Samuel Morton, the Alabamian slave owner Josiah Nott and the Egyptologist George Gliddon, was committed to finding proof of black inferiority, particularly after Darwin's *The Origin of Species* in 1859 officially discredited a polygenist argument. Abolitionists, European race supremacists, and proslavery advocates all drew on the popular scientific discourses on race for their "facts" on racial constitution. Stowe's descriptions reflect this scientific thought.

In *The Key to Uncle Tom's Cabin*, Stowe's descriptions of the "Negro temperament" show the influence of Morton, Nott, and Gliddon; no surprise, as their work was available to a popular audience. "Their sensations and impressions are very vivid, and their fancy and imagination lively," Stowe writes. Particularly evident is the influence of phrenology. This "science" proved not just that intelligence could be read from external features, but that all physical and neurological differences were dictated by the brain. "In this respect the race has an Oriental character, and betrayed its tropical origin. Like the Hebrews of old and the Oriental nations of the present . . . their whole bodily system sympathizes with the movement of their minds . . . like oriental nations, they incline much toward outward expression, violent gesticulations, and agitating movements of the body." (Key, 45) Difference was located not just on the skin but inside the body, in the nerves and sinew.

Phrenology claimed that "mental constitution, not climate or terrain was the vital factor."[41] This claim is crucial to a theory of racial inferiority in the United States, where arguments that climate dictated the temperament could not be relied on, since the "primitives" inhabited the same physical space as their masters. The reference to climate here is only to immediate environs, as there were certain inherited factors from the races' originary lands. These factors hardened into permanent features. As the noted phrenologist George Combe wrote: "If we glance over the history of Europe, Asia, Africa and America, we shall find distinct and permanent features of character, which strongly indicate natural differences in the mental constitutions."[42] Stowe describes Negroes as an "exotic race, whose ancestors, born beneath a tropic sun, brought with them, and perpetuated to their descendants, a character . . . unlike the hard and dominant Anglo-Saxon race" (*Uncle Tom's Cabin*, xiii). Stowe's thinking reflects a commonsense understanding of the relationship between civilization and geography.

According to these popular understandings of racial fact, it was these constitutional differences that led to slaves' deviance, and made the need for corporal punishment seem natural and necessary. Samuel Cartwright, in "Diseases and Peculiarities of the Negro Race," published in 1851 in the pro-slavery journal *De Bow's Review*, describes the condition "Dysaesthesia aethiopica, or hebetude of mind and obtuse sensibility of body—a disease peculiar to negroes—called by overseers, 'rascality.'" The worst symptoms of this condition, according to Cartwright, are the violation of the rights of property. The slaves are "apt to do much mischief, which appears to be intentional, but is mostly owing to the stupidity of mind and insensibility of the nerves induced by the disease. . . . [They] break, waste and destroy everything . . . paying no attention to the rights of property." Scientific data on the Negro temperament (absurd misinterpretations of slave resistance) were used to diagnose proper treatment of the race. The "facts" were used to justify and define a range of disciplinary tactics. Since Cartwright's disease is noted by a "partial insensibility of the skin," he advises to "have the patient well washed . . . anoint [the skin] all over with oil . . . slap the oil in with a broad leather strap. . . . Put the patient to some hard kind of work in the open air."[43] The lasting gift of the comparative anatomists was to render blackness more than a matter of skin, to locate race in the nervous system and the mental-emotional makeup of the brain. Prone to "violent gesticulations and agitating movements of the body,"[44] the black body's difference was not its color, but rather resided below the skin; it existed principally in the body's internal electrical and chemical composition. This black body was not internally or naturally regulated according to the same rules of time and space, and the black body's raciology was detectable in its expressivity.

A LEXICON OF TORTURES, OR, DERMIS, BLOOD AND BONE

Abolitionists drew upon the graphic depictions of slavery to galvanize support for the cause. A lexicon of slave suffering came from escaped and rescued men and women; one early narrative, that of the West Indian slave woman Mary Prince, was published in 1831 by the British Antislavery

Society. This was in the same year that William Lloyd Garrison launched his abolitionist publication, *The Liberator*. Numerous and bloody first-hand accounts were also given in Theodore Dwight Weld's 1839 book *American Slavery as It Is*.

Stowe, as did William Wells Brown in his novel *Clotel*, drew upon the personal testimonies of slavery's survivors, as well as the lectures and writings of anti-slavery activists. Both authors also drew from Weld's book. Weld "proves by a cloud of witnesses"—slaves, Northern visitors, slave-holders—that a plethora of tortures were produced and practiced under the system of chattel slavery. Many of the bloodiest renderings are from "the slaveholders themselves, and in their own chosen words."[45] In the 1890s the activist Ida B. Wells Barnett would use this strategy in her anti-lynching campaign, enlisting descriptions of post-reconstruction torture from the white press in her pamphlets, essays, and lectures.

Weld's book details the ways bodies were literally marked, written on in scars and gashes, particularly on the back, legs, and arms. These forms of demarcation were choreographed performances with a function, the inscription of ownership. Faces and backs were branded and striped, teeth were knocked out and fingers removed, to make those slaves prone to running away more easily recognizable. Ingenious tortures, invented to increase the pain of punishment, were given names. "Crosswhipping" kept the wounds from healing. When "cat hauling," the torturer was to "take a cat by the nape of the neck and tail, or by the hind legs, and drag the claws across the back [of the slave] until satisfied."[46] "Pickling" describes another torture: "The slaves are terribly lacerated with whips, paddles, & c.; red pepper and salt are rubbed into their mangled flesh; hot brine and turpentine are poured into their gashes."[47] Weld may very well have drawn from the narrative of the escaped slave Mary Prince for some of these tortures. Having worked in the salt marshes, she repeatedly describes the torture of "pickling" a slave's wounds.

The narratives of survivors such as Mary Prince were key sources for Weld, as well as for Stowe and other authors of sentimental fiction. Prince escaped while in London with her masters. Having been a slave in Bermuda and Antigua, she reports particularly grisly abuses to herself and others, inflicted not only by her masters but also by her mistresses. Prince recounts how she grew to know "the exact difference between the smart of the rope, the cart-whip, and the cow-skin, when applied to my naked body by her [mistress's] own cruel hand."[48] As in many slave women's narratives, whipping, flogging, beating, which Prince suffered most frequently, stand in as code for sexual abuse and torture. "My former master used to beat me while raging and foaming with passion. . . . [Although] Quite calm . . . Mr. D . . . often stripped me naked, hung me up by the wrists, and beat me with a cow-skin, with his own hand, till my body was raw with gashes."[49] Reading Prince's graphic renderings, I wonder why it is that current criticism should find Frederick Douglass's description of Aunt Hester's suffering, however poignant at twice the narrative remove, the legitimating representative and most resonant moment of female slave suffering.[50]

The currency of representations of violence, pain, and endurance was set to garner white liberals' charitable sensibilities. Personal testimonies were designed to prove to white audiences that black people had the ability to feel pain and suffering. Their sensate abilities were a kind of scientific measurement for how readily black Africans could be lifted up from their savage state.

Whatever the imagined black body conveyed, it ran under the skin, flowed through the blood and nervous system, and rang in the bones. The arguments against slavery were couched in bodily terms not simply as a sensational ruse, but because rituals of punishment and control were the language the system spoke in. "I have been a slave and I know what a slave feels," Prince repeats. "I can tell by myself what other slaves feel." The sensate is also the language through which forms of resistance were articulated.[51]

What is striking in firsthand accounts and slave narratives is the attention to the feet, hands, and limbs. This may seem self-evident, as they are the main moving parts of the working body. "Our feet and legs, from standing in the salt water for so many hours, soon became full of dreadful boils, which eat down in some cases to the very bone," wrote Prince of her working life in the salt ponds.[52] Images of the limbs swelling to the point of exploding are frequent. Tortures were often designed for the hands and feet. As in the case of Jonathan Walker's branded hand, abolitionists described slaves' hands and feet as Christ's, situated slaves as God's innocent martyrs.[53]

Sometime in the 1860s after emancipation a Republican rally was held in Camilla, Georgia; it ended in violence. A twelve-year-old girl was in attendance with a relative when a white man, John Gaines, attacked her and "took her hand and split each finger from its end to the center of the hand."[54] This incident reminds us that there were civic bodies in struggle also. But why would a man devise this particular torture? What was threatening about a young girl's hand, palm up? The emphasis cannot be reduced to simple sensationalism. Hands and feet have great metonymic power. Control of the hands was key to bonded labor, and unchained hands were symbolic of freedom.

In survivor narratives hands and feet take on symbolic resonance for self-preservation and liberation, for freedom and as the practical means of escape. "Feet don't fail me now" is a call for agility and stamina in dancing, but it refers to the power of escape and the jubilation of post-emancipation mobility. Feet and hands articulate extraordinary beauty and grace. Ida Forsyne describes the artistic qualities she admired in Abbie Mitchell. "She was rapacious. She absolutely—spoke. Her body spoke. Her hands— spoke." Such expressive articulations meant more than what they said.

As the fugitive slave Lewis Clarke illustrated, slavery alienated people from their own bodies. Clarke writes, "The slaves often say, when cut in the hand or foot, 'Plague on the old foot' or 'the old hand! It is master's— let him take care of it. Nigger don't care if he ever get well.'" In his narrative Clarke relates his escape. "At daylight we were in Canada. . . . Not till then did I dare to cherish, for a moment, the feeling that one of the limbs of my body was my own." Escape, relocation, meant to re-inhabit one's body, reclaim the life in one's limbs. "My hands, my feet were now my own," are the key words with which Clarke describes the feeling of freedom.[55]

In Stowe's novel and Aiken's play, Topsy receives the harshest blows. As a figure of low farce she is associated with gruesome violence, which she survives and which she is seemingly inured to. Upon her first intro- duction to the "*corps de ballet*," as Stowe words it, she is dirty, blue-black, and welted, indelibly scarred by the repeated whippings of her previous owners. On her back and shoulders stood "great welts and callused spots, ineffaceable marks of the system under which she had grown up."[56] The rhythms of the whip have marked her body—the callused welts on her back are a composition of slavery's history. Black flesh is marked by rituals of (mis)recognition at the hands of the civilized. The repetitive perfor- mance of violence on her small body has left her disturbingly callused and perverse. St. Clare explains that "whippings and abuse are like laudanum, you have to double the dose as the sensibilities decline."[57] Rituals of contact were performative interactions through which the coercive relations of power between conqueror and subject were consolidated, even while they sometimes staged themselves as forms of benevolent guidance.

Topsy's bloody insensibility resonated on the comedic stage. Several songs were written for her in the over fifty years that *Uncle Tom's Cabin* plays were staged. Her first and signature song is "Oh! I'se So Wicked," written for Mrs. Howard in Aiken's play. The second stanza reads:

> She [Miss Feely] used to knock me on de floor,
> Den bang ma head again de door,
> An' tear ma wool out by de core:
> Oh! because I wuz so wicked![58]

The second stanza from another version, entitled "Little Topsy's Song," written by Eliza Cooke, is even more sadistic:

> Whip me till the blood pours down
> Ole Missus used to do it;
> She said she'd cut my heart right out
> But neber could get to it.[59]

The sadism in the lyrics can be read as slapstick from popular stage convention and street performance. I argue that these imagined acts of violence also come from the historical moment in which they were composed and performed, drawing specifically from the lexicons of discipline and torture developed out of U.S. chattel slavery.

As Elaine Scarry elucidates, the ability to feel pain functions in melodrama as proof of one's humanity. Tom's sustained suffering, as with Christ's crucifixion, leads to transcendence. Topsy's seeming invulnerability to the whips and scorns of time appears to render her as incontrovertibly savage. Topsy's defiant invitation for abuse is retained in Aiken's stage version and several of the filmed versions. To Miss Ophelia's despairing cries as to how to discipline her, Topsy replies, "Law, missis, you must whip me; my old missis allers whipped me. I ain't used to workin' unless I gets whipped."[60] When Miss Ophelia tries "the recipe," Topsy acts out accordingly, "screaming, groaning and imploring." Soon afterward, before an audience of slave children perched as usual on the balcony, she scorns the soft lashes of her new mistress. "Law, Miss Feely whip! Wouldn't kill a skeeter, her whippin's. Oughter see how old mas'r made the flesh fly; old mas'r know'd how!"[61] Topsy's hardened condition is the result of continued abuse, yet in her appalling resilience something else resides. Topsy is impervious to the whip, her wailing a hyperbolic satire of its intended effect. Her callousness, meant to signal her dehumanized condition and her precivilized nature, also signals her escape from violent forms of discipline and coercive regulation. She has not escaped from suffering, rather she has escaped *through* it; it is her absolute woundedness that has made her body malleable enough to wind through the pain. Everything, and nothing, can now touch her, as she exists in a space beyond suffering. Topsy's imperviousness to pain, her callousness, shows her body to have become resistant to violent claims of ownership. Topsy creates herself through, against, and in spite of the disfigurement her body has been subjected to. In her performance it is as if each contortion, each unholy sound erupts from an ulcerous welt. Each of her odd guttural cries is a reverberation, a twisting out of flying flesh.

Saidiya Hartman examines the connection between terror and enjoyment in slavery's use of the captive body. Slavery engendered a "nexus of pleasure and possession."[62] In the "obscene theatricality" of the slave trade, the "agonizing groans of suffering humanity had been made music."[63] In Hartman's assessment, the captive body was made "an abstract and empty vessel, vulnerable to the projections of others' feelings, ideas, desires, and values; and, as property, the dispossessed body of the enslaved is the surrogate for the master's body since it guarantees his disembodied universality and acts as the sign of his power and dominion."[64] The black body is "fixed" by repetitive acts of terror and dominance. The slave's sense of self, her subjecthood, is constituted solely through the discursive processes of legal language and the reiterative rituals of inflicted pain.

Hartman's dismal reading is useful for understanding rituals of oppression as performative acts, by which racial assignation is stabilized and relationships of power affirmed. But such literal pessimism only holds firm if the power of the word is given sole dominion over the physical being. The fixity of discursive claims over the corporeal can never be complete, and these claims are always open to challenge. A body is never an abstract and empty vessel. Nor can individual gestures be completely controlled. Topsy's hyperactive and mercurial kinesis cannot be conscripted by language. Her mimetic faculties absorb the power of what they reflect; the objects of her interpretation pass through the alembic of her body, distilled into moments of sublime expressivity. It is through these forms of self-possession that the "truth in these limbs" is evident; a body can never truly be owned.

As Elaine Scarry elucidates, pain requires a "shattering of language."[65] But what Topsy accesses in her artistry is not "a state anterior to language, to the sounds and cries a human being makes before language is learned."[66] In the beleaguered body's play lies another discourse that is not recoverable in language. Physical gesture is anti-linguistic, resisting language, whose laws would spell her as a body owned and dependent on its terms to free her. Language affords nothing in the kind of truths, comments, impressions, and expressions only found in rituals of dance, song, and music.

Dance in this sense offers a critique of the very idea of ownership. Dance affirms an individual's entitlement to the body's grounds; it affirms a right of habitation. The body is inhabited, "theirs" in that sense, but not as the result of conquest, purchase, trade, or exploitative control. My analysis here assumes a humanist concept of the individual's natural right to the body, but a tempered version. It does not assume that the body can be excavated from an exploitative system whole or intact, nor that the theoretical end game is to find it directed and governed fully by some integrated entity. The body can neither be completely wrested from the inhabitant nor governed by the inhabitant in some space free of discursive claims. This suggests that we can find a way to retain a humanistic ethical field of concern while we guard against reinstating totalizing claims of governance based on acquisition.

DOING TIME

Stowe's text is a product of a transnational moment in theatricality, ethnographic notions of race, and colonialist mythos. The plantation is a transnational site and the New Orleans plantation of Augustine St. Clare a romantic Orientalist fantasy. The environs are presented in the text as if they were a stage set, "the galleries that surrounded the court were festooned with a curtain of some kind of Moorish stuff." The big house is an ancient mansion, likened to an ancient feudalist state, with a "court in the inside. . . . Galleries ran all around the four sides, whose Moorish arches, slender pillars, and arabesque ornaments, carried the mind back, as in a dream, to the reign of oriental romance in Spain."[67] It is marked, as are other colonial holdings, by bounty: uncontrollable fecundity and sexual access. Stowe's romantic Orientalism bears the imprint of two centuries of travel writing that, along with treatises on natural science, were shaping popular understandings of race. Fantasies of the Orient combined vastly disparate lands, describing them all as "tropic climates" that were peopled with heathens and primitives and held in a timeless past.

In both Aiken's play and Stowe's novel, St. Clare presents Topsy to his sister from the North as a lesson in physical contact with "primitives." Although Miss Ophelia is against the enslavement of Africans, she is loath to actually touch them. He offers her this "fresh-caught specimen," taunting her to take on the "labor of conversion" not among the heathens abroad, but in her own house. "It might be a real missionary work," she concedes.[68]

Her first task is to bathe the battered child; Miss Ophelia is repulsed as she undertakes to cleanse the heathen. Her first bath is a mock baptismal moment, in which the heathen is dipped in the waters of holy forgiveness. Her next task is to begin Topsy's instruction, opening with a catechism of sorts:

"How old are you, Topsy?"
"Dun no, missis."
"Who was your mother?"
"Never had none!
"Never had any mother? What do you mean? Where were you born?"
"Never was born!" persisted Topsy.
"Have you ever heard anything about God, Topsy? . . . Do you know who made you?"
"Nobody, as I knows on," said the child, with a short laugh. The idea seemed to amuse her considerably; for her eyes twinkled, and she added: "I 'spect I grow'd. Don't think nobody never made me."[69]

Topsy exists in a "primitive" state and has "no sense of time." She exists with no understanding of its chronological ordering, for she doesn't even know her own age; Topsy cannot be dated or placed. It seems as if what amuses Topsy is that she knows she cannot be contained by any of the criteria Miss Ophelia seeks to civilize her with. She cannot be figured in any relation to time or place, parentage or God.

One of the categories for classifying the heathen races was their relationship to time. According to these notions, slaves lack knowledge of time—they have no sense of it as a resource, of its division by the clock, or of the need for its efficient use. Their "lack" is measured against the conceptualization of time central to the epistemology of Western thought, from Christianity to the Enlightenment.[70] Johannes Fabian explains "time as a constitutive dimension of social reality" and explores how oppressive uses of time, from early anthropological projects, linked the field of anthropology to colonialist and imperialist agendas.[71] In the epistemological shift of constructions of time from the sacred to the secular, time was naturalized and spatialized. Time became not a measure of movement but of qualitative states of being. Within this framework, all cultures are placed on a temporal slope, and primitive peoples are assigned a stilled place in time, always in the past and always in the present, and are incapable of a complex scientific understanding of time.[72] They were ruled by nature, the seasons, and their own immediate desires.

Laws of time and its regulation were created to control national and individual bodies and the terms of their interactions. They were also designed to regulate the body's relationship to time and the body's own sensorial capacities. In this respect, Topsy wreaks "nicely timed" and vengeful mischief.[73] Stowe drew Topsy in her narrative to function as a figure of abjection. But Topsy's rebelliousness spills out around the edges with bodily moments of rejected rules and regulations. She is a little heathen whose vocal and bodily gesticulations are in keeping with a "wild fantastic sort of time."

Both evolutionary and shifting physical/chronological conceptions of time staked a claim on the black slave body. According to Mark Smith in *Mastered by the Clock*, obedience to the clock was the "litmus test of modernity."[74] He argues that there was an evolution of "time consciousness" in the nineteenth-century slave-owning south. It did not run according to rural or premodern uses of time but was aligned with modern forms of time usage developing in the industrial north, with "the equation of time and money, clock time, and the technological standardization of time, disseminated by the railroad system."[75] In the South clocks and new ideas regarding time had to take place, and this shift was a battle waged on the bodies of the unfree laborers. "It is in the very essence of this battle that ideas of who owned time, who defined time, and, ultimately, who was free from and slave to time, took place," writes Smith.[76]

For the Negroes on the plantation, "time . . . was the master's."[77] Clock time was used in tandem with physical violence and its threat to define the power of the master and his freedom. Work time was indicated by the sound of a bell or a bugle, rung or blown by a slave, and task-oriented work was meshed with clock-regulated order. Slaves sabotaged masters' time with acts of sloth and laziness, everyday manipulations by which they freed time from its bondage. Emancipation equaled independence from time obedience and the right to regulate one's own rhythms of rest and work. As the former slave Sarah Wooden Johnson put it, "Dis here the new time. Let dat be."[78]

Smith's assessment reads time only in relation to labor and its value. Black southerners are solely workers, the subjects of the shift-in-time consciousness attending industrialization, the victims of the disciplinary violence of coerced labor. His analysis leaves no room to consider the sense of selfhood over and in time of transported Africans and their descendents in terms other than as reactive defense against its exploitative regulation. Smith tacitly reproduces a hierarchical understanding of the civilized and the primitive in relation to uses of time. He flirts with a kind of folk romanticism, claiming that for slaves clock time remained a mystical concept, and that they remained, unchangingly, governed by the agrarian conceptions of time they had brought with them from Africa. Smith does not consider that their time consciousness would also be adapting, transforming, fluctuating, aware of multiple registers and uses of time. Smith's evaluation leaves Sarah Johnson's statement, "this here is the new time, let dat be," to resonate past the bounds of his analysis.

Labor in its formal definition is an insufficient category of investigation from which to think of black people in relation to their own(ed) bodies. As Paul Gilroy suggests, "Social self-creation through labour is not the centre-piece of emancipatory hopes. . . . Artistic expression . . . becomes the means towards both individual self-fashioning and communal liberation."[79] Black expressivity, the creative and improvisatory moments of bodily inflection, were enacted in a complex web of time registers, calling into question the very possibility that time, or the body, could be owned. This is not to dismiss the coercive theatricality of black performance during slavery, the rituals in which slaves were forced to dance under the lash.[80] But the very necessity of such intricate and involved practices of claiming ownership suggests that completing the conquest was impossible.

Topsy has a keen sense of time, as her body has been marked by the uses to which her body, and the bodies of other slave children, were put. Topsy has no investment in keeping the "master's time." She contorts and bends it—syncopates it, rags it, swings it. In her performance, she weaves in and out of time with her vocal inflections, losing, keeping, wasting, and displacing time with her hands and feet. She creates play zones out of its distortion. Pushing at the boundaries of time's rhythmic containing, the dancing slave takes time out of its routines, its disciplinary actions on her body. The dancing slave child's body symbolically absorbs and dodges the rhythmic violence of the lash.

The picaninnies' eccentric movements were metaphors and parodies of various human and inhuman conditions. Louis Douglas had a repertoire of "the most bewildering and eccentric tricks" and moved with lightning speed from one dance to another. His repertoire included the "skate walk," an imitation of the smooth glide across ice interpreted by many later dancers. Douglas was accompanied by the house chorus line of eight English "Pavilion Girls" for his appearance at the London Pavilion for a Christmas special in 1916 entitled "Pick-a-Dilly." For this show he performed "as a call-boy, a monkey, a drum-major." Douglas parodied European decadence by introducing his famous "Gout Walk" during the finale.[81] He also performed his famous "golliwog dance." For this act Douglas staged his own death, and "poor golly is stabbed in the back." Like Ida Forsyne in 1906 he stages death in order to defy it and "'rags' off the stage."[82] Death, dismemberment, and the ability to transcend the body's infliction provided a narrative for the protean faculties of the dance.

Later male dancers, such as Jigsaw Jackson, "the Human Corkscrew," would build upon these vocabularies of bodily contortion. "It took a strong stomach to stand the things he did to his body," *Variety* reports, "most unusual trick stuff, his midriff twisted in a knot while his head faces one way and feet another. Keeps his pedals doing a jig all of the time."[83] In the 1920s, Clarence "Dancing" Dotson was known for his ragging syncopation. "He did everything around the beat . . . and he had no imitators," remembers the dancer Charles Honi Coles. Dotson also executed a skating step in a dance entitled "Snow Time." In the middle of his act, Dotson would exclaim, "I'm gonna throw a fit, and it's gonna happen right over there."[84] In these moments of black expression, the enacted distortion of the body spelled a loosening of assumed relations between the body parts.

The black expressive body was at home in its own fragmented sense of itself.

The eccentric, impressionistic, acrobatic interpretive strategies, inherited from the picaninny choruses, became primarily bodily gestures that were gendered as male. How is it that Topsy's legacy, "raising Cain," became a male property, that the rebellious black child could so easily be figured as a boy? Tap dancing, all sorts of innovative social dances after the First World War, were thought of as authored solely by men. This shift was one reason why, when Ida Forsyne returned from Russia, she could not find work. "When I got back from Europe I couldn't get a job in any [of the cabarets] . . . because I was too dark. . . . I didn't know how to shake and I never did anything vulgar," she states. "They used to boo if you did anything aesthetic."[85] Refusing to shimmy, to sexualize her performance style, Forsyne began work as a domestic.

As I explore in the next chapter, chorus lines referenced the sexual politics of raced female bodies under slavery and imperialism. And the eccentric bodily inscriptions from early picaninny performances would appear again in the interpretive techniques of the dancers Ethel Williams and Josephine Baker as they enacted the role of the mischievous little girl at the end of the chorus line.

PERFORMING THE DOMESTIC, OR GENIUS OUT OF CHAOS

The black female body carries a significant corporeality that cannot be subsumed into a universal, normative black male body (Aunt Hester springing from the head of Fredrick Douglass) or assumed as coming into its own only in relation to an imagined normative white female body. In her *Treatise on Domestic Economy*, Harriet Beecher Stowe's sister Catherine Beecher outlined the ideal division of labor between the sexes in a family. She quoted Alexis de Tocqueville, the French traveler to America. Women, he wrote, should never be "compelled to perform the rough labor of the fields, or to make any of those laborious exertions, which demand the exertion of physical strength. No families are too poor as to form an exception to this rule."[86] De Tocqueville and Beecher were, of course, speaking only of white women. Black women were to carry the labor of the female body, to be the bone and sinew of the domestic sphere.

But domestic time could be taken and ragged to creative purpose. Perhaps we can resuscitate the image of Dinah, the "gastronomic genius" of St. Clare's kitchen. Unlike Uncle Tom's wife, Claire, who moved "in an orderly domestic harness," Dinah paid no mind to method or order in her culinary art. Dinah sits in the middle of the kitchen floor, pipe in her mouth, creating "genius out of chaos." The figure suggests the potential for sedition and for creative improvisation. One does not have to wonder why this particular rendering of the Mammy figure dropped out of circulation.

Topsy rags the same. Miss Ophelia finds Topsy with her very best scarlet India crepe shawl wound round her head for a turban, going on with her rehearsals before the glass in great style, creating a "carnival of confusion. . . . Instead of making the bed, she would amuse herself . . . she would clime the posts, and hang head downward from the tops . . . and enact various scenic performances with that—singing and whistling, and making grimaces at herself in the looking glass . . . 'raising Cain' generally."[87] Topsy's performance in the domestic site of her bondage points us toward what will be a recurring trope in the histories of African American women performers. Topsy casts off the domestic harness and transforms herself in the trappings of colonial wealth before the looking glass. Raising Cain, Topsy signifies an anarchic moment in which the working black woman transforms herself in the space of labor, reclaims her body in the place of work. In her autobiography, Ethel Waters described her own transformation from chambermaid to jazz diva. "I had the most fun at the Harrod Apartments, on the days when I substituted for one of the chambermaids," she remembers. "I was allotted half an hour to make up each room but soon became so efficient that I could finish the work in ten minutes. Then I'd lock the door, stand in front of the mirror and transform myself into Ethel Waters, the great actress."[88] The symbolic power of Topsy's raising Cain resonates in the performance strategies of black children and black women performers. The disruptive resilience of the black female child will recur in popular performance well into the twentieth century. Following these paths of black expressive forms we find the traces of many black women dancers, singers, and musicians as they traveled between the rural outposts and urban centers of the United States and Europe.

"EGYPTIAN BEAUTIES" AND "CREOLE QUEENS": THE PERFORMANCE OF CITY AND EMPIRE ON THE FIN-DE-SIÈCLE BLACK BURLESQUE STAGE

THE CREOLE SHOW

In the early summer of 1890, sixteen light-skinned teenaged girls began their stage careers in a burlesque revue called *The Creole Show*.[1] Most burlesque shows still took a minstrel format; white women—toting banjos, sometimes in blackface, often cross-dressed—replacing the blackface white male performers in the semicircle. *The Creole Show* was an innovation on the burlesque circuit, a landmark event. With its limber-legged chorus and cast of women comedians and singers, it was the first show ever designed to "glorify the coloured girl."[2] The show was managed by the burlesque wheel producer Sam T. Jack, but the veteran black actor and comedian Sam Lucas was in charge of the casting and stage production, so the result was the cooperative effort of many black artists who contributed their music, songs, and specialty acts. "The Creoles were the gateway for most every colored actor on the American stage," Sam Lucas reportedly said.[3] Several similarly organized shows would follow in the wake of *The Creole Show's* success: John Isham's two revues, *The Octoroons* (1895) and *Oriental America* (1896), as well as the seasonal revues of Black Patti's Troubadours beginning in 1896. Many of the members of *The Creole Show* chorus worked in all of them. According to Langston Hughes and Milton Meltzer, these early shows "laid the groundwork for public acceptance of Negro women and of the Negro male on stage in other than burlesque fashion. A Bon-Bon Buddy behind the footlights, handsome in brown and beige, twirling a cane, doffing a stylish derby hat and strutting in rhythm backed by a chorus of brownskin beauties, brought a sparkling new dimension to American entertainment."[4] Over the next two decades, the artists appearing in these early burlesque shows, including Belle Davis, Dora Dean, and Stella Wiley, would go on to develop their own stage acts and musical comedies (see figs. 12 and 13).

The Creole Show differed in theme and content from the black variety companies and tent shows touring the South. "Smart and up-to-date in material and costumes," the show was set in an urban environment, parting with formulaic plantation nostalgia.[5] Individual acts, such as Irving Jones's "Postman Dance" and Charles Johnson's "London Swell," reflected a black trans-urban cosmopolitanism.[6] Its themes recognized the movement and migration of African Americans in the 1880s and 1890s within the United States, primarily between cities of the southeastern seaboard and northern industrial centers.[7] The Creole Show toured for five years, from 1890 to 1895, on a relentless schedule, playing primarily to working-class audiences in the theaters of industrial cities along the eastern seaboard.[8] For the entire summer of 1893 the show ran at Sam T. Jack's Opera House, not far from the fairgrounds of the Chicago World's Fair. The show then returned to New York City, where it ran for five consecutive seasons at the Standard Theatre in Greeley Square. With its cast of black women and smart, urban witticism, The Creole Show and the shows that would follow it reflected a wide trajectory of black, and black female, mobility.

This chapter situates The Creole Show both as a threshold event in the history of urban mass amusement and a key moment illustrating the centrality of African American performing women in the development of modern modes of being and moving. In the heart of the city the casts of The Creole Show and those that came after it performed a range of female colonial subjects; they demonstrated that the city and colony (territories occupied by European and U.S. national and business interests) were intertwined spectacles. I focus on these shows in relation to U.S. imperialism and the versions of popular Orientalism it produced, in relation to working-class black female public presence and the "woman question," and in relation to the ironies of black citizenship, black migration north, and the segregationist policies instituted at the turn of the century. Centering on a popular show based on a cast of young black women demands that we think about the ways public spaces—commercial, democratic,

12 Belle Davis, carte de visite,
    circa 1905. Rainer Lotz
    collection. Used with
    permission.

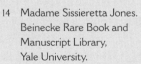

13 Dora Dean, postcard from
    Cardiff, 1905. Hatch-Billops
    Collection.

14 Madame Sissieretta Jones.
    Beinecke Rare Book and
    Manuscript Library,
    Yale University.

occupied—were shaped by sex and its currency, class and its privileges, race and its regulation. It demands that we trouble the distinctions between public and private spheres, domestic and foreign territories.

First, I situate black burlesque, with an emphasis on the particularly modern texture of sexual and racial spectacle taking place on the burlesque stage and fairground midway. I then place the shows and their casts in relation to the iconography of the sexualized Creole woman that by 1890 had long been in transnational circulation. I contextualize the light-skinned black women of the burlesque wheel in this transnational politics of fetishization and sexual commodification surrounding the mulatta. The Creole burlesque women's performances were most obviously a reference to the institution of concubinage and its fêtes: the quadroon balls of New Orleans and the Caribbean, the *bailes de cuna* in Cuba.[9] I contrast the boisterous dancing ladies with the tragic mulattos of contemporaneous black-authored literature. Robust, expressive working women's bodies offered contrast, foil, and supplement to the frail, sickly, and sexually constricted literary heroines. I then turn to the women's practices of racial delineation, alternately Cubana, Filipina, Chinese, Egyptian, as their acts mediated between and revealed the artifice of "modern" and "primitive" ideas of the feminine. These acts both celebrated and called into question the boundaries between colony and metropole and drew parallels between geographies of imperial annexation and the sexualized, racialized zoning of city spaces, the lines of which were being drawn at the same time.

The Creole Show was not a plantation "take me back" but was loosely structured on the English model of late nineteenth-century burlesque, the farcical rendition of classical heroic drama.[10] Instead of a walk around, the show's third act was a burlesque sketch entitled "The Beauty of the Nile, or Doomed by Fire," reflecting the popularized Orientalism of the era, the rage for Middle Eastern and Egyptian art and style. The male impersonator Florence Brisco played the "King of Thebes," Sarah Larue was "Isis the Queen," Sadie Watts was "Nefra," and Florence Hines appeared as a character called "Cheop."[11]

Working with and playing against the structure of a heroic drama set in northern Africa, the women in *The Creole Show* drew upon and parodied English and U.S. discourses of racialized female sensuality. An advertisement of the show on August 4, 1890 promises "Egyptian Beauties" and

"Creole Queens." It reads: "The pearly gates have swung ajar. Sam T. Jack's Creole Burlesque Co. . . . The Charmers of the Nile and the Enchantresses of the Mississippi. In the Grandest Entertainment Under the Canopy of the Heavens. Silk, Satin, Glitter, and Gold."[12] The show's chorus of black women from the United States burlesqued fantasies of Orientalist sensuality and "native women" from various sites of imperial conquest and colonial fantasy.

When *The Creole Show*'s tour manager, John Isham, decided to break with the burlesque mogul Sam T. Jack's organization, many of the women in the *Creole* chorus, including Dora Dean, Belle Davis, and Stella Wiley, left with Isham to appear in his new revues. The women performed similar acts of racial delineation in these shows as well as in the revues of Black Patti's Troubadours. In subsequent editions the revues' thematic popular Orientalism would look to Hawaii, the Philippines, Japan, and China as the United States stepped up its coercive and violent policies aimed at economic domination of the Pacific. The chorus women's malleable interchange between different racial delineations—mulatto, South Asian, North African, Filipina, Hawaiian—brought into relief the larger farce in which they were cast—the spectacles staged by racial and sexual science that buttressed geographical occupation. The shows linked the "local" to the "foreign"; the women's dancing bodies were the site at which the history of sexualized domination specific to the racial caste system of the United States was symbolically conjoined to a wider reaching and equally eroticized economy of trans-Pacific and trans-Atlantic imperial conquest. The shows both embodied these linked economies and provided space for the cast of "public women" to enact critique.

The cast alternated performances of imperial subjecthood with character sketches from African American urban life, on stage sets of the city landscape. The first act in *The Octoroons*, called "A Tenderloin Coon," was set in New York City's black populated Tenderloin district. Black Patti's Troubadours' opening sketch, "On Jolly Cooney Island," featured the naïve rural bumpkin Rube Green, who had recently migrated to the city. Staged on the boardwalk of New York's Coney Island, it featured Stella Wiley singing "The Belle of Avenue A," a brassy Irish working girls' song that would become her signature song. All of the burlesque and variety stages where the shows opened were situated within the city's territories zoned for urban transgressive pleasures. These territories were also territories allotted to both the Irish working class and African Americans. The burlesques often contained a class critique, particularly on the politics of dress reform and the "new woman's" regimes of physical hygiene. *Oriental America* featured a bloomered, bicycling quartet of chorus women, called the "twentieth-century maids" in the "march of the Oriental Huzzars."[13]

The Creole Show and the shows that followed were staged during a critical period of urban development as well as imperial expansion. Modern wealth was drawn with triumphant flourish in the building of the city. Urban planning was explicitly celebrated as the manifestation of Anglo-Americans' destiny. Edificial homages to Greece and Rome were erected in the New World to affirm cultural lineage. The ordering of space was conceived of by urban planners and captains of industry as the outward expression of the U.S. foundational democratic and egalitarian impulse. This was despite the colonial annexation of Cuba, Puerto Rico, the Philippines, and Hawai'i and the creation of its segregated zones, forcing citizens into policed districts on their own islands. It was despite the U.S. policies "at home": "dispossession" of native North American peoples and their forced relocations to arid lands, and the segregation of black "citizens." *The Creole Show* and the shows that followed all connected this experience of colonization within the "new," modern, and so-called democratic spaces to the annexation of those subjects within the occupied territories. The casts of these shows drew their acts in and around, through and against explicit discourses and often fatal practices of white racial entitlement. To understand the significance of the shows we have to consider their deft renderings in the face of the various forms of dismemberment (carnal and civic) perfected during this period.

The material of this era, such as the "coon song," can appear to us as shockingly self-denigrating. But as I argue, black artists during the 1890s were working within a particularly violent field of referents, and the burlesque shows were always multi-signifying, risibly glancing in many directions, giving the sly nod and sharp chuckle to one audience present while shucking and jiving for the other. Laughter has the potential for powerful ambivalence and may function as a form of social criticism. We need to not underestimate the power of farce. In its deepest conditions, farce disrobes authority, rendering racist hegemonic claims as a theater of the absurd.

FEMALE MINSTRELSY

As I argued in the first chapters, more needs to be written about the phenomenon of female minstrelsy. The histories of white women's racial delineations, both on and under the skin, cannot be subsumed conceptually
in discussions of white male minstrelsy. In thinking of how the female
body was gendered over the turn of the century, one obvious site for investigation (obscured by a male model) is the burlesque stage. It was around
1870 that the American burlesque wheel grew and the standard blackface
minstrel show died a bloated death (the shows became huge and monstrous). This was when troupes of white women took the stage, further
developing the lexicons of fast-paced, strenuous dancing and comic stage
foolery previously reserved for the minstrel male performers. In America,
with its puritanical sensibilities, the first women to bring burlesque to the
stage were European. Produced in 1866, *The Black Crook*, with its troupe of
over fifty European ballet dancers, is often cited as the antecedent to later
American burlesques and extravaganzas.[14] In mid-thigh pantaloons and
corsets, dancers from the continent and England brought to the American
stage a new sense of female sexuality and public presence.

Organized around the principles of excess, luxuriance, and pleasure,
the burlesque stage gave license for release into the realm of the senses.
Wealth from the colonies and as the consequence of newly developed
production technologies led to a shift in social sensibilities away from a
Victorian culture of scarcity, based on thrift, hard work, and self-restraint,
and toward a cultural climate of abundance, leisure, and self-cultivation.
Personal desire and rituals of pleasure remained illicit but were increasingly necessary. This shift, to consumerism and personal gratification,
was encoded in the commodified bodies of limber and ecstatic dancing
women appearing in sixteen-member choruses on the popular stages of
America and England.

The multi-jointed body of the female tableaux in extravaganzas of
the 1860s and 1870s symbolized corporeal desire and its fulfillment. The
erotics of their splendorous forms relied on elaborate costumes, hyperbolic metaphors of both restraint and indulgence. Bosoms burst forth
from tight corsets, layers of undergarments were covered by heavily jeweled and beaded overdresses. Buttocks, covered by layers of bright and
colorful fabrics, were emphasized by bustles; often women wore hip pad-

ding and other forms of figure-enhancing prosthetics to enlarge their forms. Burlesque women were as large as the repressed pleasures of the Victorian age. Urban working-class style and élan took the most florid and dramatic interpretations of European fashion to the streets and to the burlesque stage. This style accentuated the artificial, the decorative: bleached blonde hair and bold shiny fabrics representing a forced access to the kind of leisure the wealthy enjoyed. Their style influenced middle-class women, despite the public scorn and moral approbation of these middle-class women as they scuttled past the burlesque houses.[15]

Burlesque style was influenced by (and in turn influenced) dress reformers, as the dancers began to wear pantaloons regularly. They revealed the hidden and forbidden regions of the body, but more importantly pantaloons allowed the legs to move independently, thus giving women dancers a freer mobility and wider range of movement.

Burlesque women were robust in constitution, physically agile, and sexually expressive, combining in their acts the properties of unbounded appetite with physical stamina. What I emphasize here is that female spectacles relied on particular fantasies of the working woman's body. With their "nimble gracefulness" they symbolized the pleasures of female physical strength and endurance, properties outlawed from middle-class tenets of femininity.

In the United States, the staged reference to working-class female bodies was always racially inflected. American burlesque shows were modeled on the minstrel shows. The shows featured a minstrel show walk around in the third part; white burlesque women played the end "men" and were called principal "boys"; the interlocutor was a male impersonator in blackface. In the decade between 1870 and 1880, Michael Leavitt's Rentz-Santely shows typified the phenomena of the female minstrel show. Before establishing his own theater in Chicago, Sam T. Jack had been the manager of the Number Two company of Rentz-Santely's Female Minstrels. Female minstrel acts proliferated with such names as Ada Kennedy's African Blonde Minstrels.[16] As well as cork, the women in the minstrel semicircle often wore blonde wigs. The blonde wig became a recognizable icon for the minstrel show folded into the burlesque; white and black women performers would wear them well into the 1930s.

The meanings of white female minstrelsy cannot be represented with masculinist models; the relationship of transference was between women.

For white women, performing fantasies of African American, as well as various types of native, femaleness provided moments of immunity from restrictive social protocol, a license for physical expression and self-possessed sexuality. Later white female vaudevillians understood this, shading themselves with black and brown women's bodies to mark what was "transgressive" in their acts. With their shiny blonde tresses they both identified with and distanced themselves from the performance techniques developed by turn-of-the-century African American women performers.[17]

RACIAL SPECTACLE AND THE FORMULATION OF THE MODERN

The Creole Show played to full houses over the summer of 1893 in a hall just outside the Chicago World's Fairgrounds, a perfect location for considering the imbrication of city and colony. *The Creole Show* was one of many sites at which race was being staged in and around the Chicago World's Fair. Nowhere else was the spectacle of race and imperialism more graphically laid out and sensually imagined than at the celebration of Columbus's "discovery" of the Americas. With its monumental "White City" and mile-long Midway Plaisance, the exposition boasted the triumphs of scientific exploration, industrial enterprise, and imperial conquest, affirming the place of the United States within the pantheon of Western imperial nations. The technology of race was developing in the emerging fields of ethnology, anthropology, and museum science. Inspired by the Paris Exposition of 1889, various ethnic villages and anthropological displays were constructed on the Midway Plaisance. The fair's developers intended to "classify exhibits at the fair so as to illustrate the progress of civilization."[18] The fair was a "symbolic universe," in which the advance of civilization could be heard, seen, and felt as real. But outside and surrounding the official grounds were shows equally bound up with the ideologies of U.S. triumph. As well as *The Creole Show, Buffalo Bill's Wild Wild West Show* was running outside the fair's grounds.

Blending racial and technological spectacle, fair directors set about "to formulate the Modern," prescient that the phenomenological effects of new technologies heralded a sea change in human perception.[19] As fair organizers stated, "To see is to know."[20] But I emphasize that it was not

"EGYPTIAN BEAUTIES" AND "CREOLE QUEENS"

just the visual realm that figured in this formulation of the modern. All of one's senses were involved: the sights, sounds, smells, tastes, and haptic experience are what made this new imperial world modern.

The city and the colony were conjoined dramas, temporarily constructed on a huge scale. The Chicago World's Fair was a movable feast, constructed on the shores of Lake Michigan. Presaged by the Crystal Palace of 1851, facsimile and the power of artifice marked the formulation of the modern. The city was glittering, its massive buildings adorned in white frescoes and Greek columns, and its constructed ethnic villages, lining the midway, were stage sets, built only to be taken down when the show closed.

The midway's phantasmagoria flooded the visitors' senses, disoriented the audience/participant. On the midway, as in the emerging cities, place had become transportable; distant lands and their peoples could be relocated to the heart, or as the feet and hands, of the city. Time and space were compacted; one was able to travel vast distances, both geographically and chronologically, in less than a city block. A visitor passed through the gateway of the White City and descended into the chaos of civilization's living past. As the future was written with the assuredness of will made manifest, so the past of humankind was simultaneously written in the construction of the fairgrounds themselves. Passing the Woman's Building, guarded on the roof by gigantic white angels, a visitor then

> would pass between the walls of medieval villages, between mosques and pagodas, past the dwellings of colonial days, past the cabins of South Sea islanders, of Javanese, Egyptians, Bedouins, Indians, among them huts of bark and straw that tell of yet ruder environment. They would be met on their way by . . . camel drivers and donkey boys, dancing girls from Cairo and Algiers, from Samoa and Brazil, with men and women of all nationalities, some lounging in Oriental indifference, some shrieking in unison or striving to outshriek each other.[21]

Perhaps the most famous sideshow of all of those staged by performers on the fair's midway was Little Egypt, played by the dancing Farheda Mahzar Spyropolos of Armenia. Spyropolos embodied this era of popular Orientalism. Appearing in "The Streets of Cairo," Farheda wore a beaded midriff and low-slung skirt, her hair falling over her exposed shoulders.[22] Her dance, the "umbilical manipulation" of the "hootchy cootchy," became a midway standard.[23] Such profane racialized female movement became a stage convention and influenced the development of classic modern dance in the 1900s.[24]

Although not on the midway, *The Creole Show* was allied to this spectacle of events, and it ran very near to the exposition grounds. It opened to a full house every night, even in the midst of an economic recession and union strikes. Styled on *fin-de-siècle* commercialized Orientalist eroticism, music and dance numbers were added to the show, inspired by Little Egypt and other exoticized female acts along the midway. "Tropical Revelries" opened the show; a review described its "handsome scenery" as a "picturesque tropical scene, which introduces the ladies of the company in entirely new costumes, patterned after the soft clothing worn by the natives of the tropics, which allow perfect freedom of movement."[25] "La Dance Electrique" incorporated a gyratory dance routine, "in which the ladies of the company are dressed as native belles."[26] In 1894, the show also featured a version of "Fatima's Danse du Ventre."[27]

The Creole chorus women, as both "Charmers of the Nile and enchantresses of the Mississippi," were clad in the raiment of an imagined classical past and a future of unequaled wealth. The prosperous industrial age was made possible by the raw resources extracted from the soils of foreign, as well as domesticated, lands. The lithe, limber, free movement of the show's female dancers embodied a nodal point, where the eroticized spectacles of imperial conquest, racial subjugation, and technological innovation were shown to be interdependent.

Considering the presence of mixed-race women on the burlesque stage allows a critique of the categories "domestic" and "foreign," which were used to support raciological arguments in both imperialist and anti-imperialist camps. African American women performing other imperial subjecthoods referenced the global reach of plantation economies and the transnational migratory patterns of exploited labor. After slavery was abolished in England, for example, the workers of the Caribbean plantations were replaced with people from China and Southeast Asia. The same occurred on the sugar plantations in Hawai'i, where Chinese workers were brought in to work the fields of cane.[28] Other kinds of "colored" laborers were harder to ignore as part of the U. S. economy and culture. What is important to remember is that these colonial narratives were brought "home" to the urban centers, to the variety stages. Once again stretching the metaphor from Siegfried Kracauer, in which he likened the hands of the factory workers to the legs of the Tiller Girls, the many hands of the Asian male workers on the sugar plantations corresponded with the legs of the colored chorus girls in the city.[29]

Central to the gendered slippage within this correspondence is the concept of domestication. The business interests of the United States sought to domesticate Cuba, Hawai'i, and the Philippines in order to free U.S. trafficking in sugar from foreign importation taxes. Racialized female sexuality demarcated colonial territory; discourses of explorers and anthropologists had long characterized colonial lands as fecund and accessible, to be easily, profitably, and pleasurably penetrated. In the 1890s, the U.S. imperial invasions of the Philippines and Hawai'i and the opening up of unequal trade routes to Asia were similarly eroticized. "The Hawaiian pear is now fully ripe and this is the hour to pluck it," John L. Stevens, the chief U.S. "diplomat" in Hawai'i, stated in his address to the U.S. State Department in 1893. His triumphant address followed the coup of U. S. businessmen who, opposing governmental control, overthrew the reigning monarch of Hawai'i, Queen Lili'uokalani.[30]

The chorus of *Oriental America* was of "*twentieth-century* maids" of the "Oriental Huzzars."[31] The gendered reference to domestic/sexual service worked on many levels. It referred to the exploited labor of black women "at home," Asian women's concubinage, and the barring of Asian women from migration to the United States. But it also worked as a metaphor for the coerced contributions of sugar and labor from the domesticated islands of Hawai'i and the Philippines and signaled the profits to be made from unequal trade agreements with China and Japan. The West's civilizing mission was not aimed at the inclusion of its colonial subjects; they were meant to be domesticated only to the point of consent.

The urban presence of African Americans complicated the boundaries between the domestic(ated) and the foreign. African Americans were in, but not meant to be of, the nation just as were the new colonial subjects the United States sought to "contain." In accounts drawn up in the newly forming field of urban sociology, black urban migration during the 1890s was characterized as the colonization or invasion of the city.[32] As the United States invaded the Pacific, segregation and miscegenation panics surrounded the urban settlement of African Americans. These panics, often resulting in riots, were the fear of a "colored" invasion of the metropole, a mirror reflection of the U.S. invasion in the Pacific.

The presence of light-skinned chorus girls, in the guises of Asiatic/tropic servant women, stood in the crux of this ideology and performed a "double operation." Their eroticized presence and symbolic history as slave commodity functioned as part of the inter-discursive ideological work meant to naturalize these contradictory terms of belonging to a democratic nation. At the same time, their acts, with their malleability, played against the limitations of these proscriptions, exposing them as social constructions.

THE FANCY GIRL JIGS

"On the threshold of the women's era," the women casts of these shows emerged at the same time as did a cadre of African American women intellectuals who were active and outspoken in international politics. Black activist women formed clubs and organized interventions in the racially segregated and patriarchal political and social public spheres.[33] Agitating for suffrage and against the violent rituals of oppression regularly inflicted on African Americans, they contextualized their interventions within the larger map of imperialism.[34]

As part of their interventionist activism, women such as Frances W. Harper, Anna Julia Cooper, and Pauline Hopkins wrote works of fiction, designed in part as polemics of the moral and social responsibility of middle-class women to uplift the race.[35] Novels such as Frances E. W. Harper's *Iola Leroy* and Pauline Hopkins's *Contending Forces* centered around the figure of the tragic mulatto, providing such durable literary figures as Iola Leroy and Sappho Clark. With refined and sensitive natures, tainted only by a drop of Negro blood, these women were symbols of self-denial and sacrifice; endowed by their blood admixture to the place of race leaders, they were required to carry the moral condition or ethical virtues of their race. The triumph of these tales, and their polemic, involves the tragic mulatto dedicating her life to the uplift of her less fortunate, and darker, brethren. These novels were intended as forms of political and social intervention, but they reflected the sexually conservative agenda of middle-class reformers and their investment in inculcating working-class communities of black women with middle-class mores.

The figure of the light-skinned black woman on the burlesque stage

"EGYPTIAN BEAUTIES" AND "CREOLE QUEENS"

forms a narrative different from but adjacent to literary representations of the tragic mulatto. The robust and resilient persona of the working-class burlesque woman contrasted with the delicate and refined constitution of the literary mulatto, bringing into naked relief the fraught and anxious relationship between middle-class aspiration and black female sexuality. The literary mulatto was imagined to counteract the explicitly sexual jobs that Creole women were assigned under slavery and post-slavery oppressive regimes. She was stripped of all physicality, often frail and sickly, and sublimated her passion and eroticism into self-sacrifice. These delicate sisters were often rendered ethereal by the effort to contain and deny their sexuality. If sullied by the sexual lascivities of their male captors (which was usually the texts' dark and dirty secret) it was the literary mulatto who would often be punished for said sexual transgressions.

The explicit physicality and profane public presence of these burlesquers placed them beyond the pale of the black clubwomen's Victorian sexual politics. Stage women of *The Creole Show* were working women, not of the lettered or moneyed classes, and the shows played for primarily working-class audiences. Light-skinned and dark-skinned black burlesque women did not have to lose their flesh and were not required to faint, or die, or commit suicide at the end of their acts. The light-skinned burlesquer, "not obliged to act in concert with laws that both denied and created her," was exonerated from the narrative requirements of the mulatto as drawn in bourgeois literature.[36] The stage women both dramatized and satirized the decorative fantasies of African American affluence. Their acts parodied the pretenses of the African American middle classes. In lavish costumes, with showy high-stepping and international touring schedules, the women of the burlesque wheel were figures of self-gratification, not self-abjection and denial. From the liminal spaces of the variety and burlesque stage, the performances of light-skinned and dark-skinned black women resisted the strictures put upon the mixed-race female protagonists of uplift literature.

I maintain the important distinction between any idea of the "real" subject and the performed. The Creole woman was a persona, a performed social position, a sign. It was the *idea* of light skin that was essential to the act. Whether or not her light skin tone was "real" is immaterial, and often impossible to discern, as the mulatto/mixed-race identity was staged.

Tracing the figure of the mixed-race woman in popular literature and drama during the Victorian era, Jennifer Brody helps us to understand mixed-race and light-skinned black women's ubiquitous presence and cultural currency. Brody describes narrative representations of the figure that she terms the "mulattaroon" in Victorian literature as "especially apt representation(s) of the traffic of the triangular trade (in sugar, cotton, and slaves) and of the triangulated relationship between England, Africa and America."[37] As she argues, the mulattaroon was an exclusively feminine figure, with multiple iconographies produced and circulating transnationally.

In an Anglo-American context (as opposed to a French or Spanish Caribbean model of the mulatta) the mixed-race woman was an iconic sign for things that could not be shown. Her presence brings into relief the ambiguity of U.S. racisms, marked by legal statutes forbidding interracial marriages but clandestinely sanctioning sexual contact. She embodied the "open secret" of miscegenation, either consensual or coerced, and symbolized the sanctioned extralegal forms of sexuality.[38]

In her reading of Dion Boucicault's *Octoroon*, Brody shows how the presence of mixed-raced women destabilized racial categories. "It is the purpose of the octoroon to pose (as) the problem of racial discernment," Brody writes.[39] Qualified by gradations of skin color, the mulattaroon is the sign of interchangeability, dissemblance, and the (dis)appearance of any discernable criteria of racial codification.

Light-skinned, limber-legged, and boisterous black women on the burlesque stage carried with them the history of the fancy girl trade and practice of *plaçage* centered in New Orleans and extending across the Caribbean.[40] Their rigorous and suggestive acts carried the memory of the fancy girl slave auctions, very public rituals of bodily exposure and surveillance that their recent ancestors had endured. The fancy girl auction block was an exhibition in which the black female body was rendered as commercial territory. The ritual marketing of black women's sexuality and the involuntary sexual labor of slavery stood at the nexus of flesh and commodity. Sex, as profane desire and as the means to proliferate slave bodies, was here in its most complete moment of commodification.[41]

The slave sale was a performance in itself. The auction room suggests an obvious analogy to the public spaces of black performance. Joseph Roach writes, "With music, dance and seminudity, the slave auction, as a performance genre, might be said to anticipate the development of American

"EGYPTIAN BEAUTIES" AND "CREOLE QUEENS"

musical comedy. It certainly had important linkages to the black-faced minstrel show, which enacted the effacement of the cultural traditions of those whose very flesh signified its availability for display and consumption."[42] Roach's reading opens up the terms by which we understand how performance works to consolidate power and the ways by which pleasure and violence were conjoined. But in the case of the burlesque women, what is the "act?" It is not quite the same as the completely coerced display of women being bought and sold. How did African American women performers, on the popular stages at the turn of the century, relate in a more complex way to their own "availability for display and consumption"? In what ways did they continue to enact vibrant forms of expressive culture, even at the very sites of their subjugation?

Burlesque woman's staged artistry worked through and against the commodified inscription of the Creole woman prostitute. Like Storyville in New Orleans, the Tenderloin of New York City was a sanctioned zone of legal and sexual transgression.[43]

Popular performance, particularly for young women, was linked to the sex trade. Both were part of an alternative economy. The case of one sex worker, Estelle Russell, makes the link between these forms of labor explicit. The Blue Book flesh catalogue #27 lists "Estelle" as a former star of Sam T. Jack's *The Creole Show*.[44] Whether or not she was a member of *The Creole Show* cast, the link was made. Whether or not other performers on the *Creole* stage had worked in the sex industry is also not what is interesting here. What is interesting is the ways in which the linkages between alternative economic endeavor and the stage arts offered a space for significations with a certain license, a certain freedom. The public expressivity of light-skinned women had a resonance, a sanction for a type of public presence, both baldly commercialized and illicit.

It was at the sites of black women's sexual labor—the bordellos of Storyville, such as Lulu White's Mahogany Hall—where twentieth-century black vernacular expressive forms—called *jass*—developed. It was there that the rhythms of coerced and unfree labor were displaced in the ragged-time of male and female jazz pianists. Sites of exchange between the subjugated can be staked out right in front of, inside, and underneath the official economy.

Exploring the public presence of black women performers reveals the limitations of the gendered categories "private" and "public." The binary categories formed around the terms of the (feminized) private domain and the (masculine) public sphere don't apply in the same way to the histories of black working-class women. They had other kinds of relationships to the private spheres of hearth and home, and the public spheres of stage, city and nation. As domestics in white households, black women were the bodies at the core of the private sphere, both invisible and essential to ideas of proper white womanhood. Assigned to perform the functions of the female body (disavowed by the angels of the home) meant that they carried the sweat and labor of constructing the domestic stage. But it also meant that they carried the body's potential for pleasure and creativity, which they claimed in spite of oppressive conditions. The domestic sphere is a tenuous category when discussing the social and political forms of oppression relevant to black women. Feminized private space was inverted and actually the most public space black women could be in. The domestic space represented for most black women the public spaces of (poorly) waged work: the kitchen, the pantry, the nursery, or the "private" chambers designed to receive male clients.

Black popular music and social dance were part of the world of alternative economies—the "sporting" trades of gambling, numbers running, and prostitution. They offered a conditional release from the official forms of exploitative labor in the post-slavery era, paying much more than jobs available under the racist caste system of the United States. For women, stage performance was an alternative to the bedroom work of sexual labor offered by the sex trade as well as to the backbreaking and poorly paid scullery and laundry work in middle-class households. It offered black working-class women mobility and independence. They could earn a good living expressing themselves creatively, working alongside friends and lovers.

The black burlesque woman's incursions on the space of the public must be examined from an alternate perspective, or, rather, from many directions at once. Their presence in public space was not the same kind of insurgency as it was for white women entering the political sphere or even the popular stage, as black women had a history of both hyper-visibility and invisibility within these public spaces. But in some ways, the black burlesquers' experience was similar to that of many white actresses in this era. Juliet Blair writes of the emerging presence of the stage actress at the turn of the century. "The actresses' situation is unique in our culture in that it reverses the usual associations of women and their labour with private domains," Blair writes. "She [the actress] works in a public space where she is seen as acting in ways most women reserve for a private context. . . . The normal distinctions between 'public' and 'private' are neither incumbent upon nor possible for the actress. . . . She may be structurally located in a private relationship to society at large . . . [She is a] 'Public Woman.'"[45] Blair limits her discussion to the case of white dramatic actresses of the "legitimate" theater. However, while variety women worked in the public space of the stage, they were not reliant on the same criteria that being considered a "legitimate" stage actress required. For the legitimate actress, a "public" presence presumed the existence, or fantasy, of a sacrosanct private site for female expression. For women to disobey these rules was cause for concern for some and celebration for others. The difference is of course that the rules of public and private did not apply for black performing women. This made middle-class black women reformers nervous, as they agitated to have their womanhood assessed by the same terms of respectability as those developed for white women.

The burlesque stage, upon which *The Creole Show* and *The Octoroons* appeared, was one particular kind of public staged space. By the 1890s, forms of popular amusement had begun to separate into defined circuits. From the efforts of early entertainment managers, particularly Tony Pastor and B. F. Keith, vaudeville circuits and audiences developed during this period.[46] Vaudeville became a respectable form of amusement, offering an afternoon's diversion for the cities' white middle-class women. Very few black acts were booked, and black audiences were excluded or relegated to particular sections of the house or to certain dates and times they could attend.[47] Variety hall and burlesque houses were separated from the cleaner, more respectable vaudeville theaters, and located in and around red-light districts and were associated with the profane forms of entertainment offered in these districts' clubs and saloons. Though working classes in the burgeoning urban areas were encouraged by reformers and temperance workers to conform to the tenets of Christian clean living, it was understood that the sections of the city in which they lived were to be marked off as territories of free play—as "moral-free zones."[48] In New York City, these areas—Five Points, the Bowery, the Tenderloin—were demarcated by reformers as sex districts. As the geography of the city was increasingly delineated by race, such "interzones" were also the early sites of African American urban presence.[49] The burlesque stages were located in these interzones.

During the height of the imperialist era in the late 1890s, African American performers were self-consciously forming a noticeable artistic community in New York City.[50] Even while staged as illicit, urban black dance and song were increasingly recognized as representative forms of national cultural expression. This was at the same time as African Americans themselves were excluded from the civic body and "annexed" geographically within the urban terrain. Their expressive forms were central to the ways in which people were experiencing urban life, even as the legal, extralegal, and violent forms of their exclusion and containment intensified. As I discuss in the next chapter, the wide trajectory of the cakewalk dance phenomenon, staged in the finales of the Creole burlesques and in the huge cakewalk jubilees at Madison Square Garden between 1895 and 1898, suggests the centrality of blackened bodily expression in the development of an urban sense of self.

THE COLONY IN THE CITY: FEMALE BLACK BOHEMIA AND U.S. IMPERIALISM

The racial geography of northern industrial cities was changing during the 1880s and 1890s. African American neighborhoods grew.[51] Around 1890 African Americans previously clustered around Greenwich Village began moving up into the Tenderloin, known as a vice district situated between the West Twenties and Thirties, with its center along Sixth Avenue. Parts of the Tenderloin formed a center for black creativity and artistic community, and the area was known as "Black Bohemia" in 1902. Black composers and artists worked in and around those employed in the less savory underground economies. Unlike the insular community of middle-class African Americans in Brooklyn and the older black population of Greenwich Village, Black Bohemia "embodied the newer and more daring phases of Negro life. For it was in this neighborhood that most of the clubs frequented by both the sporting and theatrical people were located."[52] A new class of African Americans formed, the "Smart Set," made up of club owners, gamblers, numbers runners, performers, and professional athletes, namely jockeys and pugilists. The publicly celebrated figure of the black prizefighter emblematized the "social emergence" of this set. Jack

Johnson was a virile figure for this new black success. Openly spending his money and raising the roof with white women, he flouted the tenets of Victorian middle-class manly self-restraint.[53] Carousing publicly with white prostitutes, Jackson performed the most criminal of acts. At the same time, his superb athleticism was a model for a new masculinity.

The public black male presence in the heart of the city aroused white resentment. Volatile tensions erupted in mid-August 1900, as a major race riot raged through Midtown, centered in Black Bohemia. Sparked by the stabbing of a white police officer by a black man, white mobs terrorized black bystanders and residents, including the black artists living and working there. "Get Ernest Hogan and Williams and Walker and Cole and Johnson!" the crowd is said to have cried. According to James Weldon Johnson, Ernest Hogan was kept safe in the Times Square theater where he was performing. Chased by a mob, George Walker made only a narrow escape, then sprinted up Broadway before being caught and beaten.[54]

Black entertainment life centered in what was called Black Broadway, Seventh Avenue between Twentieth and Fortieth Streets. Artistic life centered around two hotels, the Marshall Hotel and the Maceo Hotel, located on West Fifty-third between Sixth and Seventh Avenues. The Marshall Hotel became a meeting point for artists. The Johnson brothers, James Weldon and J. Rosamond, lived at the Marshall, and Bob Cole, their writing partner, lived down the block. James Weldon Johnson remembers the Marshall as a "radiant point of the forces that cleared the way for the Negro on the New York stage."[55] Moving to Fifty-Third, or at least visiting it, was the strategic move for any young black stage performer. Bert Williams and George Walker moved to New York City from California in 1896. In 1898 the duo took up residence at a flat down the street from the Marshall. "The first move was to hire a flat on Fifty-Third Street . . . and throw our doors open to all colored men who possessed theatrical and musical ability and ambition," explained Walker of their planned move. "The Williams and Walker flat soon became the headquarters of all the artistic young men of our race who were stage struck. . . . By having these men around us we had the opportunity to study the musical and theatrical ability of the most talented members of our race."[56] George Walker claimed that their flat was the nodal point of the black artistic community, but this claim is more accurately made of the Marshall and Maceo hotels.

In 1908, eleven of these male stage performers organized a professional club, which they named the Frogs. Members included the best of the songwriters, producers, and performers in New York. Both James Weldon Johnson and George Walker write of their artistic community building as primarily an all-male affair. Writing in retrospect, in *Black Manhattan*, Johnson does praise the talent of both Lottie Williams, Bert's wife, and Aida Overton Walker, George's wife after 1898. He also mentions other women artists as members of the community: the former *Creole Show* chorus women Stella Wiley, Belle Davis, and Dora Dean, and Sissieretta Jones. Stella Wiley gave her detailed scrapbook of clippings to Johnson in April 1923 for use in compiling *Black Manhattan*.[57] Johnson gives Wiley one mention, calling her the "cleverest coloured soubrette of the day."[58] The composer Bob Cole later split quite publicly with Sissieretta Jones and her management, Voelckel and Nolan, over control, payment, and authorial credit of his compositions. But one wonders how many of the women's compositions have gone uncredited, and how often their choreographies have been adopted as those of their husbands and male colleagues.

Isham's *The Octoroons*, which opened in August 1895 at New York's Olympic Theatre, staged this new black urban presence (see fig. 15). The musical numbers and dance sketches in the first half were "laid in the heart of the Tenderloin."[59] The imperial involvement of the United States in Cuba and Southeast Asia also provided grounds for black farce.[60] The second act was "made up of talk about the war and preparation for the same" and took place at a fictional training camp on Long Island called Camp Black, a segregated unit where a troop of African American men were billeted. These men were eager to join Roosevelt's Rough Riders in Cuba and the conquest of Spain in the Philippines.[61] Songs included *My Filipino Babe* and *Hu-La Boolah*, both by Bob Cole and sung by Stella Wiley with Walter Smart and George Williams. Following the "Tenderloin Cakewalk Jubilee," Wiley "assists" Smart and Williams in a comedy sketch, which revolved around Smart's need of a horse in order to join the troops fighting so gallantly for freedom.[62]

Images from any of the shows are scarce. But one powerful photograph remains of Wiley, Smart, and Williams in this comedy number (see fig. 16). Wiley stands in the center, offering a small toy horse to Smart (Dewey Olympus) to her right. Smart is dressed in a snappy cream-colored suit, while Williams (Mark Hanna) to her left, is sporting a black suit covered

15 Program, *The Octoroons*. Stella Wiley scrapbook. Scrapbook of the Negro in Theatre, Yale Collection of American Literature, Beinecke Rare Book and Manuscript Library, Yale University.

in dollar signs. No book or transcription remains of this sketch. Even so, this photograph is laden with complex irony and humor. The scene plays on Smart's (the Smart Set's) association with the fast life, which included horse racing and gambling. Smart needs a horse, not to fulfill a patriotic duty but to make some quick money at the track. On the surface, this would seem to be a humiliating self-staging of Zip Coonery: black people, especially men, were hedonistic, impractical by natural inclination, and incapable of self-government or of managing wealth. But this scene, like and resembling it, was so much more than this; it is a layered satire, and this photo multi-signifies. It suggests that American imperial expansion is a form of illegal money making as unethical as gambling. It draws a parallel between horse racing and rough riding in Cuba as equally corrupt capitalist enterprises. There is a deep belly laugh here at the United States, at its unprincipled policies of capitalist expansion (in the name of protection) and its pretense of democracy.

William's suit of dollar signs also signifies in many directions. On the surface, it creates him as the newly immigrated Jim Dandy character ("From Ohio? Well, no, from Louisiana"), the black man who takes on city pretensions, who is easily seduced by money and flashy clothes. But

16 Stella Wiley, Walter Smart, and George Williams, *The Octoroons*.
Stella Wiley scrapbook. Scrapbook of the Negro in Theatre,
Yale Collection of American Literature, Beinecke Rare Book and
Manuscript Library, Yale University.

this suit of bold symbols also reminds us of the history of the black body as a commodity and commercial venture. In this new decade, the black man's body, as soldier, could be used to acquire even more exploitable land, people, and resources.

This sketch, and the theme of black soldiering in the show, are a dialogue on the long history of black struggle for civic recognition, one tactic being to fight in the nation's wars. Black participation in the military was always a politicized issue, fighting for the United States always a flashpoint. Smart's longing for a horse invites the satire to be not on the simplemindedness of black men but on the history of black contributions to the nation and the irony of black patriotism. It is a comment on the politics of national inclusion, the right for black "citizens" to reap the benefits of the nation's promised wealth and enfranchisement. The irony was that these rights, hard won during Reconstruction, were being violently rescinded in the South while systems of civic exclusion were being further developed in the North. And populations of the newly acquired territories of the United States were not being admitted as citizens but as subjects, at the same time as the nation represented to the world freedom and possibility for all. This war in particular brought out a number of positions on imperialism and rights at home. African American opinion on U.S. imperial policy was mixed. Some blacks were ambivalent about joining either pro- or anti-imperialist organizations due to racist policies upheld in both.[63] Many held onto the hope that participation in the war effort was a way for black men to earn recognition as native-born citizens. A black nativist opinion held that African Americans were actually the most civilized of the colored races and were the most suited to uplift other colored peoples, and in doing so contribute to the nation's benevolent civilizing mission. Many groups however, like the Afro-American Women's League of Boston, were outspoken against the imperial wars on the grounds that such wars exhibited the same kind of racist violence African American (Negro) people were suffering "at home" in the nation.

Bob Cole, who wrote many of the skits and musical numbers for *The Creole Show*, the shows John Isham produced afterward, and for Black Patti's Troubadours, was highly critical of America's imperial involvement. As were other artists: with James Weldon Johnson, Cole co-authored an explicitly anti-imperialist critique, a play called *Tolosa*. Although it was never staged, the complex ironies of African American nativism, Filipino native insurrection, and the policing of racial territories shaped its writing.[64] Cole was also somewhat of a nativist, believing that black people in the United States should have certain inalienable rights as native-born citizens.

The show's fifth and final season occurred in 1900. At the same time as riots broke out in Midtown, the war had taken shape as an imperial blood bath, following the battle of San Juan Hill and the poor treatment of the segregated African American troops in Cuba. Led by Emilio Aguinaldo, the Filipino people had proclaimed independence and the U.S. military had begun its violent suppression of their movement. From 1899 to 1902, seventy thousand American troops were brought in to crush the Filipino insurrection. Soldiers of the United States forced the Filipino people into designated zones. American racist policy levied violence and disease on the communities. Of the black troops, the 24th and 25th Infantries were the first to be deployed. The 48th and 49th Infantries—the black volunteers, some of whom had already been stationed in Cuba—arrived early in 1900. Soldiers sent letters from the war in to black periodicals, and many express a deep ambivalence about participation in the war. "I have not had any fighting to do since I have been here and don't care to do any," Patrick

Mason of the 24th Infantry wrote in a letter to the Cleveland *Gazette*. "I feel sorry for these people and all that have come under the control of the United States. I don't believe they will be justly dealt by. The first thing in the morning is the 'Nigger' and the last thing at night is the 'Nigger.' You have no idea the way these people are treated by the Americans here."[65] Some black soldiers recognized affiliations with the Filipino peoples and developed connections with them. Some deserted; one high-profile deserter was David Fagin, who joined the rebel army and fought as an officer commanding troops against the United States.

Emilio Aguinaldo was well aware of the inherently contradictory position black soldiers were in, fighting for a country that refused to recognize them as citizens. Aguinaldo drafted letters, addressed to the colored soldiers, that were dropped in bundles over African American encampments. One, addressed to the 24th Regiment, reads:

> To the Colored Soldier: It is without honor that you are spilling your costly blood. Your masters have thrown you into the most iniquitous fight with double purpose—to make you the instrument of their ambition and also your hard work will soon make the extinction of your race. Your friends, the Filipinos, give you this good warning. You must consider your situation and your history, and take charge that the blood of . . . Sam Hose . . . proclaims vengeance.[66]

Aguinaldo refers to the brutal lynching of Sam Hose in Atlanta, Georgia in 1899, which was brought to international attention by the anti-lynching activist Ida B. Wells.[67] The brutal murder of Hose was one of many highly publicized lynchings. Following the public announcement of plans to burn him at the stake, advertisements were posted for the event and trains were routed to the site. Such violent rituals were part town meeting, part family outing, and often, as with Hose's torture and murder, huge spectacles. They put new (or old) meaning to the idea of mass amusement. Before an audience of thousands, Hose was dismembered and his body partially burned, before being cut open. Ears, toes, and fingers, and pieces of his heart and liver were sold as souvenirs. As with other lynchings, photographs and postcards were made and widely circulated.[68] The gruesomeness of Hose's case galvanized black activists. W. E. B. Du Bois was shocked when he found Hose's knuckles on display in a shop window in Atlanta. This experience proved to be a moment of conscious awakening for Du Bois to the pitch and level of white group violence against black men. Aguinaldo was aware and well informed about this endemic violence against African Americans, as well as with black dissent.

By 1900 the hope held by African American men that fighting abroad as native citizens would bring them recognition at "home" had been disappointed. In New York City black people had begun moving northward, up from the Tenderloin district into the streets numbered in the lower 60s. Because of the race riots that took place as black people moved into the district, this area was soon nicknamed "San Juan Hill." It was probably also named as such because black veterans from the war in Cuba were said to have settled there.[69]

The contradiction between U.S. politics of racial segregation, imperialist policies of "benevolent assimilation," and claims to democracy was not lost on the black artists of New York's Tenderloin, and it informed the material for *The Octoroons*, *Oriental America*, and the Troubadour revues. Although it is impossible to recreate the show, the politics of the war and its irony for black "citizens" inflected the artists' performances and shaped the context for the audiences' reception, particularly considering the explicitly anti-imperialist position held by the shows' main song writer, Bob Cole.

Much has been written about the politics of masculinity, both white and black, during this period.[70] But a full consideration of the linkages between colonial conquest and urbanization also calls for an examination of the circulating and contested signs of racialized femininity. As Kevin Mumford argues, a sexual economy was central to the racial segregation of urban districts.[71] Black female expressive artistry carried the public history of black female sexualization. Considering the black female members of the urban theatrical community is key to understanding the ways black women's sexual subjugation under slavery and post-emancipation peonage was linked to the eroticization of colonial women, lands, and the pleasure zones within city limits. The politics of "octoroonage" is a positionality; how "real" a chorine's lineage and/or light skin was could be easily concocted through make-up and as easily rendered through performance.

Oriental America opened in 1896 and was the first such show to open at a variety theater rather than a burlesque house, and to include an operatic kaleidoscope as its finale.[72] The women performed in a variety of eroticized Asian character sketches, including a "cleverly rendered" Japanese dance. The women of the chorus yoked renditions of the New Woman, clad in bloomers and riding a bicycle, to their staged versions of Oriental-ism. Belle Davis, Mattie Wilkes, Ollie Bourgoyne, and Dora Dean formed a "quartet of cycling girls in bloomers," leading "the twentieth-century maids" in the "march of the Oriental Huzzars."[73] *Fin-de-siècle* physical culture for middle-class women utilized forms of Orientalist exoticism, a practice the chorus satirizes through its Orientalist burlesque.

Oriental America was also the first of these shows to tour abroad. In April 1897, the troupe sailed for Great Britain, enjoying an extended tour of London and the provinces.[74] This show staged the urban Smart Set; the first skit was "Blackville Derby," a race-course comedy "in which all the latest darkey melodies are sung by jockeys, touts, plungers and bookies."[75] Belle Davis contributed "a budget of Negro oddities"[76] and the show ended with a cakewalk, "one of the liveliest festivals of the American coloured native."[77] No reviews mention the bicycling twentieth-century maids, although a "girl series of musical comedies," featuring lady cyclists, was playing in nearby towns, and *A Trip to Chinatown* was playing in Manchester.[78]

Black Patti's Troubadours, headed by the operatic singer Sissieretta Jones, followed *The Creole Show*, *The Octoroons*, and *Oriental America* in its shift away from the minstrel/burlesque format. As in the other shows, its loosely themed skits juxtaposed an urban black presence with U.S. im-perialism in the Pacific. In early 1901, the first act of the show was called *A Darktown Frolic*; later that year it was renamed *A Filipino Misfit* (see fig. 17). Many of the performers from the Jack and Isham productions moved to Jones's troupe, including the future choreographer Aida Over-ton Walker, who had entered the stage as a young dancer from the *Ori-ental America* cast. Bob Cole and his then wife Stella Wiley also joined. Black Patti's Troubadours and Isham's productions toured simultaneously for four years: Wiley's, Walker's, and Belle Davis's touring schedules must have been strenuous.

The African American composer Will Marion Cook (Abbie Mitchell's husband) wrote a review of Black Patti's Troubadours for a Washington, D.C. paper, lauding it as "The Best Colored Company on the Road." Com-paring it with the other colored shows, Cook wrote:

> All four of the representative Negro companies—*The Troubadours*, *Orien-tal America* and *Octoroons* Nos. 1 and 2 are artistic successes, and reflect great credit upon themselves, their management, and upon the colored

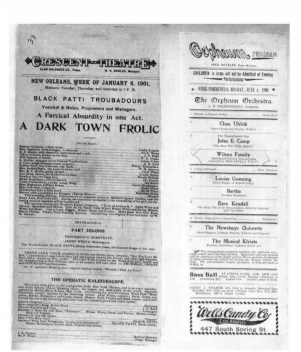

17 Program for *A Dark Town Frolic*. Stella Wiley scrapbook. Scrapbook of the Negro in Theatre, Yale Collection of American Literature, Beinecke Rare Book and Manuscript Library, Yale University.

people. They are working their way into opera houses hitherto tightly closed to colored performers, and their ambitious attempts are winning the highest encomiums from the Press, which would have, but one or two years ago, been received with the greatest derision and laughter.[79]

Bob Cole and his wife and stage partner, Stella Wiley, distinguished themselves with their acts in the Troubadours. "Mr. Cole evinces talent of the highest order," continues Cook. "His stories abound in wit, humor and sarcasm, and are told in an entirely original manner. Miss Wiley's support is all that could be desired."[80] Bob Cole would later use the sketches he composed for the Troubadours in his own full-length comedies.

An array of racy character sketches from cosmopolitan African American life appeared in the Troubadour skits. Opening in 1896, the first skit of Black Patti's Troubadours, "At Jolly Cooney Island" (composed by Bob Cole), concerned the plight of a young "Alabama sport," Rube Green, who was fresh from the country and being taken for his money by various urban character types. "Rube Green . . . with plenty of cash, in other words, a soft thing, comes to Coney Island and is at once tackled by sharpers, touts, and green goods men, who soon separate him from his money." The review continues: "This favorite seaside resort gives the various talent

18 Stella Wiley and Bob
Cole. Yale Collection
of American Literature,
Beinecke Rare Book
and Manuscript Library,
Yale University.

a splendid opportunity to display their funny talk and unique dances and clogs."[81] The show was a combination of artistic talent and comedic racial impersonations. Everything from operatic virtuosity to the self-parody of the coon song was included on the bill. As well as the operatic duets of the De Wolfe sisters, the Troubadours featured Belle Davis, Henry Wise, and Aida Overton Walker singing a coon song entitled "The Three Little Kinkies."

Following a performance playing in the nation's capital, a review probably from a white newspaper remarks on the packed houses. "The olio was opened by the De Wolfe sisters who sang a number of duets in sweet voices," but the review notes Stella Wiley's "tough girl" act as particularly memorable.[82] The character sketch of a working-class Irish girl from downtown Manhattan was a standard variety turn, a staged paean to the young immigrant women working in the city: the factory girls, seamstresses, domestics, and urban prostitutes.[83] Wiley became famous for her "lifelike" rendition of the Irish Liz Leary and sang her signature tune, "The Belle of Avenue A," in subsequent shows for years after the Troubadours' first run.[84]

At the same time that Wiley was appearing as Liz Leary, Bob Cole and the Johnson Brothers sold one of their compositions, entitled "Louisiana Lize," to May Irwin, a white vaudevillian and coon shouter. Using it in her act, Irwin appears as a Creole woman from New Orleans.[85] Such mutual acts of imitation were common; in 1897 Belle Davis rendered an imitation of Irwin in *Oriental America*.[86] These moments of female minstrelsy referenced previously linked discourses of white and black female sexuality, class identification, and competition. The popular press of the North during the 1840s and 1850s imagined both the southern plantation and the industrial metropolis as "harem-prone spaces." In the urban gothic novels and women's slave narratives of the antebellum period, abolitionist arguments called the sexual corruption of slave women the "deeper wrong" of slavery and linked it with the arguments of urban moral crusaders, who were rallying against the sexual vulnerability of young white urban women.[87]

Stella Wiley's and Belle Davis's whiteface acts and May Irwin's "Louisiana Lize" played on the "moral panic" surrounding female autonomy. Later crusaders called the plight of these young white working-class women "white slavery" and argued that urbanization had brought with it the loss of familial integrity. The chastity of young women was threatened, vulnerable to exploitation, without the protection of a sheltering family. Reformers, however, did not count black women as viable subjects for their numerous reports. Black reformers attempted to redress this situation, adopting similarly conservative tactics in their fight against the moral corruption of black women migrants to the city.[88] The acts recognized shared experience along class lines; for their working-class audiences their acts provided a public moment of identification with other women living independent lives in the city. But I argue that it is important to retain a distinction; black women's acts also acknowledged the irony of black women's exclusion from national belonging, having been so recently literally belongings.

The light-skinned black burlesque women brought to the stage the imagined strength and vitality of the working female body. "Stella Wiley, as Liz Leary, the belle of Avenue A, is tough enough to suit the most cultivated taste for toughness," reads a review. The range of representations played by the "dusky beauties" of the chorus suggests the malleability of the racialized female form, as well as the multi-valenced positionality of mixed-race women in the drama of U.S. racial and sexual relations. Wiley is cited as "one of the four Creole dancers who, later on, in becoming lingerie, are as engaging a quartet of dusky beauties as one would wish to see. The other three are the Misses Overton, Wise and Davis. It is taken for granted that their color is the real thing; it is certain that their nimble gracefulnes [sic] is."[89] The women working in the Troubadours introduced various "character types" into their specialty acts, including the "Bathing Girl," the "Bicycle woman," and the "Couchee Couchee girls from the midway."[90] The women manipulated the "realness" of their racial status through various skillful strategies of makeup application and gestural techniques; their "nimble gracefulness" allowing them a mobility between different acts of femininity. Performing in various gradations of skin tone, black burlesque dancers were figures linking the eroticized fantasies of the Louisiana octoroons, urban immigrant women, and various female colonial subjects.

In Bob Cole's musical comedy of 1898, *A Trip to Coontown*, ethnic delineation and farcical plays on typologies were what Cole and his All-Star Stock Company worked with. "The first [act] ended with the most astonishing demonstration of the facility with which the African face can be made to represent other dark-skinned races. . . . Four misses looked and acted more like Japanese girls than most white chorus girls in comic opera. A group of men made perfect Arabs. Three more girls were vivid Egyptians, with sinuous suggestion. Two men represented Chinamen. One group was of Spanish girls."[91]

Cole and his company played on the success of *A Trip to Chinatown* with their Orientalist and colonial characters, but they also performed in whiteface. As he had with Stella Wiley in the Troubadours, Bob Cole and the cast of his company captured the quality of rough urban living in their burlesques of Eastern European immigrant city-dwellers. Cole brought his most famous whiteface character, the hobo Willy Wayside, whom he had created while with the Troubadours. Cole used the character developed by Stella Wiley as the actress Jennie Hillman "mimicked the typical Bowery girl with gum and jersey," while her partner, Carter, "sang an irresistible new 'tough' ditty with rhymes so strong that he could jerk out every syllable hard and fierce." In its act, the company adopted conventions from the white working-class stage of an earlier era. "During this the ferocious pair pursued strong men and police, who fled at their threatening approach."[92] The spectacle of African Americans, disguised as white working-class women and chasing policemen through the city streets, requires that we account for the multiple levels of meaning in such acts of racialized performance.

Bob Cole's *A Trip to Coontown* was the first all-black produced show, a historical turning point in the efforts of black artists to gain control of their own productions. Bob Cole had left Black Patti's Troubadours in its first season, the spring of 1897, taking his musical compositions and sketches with him. Cole was protesting the poor compensation and lack of recognition he suffered from the troupe's managers, James Nolan and Rudolph Voelckel. "These men have amassed a fortune from the product of my brain," Cole said to the magistrate, "and now they call me a thief, I won't give it up!"[93] Cole won his case in April; by September he had organized his own production company. Many black artists left in protest of poor treatment at the same time as Cole, though Stella Wiley remained. Nolan and Voelckel "blacklisted" Cole and his stock company, making it difficult for them to work on the New York stages. Cole had organized his All-Star Stock Company in 1894, and after his acrimonious break with Voelckel and Nolan, Cole was more determined to take control of production. He wrote a manifesto, the "Colored Actor's Declaration of Independence of 1898." He and an all-black crew and cast staged *A Trip to Coontown*. Because of Voelckel's and Nolan's influence, the play had to open on the road, touring Canada, before Cole and his company found a small venue in New York.

Cole and his company adapted conventions of ethnic impersonation that typified the U.S. vaudeville stage. Developed by Irish, Jewish, and Italian players, such acts reflected the tensions and contradictions around class and cultural belonging for the new immigrants. The first wave of vaudevillians—Irish, largely pro-Democrat, and solidly working class— were later joined by Jewish and Italian performers.[94] Ethnicity itself became the medium for outrageous maskings on stage. Reducing ethnic characteristics to a set of stock traits, vaudevillians exchanged ethnic identities on stage with absurd rapidity.[95] These vaudevillians attempted to reconcile themselves with an ethnic loyalty, while at the same time divorcing themselves from their "repulsive pasts," which barred them from access to the status of whiteness that accompanied the process of "Americanization."[96] But the vaudeville stage excluded most black performers from its circuits. With their European ethnic delineations, Cole and his company critiqued African American exclusion from the more profitable venues, as well as from these processes of ethnic reconciliation.

The category of whiteness itself was the subject of intense debate and imaginative configuration among racial theorists. The Irish had been likened to African Americans in the discourses on race developed in the field of anthropology and in the popular press. According to some nineteenth-century race theories, the Irish were an inferior race; some compared them to Africans. In 1885, Beddoe called the Irish "Africanoid" in *The Races of Britain*; and the Irish were likened to "Negroes" in the U.S. popular press.[97] But the early 1900s were a transformative time for Irish Americans. In the United States, the Irish did not stay black. Although the Irish were "blackened" in some accounts of racial science, other theorists welcomed them as family capable of being civilized. Instead of being excluded they would be recovered as "the Folk," their traditions preserved. With nostalgia for an earlier, simpler agrarian era, the Irish would be absorbed, their "Celtic spirit" drawn upon.[98]

Cole was levying an explicit critique on two levels. He was critiquing U.S. vaudeville stage managers and booking agencies, which excluded most black acts from its circuits and exploited the black performers it did use. But he and his company were also acknowledging the process by which Irish New Yorkers were transforming into white civil subjects. He and his troupe were noting the irony that the Irish's so-called blackness was only temporary. This was felt economically. His farce acknowledges that Irish men made up most of the police force at this time. His white-face critique was also a recognition that Irish women were replacing black women as the favored domestics in New York. Jobs as maids were given to the poor cousins of the Anglo-Saxon family.

What Cole and his company offered was comment on the white power structure in the United States and the way citizenship was conditional on racial category. Black acts of Irish impersonation did register that both Irish and black people were excluded and contained, but it also recognized the limits of potential alliance on those terms. These forms of exclusion were not the same at all between (permanently) black and (marginally) white citizens. And as farce, these acts noticed how absurd the idea of firm racial fact was. Chasing strong men and police through the city streets, Cole and his company parodied the unstable nature of racial identity. These acts showed that racial hierarchies were politically motivated. As farce, their delineation brought into relief the contradictions of their own relation to national belonging (as property) and the condition of whiteness upon which this belonging (as citizens) was predicated.

Popular performance is not the site to find authentic folk types or instances of racial authenticity or explicit resistance. But what these acts did do was to expose race "typologies" as conceptual categories bound by time and place, produced out of relations of power. Michel de Certeau's concept of "tactics" can help us to understand the malleability of racialized performance on the black stage.

> The space of a tactic . . . must play on and with a terrain imposed on it and organized by the law of a foreign power. . . . It is a maneuver "within the enemy's field of vision" . . . and within enemy territory. . . . It takes advantage of opportunities and depends on them. . . . This nowhere gives a tactic mobility . . . but a mobility that must accept the chance offerings of the moment, and seize on the wing the possibilities that offer themselves at any given moment. It must vigilantly make use of the cracks that particular conjunctions open in the surveillance of the proprietary powers. It poaches them. It creates surprises in them. It can be where it is least expected. It is a guileful ruse.[99]

Despite de Certeau's language of battle and ownership, and his assumption of clear division between the foreign and the familiar, his theory is useful for understanding the protean mobility of such acts. However, these acts demonstrated that movements and routines could *not* be owned or kept. For years white performers had been miming blackness, circulating ideas of the "fungible" black body.[100] African American performers, moving in and among racialized roles, threw back onto the stage the power-based relational politics of their own accessibility and commodification, adopting acts of whiteness as a strategy of social critique. Mixing styles of movement from various sources was their "guileful ruse," as black performers were playing within the artificiality of racial typing.

Exercising and embodying freedom of movement, the performers emerging from *The Creole Show*—namely Dora Dean and Stella Wiley— all had dancing and singing acts, with each other, with their husbands, or with dancing partners. Despite the fact that Wiley is barely mentioned except as the wife of Bob Cole, and her presence in the archives organized under his name only, Wiley and Cole were not married past 1897. According to Cole in one newspaper report, their split was already a year old when they were working together in 1897 in Black Patti's Troubadours, aside from some highly publicized (and perhaps performed) drama. Taking a backstage quarrel out onto the street after a show, Wiley "beat [Cole] over the head with an umbrella," until a patrolman "came up in response to his cries for help and arrested her."[101] Tensions between the performers were most likely high, as Cole was to leave Black Patti's Troupe in April. But the story sounds straight out of the pages of *The National Police Gazette* and could have sat next to the numerous florid tales lining this publication of jealous wives poisoning their masher husband's mistresses. "Flowers for Another Cause Trouble between a Husband and a Wife," reads the title of one newspaper report of the publicly performed quarrel between Wiley and Cole. It offers a rare description of Wiley, as she punches Cole over the head at midnight in front of the theater. "Both were corralled by an officer, and on Cole's complaint his wife was locked up at the Central. This morning she appeared before Squire Sultzer handsomely gowned and bedecked in a superbly beautiful hat, overflowing with red roses. She is quite handsome, of olive complexion, blue eyes, luxuriant black hair and comely of form."[102] This "real" moment between the two was a continuation of Stella's stage persona, the tough, yet beautiful, city girl. The act was a comedic performance of the heterosexual couple, which was often simply a cover for the duo stage acts so many black women would work in during this era. Perhaps it plays on the expectation that the actress exists as an extension of her husband, which was certainly the case with how Wiley has been remembered historically.

> "That's my wife, said Cole, "and, though playing in the same company, we haven't lived together for 12 months. Last night I presented a boquet [*sic*] of flowers to Miss Oatman, also a singer in the company, and my wife called me to account on the street." "Yes I did," interposed Mrs. Cole. "I'm the rightful one to receive his flowers, and not she. Besides, he asked me to do some vile things, and I refused, and that's why I hit him."[103]

Stella Wiley is remembered mostly as Bob Cole's wife, despite the fact that they were not married long. Wiley's career did survive past her break with Cole, although she has since fallen into obscurity. After her divorce from Bob Cole and the close of Isham's shows, Wiley teamed up with a male acrobatic dancer named Russell Brandow. Wiley and Brandow toured widely. Billed as "the colored aristocrats," they appeared on the prestigious white Keith Circuit.[104] According to Wiley's date book, they also toured England extensively. Drawing on the earlier conventions from the children's troupes and also circus work, Brandow "specialized in grotesque dancing."[105] According to reviews, he was as "nimble on his feet as a cricket." Wiley accompanied the dancing with songs like "Rag Man":

> Got any rags?
> Got any rags? Got any rags, bottles, bones, today?
> There's a big black man a-cmon' this way
> It's the same old story in the same old way
> Got any rags? Got any rags? Have you got any rags today?

"When she has finished her singing," reads the review, "the man makes a veritable pinwheel of himself gyrating about with his hips as a pivot till one wonders how it is that he does not break himself into a dozen pieces."[106] Wiley and Brandow were a black act, performing in the convention of white working-class vaudeville. But the black trope of dismemberment and limber survival remain at the core of even the most conventional sounding of variety acts.

The women working in these early burlesque revues went on to work solo careers: some, such as Belle Davis, toured Europe with picaninny revues; others, such as Dora Dean and her partner Charles Johnson, appeared in cakewalk dancing duos. Women artists worked in shows and revues and specialty acts across Europe and America. Ida Forsyne, Mattie Wilkes, and others would go to St. Petersburg, Russia. Wiley's work and that of the other *Creole Show* women in the early chorus lines prefigures the later work of colored chorines on the New York variety stages, as well as the training black women gave to the women of the segregated white chorus lines. As I argue in the next chapters, their artistic presence signaled the modern era in particular ways.

THE CAKEWALK BUSINESS

D espite the carnal violence of lynch law and the de facto segregation of black citizenry, black expressive techniques became the chosen gestural languages of a northern urban populace. In the next two chapters I explore this contradiction and invoke a breach in the analytical shadow/silence when it comes to thinking about the strange choreographies of segregation and the uses of black dance in the articulation of modernity's civic bodies. Analyzing the *fin-de-siècle* cakewalk craze and the social dances of the 1910s, I am thinking about the politics of gendered race and social space in New York City during the decade black people were making Harlem a cultural center. "Space is fundamental to any exercise of power," Michel Foucault stated. "I think it is somewhat arbitrary to dissociate the effective practice of freedom by people, the practice of social relations, and the spatial distribution in which they find themselves."[1] In the last chapter I suggested that one level of humor on the black variety stage was about the ironies of national belonging for black people in the United States and the concept of being a possession to an imperializing democracy. I continue my argument here that the racial annexation of both urban and imperial territories, and the incursions made by the annexed, were intimately fundamental to the shaping of modern geographies.

The sociopolitical landscape in northern industrial cities at the turn of the century has been amply explored and celebrated, though studies more often than not assume a top-down model for historical analysis.[2] In many studies black culture is source material, made legitimate only through its effects on whiteness as a construction, or in relation to white class formation. In other studies it is white (and probationary white) working classes whose experience forms the defining cultural focus.[3] Almost all of these studies of cultural formation in the United States claim a "relaxation" of the boundaries between social categories (men and women, working and middle classes, Irish and Anglo) as a defining tenet of modernity and/or as proof that the United States really would fulfill, or was in the process of realizing, the egalitarian promises of its founding fathers. Some studies argue that forms of social dance enact this fundamental urge in American culture. Better studies of social dance understand danced performance moments and dance spaces as sites of sociopolitical contestation.[4]

According to many urban studies, sites of mass amusement, both participatory and spectatorial performances, were areas where new, open, and intimate forms of sociability were developing. Perhaps this is true for some constituents, but for black people civic space was just as heavily, if not more creatively, policed. Physical closeness does not imply the intent to share or the realization of natural egalitarianism. Mere physical proximity hardly denotes a breakdown in social divisions; instead, it shows the powerful ability for these racio-social, political, and economic hierarchies to recalibrate, adjust, and re-form in new moments. White people performed black dances to celebrate democratic progress, and this use served to retain and restabilize the gestural codings of such hierarchies. I am interested in how black people's performances in the center of the modern city played on this irony, as well as acted as assertive claims to social space.

The cakewalk dance craze had everything to do with the development of the modern city space and was a precursor to later forms of social dance that signified trans-urban popular culture in the 1910s and 1920s. These dances were performed and staged in critical territories within the city: the fairground midway, the park, the coliseum, the theater rooftop. These were territories where ideologies of American wealth were being ritualized. The cakewalk and the black social dances that followed shaped these territories. The various places and ways the dance was staged reveal the contestation over social geographies, both the hegemonic project to retain racial hierarchies and black people's claim to new modern spaces.

I focus here on ways the cakewalk dance craze opens up discussion along two lines. First, I consider the ways the dance invites a discussion of the politics of the cultivated modern body and the use of black gestural vocabularies (dance and style) in that cultivation. Second, I explore how the "cakewalk business" demonstrates the multi-signifying power of black performance, the agile navigation of hostile territories.

The favored version of the cakewalk's origin tale situates it as the biting satirical practice of plantation slaves in the South. This origin story recognizes the dance as counterhegemonic at its inception. The slaves would stage mock quadrilles; flipping their skirts and prancing the yard, the enslaved parodied the aristocratic pretenses of the master class. The plantation owners soon noticed that the slaves were imitating their courtly rituals, thinking it natural that they should imitate their betters. At harvest time they offered the prize of a cake for the best couples and invited them to perform up at the big house. So the cakewalk was born, a forced entertainment with satirical meanings hidden in full view of the masters. This process of mimesis has a delightful twisting irony; soon the masters themselves were attempting the dance as the enslaved had reshaped it.

The dance is now critically remembered as an iconographic demonstration of black people's manipulation of masks, a particular form of complex, multi-layered racial mimesis. I do not read this plantation setting as the sole location of the dance's authentic meaning. I am thinking about what happened to the dance, its forms, uses, and meanings, as it traveled. Considering the practice of the cakewalk in specific historical conjuncture is a way to think about how black social dance techniques develop over time and in various sites of dislocation, how they rearticulate in different sites of enactment. The spaces in which black people performed this dance—world's fair midway, midtown coliseum, skyscraper rooftop, city park—were key sites to the graphing of the urban landscape and the modern body.

How is it that black bodies came to model for a white populace the ideal bodies of urban sophistication, wealth, and fantasies of access to that wealth? It is a thick irony that a black dance supposedly originating on the plantation would become the era's signature performance at the heart of the metropole. We can make some sense of it here, as the cakewalk was part of a new language of physical development.

Over the turn of the century and into the 1910s, as the model for economic livelihood shifted from an artisanal one to industrial capital, the work force was split into working and managerial classes and the terms defining manliness and womanliness were shifting. The Victorian ethos of bourgeois manliness and the cult of true womanhood were giving way to new mores of class behavior based in leisure pursuits. The gendered body became a key terrain for these shifts in meaning.[5] New concepts of physical wellness for "ladies and gentlemen" were designed, as cultivation and maintenance of the body were central to new meanings of the self. A cadre of health professionals developed "cures," health philosophies involving exercise regimes for women as well as men. A class of physical instructors also formed. The respectable classes were encouraged to take up "purposeful exercise." Working-class cultures of the male body influenced the changing ideas of manhood—civilization as the result of the survival of the fittest was now rendered literally. Boxing, running, weight lifting, and other demonstrations of stamina and strength became important articulations of the new ideal. The model for strong, agile abilities was embodied in the natural form of the "primitive" races.[6]

But now more than ever class distinctions were important to maintain. Fine musculature must not ever be the byproduct of wage work. Achieving the ideal body must be actively distanced from the idea of becoming, or from any chance of resembling, the working class. A strong manly body was the product of exercise routines that, while as regimented, were aimed specifically at body sculpture. They also involved a service class whose job it was to tutor these new bodies into these perfected forms. Boxing and other games were now ways to get "in shape." As this was about assertions of fitness, physical culture involved competitive exhibition.

That the ideal exercise regime must not involve work was particularly true for white middle- and upper-class women. The ideal of the New Woman developed out of decades of social and reform activism: suffragist activity and the more conservative claims to public space and authority made by moral reformers. White middle-class women rebelled against the forced leisure of Victorian-era medical diagnoses. These formerly docile bodies would instead partake of liberating physical practices: stretching, toning, swimming, lifting light weights. They would take the air: playing golf and riding the park path upon their bicycles. They would dress according to the new principles of dress reform, as rational dress freed the body from corsets and other constraints that strangled the nervous system. But new physiques were cultivated recreationally, not through labor;

for white women to be "New" in this way exercise could only be for its own sake. Leisure pursuit was still the rule de jour for new wealth, for the angels of the house.

White working-class women were at the center of the contests over the meanings of female form.[7] White women reformers sought to discipline working women's bodies and behaviors; saving them from sin meant making them into good servants. But a particular philosophy of bodily freedom and dress reform was also inherent to the radical socialist thought of the activist Emma Goldman. Told that it was not correct for a political activist to dance, she is famously *mis*quoted as having said, "If I can't dance I don't want to be in your revolution." For Goldman, dress reform was in service of a woman's right to "freedom, the right to self-expression, everybody's right to beautiful, radiant things."[8]

In the United States, the ultimate icon of the laboring woman (nothing "New" here) was not only working class but black. Black working women's bodies were so associated with labor that they did not even come into discussions and contestations over female form and reform. White slavery was just that: for women who were, or would be, white. Considering the intertwined relationship among race, labor, and the various responsibilities and meanings attached to women's bodies (as the folk, the modern, the transgressive), I wonder at the marked absence of black women in the work of historians of working-class white women's culture. Many interesting studies could be made of the uses of public city space in relation to both working-class white women and black women.

The cakewalk was already part of a widely circulating set of black dances. As it was rigorous exercise, black dancers easily adapted it to these new regimes. The dance was strenuous, demanding stamina and poise. The dance's emphasis was on proper form; as a slow moving two-step, timing and control were essential. Its high-stepping movements were to appear effortless at all times. The cakewalk was a couple's dance, and it was to be done exclusively in fancy dress. Its execution must appear graceful and leisurely, no matter how heavily ones' bejeweled gown weighed on the hips. After all, it was the dance to celebrate new wealth.

With its emphasis on form and carriage it became a demonstration dance—stylized instruction of proper deportment—and black dancers codified the dances' movements to teach it to a white populace. Its exact form varied according to place—a stage form for the black revues, a ballroom style designed for white society parties, a technically more difficult and athletic form for the huge cakewalk competitions held in Madison Square Garden. Whatever the form it was always a dance of pageantry and public display, done in the processional or in the round. The performance space was always part of its meaning, as its enactment was part of claiming that space.

Ada Overton had first brought the cakewalk to England's Empire Circuit in 1897 with Isham's traveling company, in the revue *Oriental America*. She would bring it to England again six years later as the finale to the successful Williams and Walker show *In Dahomey*, only this time Overton, Williams, and Walker brought it to the West End. As the troupe's choreographer, Ada Overton gave private cakewalking lessons to many of London's leading personages. Composure and elegance—the appearance of relaxed wealth—were the aims of this version of the cakewalk aesthetic. Ada Overton described the dance to Constance Beerbohm, a correspondent for the *London Tatler*. Beerbohm paraphrases what she learned from Aida's instruction: "The step of the cakewalk is light and elastic, after it has been learned, fancy steps may be practised. Some are very intricate; but the success of cakewalking depends largely on temperament . . . the faces must be interested and joyous, and as the cakewalk is characteristic of a cheerful race to be properly appreciated it must be danced in the proper spirit."[9]

Ada's lesson is quite clever. Coding the dance as the effortless expression of a cheerful race hides the many articulations of resistance and parody the dance is capable of evoking. Such dissemblance—the naturally joyous temperament of a happy race—masks any satirical content. Six years earlier, the female cast of *Oriental America* had staged the "picturesque features of the more pleasant side of old slave life," bringing the cakewalk, "one of the merriest and liveliest festivals of the American coloured native" as one Liverpool correspondent called it, to the English working-class audiences. Now they could bring the cakewalk to the high paying public of London.[10] Talented dancers, Overton, and the other cakewalking women demonstrated lithe beauty and adroitly wrested public recognition in England for African American creative artistry and urban presence.

The juxtaposition of physical prowess, heavy wealth, and cool grace was the key to the art of the cakewalk, as modeled by the former *Creole*

Show chorus girl Dora Dean. With her cakewalk partner Charles Johnson, Dean would become famous for cakewalking in a ballroom fashion.[11] Their version of the cakewalk emphasized style and fluidity of movement. Dressed in opulent gowns, dripping with jewels and feathers, Dean performed arduous and contortionary body movements with her dance partners—back bends, high kicks and splits, irregular struts that demanded a delicate balance of body weight.

As a demonstration dance and white urban craze, the cakewalk is a perfect embodied response to this historical conjuncture. It spoke with the body to the need for renewed systems of regulation for manners, etiquette, and deportment, which were key as social hierarchies were shifting and less stable. It spoke to the increased importance placed on rules and guidelines for class and gender propriety during this era of economic and social change. It spoke to the challenges to patriarchal family structure posed by new forms of social independence for white women in the city. It could be used to stage heterosexual romance as a "natural" process, a process thought to be most deftly demonstrated by "the Negro," imagined as closest to nature and its properties.

For the white upper classes the cakewalk became a metaphor for the new importance placed on leisure pursuits and conspicuous consumption as signs of class standing. New York's Elite Four Hundred affirmed the passion of their wealth through imitating the bodily expressions of African American performers. White middle-class Americans also cottoned onto the craze, partially imitating a white elite. Under the tutelage of black practitioners both classes began to dance it with fervor. In his study *Harlem Renaissance*, Nathaniel Huggins discusses the version of the cakewalk, the rage in the fancy masquerade balls held by incredibly wealthy families dominated by such as the Astors and the Vanderbilts, as a grotesque spectacle of racial masking and class pretensions. "All was a jumble of masks and costumes covering naked uncertainties," he writes. "White men pretended to be black men of their fantasy; black men pretended to be the grotesques that white men had created, while other white men and women pretended to be aristocrats, court jesters, knights in $10,000 armor, Mary Queen of Scots, and so on. The deep realities from which they were all fleeing were doubtless more horrible than the acts they put on. It was all a theatre of the absurd."[12] Huggins's analysis is an aptly put and appropriately leveling reminder of the lack of love involved in the complex of power and pretense structuring *fin-de-siècle* U.S. cultural politics.

The history of this dance catches all of the dubious ironies produced from the terms of exchange by which an ex-slave populace teaches the new elite its dance of wealth. It also reveals the development of a choreography of segregation in northern cities, the complex ordering of space and rules of physical proximity. I could say these were doubling ironies; however, I argue throughout that the multiplying properties here exceed a binary. Rather than looking both ways, or being split by "two warring ideals," black women "glance in all directions," that is, they must consider several levels of perception simultaneously. For black women, Du Bois's set of warring ideals consisted of more than two; women were caught between several, and they were less than ideal.

Du Bois's concept of double consciousness has been marshaled into service across academic disciplines to dramatize the schismatic experience of being black in the United States. The concept, as Du Bois conceived of it, was about consciousness shaped in relation to race and nation and assumed as its main focus a conversation about national belonging. What gets lost in many contemporary uses of this concept is that, as Hazel Carby reminds us, the ideal of a national subject position, the model for which Du Bois wrote, was male.[13] I would add that national identity was not always a central organizing principle of black awareness, and certainly not a natural one. Earlier frameworks of understanding do not automatically assume a U.S. national identity for African descendents. What we find more often is multiple affiliations. These affiliations are possible—and often productively staged—where and when no civic or national or economic forms of enfranchisement are in fact really being offered.

In both demonstrated and participatory moments the cakewalk dance craze performed the paradox of national "representation." This was happening at the same time as some of the most divisive practices of civic violence and racial segregation were choreographed for its makers. That we should live as "separate as the fingers" (though not necessarily as "one as the hand") seemed the chosen truth; in 1896 the Supreme Court's decision *Plessy vs. Ferguson* naturalized an ideology of racial apartheid for the post-emancipation era. Practices for excluding black bodies from the national and civic body intensified and diversified. Segregation was enforced by rituals of fire and dismemberment. Yet black dances signaled that modern social space in the United States was democratic.

The cakewalk was formally acknowledged as a national pastime, acting as the folk expression of a nation. The satirist George Ade picked up on this irony in his *Stories of Benevolent Assimilation*, published in the *Chicago Record* in 1899. The stories revolve around the interactions between an American missionary named Conner and a rural Filipino family, the Kakyaks. In his effort to civilize the new subjects and introduce them to American national culture, Conner demonstrates the cakewalk and the coon song as representative forms of American dance and music. "You say you are imitating him," Mr. Kakyak comments,

> "I thought that the darker race always took second place and as dependent on the Caucasian, receiving instruction from him. . . . Yet now you confess that you get your songs from the negro."
>
> "You do not understand," replied the missionary. "We may borrow our popular songs from the negro, but in the important matter of handling the dollars we are still on top, and will continue to remain there."
>
> "Even when the negro has been assimilated?" asked Mr. Kakyak.
>
> "Well, we are not going to assimilate him to that extent."

The missionary then demonstrates the cakewalk dance for the Kakyak family.[14]

Ade's satire acknowledges the paradox of representing a nation's culture with the creative practices of its politically and socially disenfranchised. Cultural assessments that celebrate the "democratic" quality of American mass amusements work to suppress this alarming contradiction.[15] Certainly, moments of transformation in social hierarchical structures leave gaps that invite possibilities and spaces for contestation. But we cannot assume that social transgressions (of race, gender, or politics) are inherently radical or progressive in their intent or consequences.

The cakewalk was also a demonstration in which the civic body was contested. The dance was demonstrated in locations crucial to the sociopolitical mapping of the urban landscape. The city parks were being designed for outdoor recreation, the coliseums for physical exhibitions, while dancing white Americans were designating rooftops for the social ritualization of the new cultivated body. Black citizenry were excluded from pedestrian participation at these white sites (not permitted to stroll or sweat too near these newly urbane masses) while black boxers, jockeys, acrobats, and dancers, at a safely demarcated proximity, furnished the new languages of the body. Every white body, "strutting for dat cake," was a minstrel under the skin.

Ten-year-old Ida Forsyne danced the cakewalk, with a small boy for a partner, along the midway of Chicago's Columbian Exposition over the entire summer of 1893. Before the fair, Ida Forsyne had danced the cakewalk at various clubs and cabarets on weekends. "People had cabarets," Forsyne explains. "Saturday nights the man selected who he wanted, and we would all do a bit there cakewalking. Everybody had a job on Saturday nights, so eventually they put it in the World's Fair." As she explains it, her mother was "one of the people in the Cakewalk business" and so her family traveled from Kentucky to perform at the fair. "They rode us around in a wagon or a truck and they had a speaker saying *'we have the cakewalk over here.'* This was in a building in one part of the fair. They had several couples who danced. I did mine solo, worked there all summer."[16] Forsyne's performance and that of her family were not officially a part of the fair's exposition or midway exhibition. Like *The Creole Show*, running at Sam. T. Jack's Opera House, their performances were outside and in the interstices of the official fairgrounds.

Forsyne provides a pragmatic origin tale for the dance. "The cakewalk is something they had in the rebel war for southern people who were slaves. The man who owned them every once in a while he'd bring em out and have them do this cakewalk for him. Because my mother was one of the people in this cakewalk business, I took it up and used to make money."[17] Forsyne follows her mother in the "cakewalk business," a more lucrative choice than those offered. The cakewalk business became big business, and a cast of black professional performers emerged from these conjunctures, seizing the time to travel and dance.

Besides the midway, the dance took on meanings at other symbolically critical locations, including the urban variety stages. Beginning with *The Creole Show* all of the black variety shows incorporated the cakewalk, usually as a finale. In *The Octoroons* the cakewalk finale was joined with a military drill. Williams's and the Walker's first musical comedy, *In Dahomey*, offered directions for how to do the dance in a song called "This Is How the Cakewalk's Done" by J. Leubrie Hill. In 1898, the classically trained musician Will Marion Cook and the poet Paul Lawrence Dunbar composed *Clorindy, or the Origins of the Cakewalk*, staged on New York's Casino Roof Garden. Their show was the first time that black performers were admitted into this theater. But not a black audience: black acts in the city packed the theaters, but most were open to white audiences only. True to form, these shows held parodic meaning. On the outside, they remained confirmation of Zip Coonery, black clownish imitation of white wealth. Layered in was satire of the white and wealthy, but also of black middle-class aspiration. Lyrics to white and black musical compositions from these plays illustrate this complexity. In lyrics by H. G. Wheeler, the "The Colored Four Hundred" are clownishly rendered, but just who is imitating whom is not clear:

> We're swains of swell society, all imitate our ways
> and any fad we may adopt at once becomes a craze
> We ride and drive, we dance and pose to catch the female eye
> and as matrimonial prizes don't we set our value high.

These parodies were also of black pretensions. "I'd Like to Be a Real Lady," Ada Overton Walker sings, in a composition by Alex Rogers. "Like others I'd do silly things to make the smart set talk, get Mansfield and black Patti to lead my big cakewalk."[18]

The meaning of the dance—class parody, serious self-fashioning, intra-racial satire—depended to some degree on where and when and by whom the dance was performed. But the spaces and significations interpenetrated and rang off of each other. The popular stage, the recreational space of the city park, the panoptical space of the coliseum, the proprietary space of the rooftop theater were all prime sites for the drama of social contestation, for the recalibration of racial hierarchies as well as black incursions on public space.

AMBROSE PARK

A range of racial spectacles were held in the centers of the city over the turn of the century. *Buffalo Bill Cody's Wild Wild West Show* enjoyed a wildly successful run outside the World's Fair, in conjunction with the ethnic villages inside the fair's grounds. That next year the show's producer, Nate Salsbury, and its manager, Billy McClain, moved the *Wild West Show* to Ambrose Park, which had been planted in the middle of Brooklyn, New York. Salsbury, a former blackface performer and the leader of Salsbury's minstrels, was part owner of the forty-acre park. Over the summer of 1895

Salsbury and McClain organized a gigantic plantation reenactment called _Black America_ to be staged in Ambrose Park. The plantation reenactment joined the culture of spectacle for racialized bodies, reenacting life in their natural habitats, at museums and fairs.

The black performer Billy McClain had been responsible for the casting and management of the grounds for the _Wild West Show_. He was a seasoned performer and had previously produced his own plantation reenactment, _South before the War_. Because of this McClain very well may have pitched the idea for _Black America_ to Salsbury and been ready with a large number of people willing to cast it. Together they produced this "big novelty extravaganza," with a cast of over five hundred performers and an audience of eleven thousand coming to the staged shows at the performance tent set up in the park.[19]

Black America was advertised as a "Novel, Natural, National Colossal Afro-American Exhibition";

> A Stupendous Aggregation of Actual Field Hands from the Cotton Belt. A Veritable Invasion from the Sunny South of 500 Colored Men and Women. Representatives of a race famed for Spontaneous Exuberation of Human Humor who will present the Lovable Bright Side of the Negro Character, Living in a Village of Plantation Cabins.[20]

In the middle of Brooklyn, forty acres were "transformed into the likeness of a plantation," on which cast members built and lived in "real cabins" for the season:

> Cotton bushes . . . were transplanted. Bales of cotton were brought in and a cotton gin in working order set up. Poultry and livestock were brought in, and real cabins built, a large part of the company using these cabins as living quarters for the season. The entire layout provided atmosphere through which the audiences would roam at random before the show itself started.[21]

Winding their way through the authentic slave plantation grounds, the audience participants ended up at a "tented amphitheatre" for the musical revue at the heart of the event. The revue was split in the usual three-part format of the minstrel show. The olio featured eccentric dancers, black boxers and jockeys, a demonstration by the black division of the Ninth Cavalry, an amazon drill of women on horseback, and a women's foot race. It also included Jubilee singers and vocalists' renditions of popular favorites, such as Stephen Foster's "My Old Kentucky Home" and James Bland's "Carry Me Back to Old Virginia." Special theme days were offered, including a Cotton Exposition Day and a "Picaninny Day," a pageant held of "a thousand black babies." And of course the show ended with a cakewalk dancing competition.

Plantation recreations were part of a culture of southern nostalgia produced out of the post-reconstruction era. In these fallaciously "historical" recreations "the stage and the political forum easily merged; theatre and politics extended each other's capacity to drain African American culture of . . . civil rights while mapping it onto an idealized display of racial supremacy that transported pastoral nostalgia into a violence-ridden present."[22] These recreations staged an agrarian topos as the natural homeland for the "hewers of wood and drawers of water." These enactments were one way the plantation would return in popular cultural forms, re-versioning slavery as a prelapsarian innocence rather than as a system that needed to be enforced by violence and coercion.

Like the fairs' ethnic villages, and like the newly designed museums, these restagings required an audience. As Lori Brooks writes, "The white audience was as necessary a participant as the black performers." Strolling through, as they did through the ethnic villages at various expositions, northern white audiences "were not required to face their own complicity in . . . sectionalism or its Northern component—urban racial segregation."[23] The cakewalk was a featured entertainment in plantation reenactments across the United States. It was staged as an authentic slave dance, the dance's "origins" as the happy days of servitude, the natural effulgence of the slaves, readily demonstrated for their master's enjoyment.

Black America operated on the same principle of reenacting the real as did the *Wild West Show*. Salsbury had been influenced by the World's Fair ethnic villages, staffed by the indigenous peoples of the colonies, and he intentionally based *Black America* on them. He insisted that his cast be southern born and raised and instructed them to demonstrate, purely and without guile, the natural attributes of their race for their northern audience. "They are not show people," he claimed, "but are the genuinely southern negro in all his types."[24] This idea of the authentic, the real, was key. The "non-acting actors" (using Lori Brooks's term) were to pretend to exist in a timeless southern past.

Such a staging of "animated rural simplicity in 'Dixie'" played upon the white wish to re-member a period of national childhood innocence, a pre-industrial agrarian moment. The repetitious return to the primal scene of the cotton plantation suggests its centrality as a site at which the terms of contact and sets of exchanges making up ideas of race in the United States were founded. The repeated staging of a happy black past was aimed at erasing the memory of violent interracial relations of U.S. chattel slavery, recasting slavery's captives as the singing and dancing children of free soil.

Like the *Wild West Show*, *Black America* signaled the triumph of the civilizing mission to bring stability and guidance to the inferior races, folding them into the embrace of the nation. These stagings worked to retie Indians and black people to the land. It did the important work of rendering black people as an indigenous folk, whose traditional ways infused the modern world with childlike emotionalism and musicality. As I discuss in chapter 6, this indigenousness was not meant to be confused with a nativist right to civic belonging, but to relegate blacks to a place outside the reach of democracy. Like indigenous folk, their place was pre-industrial, or rather, extra-industrial, for their bodies were still needed to labor.

It is both troubling and revealing that Billy McClain would stage *Black America*. In a bleak assessment, such a large-scale reenactment can be read as the collusion of black artists in creating and maintaining an obscene nostalgia, a ritual of historical memory whose main function was to obscure the truth of racial terrorization. But even so, Brooks points out that Salsbury and McClain had contradictory ideas of what the event was about. Foremost for McClain, *Black America* was a place for a large number of black artists to work and get paid during the off-season. His stated vision was to provide a training ground for the newly emerging professional entertainers as well as to maintain black management and artistic control. The staff for the plantation grounds may well have been untrained as Salsbury claimed. McClain was probably able to recruit many of the same people from *The South before the War* to staff Salsbury's grounds. It was, after all, paid work for them over the summer too. All they had to do was to act as if slavery had not ended. As well as the untrained members of the cast, McClain hired artists, musical quartets, singers, and dancers, some of whom he had met while working the circuits in Australia, and for whom paid work was crucial.

The concept of "acting natural" here takes on a twisting kind of nonsensical absurdity. We can understand it as spectacle, as black masquerade, because playing in the field of white fantasy was stock and trade for African American variety artists. To create a spectacle of subjugation was a way of underlining its construction. Riffing the script did not mean being scripted by what were obvious falsities, because what black meant was not, and could not, be fixed by white fictions.

We can also think of this moment, like so many others, as black people's incursion on the pastoral grounds of urban white America. Black actors, singers, and non-acting actors were claiming a historical moment of black migration out of the South to the centers of northern industrial triumph. The pageant affirmed this moment of black migration as a narrative of racial progress, for playing at picking cotton was an affirmation that they had no intention of returning to the "down-home" of whips, chains, and fruitless labor. Ida Forsyne's comments on the cakewalk business are especially poignant here. "It was good because colored people got a job all those years and didn't have to scrub anything. Just prance around and smile."[25]

JUBILEE IN MR. WHITE'S GARDEN

Ironically, stagings of the plantation were central in the shift to what we now identify as modern mass amusements. Stanford White's Madison Square Garden itself hosted the most famous of these plantation stagings as part of the huge cakewalking pageants held there between 1895 and 1898. The Garden was the site for the full demonstration of modern cultivated bodies, and by far the most popular exhibitions of physical stamina and strength were these cakewalking competitions, for which black dancers came from across the nation and drew as many as ten thousand spectators. This is the moment when we can see how central black bodies in motion were to articulating urban style and carriage.

Madison Square Garden was originally a railroad depot. When the trains were rerouted through Grand Central Station, the depot was sold to P. T. Barnum, who repurposed it as a huge circus arena. In 1879 William Vanderbilt bought the arena and renamed it Madison Square Garden. In 1890, Stanford White redesigned the Garden, building in living quarters for himself. Boasting the largest great hall in the world, Mr. White's Garden was built for mass rituals of new athleticism, its stands providing thousands of spectators full view of the events held there.

The public display of physical achievement was key to the meaning of modern urban spaces. Demonstrations and contests of physical ability were the loci for the renegotiation of gendered bodies in the city. At the Garden's huge bicycling exhibitions, white middle-class women were claiming their bodies through new regimes of "purposeful" exercise that emphasized muscular development. The Garden became a central venue for boxing contests as the shift from a politics of manliness to one of masculinity created a craze for pugilism and other competitive physical regimes for men.[26]

Boxing and cycling were two forms of sport held at White's Garden, but "the *Prize Cakewalk* contest soon grew to be one of the city's greatest sporting events," remembers Thomas Fletcher. "The Madison Square Garden competition was always a sell-out." Fifty or sixty black couples would compete. These Garden events were advertised and covered in the *National Police Gazette*, which provided the prizes for the winning couples. The cakewalk competitions followed what Fletcher calls a "big plantation scene";

> Before the contest there would be a big plantation scene with a cast of about 150 singers and dancers and some great vocal soloist of the period. After the show was over, the judges, including many of New York's prominent brokers, sportsmen and athletes, especially prize fighters, would take their places on the stage. . . . The inside of Madison Square Garden on such occasions was arranged like a race track. The space for the cakewalkers ran alongside the boxes and loges. . . . The curtain would part and 50 or 60 couples would come from behind the stage on to the floor, prancing and dancing to the tempo of the music.[27]

These events were linked to *Black America*, the spectacle in Ambrose Park, as the city park and the coliseum were co-articulating sites for new forms of leisure. Performers from the *Black America* pageant held special performances at Madison Square Garden. McClain's star, the operetta singer Madame Flowers, appeared at the Garden as did several of *Black America*'s singing quartets. Madame Sissieretta Jones got her start singing for one of these competitions. By 1901 the staged setting for her touring Troubadours revue was a Madison Square Garden jubilee itself. The smart set of African American entertainers and athletes then forming a community in New York, including black pugilists such as Jack Johnson and others, officiated at this huge sporting event in the heart of the city.

By 1898 there were eighty-nine couples circling the track. These couples were the champions of local competitions, hosted in small cities by touring black companies. The winners of the Madison Square Garden competitions became public figures; these included the dancing couples Luke and Martha Blackburn, Dave Genaro and his wife Ray Bailey, and Billy and Willie Farrell. Fletcher explains that

> the couples that emerged winners or runners up usually formed Variety or Vaudeville acts. All of the couples that took part in the contests were good singers and dancers, and the winning of the championship at Madison Square Garden was a great help in them getting bookings from all over the world because this American dance which originated among the colored people during slavery was a sensation all over the globe."[28]

Billy and Willie Farrell, the 1895 champions of the world, went on to tour Europe; in 1898 they opened a cakewalking school in London.

Black couples, in formal dress, circled the cycling track to a two-step waltz, backs arching, parasols turning. Prizes were offered for both "graceful and straight walking" and for "fancy or grotesque walking."[29] The two-step waltz provided a framework for the improvisation of steps and interactions between the dancers. As a couples dance, it was about staging proper proximity and protocol between men and women. But, particularly in the grotesque segments, it was also about how to riff from these demonstrations of propriety into the other-worldly possibilities of the body; extraordinarily deep back bends, superlatively high kicks, multi-syncopated swishes of the dress. At first only black couples competed at the Garden, but soon white couples, after their training with the black dancers, also competed. The audience was also at first primarily black, but soon a class-diverse white audience began to attend.

What was the view from the stands at such an event? This depends on who was looking. What was the view from the boxes where the black judges sat? A politics of multi-signification nudges us here, as we must "glance in all directions" even to begin to grasp the complexity of this moment. For the black judges, audience, and dancers, one can imagine it was a vantage point to look at the self, at a new moment in black culture and mobility. To "dance for dat cake" also meant to look at the self through the eyes of others, the ubiquitous white audience.

The cakewalk competitions were sometimes accompanied by boxing matches called battle royales. Circling a coliseum, men beating each other in a cage, these diversions were historically marked from the days of involuntary performance in Rome, where slaves regularly faced death and dismemberment for the enjoyment of the masses. But certainly there had been progress since the barbaric days of the Roman Empire. This cityscape was shaped by the meritocratic triumph of American wealth. The "relaxation" around social boundaries—the wealthy seated in the same arena as the lower castes—reflected the largesse of its benefactors.

We could interpret the rituals in this arena, therefore, as working to restabilize systems of racial oppression. By this interpretation these cakewalking spectacles seem like reenactments of black servitude, unfree labor forced to entertain the master class. Lazy, tending to hedonism and sartorial excess, black people certainly could not be trusted to participate in a democracy. Brush strokes from earlier anti-emancipation arguments and contemporaneous debates about imperialism pathologized a modern urbane black populace.

But it is easy to argue for the resilience and strength of dominant regimes. Was the social fabric dynamic enough then to absorb any extant satire or counterhegemonic claim to the body, the past or the present? I say no; as the dance was grounded in the complex of mimesis, its meanings are not so easy to contain. It operated as a system of multiplicities, able to exploit a range of tonalities.

BLACK ANGELS ON THE ROOFTOP

As well as the city park and the coliseum, the very tops of the new cities' skyscrapers were social spaces where white and newly white citizenry celebrated American wealth. The rooftops of downtown Manhattan were landscaped with beautiful gardens, often around a restaurant or bar space and a stage area for performers and dancing. In the 1910s huge midnight dances would rage atop the buildings until early morning, with the turkey trot and other black animal dances the favored movements. Shows atop the roofs featured chorus girls and their drunken, wealthy admirers. Stanford White's Madison Square Garden had a rooftop garden that featured show girls. The architect of *fin-de-siècle* New York City was himself a quintessential masher and quite famously took up with the adolescent chorus girl Evelyn Nesbit. It was top tabloid news of the day when Nesbit's jealous husband stabbed White to death on the roof of his own Garden.

Like all of the key social spaces articulating the relaxation between classes and ethnic groups in the United States, the space of the rooftop theater was racially segregated. In fact, the cordons grew thicker around African Americans, allowed in these spaces only to serve and entertain. Will Marion Cook's *Clorindy, or the Origins of the Cakewalk,* booked at the Casino rooftop garden, marked the first time an African American show was admitted into the rooftop space. Despite the everyday exclusion of a black audience, following *Clorindy* almost all the signature rooftop dances and musical forms were black compositions or their imitators. *Clorindy* marked the beginning of a long season defined by white rooftop dancing to black musical and dance compositions, the season I explore in the next chapter.

Clorindy was written and conceived by the musician Will Marion Cook in partnership with Paul Laurence Dunbar, the era's noted black poet laureate. The play was the result of their shared concern, quite middle class in its naïvete and earnestness, to celebrate black folk ways, although the play, known for its classic coon songs, "All Coons Look Alike to Me" and "Who Dat Say Chicken in Dis Crowd," was a peculiar product of that agenda.

For the classically trained Cook and the college educated Dunbar, the play was the product of very difficult struggles over racial representation. Trained in European conservatories and for a short time with Antonin Dvorak in New York, Cook grew disgusted with the narrow application of his formal training, but also with the class pretensions of black middle-class cultural elitism, which he found absurd. After all, he would not be admitted to perform in the concert halls for which he had been trained. This is highly ironic, as European composers, inspired by black vernacular culture, wrote their own pieces for the cakewalk; Igor Stravinsky with "Ragtime for Eleven Instruments" and Claude Debussy with his famous "Golliwog's Cakewalk." The cakewalk became a signature designed to carry these multiple layers of irony. In *Clorindy* these layers, as well as a layer of racial masquerade and class critique, folded around the dance itself, in which the potential of satire remains its main articulation.

Black performers used the cakewalk as a lampoon of black middle-class social pretensions. It critiqued black bourgeois retention of the prim, well-behaved, Victorian models for civilized deportment and the black bourgeoisie's sensitivity to white approval. Dancers cadenced their versions of the cakewalk as a satirical comment on the self-conscious elitism of the black Brooklyn set and the Washington, D.C. elite. Members of the black professional classes were critical of variety stage performance. The black middle classes did not approve of the cakewalk dance's overt physicality and ostentation and publicly scorned participation in such decadent acts. Black performers pointedly reversed the criticism; aping the "leaders of the colored aristocracy" was a common and favorite ploy for their stage comedies.

Will Marion Cook illustrated the ironies of intra-racial class conflict and racial realness, describing his experience composing music for *Clorindy*.

> I was at [the] piano trying to learn to play my most Negroid song, "Who Dat Say Chicken in Dis Crowd?" My mother, who was cooking breakfast, came into the parlor, tears streaming from her eyes, and said: "Oh Will! Will! I've sent you all over the world to study and become a great musician, and you return such a Nigger!" My mother was a graduate of Oberlin in the class of 1865 and thought that a Negro composer should write just like a white man.[30]

Cook is not a fully reliable narrator here; perhaps he was still playing with masks, describing "Who Dat Say Chicken?" as his "most Negroid song" to a white newspaper. Cook's use of hyperbolic Negro typing (a predilection for thievery, an uncontrollable appetite) in his songs was at once a parody of white delight for black ignorance and a rebellious retort to the pretensions of his social class. For Dunbar, composing for *Clorindy* may have seemed an ideal chance to celebrate folk culture of rural black people, claimed as a national treasure. But he was adamant that this was the first and last collaboration he would attempt with the famously difficult Cook.

Nevertheless, *Clorindy* was the first show with an all-black cast to perform on a white rooftop, and it was a rave success. The focus was pure dance and song, and little of Dunbar's libretto was actually used.[31] Following this play, the cakewalk was situated firmly as the expected finale for all black musical revues. Cook remembers, with perhaps a sly dissemblance, the success of this play.

> When I entered the orchestra pit there were only about fifty people on the roof. When we finished the opening chorus, the house was packed to suffocation . . . the show downstairs in the Casino theatre was just letting out. The big audience heard those heavenly voices and took to the elevators

. . . My chorus sang like Russians, dancing meanwhile like Negroes, and cakewalking like angels, black angels! When the last note was sounded, the audience stood and cheered for at least ten minutes.[32]

Gone are the days of that "Massa Lincoln stuff!" Dunbar insists. As Cook remembers it, the singers' voices rang like those of emancipated Russian serfs.

What is important for us here is to think of the show *Clorindy* as an incursion into a space reserved for particular enactments of modern whiteness. What Cook evokes is how easily black art can take over; we are left with the image of a white audience, rising up in elevators toward the source of the music, in search of the heavenly sound. The usual spatial arrangement is inverted; whites had to rise up to meet the black angels who had alighted on their roof.

Fourteen-year-old Abbie Mitchell made her singing debut in *Clorindy*. Also from a middle-class family, Mitchell was classically trained. She had previously trained with Cook and would marry him the next year (at the age of fifteen). Mitchell sang in almost every major black stage show of this period. In addition to touring with Black Patti's Troubadours, she starred in Cook's *Jes' Like White Folks* (1899) and *The Southerners* (1904), and two of the three Africa plays of Williams and the Walkers, *In Dahomey* (1903) and *Bandana Land* (1908). She also appeared in Cole's and Johnson's *Red Moon* (1909). Mitchell toured Europe extensively; she toured from 1905 to 1908 with her Memphis Students in London. Hughes and Meltzer describe this troupe as singing musicians and "the first jazz band to ever play a theatre engagement."[33] Mitchell and her husband Cook were instrumental to the history of jazz, which takes on a different shape when not separated from the heterogeneous world of the stage. With Laura Bowman, Mattie Wilkes, and others, Abbie Mitchell would join Anita Bush's black dramatic company, the Lafayette Players, after 1914. She would have made inroads in classical opera, but this arena was carefully policed along the color line.

Mitchell performed the operettas for *Clorindy*, while Stella Wiley and Belle Davis also performed as "coon shouters." This is not to say that the ultimate value of such black popular forms as the coon song was to "break the color line" for access to the higher, finer arts. The coon song phenomenon is a fascinating example of complex dissemblance and humor. It has been usefully written about, and a full exploration would take us beyond the limits of this study.[34] But what falls out from the historical record is the importance of black women "coon shouters" from this era. Belle Davis gained notoriety by belting out coon songs for *Clorindy* and Stella Wiley was regarded as a "world renowned coon shouter," yet these women receive little if any consideration in leading analyses of coon songs.[35]

THE TABASCO SENEGAMBIANS MARCH ACROSS TOWN

Version upon version erases the possibility of an original and often reveals the originary as the most fictitious. Authentic "Ethiopian Delineation" after all, real minstrelsy, was the province of white men. So what could Williams and Walker, the self-described "Two Real Coons," the "Tabasco Senegambians" deliver? Here my argument emphasizes that the basis for understanding the changing of the joke and the slipping of the yoke is not the discovery of some solid, naked African retention hidden in plain sight. We needn't search for the really "real" to substantiate our desire for clear practices of resistance. In fact, to do so is to miss the truly crafty elusive nature, the deep strategies of laughter, embodied in "getting over." In fact, the axes of the praxes, tactics of inversion and misdirection, themselves spin off the very stern fight over the terms of the "real," the representational.

At the beginning of their careers, the black comedic duo George Walker and Bert Williams performed as native Dahomians for the San Francisco mid-winter's fair of 1893. The ship bringing over the "real" Africans was late, and the fair promoters advertised for black stage people to fill in, to live and work among the African "non-acting actors" there staffing the ethnic village. "Williams and Walker were among the sham native Dahomians," writes George Walker.[36] This performance moment is one of ultimate dissemblance, Williams and Walker, performing as non-acting actors, as natural Africans. Their "Dahomian delineation" at the fair, their stage act as the "Two Real Coons," and their comedies set in Africa are all supreme plays on the performance of blackness itself—or more accurately blacknesses, for the very point was the motility of racial fictions.

In January 1898, Bert Williams and George Walker staged a painfully hilarious gag that publicly acknowledged the physical segregation of African Americans in U.S. northern cities and the very public use to which African American dances were being put. In a highly publicized act, the

"Two Real Coons" marched across town to personally challenge William Henry Vanderbilt to a cakewalking competition. Williams and Walker marched from the Tenderloin and handed a formal letter of challenge to the butler at Vanderbilt's mansion on Fifty-Second Street and Fifth Avenue.[37] Vanderbilt had been entertaining his friends with a minstrel act and planning a huge cakewalk ball. Nothing came of the challenge, but the act was an excellent form of both self-promotion and sly critique. After all, black dance professionals were training these well-heeled robber barons how to execute the steps "in good old darkey style" and yet went uninvited to the balls.

Williams and Walker counted on their act to draw attention. They had hit it big the year before, performing at Koster and Bial's. In January 1897 their act included a cakewalk demonstration, for which they were joined by Stella Wiley and Aida Overton, both with Black Patti's Troubadours. Wiley and Overton had worked with Williams and Walker the previous year, demonstrating the cakewalk in an advertisement for the American Tobacco Company. According to William Foster, Stella Wiley was George's girlfriend at the time; this is quite probable, as Wiley and Cole had split that year, and sixteen-year-old Aida Overton would not marry Walker until 1898. Trained maestros in the art of racial delineation, Williams and Walker would appear at Keith's, booked as the "Tabasco Senegambians" in April 1897.

Their fame had been spread by their appearance in the newspaper, another public space. On August 22, 1897, Williams, Walker, Wiley, and another woman (Aida Overton was in England with *Oriental America*, so this woman was probably from either Isham's U.S. company or Black Patti's Troubadours) did a photo shoot for the *New York Journal*, demonstrating the cakewalk (see figs. 19–21). "A Lesson for Society Cakewalkers" reads the title: "Williams and Walker show How the Real Thing Is Done Before the Journal Camera." These actors will, the article contends, show "The Cakewalk as It Is Done by Genuine Negroes":

> Society at the seashore and at the mountain resorts have found a brand new pastime in cakewalking. . . . It is at Lake George this season that society first saw the cakewalk was a good thing. It was tried at one of the hotels there and made a big hit. Since then it had had a prominent place in the list of entertainments at the more important resorts . . . these pictures here presented show how the thing is done in good old darkey style.[38]

See also pages 26·27

The Cake Walk as It Is Done by Genuine Negroes

Society at the seashore and at the mountain resorts have found a brand new pastime in cake walking—an entertainment that has afforded the negro much pleasure for many years back, and which is still one of his chief sources of amusement. It was at Lake George this season that society first saw that the cake walk was a good thing. It was tried at one of the hotels there, and made a big hit. Since then it has had a prominent place in the list of amusements at the more important resorts. For the benefit of beginners, Williams and Walker, the delineators of negro characters, and the composers of "Oh, I Don't Know; You Aint So Warm," posed before the Journal camera to show what a genuine Southern cake walk is like. The pictures here presented show how the thing is done in good old darkey style.

20 Left to right: George Walker,
    Bert Williams, unknown dancer,
    Stella Wiley. Stella Wiley scrapbook.
    Scrapbook of the Negro in
    Theatre, Yale Collection of American
    Literature, Beinecke Rare Book and
    Manuscript Library, Yale University.

19 Stella Wiley with George Walker. Stella Wiley scrapbook.
    Scrapbook of the Negro in Theatre, Yale Collection of
    American Literature, Beinecke Rare Book and Manuscript
    Library, Yale University.

21 "The Cakewalk as It Is Done by
    Genuine Negroes." Left to right:
    unknown dancer, Stella Wiley, George
    Walker, Bert Williams. Stella Wiley
    scrapbook. Scrapbook of the Negro in
    Theatre, Yale Collection of American
    Literature, Beinecke Rare Book and
    Manuscript Library, Yale University.

The marked visibility of black performers in the New York press and the ghostly presence of their training at elite resorts mark more sites at which ideal modern bodies were being demonstrated through racialized gestural techniques while black bodies were relegated to the service quarters.

Much has already been written about the fame of Williams and Walker and of the Vanderbilt challenge as an ingenious form of self-promotion. What is interesting to me here is that the strategy for this attention getting was the geographical staging of black urban mobility. Williams's and Walker's march across town, from the Tenderloin to Fifth Avenue, was as much a part of the challenge as was the letter. Its comedic power is based in the politics of physical proximity between the races in the city. The fact that the "ambassadors," as the papers called them, could physically approach the front door of the "aristocrats" was supposed proof of the leveling quality of capitalist democracy, the relaxation between the castes. This shift of modernity was supposedly to a more inclusive concept of the civic body. Yet their march across town rings with irony. It reveals the kinds of policing that it took to keep the city segregated. They could approach the Vanderbilt mansion (rebuilt by Stanford White in 1905) with ease. But actual access to the caliber of class mobility enjoyed by the Vanderbilt and Astor families, or even to the suggested possibility of such mobility (granted to most Americans), was most definitely denied them. The ultimate humor of their march across town lay in their claim to supposedly democratizing city space and their symbolic claim to the carriage of wealth. It acknowledged the ways they were shaping the bodies of the very populace who insisted that physical distance between raced bodies was a natural imperative to civic order.

WITHIN THE WHIRL OF THE KINETOSCOPE: DORA DEAN IN BUDAPEST

Black culture had representational territories that existed outside of actual geographies. Its reputations and iconographic currency crossed continents. Individual cakewalking couples broke away from the larger shows and toured circuits in Europe, England, and the United States. Dora Dean teamed up with Charles Johnson, the "London Swell" of *The Creole Show*. They formed a cakewalking dance and song act, touring the winter gardens in Budapest, Berlin, and Vienna in the early 1900s.[39] Dora Dean and

22 The cakewalking couple
Dora Dean and Charles
Johnson. Institute for
Jazz Studies.

Aida Overton Walker, both of whom teamed up with George Walker in
1896 as his cakewalking partner, had iconographic power. As members
of dance duos, both women demonstrated the cakewalk for crown and
crowd in England. As a dance for couples, the cakewalk craze was not
possible without black women. This included women who worked solely
in dancing teams, such as Billy Farrell, but also the women who had been
working the circuits for some time, including Dora Dean, Stella Wiley,
and Belle Davis, following the Jack and Isham productions. "It took a long
time for colored folks to break into the theatres, but there is no more
popular feature now than the Negro song and dance team," reads a review
of 1903.[40]

In London, Dean was known as the "Black Venus," a title Josephine
Baker would later inherit (see fig. 22). As with other performers at the
time, promotional photos of black artists were placed inside boxes of tobacco. A British cigarette company printed Dean's picture as "The Sweet
Caporal Girl" and fitted it into every box, much as the American Tobacco
Company had done with photographs of Williams and Walker, and Wiley
and Overton. Returning from Europe in 1908, Dean and Johnson signed
with the William Morris Agency. Separating at the beginning of World
War I, Dean organized her own touring act of picaninny performers. In

June 1914, Dean appeared as "Dora Dean and Her Fancy Phanthoms [*sic*]" on the Loew circuit.[41]

Dora Dean was an embodiment of *fin-de-siècle* excess and decadence. "Dora Dean of the dance team Johnson and Dean is in New York for a brief stay," reads the *New York Age* in 1908. "She came to America from Europe a few days ago. Her husband remained on the other side. To judge from her appearance she is enjoying prosperity across the water. She is wearing enough diamonds to warrant people calling her "diamond queen."[42] A review written one month after their return to the States accompanies a photo of Dean posing before a mirror. "Dora Dean of the comedy team of Johnson and Dean, it can be plainly seen, is not very lean and as they have been living off the fat of the land while they were making a hit abroad it would be a big surprise to the patrons of the William and Morris, Inc., vaudeville houses if she was lean."[43] Dean was known for the luxury of her various costumes. "[Dora Dean's act] is colored and the classiest of its kind. Miss Dean for her entrance gown chose a pink satin dress with a crystalled tunic of old blue. A large black hat with aigrettes was worn." Dean brought the Orientalist craze of the previous five years to her act, but not the trim-lined, sleek style of the emerging chorines. "A second change was a harem costume. The bloomers were pale blue and the dress purple chiffon. The last gown was artistic in coloring as well as model. A foundation of salmon pink satin was covered in white net, edged in white fox," reports *Variety* in February 1915.[44] Dora Dean carried the earlier style of burlesque well into the 1910s, but Johnson's and Dean's version of the cakewalk was a precursor of the kinds of ballroom dancing styles that emerged in the 1920s.

In later years, they introduced a version of the dance using a system of lights that gave their bodies a kinetoscopic effect. "They call their dance a kinetoscope rag time dance, which is performed against a black background amid intermittent flashes of light," a reviewer writes of their appearance in London in 1906. "The corybantic movements of the clever couple are thus illustrated in a way that give them something of the effect of the Cinematographic picture. One is charmed by the ingenious way in which Johnson and Dean treat the coon business"[45] The whirling lights made the dancers "look like a crowd of hands and feet and nothing else."[46] Dean and Johnson articulated, within the whirl of the kinetoscope, the sense of physicality in the city space, fragmented, illuminated, and mobile.

Their act resonates with the innovations in stage technology advanced by the dancer Loie Fuller. The combination of the natural, free, "colored" and/or female body with the technologically clever reflects the ethos of the era, for "technological wizardry and colonial expansion" were in tandem. "Advances in technology had, of course, tremendous importance in the so called new imperialism of the second half of the nineteenth century."[47] We can extend this time frame and look for the twinning of "the modern and the primitive" as the signature for the Western currency of other dances shaped around a politics of racial geography, such as the black bottom and the Charleston. The migrations of the cakewalk presage the later years of urban social dances and the ways in which black and white people understood themselves in the new urban spaces. As we shall see in the next chapter, the complex combinations of excess and stamina were later more thoroughly policed along the color line, with "acceptable" forms of dancing demarcated through the codification techniques of white society dancers such as Vernon and Irene Castle.

EVERYBODY'S DOING IT:
SOCIAL DANCE, SEGREGATION, AND THE NEW BODY

THE *DARKTOWN FOLLIES*

In the fall of 1913 a black musical comedy called *Darktown Follies* opened at the Lafayette Theatre on 110th Street and Seventh Avenue in Manhattan. The skilled dancers were the most notable part of the show, and some of the best black steppers of the day, including the dance duo Ethel Williams and Johnny Peters, were in the *Darktown* cast. They performed African American dance movements, such as the turkey trot, the Texas Tommy, and ballin the Jack, which had been shaping northern urban nightlife over the previous three or so years. Night after night a large and fashionable African American audience attended the show. "The houses are packed from pit to dome at each and every performance, with a line stretching off down the street from the lobby and box office," one *Variety* reviewer remarked. "Outside the theatre the avenue is Broadway in light and crowds and even in the automobiles awaiting their owners at the theatre front. . . . A more appreciative audience it would be hard to find anywhere. Every joke and every gag is greeted with a roar of delight and it is a treat to watch the audience enjoy itself alone."[1] The reviewer noted a few white people in the audience but it was mostly black New Yorkers who came to the theater. They came to see and be seen, to recognize themselves as participants in this exuberant moment in their history, the making of Harlem into a black cultural capital.[2]

Darktown Follies had a female chorus line and Ethel Williams, the youngest member of the cast, was stationed at its very end.

Like Ida Forsyne, Florence Mills, and later Josephine Baker, Ethel Williams began her dancing career as a child. Born in New York in 1897, she started dancing in the streets, at the age of five joining Buddy Gilmore's picaninny troupe for a tour of Cuba.[3] In her early teens, while working as a dancer in the clubs of San Francisco's Barbary Coast, Williams teamed up with the dancer Johnny Peters. The couple won a number of contests in 1912 with a "demonstration dance" routine of several numbers they had developed while on the West Coast and then had brought to New York City's variety stages. Joining the cast of *Darktown Follies* was Williams's "first big break," as she recalls.[4] Williams became a great friend of Ethel Waters, who remembers her fondly in her autobiography.[5]

This chapter takes the staging of the *Darktown Follies* at the Lafayette Theatre in Harlem in 1913 as a critical point of departure from which to explore the race and gender politics of urban popular dance. Black women dancers—working in New York, St. Petersburg, Paris—navigated a complex geopolitics of racialization, female sexuality, and bodily pleasure. This chapter claims their artistic efforts as affirmations of modern black subjecthood.

Ethel Williams went on to train numerous white women dancers, including the chorus girls for *Ziegfeld's Follies* and the British social dancer Irene Castle, but these sessions were behind closed doors. In this chapter I continue a discussion of female minstrelsy, here the kinds of racial mimicry that did not require cork. This type of Ethiopian delineation was about bodily inflection, what I call racialized gestural techniques. For white women the meanings of modern female physicality were articulated most adroitly through their performance of "dusky" female bodies. Irene Castle furnished her demonstration dances, now considered iconographically representative of modern womanhood, by "borrowing" black women's techniques. A similar process was in action when it came to borrowing the dances of female colonial subjects, the brown women from the parts of the globe marked by European flags, particularly British and French holdings. The mothers of modern dance shaped their sexual mysticism from Orientalist fantasies, spun from the hootchy-cootchy dancers on the midway fairgrounds. Ruth St. Denis and Isadora Duncan, moving the form to the parlor and concert hall, became the noted choreographers of their age. As the dance scholar Anthea Kraut explains, choreography has a long history as a "term of privilege, functioning both to authorize and to exclude."[6] The black and brown women whose movements they imitated were "disappeared," turned to raw material and not granted the same recognition as movement interpreters.

I end with a look at the Salome craze, staged in England and the United States between 1908 and 1913. The relationship between imperialism, modern female body culture, and the politics of race has been discussed in relation to the many versions of the *Dance of Salome*. Here I consider Ada Overton Walker's rendering of the dance as a way to understand black women's subject positionality as more than one of double consciousness; as one situated behind several veils. Her versions "glanced in all directions," signified in multiple and diverging ways. As with her ballet *Ethiopia*, which she choreographed for the play *Bandana Land*, Overton's compositions, her staged blackness, worked to reattach northern Africa to the continent as an ancestral site for African Americans. But this connection was meant to be at a remove, situating her firmly as a modern woman, for at the same time her versions identified her with the modern white women choreographers. Her claim was to be considered as a serious artist, rather than as a slightly disreputable dancing girl. Her art was the result of training experience and talent, not instinct or nature. Her *Salome* was part of her larger argument for stage performance as a respectable profession for artistically inclined "intelligent and talented" black women.[7] At the same time, she used the language of uplift, reframing stage work as a positive contribution to the race. While she employed the language of bourgeois race women, with this sensual dance Overton was also explicitly offering an intervention into the staid sexual politics of the black middle class.

African American dance practices that followed the cakewalk—from the turkey trot, the bunny hug, and the shimmy of the 1910s, through the Charleston and the black bottom of the 1920s, to the Lindy hop of the 1930s—were the expressive forms by which people sought to adjust their physical sense of being to a new and often oppressive terrain. Rapid industrialization, shifting class relations, and the hardening of de facto segregation in the northern cities of the United States were all social and environmental changes acutely experienced and made reality through the body. For white people, versions of black dance practices served a particular function as they reshaped their sense of individual self to the changing larger social and geopolitical bodies. In his dance criticism, Havelock

Ellis's ecstatic celebration weds the city skyline to the utopic primitive/ primeval impulses of bodily expression. "Dancing and building are the two primary and essential arts," wrote Havelock Ellis. "Dancing came first. In earlier than human times, dancing and architecture may have been the result of the same impulse."[8] We can see the wedding of black dance formations and the city skyline in the midnight rooftop dances popular in the 1910s. These urban bacchanals took on a ritualistic power, becoming emblematic for this age of New Moderns. Their transgression of old mores, that which made them new, was dramatized through dancing what they saw black dancers doing. Black vernacular expressive forms were miscoded according to resurgent fictions of an ahistorical primitive body and were to be used as ritual correctives for the adverse effects of the modern environment. The active miscoding of black dance forms was invested in keeping the actual expressive black body as a model, and creative black bodies in motion threatened this investment. Black dance forms, in the process of "cultural migration" or "transfer," were stripped of their deeper meanings and their complex spatial and time registers.[9]

For African Americans, popular dance—on the musical stage, in the dance halls, and on the street—was a collective dialogue of cultural and social self-formation under conditions of migration. The protean resilience of black dance compositions recognized the fragmentation and disorientation of the social and individual body as the shock of the modern condition. Dancing together in the spaces of the city was a way of recognizing this condition and also of creating new rhythms of selfhood and communality within and between several timed and spatial zones. The artistry of black dancers was a form of *flânerie*, affirming a sense of multiple-sited, modern black subjectivity.

WE BRING OUR DANCES WITH US

By about 1910 African Americans living in New York City had begun moving uptown from the San Juan Hill district and settling in the area north of Central Park. They were joined by an increasing number of people migrating from rural areas of the South, people leaving behind the exploitative conditions of peonage under the sharecropping system and lands made fallow by years of overplanting. People came from across the country; they came from the Deep South following the devastation of cotton crops by the boll weevil and the flooding of the Mississippi River in 1912 and 1913.[10] When *Darktown Follies* opened, the Lafayette Theatre was a prime location for the black revue. The owners of the Lafayette leased the theater to the show's director, J. Leubrie Hill, and the usual house rule barring African Americans from the audience was lifted.

J. Leubrie Hill, a lyricist and a former cast member of the Williams and Walker Company, had put together the revue in Washington, D.C. around 1911 and brought it north. The *Darktown Follies* book, *My Friend from Kentucky*, revolved around a character named Jim Jackson, who sells his father-in-law's plantation and flees to Washington, D.C. in search of the society of the capital's black elite and to escape his haranguing wife, Mandy Lee. With comedic aplomb, a cross-dressing Hill played the roles of both husband and wife. The farcical antics of Jim Jackson and his finger-wagging six-foot wife among the colored elite of Washington was a satire on the sharp class divisions among African Americans living in the nation's political capital. In the *Follies*, such satire was the variety artists' response to the harsh criticism and public dismissal of popular forms of black music and dance levied by such groups as the Treble Clef Club, organized by black women of the elite four hundred in D.C. to honor the work of the composer Coleridge Taylor. Such satire spoke to the climate of heated intra-racial debate over just how African Americans should cultivate their aesthetic tenets, what represented the authentic black experience, and just what forms of cultural expression should be promoted as representative of the race.

Over the next three years these debates would continue. In 1914, the black musician and *New York Age* critic Lester Walton leased the Lafayette Theatre. In 1915 it became the home for a troupe of actors organized and run by the actress Anita Bush, who had performed with the Williams and Walker Company in both *In Dahomey* and *Abyssinia*. Bush's stock company had been working at the Lincoln, another theater in Harlem, but Bush, in protest of the unfair treatment by the white management, moved her stock company to the Lafayette and renamed it the Lafayette Players. The theater soon became the home of serious, "legitimate" black drama. Joining the cast in 1914 was Laura Bowman, home from Russia, who would work in the cast for many years, her roles including that of Herodias in the troupe's 1923 production of *Salome*.

With its emphasis on dance and its theme of migration, the *Darktown*

Follies show marked a critical moment in an African American culture of restlessness, as black people moved both within and between regions across the nation. Underlying the comic absurdity and deceivingly light tone of the story was the quite serious metaphorical, and historical, question of what to do with the "inheritance" of the plantation. In the form of farcical nonsense, the show reflected the anxiety of self-assessment, as African American people moved in increasing numbers within and out of the South. These collective dialogues of assessment asked what people needed to get away from and discard and what they needed to bring with them as they continued to disperse across the nation. Most notably, the show's central organizing principle was the trope of urban migration, which would grow increasingly important within black stagecraft and expressive culture.

The circle dance was the most memorable moment of the show for the performers, the audience, and reviewers. "It was the staging which made it so striking," James Weldon Johnson wrote. "The whole company formed an endless chain that passed before the footlights and behind the scenes, round and round, singing and executing a movement from a dance called 'ballin the jack,' one of those Negro dances that periodically come along and sweep the country."[11] The cast "[circled] continuously, snapping fingers with a tango jiggle . . . a moochee slide," and a "Texas Tommy wiggle."[12] Singing "At the Ball, That's All," written by Hill and arranged by Will Vodery, the dancers were folding steps and phrases associated with other geographical regions and historical experiences into the circle dance. The effect resonated powerfully throughout the theater, as the dancers wound their way through the gallery, physically hailing the members of the audience. The circle dance was a choreography of collective recognition between audience members and performers, a ritual claiming of geographical place and communality within the segregated territories of the city. It is useful to think of this dance moment not just in terms of what it may retain from a "then" of Africa, but for its expression of, and entitlement to, the here and now. This moment was the exuberant claiming and creation of Harlem as black city-space.

As the dances of the *Darktown Follies* show, dance forms were encoded moments of historical memory, re-membrances of historical shifts and their effect on African Americans' lived experiences. Certain steps from past dances were brought into new surroundings and there took on new meanings, at the same time as they referenced former moments. The search to describe and situate particular forms generates multiple tales of origin. The stories of origin are accompanying fictions, necessary for what they reveal about what the dances meant as narratives of African American cultural and social formation. The circle dance can be recognized as containing within it memories of the ring dance and for having the same linked bodies and low shuffling feet as the ring shout, a devotional dance developed primarily in rural Georgia and South Carolina.[13] But this does not mean that it is the same dance. The dance was very much about geopolitical territory, a politics of claiming community. This dance was about the streets and city spaces, and about the continual movement between "homes."

Darktown Follies moved to the roof garden of Oscar Hammerstein's Theatre later that year to perform for a white audience. The way the circle dance reverberated at the Lafayette did not translate downtown. "People didn't take kindly to the colored troupe, as the house was almost emptied when the act had finished," noted a *Variety* reviewer. "Up on the roof *Follies* members appeared to be unable to get their bearings and could not speed it up when speed was about the only thing that would help."[14] This moment suggests something about the politics of physical proximity. Rules were broken with their presence on the roof. The power of the circle dance could not be reproduced in a territory in which the rules of zoning required that actual expressive black bodies be kept at a distance, repressed safely into a fictional past. They were too close both in place and in time, claiming a physio-geographical presence in the present modern moment. White recognition of black expressive exuberance was contingent on the codification of the black expressive body as a signature for the past, for a fictional moment of pre-industrial innocence. For African Americans to lay claim to the complexities of the present, both temporally and spatially, was to overstep the terms of the contract. Claiming such rights to the territory of the city clashed with the arcane and intricate choreographies of American racial segregation.

It was Williams's behavior at the end of the line during the circle dance that distinguished her. For the circle dance segment, Williams remembers, "everybody did a sort of sliding walk all around the stage in rhythm [with] their hands on the hips of the person in front. There'd be a line [in the song] that said 'do the Tango wiggle' . . . everybody would . . . put their foot

EVERYBODY'S DOING IT

out a certain way." Everyone that is, except for Williams, who refused to toe the line. "I would be doing anything but that. I'd do the 'Ball the Jack' on the end of the line every kind of way you could think about it. When the curtain came down even my fingers were doing ball the jack outside [the curtain]."[15] Ethel Williams's disruptive behavior, ballin the jack at the end of the dancing line "every kind of way you could think about it," marks a new cycle of movement in the historical trajectory of trans-urban black expressive forms. With the dance's reference to the train, and the profane pleasures generated along the routes of black labor, Williams spoke with the audience of black restlessness and the contingency of communal moments. Her bad behavior was a continuation of the kinds of complexly uncooperative movements of earlier eccentric dances developed by dancers such as Louis Douglas and Ida Forsyne and was a pivotal influence on the choreographies of the urban chorus line.

Williams describes her stage choreography, her resistance to the uniformity of the chorus line, as the inevitable consequence of her individual artistic finesse. "I never could work in a chorus because I kicked too high," Williams remembers. "I would kick my head with my foot—and I couldn't seem to stay in line."[16] Her restless irreverence moved the audiences, and other dancers and performers remember her antics vividly. "When they finished throwing each other around in the Texas Tommy the whole cast went into the Circle Dance—except Ethel," remembered Nobel Sissle, "who was so winded or something that she just faked crazy steps that brought down the house. Josephine Baker did the same thing in *Shuffle Along* eight years later."[17] Ida Forsyne went to see the *Darktown Follies* when she returned from Russia at the outbreak of the war and recognized Ethel Williams at the end of the line. "I got back in 1914 and saw *Darktown Follies* at the Lafayette. I don't remember too much about the show except how good Ethel Williams was kicking at the end of the chorus line. They always put the best ones at the end."[18] Forsyne herself could never reckon with the chorus line formation's demand of uniformity. The choreographies of female resistance, both playful and strenuous, developed by these black women were soon absorbed into the form itself, and Williams's improvisatory disobedience would become a convention of chorus line routines in both white and black shows over the next two decades.

After seeing the *Darktown Follies*, the white stage director Florenz

Ziegfeld contracted Williams to train the *Ziegfeld Follies* dancers. He had purchased rights to the song "At the Ball, That's All" and the circle dance sequence, but he needed someone to show his girls just how to handle the rhythmically complex, yet seemingly so simple, steps. "I went down to the New York Theatre and showed the cast how to dance it. They were having trouble," Williams quips. Ziegfeld did not credit Ethel Williams for the necessary training she had provided his white chorus girls (nor *Darktown Follies* director J. Leubrie Hill for his lyrics and staging). What angered Williams the most was that Ziegfeld would not hire her, or any of the talented dancers from *Darktown Follies*, to appear in his revue. "None of us were hired for the show . . . and at that time I was supposed to be the best woman dancer in the whole country."[19] The performance of segregation, as the custom of the country, separated the talent from the talented, though periodically opening a theater side-door for deliveries. This was the case with other white dancing acts then forming in the dance-crazed city. Besides the Ziegfeld girls, Williams also trained the dance duo of Irene and Vernon Castle. Black female dancers were barred from the U.S. white stage, although their creative innovations formed the backbone of what would make black vernacular dances emblematic of urban popular entertainment.

THE INSTITUTION OF THE CHORUS GIRL

Beginning in the mid-nineteenth century, troupes of women dancers, such as the Palace Girls of London's Palace Theatre, accompanied individual specialty acts on the variety and music hall stages. But beginning in the twentieth century, their acts took on new forms and their staged presence took on a new currency. The institutionalization of the chorus girl formation was a particular condensation point for a new set of meanings associated with industrial capitalism and its disciplinary claims on the body. The principles of uniformity, precision of routine, and efficiency of movement governing this period of industrial development were reflected in the codification of rigid dance training systems and increasingly regimented dance routines. As the century progressed, the ubiquitous presence of geometrically ordered young female bodies—on stage, in night clubs and cabarets, and on screen—would seem to bear out that the bodily disciplines exacted in the industrial school, on the factory floor, and in the military training camp had found their aesthetic correlation.

The institution hit a peak around 1915, with the eighth of the *Zieg-feld Follies* revues its most successful, but it was after World War I that the chorus line system developed as a quintessential formation and the numbers of women on stage increased. Hundreds of women danced in perfect unison, forming a corridor of mirrors, the poetic reflection of the avenues of the city, the factory assembly lines, and the military maneuvers of marching soldiers.[20]

In the late 1890s, the Englishman John Tiller devised what would become his signature system for the formal training of chorus girl troupes. The Tiller schools were designed as a welcome alternative to factory work and the dangers of poverty for young working-class girls, and they operated well into the next century. From the northern industrial city of Lancaster, John Tiller had earned a fortune in the exporting and trading of cotton. While he was still a wealthy industrialist, Tiller produced shows and appeared on the amateur stage in blackface. It is both revolting and fitting that the man grown rich from cotton would appear at some point "blacked-up in the burnt-cork as a nigger minstrel."[21] Losing his fortune after an economic crash, the former cotton magnate turned to his long-time hobby of amateur dramatics. After his bankruptcy Tiller organized his first all-girl show, which opened in 1890 at the King's Theatre in Manchester. Tiller drilled a group of girls to dance in perfect unison. "We rehearsed from nine in the morning till twelve at night, and had to walk home in our stockinged feet because they were too sore for shoes," one of the dancers recalls.[22]

Tiller and his wife, Jennie, soon established a residential school in Manchester. As well as auditioning young women at the school, Jennie Tiller scouted the poor neighborhoods in nearby northern industrial towns for recruits, taking prepubescent girls away from their families to reside at the school. "The training begins when the child is nine years old . . . of course all the pupils are not that young, but I prefer to start them at that age," Tiller said in an interview in 1912. The Tiller school system sold itself as rescuing young girls from poverty and its corrupting effects. "In most cases I try to separate the children from their old home life," Tiller continued, "for in most cases their homes may not be of the best."[23] Tiller described their program as a refuge from the beckoning workhouse barracks and other houses of disrepute, and as something of a finishing school for working-class girls. "The first training is in the hands of Mrs. Tiller and her assistants, and includes considerably more than dancing. The children are taught the usual school studies by certified governesses." Stressing the instillation of manners and modesty in its young trusts, the school would provide a protective environment and a program designed for the cultivation of the feminine arts to guide the girls through the tender years of their adolescence. "They are impressed with the importance of personal cleanliness, of regular hours, and of good morals," Tiller emphasized. "Their hands and feet receive particular attention, because of course a dancer must have strong feet."[24] Their meticulously rendered dance routines reflected the disciplinary training young girls should receive to become productive workers, as well as to avoid the temptations of the streets—the evils of sex, drink, and idleness—which they were seen as particularly vulnerable to.

Separated from their families, the young girls were then put through a short but intense training period before the finalists were chosen. "The first period of training lasts about a month, and then a weeding process takes place," Tiller explains (45). The Tillers would then hire out the chosen troupes of girls to various theaters and revues across Britain. Tiller assured the press that the girls were accompanied by a governess to tutor them between performances (45). Tiller soon opened a school in London. When the African American dancer Ida Forsyne appeared at London's Palace Theatre as Topsy in 1905, the house troupe of female dancers (known as the Palace Girls) had all come from Tiller's school. Before long the Tiller girls were touring America and Europe. Tiller Girls appeared in shows across the United States and Europe well into the 1930s, and Tiller's grueling and meticulous system of training inspired the next decades of dancing school instructors and stage production managers.

In the United States, the women working in the shows produced by Florenz Ziegfeld after 1907 soon became an analogue for the chorus girls of the 1910s and 1920s. The French dancer and music hall artist Anna Held, Ziegfeld's wife, led the chorus of women dancers in his early shows. The first show, on the roof of the New York Theatre in 1907, was like other variety revues of the era; the chorus was a bosomy congregation still reflecting a burlesque-era sensibility. But Ziegfeld, the stage director Julian Mitchell, and Anna Held sensed the change in modern concepts of sexuality and designed a new ideal: the slim, athletic, and definitively Anglo-Saxon beauty.

In the United States, stage directors such as Ned Wayburn, Bobby

Connolly, and Busby Berkeley opened up their own institutions for the training of young white women for the stage. For these directors, "The girl business was strictly a commercial affair, and the girls were the product" (53). The dance director Busby Berkeley assessed "the horde of gorgeous creatures who apply to him for jobs, the way a nut-and-bolt manufacturer regards his products" (55). Ned Wayburn directed for Ziegfeld through the war years, from 1916 to 1919, and established his own dancing institutes in Chicago and New York, training such dancers as Fred and Adele Astaire, Gilda Gray, and Eddie Cantor. Wayburn incorporated the African American art of tap dancing into his dance routines and offered codified versions of black tap styles in his book *The Art of Stage Dancing*. But he took credit for these dance techniques and would not work with African American dancers.

Wayburn's school promised "Health, Fame, Popularity, Independence"; his training system for chorus girls was designed to mold their flesh into the ideal physical manifestation of the new modern ethos—self-cultivated, entitled, and white (48). Beauty was mass-produced for the consumer. "In our school we make it a business to produce beauty," Wayburn declared. "Neither sentiment [n]or art enters the question. Audiences will not come to the box office with their money to see ugly, misshapen girls on the stage. Therefore it is up to me to make them right" (53). Wayburn's system ranked and classified the women dancers according to their physical attributes and their function in the routine. The "showgirls" were tall and thin, while shorter women were called "ponies" and did most of the solid dancing. In between these were dancers categorized as "chickens and peaches" (53).

Brought to market, women were the product described in terms from both merchant and industrial capitalism. The dance instructor David Bennett assessed the women applicants as a horse trainer would his livestock. "To get into my chorus . . . a girl must be close to five feet four inches in height and weight from 105 to 115 pounds," he stated in an interview. "I look first at their teeth. Good teeth are the initial beauty essential of the chorus girl. . . . I have always chosen girls with the idea, first, of getting healthy ones. Posture has much to do with my selection. If the girl doesn't sit well, I know she has let herself become slouchy. She probably has been too lazy to brace herself properly at the waist, where the vital organs are" (54).

For the cultural critic Siegfried Kracauer chorus girls were a symptom of the global presence of American capitalist and cultural hegemony. "The hands in the factory correspond to the legs of the Tiller Girls," he wrote in his article "The Mass Ornament," published in the *feuilleton* section of the *Frankfurter Zeitung* in 1927. Female chorus lines were the "product of American distraction factories." Their bodies formed "indissoluble girl clusters . . . ornaments composed of thousands of . . . sexless bodies in bathing suits."[25] De-erotized, fragmented into disparate body parts, female bodies became the ultimate representation of the "core defect" of capitalism.[26] In "Travel and Dance," another of Kracauer's *feuilleton* articles, both of these activities were the symptomatic pathologies of the mechanized modern world. Dance steps "cut to measure" by dance teachers were "hardly more than rhythmic offerings, temporal experiences whose ultimate joy is syncopation."[27] Not even the use of "Negro rhythms" could allay the degenerating effects of modern rationality. For Kracauer, "the secret aim of jazz tunes, no matter how negroid their origins may be . . . strive[s] to extinguish the melody and spin out ever further the vamps that signal the decline of meaning."[28] Capitalism's corruption of the human spirit was represented by clusters of female bodies vamping to derivative Negro rhythms across the popular stage.

Historically, female bodies bear great symbolic utility, for they yield completely to outside meaning. As cities grew, the pleasures and dangers of the urban industrial age were dramatized through depictions of various female forms. "Berlin . . . served as the decisive metaphor for modernity," writes the feminist critic Patrice Petro. "Modernity, in turn, was almost always represented as a woman."[29] Critics used the metaphor of the woman as city to describe the hypnotic, seductive, and sometimes cruel power of the city, its phantasmagoric distractions and diversions, its promise to fulfill every sensual desire. The female dancers of the chorus line represented the regimentation of experience but also embodied shifting understandings of pleasure, relocated to the body, the result of intense sensory stimulation. The chorus girl phenomena expressed the way people were training themselves to experience excitement and the city as "a place of freedom rather than entrapment."[30]

Young, single women were living and working in the city in increasing numbers, and the women in the chorus lines were public symbols of modern working women. Lewis Erenburg, in his study of New York's

23 Chorus girls from the
    show *Blackbirds* at the
    Coliseum Theatre,
    London, October 5,
    1934. Photo by Sasha/
    Getty Images, Hulton
    Archive, Getty Images.

dance and club culture between 1890 and 1930, said African American women were not part of this critical constituency. For him they were not the "modern shop girls, clerks, and secretaries" who found their model forms mirrored in the "health, fame, popularity and independence" of the *Follies* chorus lines. African American women were barred by the custom of the country from most white-collar jobs, just as they were barred from the white stage. Despite this they were a critical presence in the city and outnumbered black men. Working as domestics and as stage performers, and training white choruses, their presence was central to the meanings of urban culture, despite their erasure from the critical record.

Dance techniques developed by African American women vitalized the white dance instructor's choreography. The men added tap steps, modified shimmies, and a dampened version of the "little girl at the end of the line" to their codified regimens. These adoptions signified what was new about the female modern body: they were a license for the white (or becoming white) woman to transgress, in moderation, the sexual mores of her mother's generation. Adding named sequences such as the Charleston and the black bottom was an enacted restoration of spontaneous physicality "lost" in the regimented time sequences of modern life. But such "semibarbaric dances of America" had to be contained and controlled.[31] The dance director Seymour Felix insisted that a "girl . . . kick no higher than the length of her legs," and that she "only dance a Charleston or a Black Bottom when she is supposed to dance a Charleston or a Black Bottom."[32] Felix does not address black dancers directly, and gives only an oblique nod to the techniques of disobedient spontaneity developed by Ethel Williams and scores of other black women dancers to whom his codes of female deportment did not apply. As illustrated by Ethel Williams's experience, African American women themselves were not included in the closed geometrics of his masterful stagings.

THE GEOPOLITICS OF BLACK DANCE

When the *Darktown Follies* opened in 1913, the craze for social dance in the city was at its peak. That winter, the midnight roof gardens of Times Square were alive with "rag dancing contests."[33] White city dwellers danced until the morning hours atop the skyscrapers of central Manhattan. Dance professionals were in demand, and a culture of popular dance instruction and demonstration sprang up. "Dancers are Fashionable: Go From Fad to Craze" states a December article from *Variety*. "Society Taking Up Professional Steppers Send Salaries Soaring."[34] Although African American dance movements were the mainstays at these events, the dance instructors for whom the salaries were soaring were white, and the roof garden venues were closed to African American audience participants. However, society dances and roof garden events were lucrative places to work for the African American musicians who could get gigs there. In 1913 Irene and Vernon Castle contracted James Reese Europe and his Society Orchestra to provide music at the private dance functions they hosted for the northeastern elite. Following the black orchestra's engagement by the Castles, high society would hire only black musicians. But black dancers, with a few exceptions, had to work behind the scenes, informally and unrecognized, training the white dance instructors in how to master the feeling and tempo of the modern rhythms.

White dance professionals scouted out black dances to be interpreted into their own acts. Animal dances were the rage in 1910 and 1911, despite social approbation as to their immoral influence. The chorus girls of the *Ziegfeld Follies*, for example, performed the grizzly bear in the Follies in 1911.[35] At James Reese Europe's seventh semi-annual Clef Club Orchestra concert, held at the black theater the Manhattan Casino in May 1913, Ethel Williams and Johnny Peters demonstrated the Texas Tommy for a black audience. Sometime after this event, Irene Castle took a trip across town to ask Ethel Williams for some instruction. "Mrs. Irene Castle has even been to my house and asked me to teach them some steps," Williams remembers.[36]

But these moments of cultural "exchange" were not necessarily moments of respectful recognition, as illustrated by Irene Castle herself. "We get our new dances from the Barbary Coast. Of course, they reach New York in a very primitive state and have to be considerably toned down before they can be used in the drawing room," Irene Castle reported to the *Dancing Times*. "There is one just arrived now—it is still very, very crude—and it is called 'shaking the Shimmy,'" she continues. "It's a nigger dance, of course, and it appears to be a slow walk with frequent twitching of the shoulders. The teachers may try and make something of it."[37] Irene Castle's explanation of the dance that had "just arrived" (from where? And who "delivered" it to the "teachers?") reveals the process of mimesis and erasure in popular performance, the right to represent. The Castles codified the dances they were taught, by black dancers, and their attention legitimated the dances for a white audience. White Americans coded their bodies through and against their own abject projections of racialized femininity.

Irene and Vernon Castle would model elegant deportment, a new etiquette for an upper-class clientele. Vernon Castle's smooth yet elegant carriage helped to ameliorate the moral panic surrounding the "parasitic male social dancer," the "male dandies" who lived off of rich female socialites and preyed upon innocent young girls.[38] Irene Castle, blonde, slim, athletic—revitalized the icon of the New Woman. "Through her association with expressive social dance, Irene promoted the image of the new woman as distinctly freer than her mother's generation, yet still essentially wholesome," Lewis Erenburg writes. "Reversing nineteenth century's view of women as frail and motherly, Irene symbolized the active, free, and youthful women of the twentieth century."[39]

Black women dancers' complex articulations were of bodily free-dom, the possibilities of multi-jointed resilience, the recoding of black female bodily expression. Interpretations of these articulations formed an essential part of the process of becoming "new," but in distorted and misread ways. Black social dances were an imagined source of rejuvena-tion and revitalization, but only as "natural" urges of the body. As expres-sions of "primitive" essence, these urges had to be vigilantly controlled. (Mis)codifications like those of the Castles sublimated these articulations into constrained movements.

The threat of increased bodily contact encouraged by these dances was a critical concern for social reformers. A Western discourse on the place of dance in relation to social formation—in the form of historical accounts, anti-dance treatises, and instruction manuals—extends back into the seventeenth century. Christian manifestos, such as the anonymous tract "The Immorality of Modern Dance," published in 1904, condemned social dances as the breeding ground for the sins of the flesh. The lustful temp-tations invited by close bodily contact must be prohibited. Many a cleric had been "justified in seeing, albeit with secret indignation," the "Sinful Poses" enacted by "men and women whirling each other about furiously in the mazes of the seductive dance." How could these churchmen "re-main silent when they see souls which have been entrusted to their care being lured to destruction by the sinful pleasure of the ballroom?"[40] The female body was the critical site of social contestation during this period. In *From the Ballroom to Hell* (1894) and *The Lure of the Dance* (1916) the ex-dancing instructor Thomas Faulkner credits social dance as the means by which the white slavery trade lured young women into its grasp. The dance halls were "nothing but the 'Devil's Playground,'" and a hotbed from which the brothels were kept replenished by the "White Slaver."[41] The ruination of "unsophisticated young working women" was not simply co-erced, however, but made possible by the awakening of the young women's own lustful urges. "The dance is indulged in by many of our so-called 'first families,'" Faulkner writes, "and yet, it is one of the most dangerous of social pleasures because of the fact that it arouses, to an alarming degree, the demons of lust."[42] This acknowledgment of female sexual pleasure was at the crux of the moral panics surrounding social dance in the 1910s.

The vulgar practices bred in the dance halls were also a concern for black middle-class social reformers. "The Negro Race is Dancing Itself to

Death," Adam Clayton Powell proclaimed in his New Year's Day sermon of 1914. "You can see the effects of the Tango, the Chicago, the Turkey Trot, the Texas Tommy and ragtime music not only in their conversations but in the movement of their bodies about the home and on the street," Powell warned. "Grace and modesty are becoming rare virtues."[43] Reformers attempted to police the forms of interaction between bodies at home, in the street, and in the public dance halls. Even the Castle walk, the signature piece of the respectable couple, was dangerous when danced improperly. This dance "requires the partner's feet to be placed in a position, which while it may be taken without bodily contact, usually results in the public dances of the city in an interlocking of the partner's lower limbs and a continual rubbing together of the bodies."[44] The "continual rubbing together of bodies" spoke to the fear of increased contact in city space, which threatened to destabilize societal mores already in a shifting state. Imbedded in this concern was the potential contact between the races when enacted in the potentially uncontrolled spaces of the public dance halls.

The Castles, urged by their manager, Elizabeth Marbury, to distance themselves from the prurient association being made with modern dances, published their own tract in 1914, entitled *Modern Dancing*. "Do not wriggle the shoulders. Do not shake the hips. Do not twist the body," the Castles suggest. The terms of their instruction are prohibitory, paying careful attention to the restraint of particular parts of the body and the importance of maintaining distance between partners. "Do not flounce the elbows. Do not pump the arms. Do not hop—glide instead," they advise. "Avoid low, fantastic, and acrobatic dips. Stand far enough away from each other to allow free movement of the body in order to dance gracefully and comfortably. . . . Remember you are at a social gathering, and not in a gymnasium."[45] The animal dances of the last few years were to be avoided. "Drop the Turkey Trot, the Grizzly Bear, the Bunny Hug, etc.," they warn. "These dances are ugly, ungraceful, and out of fashion."[46] Areas of the body, particularly the pelvis, the hips, and the chest, were hot zones, body parts that, when in full use, spoke undeniably of the natural urges that a civilized body should restrain. The expressive uses of these "zones" in dances were the language through which the gendered definitions of race and class were formed and contested in the body.

The way they were used in the dances defined class and racial belonging. This is why the codification of dances was crucial, and a "how to" discourse formed around the dances. This "how to" discourse demanded demonstration. The Castles' instruction manual was published in tandem with their twenty-eight-day Whirlwind Tour of the United States in 1914. The tour was designed to assuage popular fears about the moral condition of young people swept up in the dance craze. Irene and Vernon were to model the proper forms of deportment and demonstrate commonly made "mistakes." After their demonstration, the audience was invited to participate and practice what they had just been instructed.[47]

As explored in the previous chapter, a politics of racial segregation shaped the language of "interracial exchange" between black and white bodies in the cities of the United States. New forms of contact between peoples were central to the concept of the modern and the emergence of metropolitan modernity. With ever more efficient means of transportation and production, the relationship between time and space had radically shifted. But only certain forms of touching were to be possible between certain peoples. The dances codified by white instructors—the fox trot, the Texas Tommy—to express the freedom of the new modern moment were extrapolations of expressive forms practiced by the most unfree populations of the city, those citizens penned in by segregation and social prohibition and assigned to fallow urban sectors inaccessible by mass transportation. Such moments of cultural transfer were not celebrations of African American creative resilience. Instead they affirmed a politics of white racial privilege, cultural access, and willful misrecognition. Condensed in such moments of "exchange" was the fetishization of racial expressivity, which worked to replace the presence of black expressive bodies. The form of cultural transference was structured by the property of *erasure*, the effort to contain the agency of racialized expressive bodies. The black subject is evacuated, removed.

The principle of *absorption* is lodged in cultural memory, is at the heart of this disembodied contact between white Americans and African Americans in the urban dance spaces. At the basis of white social dancing, in polite society, were the bodies of the slaves, the disenfranchised colonial subjects. But white dancers did not seek to "become" a colored body. To dance the tango, versions of which were developed by slaves in Cuba, was not to desire to be in the slave body. It was to absorb its power, and, through eroticized ritual, affirm its servitude. The dances of the internal colonial subjects could be accessed, disembodied from their actual forms.

The interpretive strategies of codification, and the stratification of the body, a process that zoned the body according to appropriate and inappropriate ways to move, were structured in terms of the primitive and the civilized. Dances miscoded the black expressive body as primitive and then sought to sublimate these fantasies of originary energy. Locking black dance and music into a framework shaped in terms of the primitive worked to deny what was modern about them.

At the same time, white use of black dances spelled the imagined restoration of cohesiveness to what felt like fragmented bodies. To counteract the mechanization of the white body, in the shifting moment of industrialization, white people used black dance to restore their bodies with the spontaneity and exhilaration promised by the dream of a new democracy.

SALOME, BEHIND THE (SEVEN) VEILS

The recognized founders of classic modern dance, including Ruth St. Denis and Maude Allen, organized their signature works around popular Orientalist imaginings of the native woman's sensuous freedom. Staining their bodies brown and dancing in bare feet and bangles, they created acts of female racial mimicry that embodied a new era of freer physicality for western women. The dance scholars Jane Desmond and Amy Kortiz have very usefully analyzed this phenomenon. The Orientalist dance craze, while pointing to the emergence of the New Woman, was an eroticized enactment of European colonial access.[48]

As seen in the creative efforts of dancers such as Ruth St. Denis, white women were reinscribing their own bodies' sensual potential through the rubric of Orientalist fantasy. The native women's body was not new territory, but it took on a new function in the many versions of *Salome's Dance of the Seven Veils* and the popular craze for all things Salome from about 1907 until 1913. The Salome craze on the popular stages in Europe, England, and the United States over the turn of the century marks a moment in dance history as white dancers used the mythical Salome as a vehicle to elevate dance as a serious art form, a drama of the body. They brought the hootchy-cootchy dances middle-class women had first seen on the fairgrounds to the safer confines of the concert stage. With dance poised at the threshold of becoming a "respectable" medium, this moment marks its entrance into the company of legitimate theater arts.

Sir Frank Kermode, the eminent Shakespeare scholar, writes at length of the "particular prestige of dancing" in artistic circles of *fin-de-siècle* Europe. Qualities associated with the "primitive" figure prominently in his critical recognition of the "cult of music hall" in Paris and London. "The circus, the vaudeville, the *bal*, were serious pleasures," Kermode writes. "The primitive, the ugly, the exotic were in demand." For many male artists, the female dancer/prostitute of the Parisian music halls—La Goulue and Jane Avril as drawn by Toulouse-Lautrec—embodied the aesthetics of *fin-de-siècle* decadence, the rejection of bourgeois complacency with an unbounded embrace of pleasure and beauty. Kermode celebrates the appearance of the American dancer Loie Fuller in 1893, dancing as Salome at the Athénée in Paris. In her "smiling nakedness," Fuller "had the power of fusing body and soul, mending all our division." Poets including Stéphane Mallarmé (who saw her perform at the Folies-Bergère in 1896) and Paul Valéry, were so inspired by Fuller as to reconsider this new kind of solo dance the "emblem of true poetry." The source of this true poetry was the primitive urge, embodied in women's passionate dances. The power of Fuller, Kermode assesses, is "rooted in the terror and joy of the obscure primitive ground from which modern poets draw strength for their archaic art."[49] The dancer became the modern poet, drawing on a primitive source of raw energy and strength. Such "terror and joy," the sublimity of female pleasure and suffering, were to be found in the narrative of the harem dancer, both enthralled and enthralling, behind her seven veils.

As Rhonda Garelick writes, Loie Fuller shaped this new possibility at the juncture of technological display and colonial commodity. Her "veils" were a series of clever manipulations of light and reflection, made sensuous through the suggestion of harem incense and naked skin under yards of muslin.[50] While she dramatized the colonial subject, she also gave shape to the figure of the colonizing women of empire, and to the sensuous possibilities of modern consumer spectacle.

As argued in earlier chapters, over the turn of the century the form of the ideal female body had changed. The large and luxurious yet tightly corseted female body of the burlesque age, held in by rigid whalebone and layers of crinoline, was rejected in favor of a more active (white) female form, able to move more freely through the city streets. White women rebelled against the Victorian era's diagnoses of female hysteria and its treatment by punitive confinement. Dress reformers, suffragists, and utopian freethinkers (in America inheriting the principles of abolitionist radicalism) sought to free the female body from its Victorian restraints.[51] The costume versions of the loose clothing of the harem girl, still concealing yet allowing a fluidity of movement, were a perfect transition into the new era of freed and freeing dress for women. Any variation too shocking (the exposed midriff) could be explained as faithful ethnographic rendering. Principles of freedom were associated with alternative health practices, as well as different conceptions of the body and its properties. In the mid-1800s, the French singing, acting, and aesthetics teacher François Delsarte devised a system of codification for human gesture, labeling the parts of the body "according to certain zones—Head, Heart and Lower Limbs which corresponded to Mind, Soul and Life."[52] Upper- and middle-class white dress reformers and feminists championed the Delsartian approach, as they sought in their politics to reclaim for the woman a right to her own mind, soul, and body and to re-establish a connection between them.[53] But new forms of physical cultivation—health spas, diets, and other nutritional philosophies—were not meant to be confused with increasing the bodies' efficiency or productive abilities. These cultivated bodies were constructed against the (racialized) working body.

New emancipatory body politics did not extend evenly to those bodies assigned the task of labor. African American dancers spoofed on this absurdity and the lofty claims of new health regimes. Appearing in a skit as "Delsartean dancers" in Black Patti's Troubadours of 1896, Stella Wiley, Bob Cole, Henry Wise, and Tom McIntosh satirized the development of such body philosophies, which were moving certain kinds of dance, and only certain dancing bodies, to the concert stage.[54]

Initially inspired by the exotic spectacle *Egypt through the Centuries* at the Palisades Amusement Park in 1892, the American vaudevillian dancer Ruth St. Denis became famous in 1909 with a group of three dances she called *Egypta*. Her third act, *Radha*, was her signature piece, in which she imitated the native dances of the Hindus of a staged Indian village she had seen on Coney Island. Her inspiration, the basis for dance modernism, therefore, sprang straight from the racialized spectacles developed on the fairground midway. For the dance, she "garbed herself in a gauze skirt with a gilt rim; she covered her midriff bodice with dimestore brooches and 'decapitated hatpins,' she put two jeweled circles in her hair at the nape of her neck, and she stained all the skin of her body brown."[55] Society women filled the matinees for Denis's temple dances, in which she "impersonated a waiflike snake charmer, surrounded by her recruit of 'real Hindus.'"[56] With this kind of Orientalist blackface, Denis took the licentious hootch dance of the world's fairs and elevated it into the realm of high chic. Surrounded by other versions of the female native, it was the figure of dancing Salome, the daughter of Herod, who would epitomize the native dancing for this generation of women.

The American Salome craze followed the outraged critical rejection of Richard Strauss's opera *Salome* in January 1907 at the Metropolitan Opera House in New York City. The myth then made its way to the variety stage; Florenz Ziegfeld adopted it for the early edition of his *Follies* that same year. The *Follies* Salome, Mademoiselle Dazie, then set up a school for Salomes on the theater roof garden. By 1908, her school was "sending approximately 150 Salomes every month into the nation's vaudeville circuits."[57] Ruth St. Denis would stage her own version of Salome in 1909, after the craze had peaked in London in 1908. Layer upon layer of imitations ensued, as Gertrude Hoffman, the renowned imitatrice, staged her own version of Denis's show at Hammerstein's Theatre in New York, surrounded by "thirty Cingalese natives."[58] Eva Tanguay offered a more conventionally minstrelized version, with the head of a Negro boy on her plate.

In England, Salome had been re-versioned in the preceding decade as a cult figure of the decadents, epitomized in Oscar Wilde's play of 1894. The innocent yet sexually insatiable seductress "personified the old society on the brink of radical reform or dissolution."[59] In Wilde's play Salome was a "figure in whom perversity and virginal innocence are piquantly mixed."[60] The popular craze for Salome came years later and hit its peak when the thirty-three-year-old musician and amateur dancer Maud Allen brought her version, *Vision of Salome*, to the Palace Theatre in 1908. London saw an abundance of American "barefoot dancers" on the popular stage that season. St. Denis was performing her *East Indian Suite* at London's La Scala Theatre. Isadora Duncan was performing *Orpheus* at the Duke of York Theatre. But Maud Allen's middle-brow version of *Vision of Salome* overshadowed them all, playing 250 performances at the Palace.[61] Allen appeared at the Palace on the same bill as Belle Davis and Her Picanin-nies.[62] As with Ida Forsyne's appearance at the Palace three years earlier, Allen was accompanied onstage by the Palace Girls. "There is . . . a robust, breezy satisfaction in watching the well-drilled 'Palace Girls' in their violent prancing and whirling and high-kicking," reads a review from the *London Times*. "Downright gymnastics of this kind form . . . a piquant contrast to the wonderful instrument of expression, the revelation of beauty, the mysterious power, that dance becomes with Miss Maud Allen."[63]

In her study of Maud Allen's *Vision of Salome*, Amy Koritz frames Allen's interpretation of Salome as a particular enactment of English colonial dominance. "Descriptions of this dance by critics and others, including Allen herself, reveal an interaction of racial and gender stereotyping that reinforced English assumptions about the 'Oriental.' This Orientalism (in Edward Said's sense of the term) in turn depended upon a rhetoric that characterized as female those attributes that denoted the inferiority of England's colonized peoples."[64] Enacting fantasies of the native woman's body, and the imagined absorption of her natural properties, was an affirmation of colonial access and power. But however inferior occidentals thought the colonized peoples, taking on the shape of a native woman's body also acted as a criticism of the rigid and imprisoned roles Western women were required to play. It was only in disguise as native women that white women could be nude. The connotations of sexual transgression were mediated by the depiction of "Oriental" women's sensual power as purely natural, innocent of western corruption, a source of physical rejuvenation. Dancing as native women was one way that white women were exploring what urban freedoms meant to them. This did not mean that white Western women desired contact with actual South Asian, Middle Eastern, or North African women (and certainly not women of the sub-Saharan regions). To the contrary; as Amy Kortiz makes clear, the act of impersonation served to *consolidate* colonial relations in the popular imagination and to affirm European women's caste relations to women of the darker races.

As in the *fin-de-siècle* burlesques (*The Creole Show, Oriental America*) black women performed multi-signifying versions of imperial fantasies about the "Orient." These stagings, such as the bicycling maids of the Oriental Huzzars in *Oriental America*, were also demonstrations of the changes in female body culture. As black women's public presence reso-

24 Ada Overton Walker,
    Abyssinia. Billy T. Rose Theatre
    Collection, New York Public
    Library for the Performing
    Arts, Astor, Lenox, and
    Tilden Foundations.

nated very differently than for white women, the spectacle of teenaged mulatto cycling concubines generated a perverse chuckle because the new rules being designed for appropriate physical exercise did not necessarily include the colored women of the nation. The variety act's humor, for a working-class and/or black audience, comes from an understanding that these new forms of physical hygiene (exercise for the sake of exercise, never work) were designed for women of leisure, women of the upper classes with time for such self-cultivation.

The dancer and comedian Ada Overton Walker danced *Salome* from 1908 to 1912 (see fig. 24). Overton had been developing as a choreographer since her cakewalk days; she had been responsible for the dance sequences in the three Williams and Walker African plays, *In Dahomey*, *Abyssinia*, and *Bandana Land*. Overton introduced her version of *Salome* in *Bandana Land* for which she also choreographed a ballet titled *Ethiopia*. Following George Walker's death, she continued to include it in her own variety act. *Salome* was a strategic choice for Overton. By claiming the dance that by 1908 had become a signature for a new generation of modernizing white women, Overton was insisting that she be respected

EVERYBODY'S DOING IT

as an artist and choreographer. Overton remains one of the only black women dancers given critical recognition for her professional work.[65] This recognition was the hard won result of her struggles against the scorn of a black elite for the popular stage, the racism of white women modern dancers, and the demands of white, and black, variety audiences. Her decision to stage her own version of *Salome* was a strategic move. With her version she claimed a right to black female self-representation and at the same time aligned herself with white modern choreographers and dancers.

Isadora Duncan, the foremost "mother" of modern dance, would probably hotly disavow any kind of association with Ada Overton or any other black dancer. Duncan conducted her own ethnographic, Orientalist adaptations, but there was a generous gap for her between the primitivism of a distant, vague, and timeless "Orient" and dances created by actual dancers from Turkey, Syria, or the Maghreb. And she maintained a very wide gap between Orientalist inspiration and the "savage" dances of the colored bodies in her own nation. She railed against the idea that black American rhythms represented national art. For her it was "monstrous that anyone should believe that jazz rhythm expresses America. Jazz rhythms express the primitive savage," the Charleston a set of "tottering apelike convulsions." American dance, as she defines it, will be "clean" of any "sensual convulsions of the Negro," any dictate from the "lower instincts of mankind" represented by "half-clad chorus girls."[66]

The artists working during this period of urbanization and imperialism played with immense slides in popular thought, in which cultures as disparate as mainland China, Turkey, and North Africa were conflated or related within the concept of the Orient. The biblical figure of Salome was not from the continent of Africa but from a region around the Sea of Galilee. But the rings around concepts of blackness, the lines between brown and black, were often gray. Racial science and popular Orientalism separated North Africa from the rest of the continent.

Salome was not Overton's first nor only Orientalist interpretation, and she continued to render Orientalist delineations after her first staging of *Salome* in 1908. In 1909, with a chorus of eight women called the "Abyssinian Girls," Ada Overton Walker appeared in New York, offering her pieces "Kara Kara" and "Dance L'Afrique."[67] The division between high and low was not always clear cut, nor the welcoming inclusion in the eyes of the critics forthcoming. But her dances were also about a politics of black self-representation. Her efforts presage the efforts of later black dancers, such as Katherine Dunham and Pearl Primus, at cultural recovery. These efforts are always mediated and shot through with contradictions.

According to the fictions of racial characteristics, Overton was ideally positioned to interpret *Salome*. As a black woman she could claim to be a more legitimate interpreter of native dances. This perspective would seem to place Overton as a kind of native informer. After all, in spite of Duncan's distinctions, didn't all primitive peoples have a proclivity for bodily expression and access to the free spiritual and sensual realms? Overton therefore had a natural right to represent the native woman and could most effectively translate native movement for a white audience. Overton's "Ragtime to the Judean Veils" was noted in the press by her racial affinity for the role.[68] "It's not such a bad idea, at that," writes a reviewer in *Vanity Fair*. "It is quite possible that Herodia's daughter had the blood of Sheba in her veins, and there is no gainsaying the fact that Ada is one of the most graceful and sinuous dancers on the American stage. Her Pantherine movements have all the languorous grace which is traditionally bound up with Orient dancing."[69] Staging Orientalism, Overton and other black women dancers could play against the assumption that black and brown people had natural access to the physical and sensual realms.

Walker's Salome culminated in 1912 with a revival at Hammerstein's Theatre Roof Garden (see fig. 25). "This will be the first time since the inception of the much talked of dance that it has ever been interpreted by a colored artist, or that a colored artist has ever attempted classic dancing," a trade review erroneously reports.[70] "Mr. Hammerstein, after witnessing several performances of Miss Walker, surrounded by real Negroes . . . was so impressed with the artistic mannerisms and grace of this colored artist that he came to the conclusion that she was capable of graduating form [*sic*] this environment."[71] Revealing all the irony from the circular borrowing and erasure of black artistry, another reviewer claims that "Miss Walker is the only colored artist who has ever been known to give this dance in public, despite that fact that the original Salome's skin may have been a hue resembling that of Miss Walker's."[72]

Yet Overton's identification with native *jouissance* only went so far. Hers was an incursion on who could hold artistic authority. Her insistence was a claim to an artistic interiority denied black dancers. Asserting

25   Ada Overton Walker, *Salome*. Billy T. Rose Theatre Collection, New York Public Library
      for the Performing Arts, Astor, Lenox, and Tilden Foundations.

herself as first and foremost an interpreter, she was challenging the idea that black acts were simply instinctual or purely emotional. She stood as a choreographer whose conscious body responded with its intelligence to music and emotion, not simply to the dictates of its innate (primitive) gifts. Such a move gave her an authority and situated her as a professional dancer. But hers was not simply a move for inclusion to the old girls' school. Overton's alignment with the mothers of modern dance was with a difference; white approval was not her only objective. Overton was also negotiating some control over the terms by which brown womanhood would and could be imagined. At the same time as she was enacting her right to the Western world, she could reclaim the meanings of certain types of (North) African womanhood.

Overton's version of *Salome* was also part of a larger movement among black artists and writers to reclaim Africa in their work. As Daphne Brooks illustrates, Overton's versioning of Salome was part of a "cultural Pan Africanism of the period." African American artists, in painting and literature, developed a pantheon of "dark princesses." As Brooks points out, Overton was most likely familiar with these renderings, and her ballet *Ethiopia* was an earlier instance of this "romanticized 'African' iconography."[73] A wide array of racialist thinkers—philosophers, statesmen, scientists—had argued to detach Egypt and the Maghreb from the rest of the continent. Black literary and artistic ventures were interventionist in that they claimed North Africa as located on the continent and as a vibrant part of the sociopolitical and cultural black diaspora. As Kevin Gaines argues, at the same time, this pan-Africanism was deeply invested in the idea of Western progress. By associating themselves with the civilized territories of North Africa in their forms of fine art (at a distance from less fully evolved sub-Saharan peoples), African Americans situated themselves as an avant garde, the rightful inheritors of a proud aristocratic African past.

Walker's and Overton's earlier African comedies, *In Dahomey* and *Abyssinia*, were not firmly a part of this serious artistic intervention, although they recognized a connection between Africans across national lines. These comedic farces were witty class critiques, poking fun at American racism, consumerism, and enthusiasm for capitalist expansion. In *In Dahomey*, for instance, critiques were lodged in the lyrical content of the musical numbers for the show. The main characters plan a development scheme to build a "Broadway in Dahomey" for the king. The entire cast travel with the African Colonization Society to Dahomey, where, as Paul Lawrence Dunbar's song asserts, "Evah Dahkey Is a King." This song and others written for this show subverted class hierarchies in two ways. They spoofed African American avant gardism, the heady responsibility certain Western blacks felt they had to save their heathen brethren, to bring light to the Dark Continent. Instead they depicted African American interest in Africa as much more about potential pecuniary gains to be made from capitalist ventures there. But they also satirize white claims to all civilized societies. "White folks whats got darky servants/Try and get dem everything/You must never speak insulting/You may be talking to a King," a stanza from Dunbar's "Evah Dahkey Is a King" reads.[74]

In staging their Africa plays, Williams and the Walkers' performance tactic involved a complex relationship of identification and distance between themselves and native Africans. Their performance as "sham Dahomians" had given them exposure to "real" Africans. George Walker writes:

> After the [belated] arrival of the native Africans, the Afro-Americans were dismissed. Having had free access to the fairgrounds, we were permitted to visit the natives from Africa. It was there, for the first time, that we were brought into close touch with native Africans, and the study of those natives interested us very much. We were not long in deciding that if we ever reached the point of having a show of our own we would delineate and feature native African characters as far as we could, and still remain American, and make our acting interesting and entertaining to American audiences.[75]

Race is staged, but it is also historically lived. Black performers were not "minstrels" in the same sense as were whites in blackface, for there was the formation of and recognition of diasporic kinships here. These involved both a claiming of affinities as well as a distance kept. Ada Overton's interpretive African dances employed a similar tactic. It allowed her to defend the reputation of African women as central figures in the history of civilization but also "remain American," distancing herself, as a modern dancer, from association as a hyper-sexualized primitive.

Since her adolescent appearance as the cakewalk partner to George Walker, Ada had been a charter member of the black theatrical community in New York, and she remained active, working in conjunction with the Frogs' theatrical club, the organization of black performers of which her husband had been the president before his death. Overton had her own company through the 1910s after the deaths of her husband and her close colleague Bob Cole. Up until August 1914, two months before she died, Overton was performing "modern society dances" in white variety theaters around New York.

Like Williams, Overton survived Ernest Hogan, George Walker, and Bob Cole, key members of the artistic community whose passing marked the end of a vibrant era in black stagecraft. All three men launched pivotal productions and were business leaders of the theatrical community. All three men could no longer work after 1908. Ernest Hogan died of tuberculosis in 1909, just a year after the successful opening of his production *The Oyster Man*. Remembered as the man who coined the term ragtime, Hogan was already an important player when Williams and Walker arrived in New York. He was a generation ahead of them and much older than Ada Overton, but all three had worked with him often. Both George Walker and Bob Cole fell ill with syphilis in 1908, and after years of slow degeneration both died in 1911. Williams's and Walker's *Bandana Land*, which opened in December 1907, would be their last production together. As Walker succumbed to syphilitic dementia and muscular failure, Overton replaced him in several of his numbers in the show. In 1908 Overton was also working with Bob Cole in his large show *Red Moon*. This would be Cole's last big production; he entered a sanitarium in 1910 and committed suicide in 1911.

Despite her identification and work with the men of the stage, Ada Overton's own serious artistic goals were not always a fit with the agendas of Williams's and Walker's black comedic farces. This is shown in the two versions of Salome staged in *Bandana Land*. Appearing after Overton performed her version of Salome, Williams performed a wench role version. The reasons for this staging was perhaps twofold: the ridiculously wenched version, with Williams emphasizing his huge feet, was staged partly to appease a white audience that did not come to see serious black artistry, but expected simple comedic relief. But the fact that it offered a version that ridiculed Overton so directly and so immediately (in the same show) suggests a more critical concern with the actors' choice. This dual staging was to allay the conflict between Overton's version—"serious" art that aligned itself with the black bourgeois agenda—and the need for black comedic farce to retain one of its key functions, to offer satirical renditions of such black middle-class aspiration. This aspiration sought recognition for black ability to produce "high art forms" and scorned the vulgar goings on in the clubs and on the variety stages.

But despite this juxtaposition between Salomes, both straight and wenched, Overton's *Dance of the Seven Veils* also intervened on black middle-class concepts of womanhood in a number of ways. First, Overton sought to claim stage work as a respectable job for black people. "Some of our so-called society people regard the Stage as a place to be ashamed of," she writes. "Whenever it is my good fortune to meet such persons, I sympathize with them for I know that [they] are ignorant as to what is really being done in their behalf by members of their race on the Stage. In this age we are all fighting the one problem—that is the color problem!"[76] But in particular Overton was working hard to change attitudes about stage work for young black women. She argued that the stage was a space for artistically gifted black women, not afforded many avenues for self-development, to realize their talents. She argued in the language of uplift available to her because invoking the uplift narrative legitimated her cause. This tactic was meant to loosen the connection between popular dance and comedy from association with the dangerous elements threatening black womanhood: permissiveness bred of unguided independence, the threat of corruption as young women traveled unprotected through the bad parts of town where many theaters were located. "You haven't the faintest conception of the difficulties which must be overcome, of the prejudices that must be left slumbering, of the things we must avoid whenever we write or sing a piece of music, put on a play or sketch, walk out on the street or land in a new town," Overton told an interviewer, following the success of *Abyssinia*. "No white can understand these things, much less appreciate them."[77] Overton refers here not only to the difficulty of composing and performing as a "negro," but to the doubled injunction she and others faced as black stage women. Overton argues that the popular stage offered an exciting avenue, and one avenue of very few, for women to realize their creative potential. In the case of black women artists, "the greatest of all gifts is negated or suppressed," she wrote. "How many intelligent women have we whose parents educate them to follow their artistic yearnings[?]"[78] It was imperative for their sake that popular stagecraft—dance and song as a paid profession—be rendered as a respectable endeavor for young women.

Her version of this risqué dance also negotiated the limits of the sexually repressed politics of the black middle-class uplift movement. The dance could be rendered as both dangerously sensuous and safely classical, the romanticized "dark princess" offering a respectable version of female sexuality. Black women, too, could be freed of the Victorian corsets, free, at least within reason, to express their eternal passionate souls through their bodies.

"The dance of the seven veils" was a language with which Overton could recover a quality of sensuousness not marked as dangerous and animalistic, as it was marked for African American women in their lives "behind the veil." Dancing in the guise of other colonized women was a forum in which African American women could simultaneously celebrate their own sensual barefootedness and claim their bodies as modern.

BABYLON GIRLS:
PRIMITIVIST MODERNISM, ANTI-MODERNISM,
AND BLACK CHORUS LINE DANCERS

Throughout the 1920s and 1930s, troupes of colored cho-rines hinged together the revues and floor shows in the clubs, cabarets, and dance halls of the United States and Europe. Women worked in whites-only Manhattan nightclubs such as Connie's Inn and the Cotton Club, as well as clubs such as Small's Paradise that catered to a black clientele. In Chicago they danced at clubs such as the Grand Terrace; each week any number of them graced the stage pages of the *Chicago Defender*. They were important to both white and black audiences, who loved them and anticipated their presence. "There were stars in the show, but we held those shows together because the audience came to see us. We got to know their faces," remembers the former Harlem chorus dancer Elaine Ellis. "[The chorus lines] had some of the best female dancers in the world, and you don't hear about them. They were really the backbone of show business," remarks Geri Kennedy. "They've always been the biggest stars."[1]

Many of the chorus girls working in the 1920s started out in the black musical stage revues based in New York beginning with *Shuffle Along* in 1921 (see fig. 26). Some of these women—Cora Green, Florence Mills, Adelaide Hall, Ethel Waters, Josephine Baker, Fredi Washington, Valaida Snow—became influential solo artists. Both black and white impresarios expressly organized black revues to tour overseas, and like the previous generation of show women many enjoyed their most gratifying and sustained

26 Program from *Shuffle Along*. Beinecke Rare Book and Manuscript Library, Yale University.

successes in Europe. Between 1926 and 1935 many women worked in the yearly editions of Lew Leslie's *Blackbirds* revues. Florence Mills, Adelaide Hall, and Valaida Snow toured France and England as the featured singing stars in consecutive editions of the *Blackbirds*. Ethel Waters starred in the short-lived edition of 1930, which did not make it out of New York City, but she did perform for several weeks at London's Palladium that year. Icons of an era in modern black creativity, this generation of women performers—chorus line women, singers, comediennes, actresses, musicians—embodied the pleasurable mobilities of the modern age; their urban élan shaped the so-called Jazz Age and the Swing Era.

As with the women in the *fin-de-siècle* burlesque shows, this new generation of performers worked within and against familiar versions of racialized femininity; this new period of European imperial expansion recirculated fantasies of African and colonial female subjecthood. "We did every kind of dance imaginable," remembers Marion Coles. "Hawaiian, Indian, African, we did it all!"[2] The "native" dancing girls were key figurations of primitivist rejuvenation in the white American and European imagination, the primitive infusing the modern with its resilience.

In this chapter I focus on these casts of itinerant black women expressive artists and explore the cultural and political climates they navigated. As well as being icons of modern movement and pleasure, they also figured centrally in contestations, within both white and black discourses, around miscegenation, cultural heritage, nationalism and the folk, and the consequences of capitalism. For a black constituency during the 1920s, black chorus women were important figures of hopeful migratory movement, urban ebullience, and promise. Moving in sinuous unstoppable unison, black chorus girls' agile mobility became the triumphant and pleasure-filled affirmation of opportunities gained. But during the Great Depression intellectual assessments of the black female dancer changed. Black anti-modernist sentiment in the 1930s instead framed the colored chorus girls as the quintessential symptoms of modernity's failings.

The era following the Great Depression demanded a return to pure folkways. Forms of romantic nationalism constructed fantasies of a black "folk" sprung from the soil of the United States. This trend, for a timeless people in the midst of the modern, took on a crucial importance after the sudden and devastating failure of the U.S. economy in 1929. Black folkways soothed both white and black anxieties. The United States had a caste to represent a pre-industrial innocence, immune to the corrupting seductions of commercialism. For black cultural arbiters, black folk culture represented the recovery of lost community and cohesion. Rules and regulations for black expression were increasingly important, and the trade in black popular culture came under scrutiny. The light-skinned, rootless, single, and independent chorus girls became symbols of decadent cultural dissipation. They were seen as colluding with the very system that oppressed black people, as the embodiments of the corrupting seduction and betrayal of capitalism.

At the same time, the figure of the dancing girl carried great cultural significance. The figure of the "native" dancing girl was a central trope used in the discourses of primitivist modernism as New Negroes sought a modern subjectivity and a usable past. Self-definition called for the conscious construction of historical memory, a cultural source of self; this process was essential to the collective affirmation of modern subjecthood. As the feminine yielding up, and to, the rhythms of an ancestral past, the black female dancer was a <u>potent figure of self-reclamation</u> for black American artists, writers, and intellectuals. Representations of black women performers took on particular meanings in African American narratives in relation to such collective self-fashioning.

Both the 1920s and the 1930s were decades of crucial, often anxious, critical self-assessment for African Americans regarding the trajectories of their expressive forms and the consequences of their commercialization. Black women popular performers—dancers and blues singers—were caught in the crux of these shifting cultural assessments.

The black backstage musical film *Swing!*, directed and produced by Oscar Micheaux, offers a rare filmic illustration of the crisscrossing of these intra-racial politics. As with all of Micheaux's films, particularly those made in the 1930s, this film was done on a shoestring, and it is perhaps all the more powerful for it. *Swing!* survives as a document of the 1920s black theatrical renaissance, offering rare footage of African American stage and cabaret performers from the former decade.

The main plot line in *Swing!* revolves around the character, Mandy Jenkins. Recently migrated to Harlem from Birmingham, Mandy saves a black musical production from failure with her down-home authenticity. When the hard-drinking and harder-fighting lead singer succumbs to dissipation (breaking her leg while falling down the stairs of a speakeasy), Mandy saves the day, replacing her as its lead singing blues woman. The cast includes a number of black stage performers. Cora Green, a former *Shuffle Along* chorus girl, plays the film's central character. As a young woman, Cora Green had been one of a variety trio, the Panama Girls, with Ada "Bricktop" Smith and Florence Mills. Coming out of the chorus line, she worked again with Mills in the *Blackbirds* revue of 1926. Green was working as the featured singer at Connie's Inn while making the film with Micheaux. The tap dancer U. S. "Slow Kid" Thompson—Cora Green's colleague and Florence Mills's widower and partner from the Plantation Club—taps a routine in the film's audition sequence. The blues singer Trixie Smith—who sang in *Shuffle Along* and toured with Mae West—appears in a small role. The female trumpet player Dollie Jones, the daughter of Dyer Jones, performs twice as the "little girl from Birmingham."

As well as the credited women performers, such as Green and Jones (credited as Doli Armenra) many unnamed women appear in the film, including a chorus line of twelve, complete with a "little girl at the end of the line." These dancers were most likely donating their time, coming to Micheaux's film set after their long shifts dancing in Manhattan's night-clubs. Having traveled across town after work, the twelve tired chorus women perform, "auditioning" for the black musical revue being staged within the film.

Micheaux would never have affiliated himself with the artistic leader-ship in Harlem, and he reserves some of his harshest and most conserva-tive criticism for its members. But what he films in this picture is part and parcel of this moment in black self-assessment in the 1920s and 1930s. *Swing!* is a "show within a show," but it is more importantly an audition within an audition. A stationary camera faces the audition space of the rehearsal hall, its central focus a long couch lining the opposite wall, upon which nine or ten black women sit. They are watching the auditions as they audition themselves. The row of black women is therefore a mirror reflection of the film's audience, who are thus invited into the process of audition and rehearsal. This staging strategy, in which the film audience is situated as part of the rehearsal process, speaks to the place of African American cultural producers within the burgeoning culture industries and the complex politics of black self-recognition. To watch the audition-ing acts, viewers must include in their view the couch of black women also watching. Viewers thus see themselves watching themselves in this act of self-representation.

Solo acts also audition, one woman in particular enters from stage right and is introduced as "the girl from Los Angeles." Clad in a feathered bikini and silver tap-shoes, the dancer undulates with smooth back and arm movements, punctuating her body dips with a two-bar tap phrase. Seem-ingly wrapped in the throes of sensual abandon she does not miss a step in her complex tap routine even as, in the midst of her ecstasy, "the girl from Los Angeles" quickly adjusts the strap to her bikini top. With this telling movement the dancer demonstrates supreme skill, as she balances the prosaic with the ineffable.

Such enactments of "primitive joy" were rituals of racial reclamation for an urban black populace seeking to redefine the terms of their racial inheritance in their struggle for modern freedoms. Expressive rituals, particularly dance, sat at the heart of contemporaneous debates around what comprised a usable past and what forms of access should and could be developed. What was at stake in evoking a connection to a primitive (and/or primal) source? When was this evocation colluding in the commodification of particular fantasies of blackness? When were such enactments useful in reclaiming history, redefining the black self with dignity? Where lay the difference between the fast-stepping "pep" expected by the white theatrical reviewers and the quality of exuberant movement black scholars such as Zora Neale Hurston evaluated as principles of a black aesthetic, as privileged moments of cultural identification? Black artists were anxious to identify dignified forms of cultural expression. *Participation*—the level of interaction between dancers and audiences—as well as *location*—the specific site of performance acts—had much to do with how these acts were evaluated along a continuum between the authentic and the corrupt. But uncomfortable ambivalences remained and required a line to be drawn in the aesthetic, and therefore political, sand. In the discourses of black and white artists and intellectuals, this line was drawn through the chorus of light-skinned chorines.

For the black writers centered in Harlem during this period, black women performers were figures through which evaluations were made and contestations were enacted around the meanings of geographical and class mobility, racial memory and refiguration. Black women dancers and jazz and blues singers represented both racial inspiration and the public recognition of African American's modern presence. The figure of the black female solo dancer appears throughout the poetry published in *Crisis* and *Opportunity* during the 1920s. Some poems, like those of Langston Hughes, were celebrations, but in many works fear and blame were mapped onto the bodies of the black women dancers: fear of what was being left behind as black people diffused into urban industrial environments, and blame for the perceived loss of community structures and stable cultural traditions.

This happened with increasing vehemence in works written during and after the Depression, as African American's desperate living conditions were compounded. Intellectual and cultural responses valued a revival of the concept of the folk as a therapeutic restorative to the death knell rung by this crisis of industrial capitalism. Black nostalgia, the desired return to a simpler time, ran alongside white romanticized versions of the black folk. Once the symbols of black urbanity and opportunity, chorus girls now represented an acquisitive cosmopolitanism. They stood in as figures of capitalist seduction and betrayal. Embedded icons of the city, they refused to go back home to the South and so were held responsible for the loss of racial unity and community formation associated with earlier urban migration. They symbolized assimilation, threatening the recovery of a racial authenticity. For Zora Neale Hurston, the octoroon chorus girls signaled cultural corruption. "Negro shows before being tampered with did not specialize in octoroon chorus girls. . . . The bleached chorus is the result of a white demand, and not the Negro's," she wrote.[3] In their collective person, black commercial collusion with white appropriative interests was sexualized.

The policies of colorism Hurston so sternly criticizes, the preferential hiring of light-skinned women, was true to an extent, but only to an extent; the women of the chorus line came in all shades of brown. Most importantly it was the *idea* of "light skin" that had been scripted into the definition of a colored chorus line. As in the *fin-de-siècle* choruses, it was an important function of chorus lines that they be scripted to suggest racial admixture. The chorus girls' light skin—both "real" and imagined—troubled concepts of an authentic black "folk" by raising the fleshly ghost of miscegenation. The best assessments from white critics considered the chorus a refreshing mixture of the modern and the primitive, while many gave a sly nod to the titillation of interracial desire and the erotic history of a master's access. In popular black films as well as the "serious" literature of the Harlem literati, the light-skinned showgirl was an ambivalently rendered figure. She referenced urban pleasures and freedoms, but she also stood for white privilege of access and immoral desire and for African Americans' collusion in their own cultural contamination. In Sterling Brown's Depression-era poem of 1932, "Cabaret: Chicago 1927," light-skinned chorus women are sentenced as the concubines of Babylon, as pathological symptoms of the fall of civilization itself.

In the works of Hurston and Brown, by contrast, blues-singing, dark-skinned black women were the organic intellectuals of an authentic southern constituency. They were firmly rooted in the "real" rural south, while the "light-skinned" chorus girls and variety hall crooners represented the deleterious effects of the city on forms of black cultural communality and resilience. But consider how the history of the variety stage reveals the ways blues singers, variety crooners, and chorus girls all worked together on the urban stages as well as the ways the TOBA circuit allows for a more supple analysis of the historical and geographical trajectories of expressive forms developed between women. The blues singer Trixie Smith started out on the variety stage revue, working in cork. Josephine Baker began her career touring as a young teenager with the Dixie Steppers, who accompanied the blues singer Clara Smith. Throughout the 1920s, troupes of female backup dancers and singers toured the TOBA circuit with the famous blues women Mamie Smith, Clara Smith, and Bessie Smith.

Bessie Smith, at one point, had the young singer and dancer Ethel Waters in her troupe. When Waters became the first woman to record for Black Swan records, reports of a feud between the two women were publicized and arguably overblown. "I'm not Bessie Smith!" Ethel Waters had exclaimed while on tour with the "queen." Waters's words continue to resonate in contemporary criticism as a staged antagonism between the (dark-skinned) representatives of a southern-based black constituency and the (light-skinned) representatives of a citified, white-influenced, middle-class audience. This drama was useful; it gave a shape to the anxieties around the consequences of migration and the effect of new technologies—film and recorded sound—as they created new geographies and listening communities. But it must be understood as a drama, not a reflection of true class conflicts or easily or evenly drawn divisions between shades of brown.

Hurston quite rightly acknowledged white and black producers' preferences for lighter skinned women. But the problem of the color line cannot be so clearly drawn. Whatever the musicologist debate about who was a better blues singer, the staged feud between Smith and Waters is not an accurate barometer of divided loyalties, for black people knew that class and caste did not always evenly follow skin tone. Ethel Waters grew up in poverty just as had many other women finding freedom on the road. As much as black audiences loved and identified with Bessie Smith and other blues singers, they also loved the stage warblers and the high-toned chorus girls. One white reviewer was dismayed at how, when he considered the audiences for two shows that were running simultaneously in 1927, black audiences preferred the frothy comedy and scantily clad chorus of Miller's and Lyles's *Keep Shufflin* to the socially engaged message and "real" folk renderings of Gershwin's *Porgy and Bess.*[4] He could not see or understand that black audiences recognized these yellow gals as sisters, cousins, nieces, as fellow children of both rural sharecropping migrants and the urban working poor. No matter what their (perceived) skin tone, black women performers' expressions of urban sophistication were sleek-haired celebrations of working-class resilience, of the restless, multi-directional forms of survival black women forged for themselves.

SHUFFLE ALONG, OR "WE CAUSED IT TO BE BROADWAY"

As *The Creole Show* had marked a threshold moment for black women on the stage and in the city, so *Shuffle Along* of 1921 heralded a new era of black female cultural presence. The show had a cast of talented actresses playing the lead roles, but the women of the chorus "were the heart of *Shuffle Along*."[5] Multi-talented women formed the chorus lines in the wave of black revues that followed, framing the shows' skits and musical numbers. "It was the musical revue, *Shuffle Along*, that gave a scintillating send-off to that Negro vogue in Manhattan," Langston Hughes wrote in his autobiography, *The Big Sea*. "To see *Shuffle Along* was the main reason I wanted to go to Columbia. . . . I was in the gallery of the Cort Theatre every time I got a chance. . . . It was always packed. . . . It gave just the proper push—a pre-Charleston kick—to that Negro vogue of the 20's, that spread of books, African sculpture, music, and dancing."[6]

Even as the Jazz Age dawned, the theater district pushed black performers and revues into its dusty corners. Despite *Shuffle Along*'s notoriety as the first black show to make it to Broadway, the run-down Cort Theatre was on West 63rd Street, not within the Broadway theater district. It was actually a lecture hall that was badly in need of repairs and lacked a stage. In addition, the show's opening date was after the close of the regular Broadway season in New York, at the onset of the hot and sweaty summer months that made the theaters insufferable. The racial and cultural geographies being carved in the urban terrain forced black performers to do some quick stepping to navigate the complex politics of northeastern urban segregation. In doing so, they rezoned Broadway. "It was really off-Broadway, but we caused it to be Broadway," stated the show's producer, the lyricist and composer Eubie Blake.[7]

The cast's improvisational talent fit itself around material and thematic compromises black performers had been contending with for years. The chorus women inherited a pile of used costumes that, as Blake remembers, "still had sweat-marks under the arms" (see fig. 27).[8] Included in this pile of hand-me-downs was a set of fantastical Orientalist gowns left behind from an unsuccessful play called *Roly Boly Eyes*. To suit the outfits, Blake and his co-producer, the orchestral conductor Noble Sissle, wrote a composition called "Oriental Blues," a song, Blake clarifies, that was "neither Oriental nor a blues"(see fig. 28).[9] Among the piles were some "cotton pickers costumes" that had been made for a plantation number, for which Sissle and Blake quickly composed "Bandana Days" together over the phone.[10] After rehearsing in Harlem, the show went on the road before returning for its New York opening. Despite the conditions of the Cort Theatre, the show drew huge crowds and good reviews, running for 504 performances in New York until the summer of 1923 (see fig. 29).

Women performers began auditioning for the cast of *Shuffle Along* in New York City early in 1921 as news of the production spread. Actresses from the Lafayette Theatre and dancers and singers from the Williams and Walker and Cole and Johnson companies all signed up to participate. The singer Lottie Gee played the female leading role. Reviewers duly noted Gee's trilling soprano voice; in 1925 she would travel to Germany and Russia with a show called *The Chocolate Kiddies*. Gertrude Saunders played *Shuffle Along*'s second lead but fell ill during the second season and was replaced by the young singer Florence Mills. Playing the role of "Mrs. Sam Peck, Suffragette" was Mattie Wilkes, who had returned from Russia in 1914 and joined the Lafayette Players. But the show was noted in particular for its cast of chorus girls.

As with shows of the previous decades, it was the dancing chorus that articulated the new urban moment. "*Shuffle Along* . . . brought so many of us happiness," recounts Josephine Baker. "Freddie [*sic*] Washington, the exotic dancer; Elida Webb, now a choreographer; Katarina Yarboro, headed toward an operatic career; Florence Mills, triumphing at the Plantation . . . and above all, me."[11] The *Shuffle Along* colored chorines were organized into three ensembles: the Jazzy Jasmines, the Happy Honeysuckles, and the Majestic Magnolias (see fig. 30). The dancers Josephine Baker and Fredi Washington were in the replacement cast of the Happy Honeysuckles. Although she was a dancer, Fredi Washington would later work as an actress, her most notable role that of Pecola in the film *Imitation of Life* (1934). The dancer and choreographer Elida Webb was in the original cast of the Jazzy Jasmines. To date Webb has received little if any recognition, although she would go on to stage and choreograph many Broadway shows. In 1923 she staged what would become known as the signature version of the Charleston dance.

27 Chorus girls from *Shuffle Along* with Noble Sissle. Billy T. Rose Theatre Collection, New York Public Library for the Performing Arts, Astor, Lenox, and Tilden Foundations.

28 Three chorus girls in costume, *Shuffle Along*. Billy T. Rose Theatre Collection, New York Public Library for the Performing Arts, Astor, Lenox, and Tilden Foundations.

29 The Jazzy Jasmines, *Shuffle Along*. Elida Webb is at far right, Adelaide Hall second from right. Billy T. Rose Theatre Collection, New York Public Library for the Performing Arts, Astor, Lenox, and Tilden Foundations.

30 Entire cast of *Shuffle Along* in satin. Billy T. Rose Theatre Collection, New York Public
Library for the Performing Arts, Astor, Lenox, and Tilden Foundations.

Despite her lack of humility, Josephine Baker was really just one of the
many women working in chorus lines during the 1920s and 1930s. "People
always say she was in the Cotton Club. She wasn't in no Cotton Club," one
former chorus worker commented, regarding Josephine's later notoriety.
"She was just a chorus girl, baby, we all was chorus girls."[12]

The chorus women of the clubs were the lowest paid members of any
cast. And they worked hard. Members of the Apollo Theatre revue, the
Apollo Rockets, remember these conditions. "You didn't take a week off,
[because] when you came back, somebody'd be in your place. . . . [We
worked] from ten o'clock in the morning to eleven o'clock at night," remembers Cleo Hayes. "[We worked] four, five, six shows a day," recalls
Marion Cole, "with rehearsals after the second and the last show." Bertye
Lou Williams remembers, "You'd be there rehearsing sometimes until
three o'clock in the morning. That's why they put beds upstairs." Protesting the punishing work schedule and conditions, Hayes, Cole, Williams,
and other Apollo dancers organized a union in 1940 and picketed outside
the theater. "The Apollo theatre chorus girls made this house, and closed it

up one Saturday night because they didn't want to pay us enough money," states Hayes. "We established AGVA right here." The women picketed the Apollo for twenty-four hours. "It was snowing like crazy when we closed this theatre up. The people loved us here and when they saw us standing out here and not coming into work they said, 'later!'" Hayes remembers. When the owner of the theater, Frank Schiffman, settled, the women received $25 and payment for rehearsals. "They went downtown to Radio City and paid them $10 more than we got," Hayes remembers, "but we established the union. I don't forget. Sixteen chorus girls closed that theatre. We shut it down."[13]

As many women recall, there was great camaraderie among the members of the chorus. More seasoned performers would freely guide and train the newer members. Bertye Lou Williams was captain in charge of the show. "I must have been about seventeen," remembers Marion Coles, "and Bertye Lou was so generous. She absolutely guided me through." Cole and others would often pick up steps from male dancers and then teach them to the other girls. "All the top dancers were very generous. If an act came in the theatre . . . I would pick up something from them then take it down to rehearsal and teach it to the girls," Cole says.[14]

Jazzy Jasmine Adelaide Hall remembers being a member of various choruses over the years. In the early 1920s, before beginning her solo career, she was captain of the chorus at the Cotton Club. "I was the head of the show. I was in the first one, at the beginning of the Cotton Club," she recalled in a later radio interview. She appreciated the earlier sense of camaraderie she felt while with the chorus and missed the sense of community in her solo career. "I remember [that] when they took me out of the chorus line my heart was broken to be away from all my pals, I didn't like that at all . . . I'd rather be with the girls, all in one big dressing room, much more fun." This was over the years that it was owned by the Mafia, "Al Capone's gang," as Hall states. The Cotton Club was segregated. "They didn't want the colored people there, because they didn't have the money. Unless they were Joe Lewis or someone with lots of money," Hall explains. When asked about the color line policies she replies,

> I didn't like it at all but we looked at it as an engagement. . . . We knew that
> the color bar was there but it was the case of having the chance of being
> first and foremost. You were paid more, you met the best artists; we knew
> of the conditions but it didn't mean very much as we didn't have to come

in contact with them [the audience]. . . . I'm not angry at all. I couldn't be bothered with what was going on in the audience. After we performed we got dressed and went home.[15]

Hall would work again with friends from the *Shuffle Along* cast. She worked with Elida Webb at the Cotton Club. "Elida Webb . . . looked after all the salaries, made sure they were safe," Hall remembers.[16] In 1925 Hall sailed to Hamburg along with her colleague Lottie Gee in the cast of *The Chocolate Kiddies*. This was Hall's first trip abroad. "We went to Denmark, Prague, Budapest, Germany. It was my first time away from home but I had a good friend, Lottie Gee; she was the star of the show, and a good friend."[17] Returning briefly to the United States in 1927, she recorded "Creole Love Song" with the Duke Ellington Band, establishing herself as one of the first female jazz singers. But Hall did not stay in the United States. In 1928 she replaced Florence Mills as the lead in Lew Leslie's *Blackbirds* revue and went back to Britain (see figs. 31 and 32). In the 1930s she toured the RKO circuit, on a long touring contract, in which she would "go from one place to another, there was no going back to [the] main office. For one entire year you traveled. It was beautiful. I had a very good car then. [I traveled] sometimes by train, sometimes by car."[18] Hall decided to stay in Europe. In 1934 she and her husband opened a club in Paris, which they named La Grosse Pomme, on the Rue Pigalle; "only a tiny little place, only about 100 seating capacity, but it was such a success," Hall remembers. "We had Maurice Chevalier, Charles Boyer, Josephine, Mistinguette, quite a few people would come. We had lovely crowds of people there."[19] Hall continued to perform in London and sometime after 1938 decided to settle there. Closing La Grosse Pomme, she and her husband, the former merchant marine Bert Hicks, opened a club in the Mayfair district of London called The Spotted Dog. But both the club and her home were destroyed during the London blitz. "I lost my home on Bruton Street. We had the old Florida Club there. We lost everything . . . it was landmined."[20] She and Hicks stayed in London, where Hall became a well-known radio broadcaster. A fixture in Britain, Hall died there in 1993.[21]

Many of the chorus women stayed in the New York choruses, appearing in the New York shows that immediately followed *Shuffle Along*, including *Put and Take*, *Strut, Miss Lizzie*, *Liza*, *Oh, Joy!*, and *Runnin Wild*. These shows also opened during the hot summer months and/or in less than ideal theaters.[22] In 1921 and 1922, the variety blues singer Cora Green

31 & 32   Adelaide Hall, *Blackbirds* of 1928. Billy T. Rose Theatre Collection, New York Public Library for the Performing Arts, Astor, Lenox, and Tilden Foundations.

appeared in *Put and Take*, the first to open after *Shuffle Along*. Green also worked in Creamer's and Layton's show *Strut, Miss Lizzie*, which opened in the summer of 1922 at an Eastside burlesque house. *Strut, Miss Lizzie* was advertised as "Glorifying the Creole Beauty," and many of the songs and skits—such as "Hoolah from Coney Isle," described as "a Hawaiian style number"—were direct borrowings from *The Creole Show* and other *fin-de-siècle* black burlesque shows.[23] Themes of popular Orientalism still had currency. In 1923 actresses from the Lafayette Players joined Mrs. Sherwood Anderson and Raymond O'Neill's Ethiopian Art Players in staging a version of Oscar Wilde's play *Salome*. Laura Bowman, who had joined the Lafayette Players after returning from St. Petersburg, starred as Herodias, and Evelyn Preer, who had starred in Oscar Micheaux's silent films, played the infamous Salome.[24]

   Importing a rural southern tent show to the heart of Manhattan may have been calculated as a lucrative novelty by the producers of *Oh Joy!*, the brothers Salem Whitney and Homer Tutt, to make the most of New York theater owners' discriminatory segregationist policies toward black shows. It was not so to Ethel Waters, who had been asked to join the company. "It ain't no novelty to me," she stated. "The days when I worked in a tent are over. I have slept with horses for the last time, I trust."[25] *Oh Joy!* was staged in a tent named "Bamboo Isle," which had been set up in a vacant lot on 57th Street and 8th Avenue. The tent show attracted black audiences as well as white. Like the Cort and the Colonial Theaters, it was situated near San Juan Hill.[26]

The show *Runnin Wild* opened at the Colonial Theatre in October 1923, with Adelaide Hall as the featured singer. The chorus girls of *Runnin Wild* were noted in the newspapers as being particularly bare fleshed. "A lot of money has been saved on tights and a little on brassieres, the light chocolate chorus ladies being as bare as their white sisters downtown. And rouged as highly," reads a newspaper review.[27] Critics often drew comparisons between black and white chorus girls, but the comparison here was expected, as Miller and Lyles produced the show with financial assistance from George White, the producer of the yearly white chorus girl revues *George White's Scandals*, then playing downtown.[28]

But this show was memorable for another reason. Elida Webb directed all of the show's staging and choreography, and Webb's choreography for the Charleston was the show's critical highlight.[29] Her set of movements was accompanied by the tune "The Charston," composed by James P. Johnson and Cecil Mack and sung by Elizabeth Welch. According to James Weldon Johnson, *Runnin Wild* "started the dance on its world-encircling course." But Johnson credits the producers, rather than Webb, for the distinctive dance sequence. "Miller and Lyles . . . did not depend wholly upon their extraordinarily good jazz band or the accompaniment. They went straight back to primitive Negro music and had the major part of the chorus supplement the band by beating out the time with hand-clapping and foot-tapping. The effect was electrical."[30] Directive credit should be given to the chorus of chorines, "beating out the time," bringing the strains of a "primitive Negro music" to an electrical effect in the heart of the city.

Mattie Wilkes and Lottie Gee were in the cast of Sissle's and Blake's second big show, *Chocolate Dandies*, which opened in September 1924 at the Colonial. This show began as *In Bamville* and toured extensively before its New York opening. The multi-talented musician Valaida Snow joined the cast as a singer, and Josephine Baker was in the chorus, at the end of the line. According to one review of *Chocolate Dandies*, "The chorus did everything from acrobatics to ensemble work which compares well with

33 Valaida Snow, *In Bamville*.
    Billy T. Rose Theatre Collection,
    New York Public Library for the
    Performing Arts, Astor, Lenox,
    and Tilden Foundations.

34 Southern belle from *Chocolate
    Dandies*. Billy T. Rose Theatre
    Collection, New York Public Library
    for the Performing Arts, Astor, Lenox,
    and Tilden Foundations.

the precision of John Tiller's minions."[31] The reviewer probably drew this
analogy because Sissle and Blake had hired Julian Mitchell, the stage manager for Florenz Ziegfeld, and the white producer B. C. Whitney to work
on their project.

   Like so many other revues, the show was a fantastical rendition of a
strange and mythical Southland. The costumes were lavish, evoking less
a rustic rural "homeland" than a faux Versailles. Women wore sleek satin
gowns, men sported three-cornered hats and spats on their shoes, and
both wore platinum wigs. Valaida Snow wore a ruffled satin pageboy out-
fit for her act (see fig. 33). The luxuriant stage sets suggested eighteenth-
century French baroque. The choices made by the set designers show how
the fantasy of the South was still as a land stuck in a feudal past. Plantation
life was compared to pre-revolutionary French aristocratic decadence. For
their number "Dixie Moon," the chorus girls were cocooned in huge white
lace gowns underpinned by hoop skirts, dressed as so many white ladies
of the U.S. southern states (see fig. 34).

35 Josephine Baker with a banjo
    player, *Chocolate Dandies*. Billy
    T. Rose Theatre Collection, New
    York Public Library for the
    Performing Arts, Astor, Lenox,
    and Tilden Foundations.

36 Florence Mills in "Jungle Nights in
    Dixieland" from *Dixie to Broadway*.
    Billy T. Rose Theatre Collection,
    New York Public Library for the
    Performing Arts, Astor, Lenox,
    and Tilden Foundations.

Josephine Baker made her solo debut in a number called "Land of the Dancing Picaninnies." In full blackface, picaninny pinafore and gigantic clown shoes, Baker mugged cross-eyed through her first solo appearance. "At $125 a week, I was the highest paid girl in the chorus," boasts Baker. "All because I could cross my eyes!"[32] Earlier, while touring with Clara Smith and the Dixie Steppers, Baker had brought the gestural strategies of a picaninny performance to the chorus line. The precedent for this had already been set by women such as Ethel Williams, but Baker does not mind taking credit for the picaninny conventions that made her name. "Mr. Russell decided to keep me at the tail end of the chorus line to make people laugh," she remembers. "As quick as a monkey I had learned that when I rolled my eyes and made the very faces that had earned me a scolding at school, the crowd burst out laughing."[33] Drawn with comic hyperbole, the figment of the plantation was still being staged in the metropole. The scampering picaninny dancer still held a particular currency (see fig. 35).

"Any time a white person wanted to get rich he'd put on a colored show," commented Ida Forsyne. "Lew Leslie got wealthy that way."[34] Leslie (formerly Lessinsky) was a crafty businessman and succeeded in making a fortune, claiming that the white man "understand[s] the colored man better than he does himself."[35] But it wasn't black men Leslie considered as the buttered side of his bread. Colored chorus girls formed the core of his lucrative revues. In 1922, Leslie opened a supper cabaret called the Plantation Club. After two seasons, Leslie moved it to the 48th Street Theatre on Broadway. He hired a cast of light-skinned chorines and Florence Mills as his plantation star, after hearing her sing "I'm Craving for That Kind of Love" in *Shuffle Along*. Before long, Mills "had become the sensation of New York . . . a public idol," as Ethel Waters wrote.[36] The Plantation Club thrived. Florence Mills's husband, the tap dancer U. S. Thompson, was also dancing at the Plantation. He remembers, "Watermelons . . . and lights—little bulbs—in the melons. There was a well you could draw the water out, and statues of hogs and corn. The place was packed every night to see Florence."[37] In the spring of 1924, while Florence Mills was touring, Ethel Waters worked as her replacement. Josephine Baker danced in the chorus, stepping out of line for her usual picaninny comic routine.[38] "I'd never seen anything as magnificent as the Plantation," wrote Baker. "It looked like paradise, with its bright lights and starched tablecloths."[39] Like earlier inner-city versions of cotton plantation life, such as Billy McClain's *Black America*, this plantation moment staged rurality, but here it was intentionally artificial. The staging was an indoor affair. Unlike the tent show in *Black America*, this was all satin and chiffon, the watermelon fairy lights a stylistic conceit to bring into relief the sleek chic of urban wealth. The surreal juxtaposition of the rural and the urban led to strange assessments from the Plantation's well-heeled clientele. "The plantation is CLASS personified," wrote Nora Bayes. "The Plantation does not grow cotton but silk," commented Samuel Shipman.[40]

As in previous eras, U.S. southern plantation fantasies carried overseas. Black cast shows were popular in London. In 1923, a chorus line from Leslie's club toured London as the *Plantation Revue*. Lew Leslie then organized a touring company around Florence Mills and a chorus line, the Plantation Steppers, led by Cora Green. He brought this cast to England in a show called _From Dover to Dixie_, which opened in 1924 at London's Pavilion. Its first act, set in Dover, England, was performed by a British cast, but the show returned to the segregationist United States in 1925 as the all-black-cast _Dixie to Broadway_ (see fig. 36) and the British format was dropped to avoid the shocking chance of a racially shared stage. Leslie began producing the _Blackbirds_ revues in 1926, and Florence Mills's status as the "sensation of two continents" was confirmed.[41] Opening in September at the London Pavilion, the show included such absurd musical numbers as "Jungle Nights in Dixie" and "Hottentot" (see figs. 37 and 38). Mills sang what would become her signature song, "I'm a Little Blackbird Looking for a Bluebird," and led the Steppers (as the "Plantation Cossacks") in a parody of Balief's Russian ballet _Le Chauve Souris_, which was perhaps a muted homage to the black artists who had lived and worked in _fin-de-siècle_ Russia.

The shows were organized around plantation staging conventions long circulating throughout Europe. In the 1934 edition of _Blackbirds_, the first skit was entitled "A Futuristic Idea of Down South," confirming the durability of the plantation mythos and its imbrication within meanings of the fantastic future.[42] By the 1930s audiences expected to see increased numbers of chorus women and faster and more frenetic dance sequences. "'Blackbirds of 1934' is blatant and jazzy, but the show has vitality and colour," reads a review in London's _Daily Telegraph_. "It is the last word in speed and noise—and a long, long way from _Uncle Tom's Cabin_ and the Old Kentucky Home."[43]

For European audiences the speedy legs of the colored chorus women represented the ethos of travel, the power and potential new modes of transportation promised. But the women's physical vitality also spoke to a renewed period of British colonialism. The trumpet player Valaida Snow was the featured performer, but a new dancer, "Kahloah, a Carib girl from Martinique," was flown in as an added attraction. "She has no passport," the _Telegraph_ reported, "but was allowed to proceed to London after a delay of about an hour."[44] Although the English audiences were meant to believe that she was a "Carib girl," this dancer was actually Elizabeth Kelly, a "shake dancer" from the Grand Terrace in Chicago. "The Londoners are going for her hook, line and sinker," reported the _Chicago Defender_.[45]

Twinkling watermelon lights, statues of hogs, huge grinning Mammy

37 Chorus girls, "Jungle Nights in
    Dixieland," from *Dixie to Broadway*.
    Billy T. Rose Theatre Collection,
    New York Public Library for the
    Performing Arts, Astor, Lenox, and
    Tilden Foundations.

38 The cast of *Dixie to Broadway* in "Jungle Nights in Dixieland," 1927. Billy T. Rose
    Theatre Collection, New York Public Library for the Performing Arts, Astor, Lenox,
    and Tilden Foundations.

figures adorning the stage curtains all comprised a cruelly absurd and humiliating iconography, easily identified as fortification for structures of racial oppression. These conditions were the very grounds for the comedy itself, the absurd surrealistic stage settings reflecting a wider spectacle of raciological irrationalities. This signified in a number of ways, as live performance moments are, at their structural level, multi-signifying events. They invite many levels of interpretation, and their ultimate power derives from their elusive impermanence. Black audience members and artists understood these conditions as a given, suggested by their laughter and the ease with which colored performers slipped between their satin gowns and their corn-shucking coarse-spuns.

A politics of dissemblance and recognition are evident in one *Variety* reviewer's comments on the acts in this show. This is one of the rare mentions of the black drag artists in Harlem in mainstream reportage. *Variety*'s reviewer describes the female impersonator Julian Costello, who came out with an "Oriental song, and dance, the Valley of the Nile." The reviewer calls "Julian's 'snake dance' . . . very feminine, though his arms are quite muscular. The 'boy' has some fins," he comments, then remarks on the fact that "someone out front must have known him, calling out 'Marjorie.'"[46]

The choices artists made had critical forms of payback. As an artistic space, the variety stage was a space to further develop skills and work with other artists. As a work place, the pay was often good and the opportunities for travel frequent. As a lifestyle, the stage life offered women and men a freedom from middle-class (and heterosexist) tenets about how to spend one's money and time. But most saliently, fame—claiming a public presence—was an important form of demanding historical recognition. In the city, stage performance was also territorial insurgence.

THE GREAT WHITE WAY

The fear of a black invasion on the Great White Way was encapsulated in a song sung by the shimmying white star of the *Ziegfeld Follies* of 1922, Gilda Gray. The fear lies in the space between representation and the potential for "actual" black bodies, "real dark town entertainers," to not just appear in but to define public and artistic space. "Just like an eclipse on the moon," she sang,

Ev'ry café has a dancing coon,
Pretty choc'late babies
Shake and shimmy ev'rywhere
Real dark town entertainers hold the stage,
You must black up to be the latest rage.
Yes, the great white way is white no more
It's just a street on the Swanee shore.
It's getting very dark on old Broadway.

As with the cakewalk craze and the rooftop garden midnight dances, such cultural territorialism reflected the politics of racial mimesis, which required geographically circumscribing the physical presence of black performers in order to absorb the imagined qualities of spirit housed in their bodies.

A telegram sent to Florence Mills from Irene Castle during Mills's appearance in London with the show *Dover to Dixie* precisely illustrates these politics. Both Castle and Mills had been invited to a fancy dress ball hosted by the heiress and famous Negrophile Nancy Cunard. (It was in fact the Cunard family's ships in which Mills and her colleagues sailed over to England.) Irene Castle made a particular request of Florence Mills; in a rushed telegram Castle asked to borrow Mills's costume from the opening act of *Dover to Dixie*: "May I borrow the costume you make your first appearance in as I wish to go impersonating you to Lady Cunards party tonight I can send for it at eleven oclock and return it tomorrow morning telephone answer Embassy Club this evening will appreciate it very much."[47] Both Mills and Castle attended Cunard's fête. Castle appeared in full blackface and clad in Mills's opening act costume.[48]

The faint pencil scrawl of Castle's missive provides the program for a complex performative moment. A kind interpretation can read the impersonation as a conspiratorial, even transgressing chuckle between Castle and Mills over being invited to such a party, where they were often expected to perform. It can also be understood as Castle imitating Nancy Cunard, who was known for her own outlandish versions of racial delineation. Perhaps, and this Castle would support, it was simply a compliment to Mills and acknowledgment of her success in London. Yet I argue that much besides a playful compliment rests upon it, as Castle's request is a crucial index of white anxieties over black people's artistic presence and mobility. Castle's performance in cork perhaps allayed her tension, allowing her to attend the ball as the black woman whose fame in London challenged her own. It could also be her nervous response to the way the stage was integrated in Britain for Mills: in *Dover to Dixie* both white and black cast members shared the stage. When the show came back to the United States (the white cast members dropped), the show changed direction and went instead "from Dixie to Broadway."

The Cunard ball itself became contested territory over who had the right to play black for high-society Britain. Castle had made quite a good job of it as an interpreter and refiner of black dances. She had the historic right to inhabit the imagined territory of a racialized body. Who had the right to be Florence? Certainly not Florence.

That Castle would make such a request illustrates the precedent of entitlement and the process of imagined absorption at the heart of what has been euphemistically called cultural exchange. It needn't reflect or determine an individual white artist's political stance per se, or preclude conditional "friendship" agreements between artists. But it does operate as a fundamental condition of all interchanges, shaping any of these friendships' actual possibilities. There is a recognition, even an open admiration in Castle's missives to Mills. As well as her request to borrow Mills's costume to stage her own Ethiopian delineation at the Cunard fête, Castle sent a glowing letter to Mills, thanking her for her performance. "Please congratulate your little company for me—they are all artists and deserve the success they have won. . . . I only wish I tho't [*sic*] I could make half as big an impression tonight, but success and talent like yours are not to be had every day."[49] Yet Castle's words intimate, and remind, that she *would* have it, as black cultural forms were to be "had" by principle. Castle's slightly sycophantic, subtly covetous words may well house an honest admiration. But what I want to emphasize is that we not get too excited over the prospect of interracial goodwill. Whatever Castle's acknowledgement of Mills's talent and success, it remains well within the bounds of the rules policing actual mutual recognition or artistic contact. Impersonation is not the same as, nor is it an invitation to, artistic exchange in person.

Often with their black personal maids backstage (who were often their dance instructors) vaudevillians such as Gilda Gray would distill the gestural vocabularies of "shaking and shimmying" into a therapeutic dose of the naughty, the forbidden, the rebellious. It was the Jewish coon shouter Sophie Tucker who first coached a young Miss May Gray, renaming her

Gilda and introducing her at Reisenweber's in New York. "May was a little Polack, with frizzy blonde hair. . . . Her hit number was 'St. Louis Blues' in which she did the shimmy. She brought the word shimmy from Chicago, and New York picked it up. It made her famous overnight."[50] All of these women learned their dances, including the shimmy, from watching Clara Smith and other black women performers on the TOBA circuit through Chicago. Tucker, Gray, and many other women on the white vaudeville circuit, including Eva Tanguay, Fanny Brice, and Mae West, had been watching black women blues singers and variety performers for years.

When working on the stage, black women performers performed these dances and gestural vocabularies in several registers, considering white as well as black paying audiences. They employed the same kind of gestural multi-signification, "glancing several directions at once," as they did when engaging minstrel conventions on the variety stage.

Many black women performers formed complex working relationships with women of the white vaudeville circuit. Working the white circuits as a personal maid was a common gig for black women performers, as was service in general, and the roles of mistress and maid often operated both on and off the stage. Of her youth, Ethel Waters wrote, "Getting into a stage show was my greatest ambition, next to becoming a lady's maid and globe trotting with her."[51] A performer of sorts, Zora Neale Hurston worked as a maid for a white actress in a Gilbert and Sullivan troupe between 1915 and 1916. In her autobiography Hurston describes her year traveling with the Gilbert and Sullivan actress, "Ms. M—." She fondly remembers their friendship and relates her experience staying with the actress in the home of her Irish working-class family outside of Boston.[52] Hurston was also in service for a time with Fanny Hurst, and their relationship was the inspiration for the central protagonists Bea and Delilah in Hurst's novel *Imitation of Life*. That *Imitation of Life* was adapted into a major Hollywood film in 1934 and again in 1959 attests to the cultural longevity of the white mistress/black maid contract.

From 1922 to 1924 Ida Forsyne toured with Sophie Tucker as her personal maid as well as part of her act. Having a difficult time finding work on her return from Europe, when given a tip that Tucker was looking for a maid, she auditioned. "I got $50 a week and did the maid part on and off stage. I was dressed in a black dress and white apron," Ida Forsyne recalls.[53] Forsyne's job included dancing at the end of Tucker's routine in order to whip up the audience applause. "She'd take the bow at the end. The colored people thought I was wrong not to be taking the bow because I was the one getting the applause at the finish," Forsyne remembered. She also recounts how these shows were segregated. "As soon as the show started they'd put down a curtain so the colored help couldn't watch the show."[54] Although she could not (or would not) dance in the New York cabarets, Forsyne worked the next four years on the TOBA circuit. In 1924 she danced in the chorus touring with the blues singer Mamie Smith. In 1927 she toured in the chorus that accompanied Bessie Smith's TOBA act.

In contrast to and in combination with her relation to black women performers and backstage maids, Sophie Tucker shaped her stage persona against and through versions of racialized femininity. Sophie Tucker left off singing in the rathskellers of the Tenderloin for her dreams of show business: following the convention of female minstrelsy, she found her feet and established her name as a blackface comedian. Tucker worked in full cork, makeup, and wig, and she adopted a southern accent for her act as "World-Renowned Coon Shouter."[55] She yearned to be free of the makeup; in her autobiography her first appearance on stage without it marks the beginning of her professional ascent. "You-all can see I'm a white girl," Tucker tells her audience. "I'm not Southern . . . I'm a Jewish girl and I just learned this southern accent doing a blackface act for two years."[56] Although she dropped the cork and the accent—"I'm through with blackface. I'll never black up again," she exclaims—Tucker kept her repertoire of ragtime songs and was later booked as the Queen of Jazz.

Yet African American performers remember her fondly. Sissle and Blake sold Tucker their first collaborative piece, "It's All Your Fault," and often worked on her bill as the Dixie Duo. Tucker was one of the few vaudevillians who would appear in conjunction with black acts. Ida Forsyne remembers Tucker defying management, sticking up for Forsyne's right not to appear in cork during their act. Tucker was openly working class and Jewish, and she interpolated Yiddish expressions into her songs. She regularly returned to her hometown of Hartford, Connecticut, and is remembered for her generosity to various Jewish causes and foundations. In the 1930s Tucker would also donate her time to African American causes. Tucker's case furnishes one of the strongest arguments for the historical precedent of cross-racial/interclass alliance, involving cooperation

alisms and white supremacist rhetoric extended between Europe and the United States. In 1921, the year *Put and Take* was staged in New York, white reactionaries staged a white supremacist rally at Madison Square Garden, protesting occupation of the Rhineland in 1917 by French African troops. Lait's review also reflects the decade's eugenicist movement in the United States, which sought to classify the Eastern European immigrants settling in the United States as an inferior people by offering pseudo-scientific codification for anti-Semitic and anti-Catholic sentiment.[60] Paradoxically, certain nativist arguments would claim African Americans as the folk of the nation in the effort to exclude Irish and Italian immigrants. Lait's review reflects the kind of peculiar jostling that making this claim required. He compares *Put and Take* to a white show then playing on Broadway: "On 39ᵗʰ Street another show flivved the night before (the Mask of Hamlet) because Italians were trying to out-Americanize Americans, and here colored folks seemed to have set out to show the whites they are just as white as anybody. They may be as good, but they're different—and, in their entertainment at any rate they should remain different—distinct—indigenous."[61] While Lait meant that "colored folks" should remain true to their native (as in primitive) ways, he certainly does not mean to imply that these "colored folks" had nativist rights. There is an irony here. The assumption underlying the proscription that "colored folks" should "remain indigenous" is that the "colored folks" somehow sprang from the southern soil.

In the United States, the concept of the folk took on a strange cast during this era. In Europe the nation-state model naturalized the connection between the temper of the people and the climate of the lands of their birth. But the United States was a settler colony, and so racist discourses of nativism could not rely on such an ethos. Manifest Destiny drew conquest and domination as the right and the responsibility of the Anglo-Saxon race. Nativist arguments in the United States in the 1920s were leveraged to marginalize Eastern European immigrants, but these discourses of U.S. nativism were constructed in opposition to, rather than out of, the people's direct relationship to the soil. In conquering the original inhabitants of North America, settler colonials utilized a tactic similar to that of the British colonials when they planted their penal colony in Australia. In both colonies, the indigenous people of the "new" land were classified as a people caught in an earlier time, without history. Classified as therefore pre-national, they were disqualified from membership in the civic body.[62] Claiming the inevitability of Anglo-Saxon conquest, discourses of U.S. nativism had to uproot, absorb, or redefine "the native," the indigenous.

The Negro, as one reviewer explains, was an imported indigenous people. But reviews reveal a conundrum inherent to U.S. racist politics: How could African Americans be claimed as the nation's folk, a "people of the soil," while keeping them outside the boundaries of what it meant to be American? In cultural terms, this bred an anxiety of influence. In 1927 after seeing both George Gershwin's *Porgy and Bess* and Miller's and Lyle's *Keep Shufflin* (which ran simultaneously) a writer named William Houghton wrote a long commentary on race and the nation's folk culture. "The conquering colonist arrives, assumes the reins of economic and political power and struts his little day upon the backs of his indigenous victims," he explains. "But unless they refuse his sway and melt away like the North American Indian, he finds himself gradually engulfed in their folk ways and by a process of cultural absorption conquered in his turn." The Negro had then been "imported" to replace the "retreating aborigine" as a peasant class. But the aboriginal's function is not simply physical labor. "Besides occupying the physical and economic gap left by the retreating aborigine, he has taken upon himself his cultural and spiritual function also, so that now most of our folk tales are his and all of our indigenous music."[63]

Houghton describes the effects of "cultural absorption," through which the former slaves have conquered their masters:

> We talk his dialect, we sing his songs, we dance his dances. His drink, gin, is the national drink; his tempo, jazz is the universal rhythm. Whenever we relax we fall under his spell; it is only in our tight working moments that we are free of it. And perhaps not entirely then. In the hum of the machinery that surrounds us, the click of the car rails, the rattle of typewriters, the rataplan of riveters, we are becoming increasingly conscious of that surging syncopation with which the Negro, our former slave, has enslaved us.[64]

Transposed to the urban terrain, the Negro's "surging syncopation" spoke through the rhythms of the industrial climate, and infused the new machine age with a nourishing organicity. Houghton assures that Negroes in the United States, as they "drift[ed] from land into city and factory," would never be able to adapt to the complexities of modern life adequately enough to survive the transition of migration in large numbers, thus retaining a timeless connection to the nourishing soil even in the midst of the city.

Houghton mourns the bleaching of Negro authenticity, which was embodied in the chorus girls. Houghton describes the "engagingly handsome girls" of the *Keep Shufflin* chorus as "so nearly white, many of them, in their rouge and powder that they might almost pass as such." Houghton expressed dismay that black people seemed to prefer going to see *Keep Shufflin* over *Porgy and Bess*. According to his observation, black people formed "a conspicuous element" in the audience for Miller's and Lyle's light comedy, making up almost half of its numbers and even occupying the expensive seats, while they were almost totally absent from the audience for *Porgy and Bess*. The black audience member would rather "feast his eyes upon" the nearly white dancers than attend to the serious tragedy of his race.[65]

COLOR LINE/CHORUS LINE

(Light-skinned) chorus women danced in the crux of a bewildering illogic. Bringing to life the titillating "problem" of miscegenation, the chorus women's dancing forms showed that the color line was sexually drawn through the nation's social geography. Their staged urban presence was a physical spoof on the serious business of color codification in the United States, particularly on the use of color caste to define the nation's "folk" (see fig. 39)

Lew Leslie's show of 1924, *Dixie to Broadway*, elicited a burst of critical commentary. Years later, in *Characteristics of Negro Expression*, Hurston used it as an example of white taste for light flesh. Most contemporaneous white reviewers assessed it primarily as a "well-dressed revue . . . fashioned on the paler things of its kind."[66] Reviews focused their descriptive flourishes on the talents of the Plantation Steppers. For white Harlemites such as Heywood Broun, the chorus women evoked a pleasing mixture of the modern and the primitive. "Although not very much is pure African" in the show, he wrote, the chorus dancers still retained enough of the primitive spirit to exhibit a "passionate fidelity to the eternal verities of tempo not in the inheritance of Nordics." Nature, mimicking modern rhythms, mesmerized and seduced. Broun uses the consumerist side of a

39 The chorus girls from *Shuffle Along*. Billy T. Rose Theatre Collection, New York Public Library for the Performing Arts, Astor, Lenox, and Tilden Foundations.

Fordist metaphor to describe what watching the chorus girls of *Dixie to Broadway* was like: "It is like riding in a racing car through the country in which the landscape cries out to you and in which the beat of the engine is magnified and mimicked by every slim tree along the road." He follows this with a reference to *Salome*, staged by the Lafayette Players in 1923, which he had also reviewed, to explain his intoxication. "Only here does every member of the chorus dance as if she were asking for the head of John the Baptist. And if I am, for the moment, Herod, John is done for." A friend to prominent African Americans making the Harlem scene, Broun gives a blasé, urbane comment on the question of racial difference. "I have always felt that the nearness of Harlem to jungle mood or thought was slightly exaggerated. . . . When I see a Negro child two or three years old come out and dance a litle [*sic*] better than anyone at the New Amsterdam or Winter Garden I grow fearful that there must be certain reservations in the theory of white supremacy."[67]

Reviews of *Dixie to Broadway* written by Harlem's "Negrotarians" offered favorable assessments of the chorus girls' talents and appeal.[68]

Alexander Woollcott—a reviewer for the *World*, a frequent guest at Carl Van Vechten's soirees, and a friend of James Weldon Johnson and other members of Harlem's elite—wrote that Leslie's revue had captured the "spirit of some of [Harlem's] milder honk tonks . . . and brought [them] on downtown . . . which means, of course, that the songs are rather better sung and the dances far, far better danced than they would be if the color line had not been drawn in the casting." He notes with care the chorus girls' refreshing energy. "The entire chorus seems animated with a special delight in being there on that stage at that minute, a fresh and communicable state of satisfaction which the paler sisters of Broadway never seem able to capture," Woollcott concludes.[69]

For sympathetic Negrophiles, the colored chorus girls embodied an innocent, mischievous sexuality. "They are animal in their wantonings, rather than bestial," writes the *Herald Tribune*. "The russet, cinnamon, sorrel, and nutbrown maids . . . get away with the rough stuff better than their blonde associates do. . . . There is a little audacious undressing in the play, but it has an insouciance . . . which makes it subtly incidental, instead of deliberately brazen."[70]

Racialist/primitivist schemas ordained rituals of racial transgression (particularly sexual) as guaranteed sources for spiritual and physical rejuvenation, as native women (like animals and children) were imagined to be more directly in connection with the originary energies of all organic life forms. But taken too far, such transgressions (particularly sexual) could lead to racial contamination and degeneration. The popularization of scientific race thinking made available a host of biological metaphors; even in praise black female bodies were equated with pathogens. *The Herald Tribune* describes Florence Mills as "like a nimble microbe, and she was equally infectious."[71] Watching the women from the safety of the white's only section of a theater, a white spectator was safe from infection. Instead, such one way ocular contact had the power to inoculate. The stage offered a controlled space for ritual forms of racial contact, while the cabaret offered a closer, yet still contained, proximity (see fig. 40).

MONKEY, CHILD, WOMAN, BEAST

The United States emerged from the Great War as a center for technological development and world economic markets, and European nations expanded their empires in Africa and Asia. As the wealth of the colonies

40 Florence Mills. Billy T. Rose Theatre Collection, New York Public Library for the Performing Arts, Astor, Lenox, and Tilden Foundations.

was desired in the city, European audiences took a new shine to black expressive forms. African Americans were the internal subjects of a very wealthy settler colony. African American troupes, particularly chorus women, were in demand, as the erotics of empire were a transnational affair.

During this period of European imperial expansion, particularly disturbing racio-sexual pathologies were forming. Scurrilous misuses of Darwin continued; ideas of race and its sexual transmission were readily imported to and fro across the Atlantic. Such ideas had long been part of the popular imagination as an erotic complex of colonial access. Traveling troupes of chorus women promised racial vitality as well as threatened racial dissolution.

For white people desiring a staged erotics of pure primitivism, the light-skinned legs of the chorus girls showed that the primitive had been tainted, not blessed, by the brush of civilization. In his review of *Put and*

Take, the white reviewer Lait found that the girls "did not turn out the pep expected of colored choruses, which should be wild and in perpetual motion." Much to Lait's frustration, these "children of nature" did not provide enough bare flesh. "There was little display of limbs and arms . . . these children of nature might be expected to bare an occasional knee, at least," he complained. Only the show's finale adequately stimulated Lait. Cora Green "shone like a gem, working with a sinuous abandon that was both nature and art—both jungle and theatre." The ensemble went into a "rabid mob scene of prancing, shouting, moaning, yelling, hopping, shimmying, eye-rolling, wiggling, leaping and fit throwing. At last it was regular darky business," he wrote.[72]

These "fast stepping step children of the south" performed a re-version of the nation's folk, but, according to scientific thought—which was gaining renewed cachet in the field of anthropology and recirculating into the popular—the "children of nature" were also closer in ancestral lineage to animals. The Plantation Steppers from *Dixie to Broadway* were celebrated in the *New York Evening Mail* as nearly bestial "extemporizing on the bambolina, legs and arms slashing about with a fierce, lunatic grace and the whites of eyes and teeth gleaming in animal exultation."[73] Black women had suffered comparative assessment with human's closest cousins, the primates, from the early 1800s onward.[74] With the new era of European colonial domination in Africa and nationalism in Europe came renewed waves of racialist thinking. In 1927, the Berlin Zoo displayed an orangutan, the so-called Red Man of Berlin, whose presence was part of yet another generation of "scientific" discussion of the links between black people and apes. One strain of these discussions depended on a classification system that placed apes, specifically orangutans, as the most evolved species in the animal kingdom, and Africans as the least evolved type from the human species. De Blainville stated that his purpose in examining the (living) Saartjie Baartman, who British and French natural scientists called "the Venus Hottentot" in the early 1800s, was to draw a comparison between apes and Negroes.[75] This thinking led to ridiculous interspecial speculation. An early eighteenth-century rumor went that a group of French scientists had gone to Africa to "experiment with breeding an orangutan and an African woman."[76] The claims of the possibility of interspecies breeding had also come from Britain; in *The History of Jamaica*, Edward Long calls African women as "libidinous and shameful as monkies," taking these "animals frequently to their embrace."[77] Another claimed that the orangutan "was born of the lust of the women of the Indies who mate with apes and monkeys to satisfy their detestable desires."[78] Interspecies breeding was usually assumed to be most probable between black women and apes, but one scientist, Edward Tyson, actually adapted the facts to fit a familiar tale, claiming that male apes preferred blondes.[79] Such pathologically racialist thinking on the results of interbreeding and miscegenation bred a host of animalistic descriptives for the light-skinned chorus women. They were delicately innocent children, playful animals, and bestial sexual carnivores—most often they were all of these qualities combined.

Reviewing the *Blackbirds* revue of 1929 in Paris, a white reviewer named Bolitho, who was purportedly from the South, waxed confessional, perhaps in an attempt to ally himself with the cosmopolitan esthetes he touted as his friends. "I have many reasons to be interested in what happens to the African race," he claims. "I was brought up and schooled among the southern branch of them. . . . I was all stirred up and mixed in the post-war craze in Paris for Negro art that my friends, Andre Salmon and Appolinaire, led." The reviewer works to align himself as racially progressive, but it is obvious that he can only talk of racial difference in the language of intertwined processes of violence and eroticism. As a child, he explains, he received a "cataclysmic thrashing" for having spoken up about the "obvious fact of racial beauty. . . . Truth was too fascinating to me even then, and I had to tell it . . . in a comparison between the lumpy, hairy, bleached coarse-boned, tow haired and common pure whites around us and the infinitely shaded varieties of the brown, black and yellow people too bold for any reply but blows. I still admire not only the fractional mixtures of European and African, whether Bantu, Hottentot or Krooman, but the aboriginal."[80] His autobiographical anecdotes are modeled on the self-explorations of French writers and anthropologists traveling abroad, as well as the long history of scientific fantasies made fact by natural scientists.

Following the defense of his sexual attraction toward colored women, Bolitho describes his trip two years before to visit the famous orangutan at the Berlin Zoo. Like museums, zoos are metropolitan outposts of colonial exploration and anthropological curiosity. Like museums, they stage proof of evolutionary progress and buttress evidentiary claims for white rule, the "territorialisation of a history" extended past national boundaries.[81] This reviewer's trip to the zoo is situated as "fieldwork." The reasoning behind his narrative choice is disturbing, to link the orangutan, the "red man of Berlin," as the "unhappy, tragic progenitor" of the chorus women before him on the stage. He shares his impressions as if they were progressive. "Any one who thinks a monkey is a parody or a joke has never seen the red man of Berlin. Any one who is blind to the sublimity of the ugliness of the Negro at his purest has never looked at him, or never, as I have often done, gazed with awe on the terrific spectacle of the Masai warrior in his own setting." The zoo, the plains of eastern Africa, and the variety stages of Paris are all interchangeable for Bolitho, the connection between the orangutan, the Negro, and the Masai warrior an indistinctly defined lineage. The colored women of the chorus become his next objects of study as part of his "fieldwork" in the city, which was infused with the libidinous language of natural science on the topic of miscegenation. "What a strange, wonderful novelty this octoroon is in the human family," he comments. "There was nothing ludicrous or loathsome then in the unhappy, tragic progenitors of the Negro to-day. . . . The living proofs of the latter fact . . . are these little octoroons. . . . There is an unescapable [sic] morbidity in the beauty of these women, whatever the stock and whatever the proportions of the mixture of bloods."[82] It is unclear where and by whom the bloods were mixed to create the "little octoroons." Their paternity could be the orangutan, the Negro, or the Masai warrior; either way they are half-creatures, abominations. The octoroons bear the signature of morbid pleasures pursued and satiated.

Bolitho was most likely imitating the kinds of racialist language being used in French theater and art criticism during this heady colonial era. Descriptions of black/native dancing women figured as prominently in these discourses as they had, and did, in literary and scientific voyages of discovery. Bolitho was probably reading the work of the anthropologist Michel Leiris, who also greatly admired the *Blackbirds* revues. He most definitely had picked up a copy of Paul Morand's *Magie Noire*, translated into English as *Black Magic* that year, a series of short stories Morand wrote in 1927 and 1928 as he toured the Americas and Africa reading the works of Gobineau.[83] As Brent Hayes Edwards elucidates, such "colonial literature" had a "pretension to social scientific verisimilitude," and true to form, Morand depicts black women as particularly susceptible to atavism.[84] Bolitho had also probably read Andre Levinson's 1927 essay, "The Negro Dance: Under European Eyes," in which Levinson evoked the bestial bloodline of the chorus women. Levinson focused on Baker's performance in *Revue Nègre* for his longer assessment of Negro dance. "Thanks to her carnal magnificence and her impulsive vehemence, her unashamed exhibition comes close to pathos," Levinson wrote.

> The Negro frenzy, although it is completely devoid of any nobility and almost "pre-human," if not actually bestial, can attain to a positive grandeur. Josephine Baker, who was responsible for the Charleston rage in Paris, is an extraordinary creature of simian suppleness—a sinuous idol that enslaves and incites mankind . . . there seemed to emanate from her violently shuddering body, her bold dislocations, her springing movements, a gushing stream of rhythm. It was she who led the spell-bound drummer and the fascinated saxophonist in the harsh rhythm of the "blues."[85]

It was in such reviews as these, Baker says rather facetiously, that she could barely recognize herself.[86]

Baker inherited the title Black Venus, the legacy of Saartjie Baartman. Conjoined with practices of bloody voyeurism, the inherited soubriquet carried with it romantic reveries of white male poetic lust; Levinson linked Baker to the urban romance of Charles Baudelaire and his long-term black model and lover, Jeanne Duvall. Baartman's fame, the collective gift of thousands of Western eyes, was earned first on the museum stage where she was on display in London and Paris between 1810 and 1815, her "callipygian nature" the spectacle of scientific exploration. Whatever verdict may be drawn regarding Baartman's complicity or agency in her own spectacularization while she was alive, the revealing facts remain that her lasting fame was borne out of her dissected body. Autopsied in 1817 in Paris, Baartman was immortalized, postmortem, in another kind of theater. The scientific essays written by Henri De Blainville and George Cuvier after dissecting her body and the essay "Nègre" by J. J. Virey, published in the *Dictionnaire de sciences médicales* in 1819, provided the book for this staging of Euro-racial pathology. They used their anatomical studies to establish the terms of racial difference, inferiority, and sexual deviancy of the darker races. Artist's renderings, engravings, and etchings, as well as the public display of Baartman's "primary and secondary" genitalia, were used as visual evidence of hypersexual black female physiognomy.[87] Baartman's genitals were cast in wax, her brain preserved in a bottle, and her skeleton wired together. Her dismembered remains were then put on display, as were many other preserved cadavers, bone collections, and body parts of Africans and Native Americans kept in museums across Europe and the United States. It was not until May 2002 that France released Baartman's remains from the Musée de l'Homme and returned them to South Africa.[88]

TRAVEL AND DANCE

With every new era of brutal and bizarre raciological proscription, ritual, and practice, African Americans devised various strategies through which to reclaim and define themselves. Forms of mobility were key in claiming subjecthood. Moving around the United States, migrating to and between cities, other nations, and continents, black people countered the claims to their personhood made by tethering geographies: plantation slavery, land-grafted servitude, debt-peonage, segregation. Increased urban migration in the 1910s and 1920s enabled a new phase of self-definition. The urban terrain promised to be a place of innovation and self-invention, the modern age to provide new understandings of what it meant to cultivate the self.

In this era of momentous migrations, African American cultural producers were looking for ways to claim modern subjecthood. To become a people required the construction of a usable past, the claiming of a racial inheritance. African American artists and intellectuals responded with various reassessments of their relationship to the African continent as well as the rural southern United States. Reconstructions of both "homelands" became privileged sites of both literal and literary return. Discourses converged and diverged as to the appropriate strategies for going back or going home, as well as to the potential meaning of these journeys. Going back meant voyaging to actual lands, but it also required flights back in time. To go home, to return to the self, involved chronological leaps into an imagined past to claim lost and disregarded ancestral heritage.

Alternative sources for self-definition were an imperative, but a truly restorative return was impossible. This impossibility was denied, sometimes acknowledged, and often mourned with an urgent nostalgia. Sometimes black artists and writers cleaved to understandings of origin that were often just as fictional as the ubiquitous and virulent racial schemas being drawn around them. Sometimes they capitalized on the dominant versions then circulating, concepts of the folk coming out of European nationalisms as well as celebratory primitivisms. Some forms of Europeanist primitivism were useful in black self-fashionings, but African American interest in these forms was not the same kind of rejuvenation; theirs was a move to reclaim their own folk past and the African lineage of which they had been robbed.

Literary efforts at representing the race were the fruit of fantastic voyages of discovery and return. African American artists rendered some of the most eloquent expressions of black life in the United States while traveling and living outside of the country. Langston Hughes wrote "The Negro Speaks of Rivers" as a nineteen-year-old-boy on the train to his father's home in Mexico and drafted poems for his collection *Weary Blues* while at sea aboard the S.S. *Malone*, traveling between New York and the West Coast of Africa.[89] He wrote jazz-inflected verse while working as a waiter for Bricktop at the Grand Duc in Paris. Here he observed dancers immersed in the music being produced by the African American musicians working there; they too had brought the sound of home (or homelessness) with them. In 1927 and 1928 Claude McKay wrote his novels *Home to Harlem* and *Banjo* while in Marseilles, among the African and West Indian men working the seaports there. Ten years later Zora Neale Hurston wrote *Their Eyes Were Watching God* while doing fieldwork in Haiti. Their eloquent renderings were at times nostalgic, but they were always the result of a change in perspective, the development of a modern view, which was the result of purposeful travels. The modern view combined intense intimacy and unbrookable distance, and it required the ability to record what one saw or felt from above, below, inside, or outside. Modern black self-definition claimed these views, and, most importantly, rights to various black diasporic proximities.

Many of the participants of Harlem's artistic movement were self-consciously drawing on romanticist concepts of the primitive in declaring their cultural legacies. These were familiar, ahistorical notions of the Negro's "psychological complexion," which he had "inherited from his primitive ancestors" and still maintained. Negroes were not a threat to civilization; rather, they brought restorative properties to the modern world, an emotionalism, a "luxuriant and free imagination," as well as a close connection with nature. Negro art was great because it remained inspired by a primitive source.

But according to the black architects of the moment, art needed to travel away from its primitive source in order to, as Albert C. Barnes put it, "bear comparison with the great art expressions of any race or civilization."[90] The fine arts of literature, poetry, painting, and sculpture were assigned as the appropriate forms through which African Americans could shape their cultural heritage as well as affirm their place in the civilized world. Influenced by nineteenth-century European models of cultural nationalism, Alain Locke and other Harlem intellectuals were invested in taking the national stage with their best and finest.[91] Intellectuals such as Barnes stressed the spiritual proclivities of their people. Carnal, fleshly, and profane manifestations of the primitive within had to be trained, or at least contained.

The fathers and midwives of Harlem's New Negro movement therefore tread anxiously when it came to the expressive arts, as did many of the earlier generation of race men and women, with the notable exception of James Weldon Johnson. Among many of the cultural arbiters, popular developments in stagecraft, music, and dance were contentious.

Expressive arts were arts that lived in the body and were therefore far less controllable than the written word. Forms circulated promiscuously between the clubs, the cabarets, and the popular stage. In music, sentiments articulated by Bob Cole in 1903 were echoed in 1925 by J. A. Rogers in his article "Jazz at Home."[92] For Cole, the untrained "Negro spirit" should be retained as the basis for musical form, yet must undergo a process of refinement to "be sophisticated enough to appeal to the cultured musician."[93] Twenty years later Rogers would describe jazz as "a rejuvenation, a recharging of the batteries of civilization with primitive new vigor." However, "the wise," he claimed, must "try and lift it and divert it to nobler channels."[94] Jazz had to be guided out of the cabarets and nightclubs, the dens of dissipation.

But not all black artists felt responsible for filtering the raw material of the folk through the refiner's sieve. Zora Neale Hurston, Claude McKay, and Langston Hughes, all in different ways, rejected with their work what they considered an elitist cultural politic. Any real look at black culture, their work acknowledged, had to celebrate collective music, song, dance, and dramaturgy.

Hurston and Hughes both had music, the popular stage, and drama on their minds. As is common knowledge, Hughes used jazz music and rhythms in his poetry and found both legitimate and variety black theater to be important sites of black expression. Hurston's involvement in expressive arts is less recognized. Hurston did her first stint of travel at the age of twenty-four."[95] In 1925 she penned the play *Color Struck*, a satire of the politics of southern racial segregation that follows a troupe of performers on the way to a cakewalking contest. She continued writing plays, and in 1927, as part of her fieldwork in Eatonville, Florida, Hurston directed a documentary film, capturing footage of such "folk" practices as children's games and a baptism. In 1939, after a disastrous collaboration on the play *Mule Bone* with Langston Hughes, Hurston worked briefly as a drama instructor at the North Carolina College for Negroes in Durham. Her attention to expressive forms continued. In 1942, while living in Los Angeles and writing *Dust Tracks on the Road*, Hurston worked as a consultant for Paramount Pictures and spent time on the film set of the black cast musical film *Cabin in the Sky*, where she met and befriended Ethel Waters. The young choreographer and anthropologist Katherine Dunham choreographed for and danced with her dance troupe in this film.

In her autobiography, Hurston acknowledges just how much the younger generation (implying Katherine Dunham) owed to her own pioneering field research, as well as to her own concert dance productions. For Hurston as an anthropologist, dance was a central form of folk transmission; her theater was related to her fieldwork.

Dance figures in particular ways in the works of Hurston, Hughes, and McKay. Until recently Hurston's connections to dance have been historically obscured. In 1932 Hurston staged a dance concert, *The Great Day*, based on her anthropological work in the Bahamas and in the South.[96] Hughes makes regular poetic references to dance in his poetry. For McKay's characters dance was a fundamental enactment of race recovery.

Dance occupies a specific place in black expressive arts. The utopian primitivism of the 1920s saw dance as the most direct access to the primal originary energies of humankind. In the critical appraisals of such white critics as Havelock Ellis, the primitive had access to the "universal," primal human drives—particularly that of sex, but also of death and hunger—upon which civilization had imposed artificial restraints. For Ellis dance was a fundamental pattern of life.[97] For black art, it provided the most direct rituals for cultural and racial awakenings.

Although live dance performance fell below the mark for the black cultural elite, literary explorations of female dancers and dance rituals were central to projects of racial celebration. The female dancer was a baroque symbol for a state of sexual and spiritual ecstasy. Woman was governed by nature and helplessly receptive and susceptible to outside influences. Her body was a plastic medium, yielding to the influences of rhythm; music opened the channels to the primal drives and her dance embodied them. In black poetic argot, her natural bodily condition granted her mediumistic powers by which she could transubstantiate the sanguinary strains of ancestral legacy called forth by the rhythms of black music. The blood was stirred—discourses of racial inheritance and recovery circulated through her.

In poetry published in *The Crisis* during the 1920s, the female dancer figured centrally in the uneasy enterprise of a search for contact with ancestry. In his poems collected in *Weary Blues*, Langston Hughes celebrated the individual female dancer as an icon of ancestral beauty, whose lithe form restored the rightful presence of black women in history. In his poem "Jazzonia" of 1924, Hughes wrote,

> In a Harlem cabaret
> Six long-headed jazzers play.
> A dancing girl whose eyes are bold
> Lifts high a dress of silken gold . . .
> Were Eve's eyes
> In the first garden
> Just a bit too bold?
> Was Cleopatra gorgeous
> In a gown of gold?[98]

Hughes's poem "Danse Africaine" seeks out the rhythms of black music, the effects of which are captured in the figure of a "night-veiled girl."[99]

> The low beating of the tom-toms,
> The slow beating of the tom-toms,
> Low . . . slow
> Slow . . . low—
> Stirs your blood.

Dance!
A night-veiled girl
Whirls softly into a
Circle of light.
Whirls softly . . . slowly,
Like a wisp of smoke around the fire—
And the tom-toms beat,
And the tom-toms beat,
And the low beating of the tom-toms
Stirs your blood.[100]

In "To a Black Dancer at the 'Little Savoy,'" the female figure of Hughes's reclamatory adoration is a "wine-maiden/Of the jazz-tuned night." This maiden is a full-grown and sexual woman endowed with "Lips/Sweet as purple dew/Breast/Like the pillows of all sweet dreams."[101] Hughes was not afraid of the flesh, but for such aesthetes as Alaine Locke and Jessie Fauset literary representation was a thing apart from actual physical demonstration. Bound in ink, the bodies of the dancing women could be kept safely under control.

When channeling the primitive nature, unharnessed, women dancing freely threatened most directly black claims to a modest cultural propriety. But black women poets also used the iconic power of the dancing woman to dramatize their own black and feminine joy. Sensitive to the ways discourses of racialized femininity depicted black woman as hypersexual and even bestial, their poems were ambivalent about black women's sensual experience. They clung to Victorianist strategies for encoding female eroticism; "spiritual" ecstasy stands in for all sexual expression, or any ecstatic primal animality. Ethel Caution's poem "Last Night" lacks the voyeuristic structure of Hughes's works. Instead the poem's narrator is the dancer herself. The dancer's soul finds an ecstasy in its whirling and twisting body, but this ecstasy is contained:

"Last night I danced on the rim of the moon
   delirious and gay
Then slipped into my sober self
Just ere the break of day."[102]

The ecstasy of Caution's dancer is contained by a return to the white light of day; the ecstasy of Marjorie Marshall's dancer in "To a Dark Dancer," whose "Nile-born grace" challenges even the beauty of the moon, is stilled by death.[103] As a Victorian verse, it implies that it was the dancer's own transgressions that brought her to her gothic end. This poem could also very well have been read as a fearful paean to Florence Mills, who had died just two months before the poem was published.

Zora Neale Hurston outlines one of her own ritual moments of ecstasy in *How It Feels to Be Colored Me*. Hurston sits in the New World Cabaret with an unidentified white friend listening to jazz music. However, she carefully distances herself from identification with the mythotype of the female primitive yielding up her body to the strains of African rhythms. Her instincts having been awakened by the male jazz musicians, Hurston heavily masculinizes her narrative of primal self-discovery. Awakened in the jungle in full battle regalia, Hurston lives "in the jungle way" in the masculine form of a blood-thirsty warrior. Hurston pointedly ignores the most probable presence of the light-skinned chorus there in the cabaret. In fact, she is seemingly the only woman present.[104]

The cabaret figures importantly in Claude McKay's novels *Home to Harlem* (1927) and *Banjo* (1928) as well as in his poetry. In these two novels, instances of pure Negro expression were incarnated most potently in the dancing rituals of Harlem cabarets such as "The Congo," which was patronized by the "unwashed of the Black Belt."[105] But these forms of rejuvenating power were ultimately a homosocial male fantasy. Communality was forged out of rituals of male virility; truly transcendent dancing was a "sacred frenzy of phallic celebration."[106] Restorative racial authenticity was only effectively generated between men, by the sweat and heat, friction and frisson, of male bodies pulsating to the beat of the drums.

In McKay's fictional works women were never so free, as their bodies were always already mediated by the market value of their sexuality. Femininity stood in for the contamination of commercial exchange.[107] In his poem "Harlem Shadows" a young woman represents his "fallen race," forced to "bend and barter at desire's call."[108] In "Harlem Dancer" the lascivious seduction of commercialism in the city is feminized, as the "falsely smiling face" of the lone woman dancer reveals the condition of estrangement from self and community bred in the modern world.[109]

While the individual woman dancer held iconic status in black fiction and poetry, the chorus line remained a figuration from the stage. The women of the chorus stood for a kind of rootless female independence and affirmed the 1920s ideal of pleasure without consequence, of the freedom to cast off the past, of defiance of traditional familial forms and their responsibility to them. By the 1930s their transgressions had to be reversed.

BABYLON GIRLS

It was after the crash of New York's Stock Exchange of 1929 (but before the Harlem "Riot" in 1935) that Sterling Brown wrote his most stinging indictments of the modern age. "Nineveh, Tyre/Babylon/Not much lef'/ of either one," he wrote in "Memphis Blues." "All dese cities/Ashes and rust/De win' sing sperrichals/Through their dust." Cities such as Memphis on the Nile were destroyed by natural disaster, God's wrath visited upon the hordes of sinners.[110] In poems such as "Tin Roof Blues" the poet/ singer states his intention to leave the "do-dirty city," where black people have become a "Gang of dicties an' de rest wants to get that way." He yearns for a return to the South, where "the shingles covers folks mo' my kind."[111] Blues singers like Ma Rainey in Brown's poem "Ma Rainey" were figures who belonged to the South, who spoke to and for the ethos of her people.[112]

Brown's poems acknowledge that the Southland they remember no longer exists, and they mourn its dissolution. Return to a place of collective and self-recognition was no longer possible nor desirable, as the mudsills of rural poverty and racial oppression threatened slow death and suffocation. "Still it's my home sweet home," the singer-poet mourns in "Cabaret."[113]

In 1927 disaster struck on the Mississippi River, when a series of levees broke, flooding the lands below it. Black men were forced into chain gangs and made to clean up the damage. The levee in Caernavon, Louisiana, was intentionally breached with dynamite in strategic places, so as to save affluent areas from flooding by directing the raging waters to lands inhabited by the poor and black. After Greenville, Mississippi, flooded, tens of thousands of black people were stranded on the crest of the levee in muddy water with no food or drinking water. Forced by the National Guard to stay, they were subjected to more violence; women were raped and men forced to labor.

Quickly, in sermons and blues songs and in Brown's poems, the flood took on religious, poetic, and political weight. The flood was both nature's revenge and the concrete effect of the racist and neglectful policies of the industrial United States toward its black population. The flooding of Mississippi in 1927 became a trope of Old Testament judgment (aimed in the wrong direction) for the self-serving materialism of civilization.

Brown embodies his damning ire most directly in the forms of light-skinned chorus girls. A troupe of chorines winds through Brown's poem "Cabaret (1927, Black & Tan Chicago)" as symbols of the seductive, corrupting influence of modernity. The chorines are symptoms of the sins of civilization, which shall make the cities fall, as have the citadels of ancient times. The cabaret is a metaphorical space, recalling Babylon, in whose court the "Rich, flashy, puffy-faced/Hebrew and Anglo Saxon . . . overlords . . . sprawl here with their glittering darlings." The light skin of the chorus girls, the "'Creole Beauties from New Orleans,'" is a reproach of sex and commerce, their beauty the result of lust and artifice.

> The chorus sways in.
> The "Creole Beauties from New Orleans"
> Their creamy skin flushing rose warm,
> *Oh, le bal des belles quarterounes!*
> Their shapely bodies naked save
> For tattered pink silk bodices, short velvet tights,
> And shining silver-buckled boots;
> Red bandanas on their sleek and close-clipped hair;
> To bring to mind (aided by the bottles under the tables)
> Life upon the river . . .

Along with the bootlegged liquor, the cabaret offers up the sale of black cultural memory, corrupted in the form of half naked women with "sleek and close-clipped hair." These women are not rooted in the rural south, but are the products of a rootless roaming trans-urban condition. They come "By way of Atlanta, Louisville, Washington, Yonkers/With stop-overs they've used all their lives."

Brown juxtaposes the chorus line with a chain gang forced at gunpoint into servitude. Beleaguered figures of black manhood, they are "poor half-naked fools, tagged with identification numbers / worn out upon the levees / And carted back to the serfdom / they may never leave again." The immense suffering mourned in this poem does not include the sexual abuse and servitude endured by many black women. Instead the poem pathologizes the young chorus women, directly situating them as willful and uncaring urban courtiers against their poor rural brethren. The "too/ proud high-stepping beauties" bring no relief to the "the black folk" who "huddle, mute, uncomprehending," sheltered at the mouth of the Mississippi River as the flood line recedes. As "the chorus leaps into weird posturings . . . seductive bodies weaving/Bending, writhing, turning," their dancing forms in fact seem to be enacting the demise of their people. The chorus women embody the modern condition as an illness of spirit and a cultural death. The poet's heart cries out for "MUDDY WATER"; he wishes to be freed from the city's limits, to be down in the mud and sacrifice himself with his dying brethren. *"Down in the valleys/The stench of drying mud/Is a bitter reminder of death."*

Brown's literary use of the female chorus line was a dramatization of the class anxieties regularly displaced onto the figures of female chorus line dancers in films and literature produced after the stock market crash. Cultural workers, such as those in the WPA projects of the 1930s, were intent on restoring a heartland to black culture, to the staging of southern black folkways. As the stage reviewer for *Opportunity*, Brown commented and critiqued the forms of folk recovery these cultural workers engaged in. He was often critical of Zora Neale Hurston, accusing her of a blind nostalgia. But he was also a supporter of many of the folk plays written during this period. Brown's poem "Cabaret" is most directly shaped by one of the most popular folk plays of the 1930s, a play called *Green Pastures* by the white playwright Marc Connelly, which was staged in 1930. Brown loved the play, calling it "movingly true to folk life" in his review, and he crafted his apocryphal verse "Cabaret" the same year that the show opened.[114] The folk/biblical tale ran to rave reviews for five years. As *Green Pastures* was incredibly popular, the Warner Bros. studio in Hollywood produced a film version that came out in 1936.[115]

The play and film are framed as stories from the Bible recounted by the minister of a rural Baptist church to a circle of children. It is the story of Babylon and its fall, a narrative that clearly resonates with Brown's poem. The court of the king of Babylon is set as a cabaret, complete with courtesans. Three dancing women enter the court and the king exclaims, "Nobody in the world can squirm like those Babylon Girls!"[116] It seems civilization will indeed fall, prey to hedonism and the seductive wiles of the young women.

Gabriel comes to warn the king to mend his ways before his kingdom falls. With his poem, Brown enters the court as had Gabriel, offering his own vivid warning against the seduction of civilization.

In the film version of *Green Pastures* one of the lovely courtesans working in the king's court, clad in a grass skirt, performs a dance I recognize; this is the same supple dance that the "Girl from Los Angeles" offered in Micheaux's *Swing!*, which was also released in 1936. She is not the same woman, or is she? What her name is, where else she danced, we may never know, but she has traced our steps on the boards.

Despite the ways they were figured as symbols of urban decadence, the sleek-haired girls of the chorus line remained public figures of black mobility. They traveled, purposefully, training in shows on the road, making their way to Chicago and New York "By way of Atlanta, Louisville, Washington, Yonkers/With stop-overs they've used all their lives." The women of the Apollo Rockets recall their own migrations, away from rural peonage. "I was born in the state of Louisiana. I picked cotton when I was a kid, and I knew if I didn't make some kind of change some kind of way I don't know what would happen," remembers the dancer Faye Ray. "I was eleven or twelve when I left home. I wore knickers and cap like a boy, and I rode the rails. I made my way to Shreveport, stayed there and worked. These people came in from Kansas City, they had a show on the road, and they wanted young girls. I was the first one to step up and say, 'take me!' We traveled by train and I made every state just about on that show."[117]

Cleo Hayes is from Greenville Mississippi, and was a dancer at the Grand Terrace in Chicago. "I don't have to tell you why I left. I had stars in my eyes. When I left Mississippi I went to Chicago. I just thought that I had arrived. Like I had stepped into another world."[118] Many in the *Shuffle Along* cast were happy to get out of the United States, and many established themselves in Europe, where they could be loved by their U.S. constituents from afar. After World War II, women still made that move and found work in Europe. Faye Ray remembers, "I started writing to agents abroad. I danced in Paris, and I went to Tehran, I went to Cicely, to Tripoli and Beirut. I learned a song in everybody's language."[119] As had the dancers from a previous generation, Hays, Ray, and countless other young black women provided the black world with a language of the resilient, mobile modern body constituted betwixt and between nation-states and their colonial outposts.

TRANSLOCATIONS:
FLORENCE MILLS, JOSEPHINE BAKER,
AND VALAIDA SNOW

During and after World War I, African American musicians and dancers traveled performance routes carved by earlier performers. They deepened these routes, developing the jazz and jazz dances that took hold as the rhythm and movement of the modern age. Younger artists joined those of the previous generation already working and living abroad. In the decade following the Great War Paris became an important nodal point for black artists and their compositions, although as I point out their presence preceded the war and their itineraries reached much further than France. Through World War I, Belle Davis, Fernandes "Sonny" Jones, Irving "Sneeze" Williams, and Louis Douglas remained in Europe and sometimes worked together. Before moving to London, Belle Davis was directing shows at the Casino de Paris, and Sonny and Sneeze were playing music for Florence Jones at her Paris club, the Chez Florence. They took occasional trips to the American continent. In 1921 Sneeze went to New York as the fifth president of the *Clef Club*, which by this time was an organization of several orchestras touring around the world, appearing in Asia, Australia, Africa, and South America.[1] In the summer of 1923, Sonny Jones, Louis Douglas, and his wife and stage partner Marion Cook toured South America with Mistinguett and sixteen Tiller Girls, appearing in Uruguay, Argentina, and Brazil.

In 1925 new troupes arrived in Europe; a cast including Adelaide Hall and Lottie Gee began touring through Germany in the

41 Louis Douglas and Josephine Baker,
    Revue Nègre. Rainer Lotz collection.
    Used with permission.

Chocolate Kiddies. A few months later twenty-three performers, including Josephine Baker and the clarinetist Sidney Bechet, arrived in Paris to
appear in another New York-based black revue organized to tour overseas.
Louis Douglas had sailed to New York to help the impresario Caroline
Dudley Reagan get the show together. With Douglas's choreography and
direction the *Revue Nègre* made quite a splash in Paris. Douglas didn't
think Baker was the best choice as star for the revue, but he was proven
wrong by the rave reception she received (see fig. 41).[2] Before the year was
out Baker had left the revue, going as the headliner to the Folies Bergère.
Douglas went to Berlin and formed a new troupe, which he named, simply,
Black People. Douglas formed the core of this troupe with key members
of the disbanded *Revue Nègre* cast—Sidney Bechet, the singer Maude De
Forest, and the composer Spencer Williams—as well as members of the
cast of *Chocolate Kiddies*.

   In September 1926, black artists were everywhere. *Black People* was
touring Scandinavia and the Netherlands; the jazz trumpeter Valaida
Snow was in Shanghai. Traveling back to the United States from London earlier that year, she had joined her sister Lavada, the conductor Jack
Carter, and an orchestra of Chicago-based jazz musicians for a tour of

China, the Philippines, and the Dutch East Indies.[3] Florence Mills, Edith Wilson, and a cast of chorus girls from the New York shows were opening in the first of Lew Leslie's *Blackbirds* revues in London.[4] Black expressive culture continued to travel with a transnational currency.

This chapter continues a consideration of the relationship of black women artists to the formation of modern space and bodies. I return to the problem of national belonging (to and in) for black Americans as well as for subjects of European colonial rule, with a focus on Florence Mills, Josephine Baker, and Valaida Snow, each of whom were in complex representational relationships to multiple places and constituencies. I consider here the contingencies of national belonging for Mills, Baker, and Snow in the contexts of British and French colonialism, European jazz culture, and World War II.

Florence Mills was an elected favorite among black stage people; she was an artist's artist: in their memoirs black performers and writers recall Florence Mills with admiration. Despite of, and perhaps because of, her fame in white-produced stage revues in London, black Harlem loved Mills. Her outspoken race loyalty seemed to quiet black anxieties about the deleterious effects of cosmopolitanism and commercialism. Before her sudden death in 1927, Mills represented black urbanity and cultural capital, Harlem's extension into and influence upon the rest of the modern world, both its self-conscious import and its equally self-conscious return to itself.

Throughout the book I have been reading Baker not, as she is often read, as the distillation of black creativity from this period but as another artist within the transnational stage community as well as in relation to the long-circulating stage techniques from which she drew. In this chapter I consider what I find to be Baker's most interesting moments, her public performances of loyalty to France, focusing on her travels and tours in the French colonies of North Africa. Raising money for the Free French Forces, she staged herself as a representative of de Gaulle's resistance. Her role was as an ambassador for France's *mission civilisatrice* in that country's colonies.[5] "J'ai deux amours," she sang, but her representational roles cannot be understood as simply dual. They were multiple and contradictory; she represented the United States abroad, most visibly troubling and doubling during the war as she performed at segregated U.S. officer's clubs in North Africa. While she represented the colonies in Paris, she also represented Paris in the desert, even as France's colonial subjects remained unfree.

Leaving, or decentering, Paris lets us remember another artist, the jazz trumpeter Valaida Snow, who was best known in London and Scandinavia. While Baker is the most well known of the black women performers who cross-patriated in the first part of the twentieth century, Valaida Snow's European tenure has remained the most obscured. While the French embraced Baker, Scandinavians were Snow's most enthusiastic European constituency. This chapter sorts through the ambiguous terms of her detainment in Nazi-occupied Denmark, which Snow herself skillfully obscured upon her return to the United States. Such a project raises questions regarding the politics of historical recuperation. How can histories—particularly lost histories—of black women be constructed in ways that remain sensitive to the slippery properties of fact (and its often unsupportive banality) and wary of the temptations of recuperative triumphalism? This last chapter raises and perhaps leaves us alone with such questions.

HOME AIN'T NO PLACE FOR ME: THE CONTINGENCIES OF NATIONAL BELONGING

Black urban artistic itinerancy was forged out of the ambivalent terms of black belonging to and in Europe and the United States. For many African Americans, the United States was not a safe place to return to; rather, it was a place one was glad to have the opportunity to leave. "Home Ain't No Place for Me," ran an early song by James Weldon Johnson. On the one hand, traveling abroad was an extension of African Americans' already multi-sited lives. In her autobiography, Ada Bricktop Smith recalls her impressions of her first trip to Europe. "I barely knew where Paris was and I didn't know a word of French, but I'd traveled a lot of cities in the United States, and it didn't seem to me that Paris would be much different."[6] But on the other hand, there were marked differences. At home artists' survival depended on vigilant newsgathering regarding the climate of racial violence in the towns on their performance circuits. Going abroad was a chance to leave behind such overtly life-threatening conditions, but artists knew full well that a different set of negotiations was required. On the light side, this meant wrangling a passport and a birth certificate (a challenge for many black people in the United States). And there were decided benefits unavailable stateside. Learning new languages, artists developed cultural mobility. Many artists were able to improve the lives of their family members, arranging for mothers, fathers, and siblings to join them abroad. At a remove from stateside caste relations, members of the European and British aristocracy often loved them, albeit with forms of love shaped by questionable agendas. During the interwar period, the moneyed elites were Bricktop's main clientele at her Paris club. Whatever concessions were to be made in her complex professional relationships with these people, the United States, with its institutionalized forms of racial oppression, remained an even more troubling place to call home.

But artists were not so naïve as to believe life abroad was a free and clear escape from racial terrorism.[7] Nor can the varying terms of their contracts with other countries be assessed simply as the trading of one set of racisms for another, a set of Faustian compromises. Black artists understood that freedom for them was a fragile thing, and that its instability crossed, or disregarded, national boundaries. The terms of "freedom from" and "freedom to" were always conditional and contingent, subject to turn quickly and sometimes lethally against them. Because they were at home everywhere and nowhere, their survival required spontaneity, agility, and awareness of the political conflicts and currents around them. National boundaries often provided crucial defense, but just as often they left little protection against the complex webs of race pathologies.

Beginning in the mid-1920s, all over Europe nationalistic and eugenicist movements were forming at the same time as European colonial control increased. By the mid-1930s, the National Socialists in Germany had begun their parade in earnest. When the defense of Free Europe commenced after the Nazis occupied Poland in 1939, the experiences of African American artists working abroad bore out the complexities of their navigations between the changing tides of globally circulating race discourses and the rocky shores of arbitrary and shifting nation-state alliances. In the century of camps, forms of racial oppression were global, the dialectic accompaniment to the realization of the Enlightenment's promises.[8]

Conditions quickly changed for Bricktop and other black musicians and performers centered in Paris after Nazi Germany's invasion of Poland in 1939. Artists were faced with the instability of their status in Europe, aware that they were particularly vulnerable, as both racialized subjects and representatives of the United States, in the flux of French ambivalence regarding German occupation. Bricktop remembers the anxieties shared by black entertainers in Paris when they were warned by the American consulate to leave. Bricktop had to make the difficult decision whether or not to return to the United States, which, after sixteen years, had become for her an "unknown world." She writes, "As foreigners, we were subject to internment in a concentration camp. Some entertainers, like Charlie Lewis and Arthur Briggs, decided to take their chances—and they wound up in prison. Opal Cooper decided to go back 'home.' I didn't know what to do."[9] Bricktop ultimately chose to stay living abroad. She went to New York for the duration of the war, but after a failed attempt to reestablish herself there she went to Mexico City. Finally she settled back in France, returning to Paris in 1952.

The jazz trumpeter Valaida Snow was one of the artists who decided to "take their chances," remaining in Europe despite the impending war. Snow worked and lived abroad for the greater part of her career and the war shaped her experience there.[10] Snow did not return to the United States when Americans were encouraged by the French consulate to leave in 1939 but went instead to Scandinavia. Following the Nazi occupation of Denmark, Snow was unable to leave, remaining in Copenhagen until May 1942.

Despite the absence of segregationist policies and the presence of enthusiastic European fans, strains of racialist thinking, both ridiculous and virulent, met the artists at every port. "The dark world is about not to conquer but to subdue Europe culturally," wrote one paranoid Dutch reviewer of Black People. "There is swing in those syncopes, in that tremendous pace, in the capers of those elastic bodies. But this is the curse of the Nigger music. It thoroughly shakes us, stretches our already overstrained nerves, has an affect on us vexed Europeans like cocaine does."[11] In his fearful view, the cross-Atlantic transmission of jazz threatened cultural impotence and regression. "They have got us all (by the balls!). . . . Is this the last symptom of the disease which began during the war and which we in the Old World still have to go through in order to emerge as being cured? Or is this the sure sign of an irreversible decline?"[12] As black artists picked up European instruments and methods, the danger of European cultural decline loomed.

They have adopted our bad habits . . . the ladies have greased their curly hair and appear with Titus heads or a man's crop; they accompany their cannibal dances with adaptations from European classics and they do not use any longer their drums but rather violins and clarinets, and a Steinway grand. This is how they catch us and bring us back to a cultural level which is thousands of years closer to that of our ancestors according to the theories of Darwin.[13]

Forms of cultural and racial assimilation threatened to infect an imagined European purity, as black people insinuated themselves into European culture. Considered a race susceptible to sensual pleasures, they assimilated the "bad habits" of European decadents, catching Europeans in a web of their own weaknesses.

With the involvement of the United States in the war had come a shift in the balance of power between the United States and European countries. Europeans to both the left and right of the political prism were wary of U.S. dominance, believing that the United States was poised to eclipse European cultural preeminence with its shiny new products. European reviewers called on the developed cultural and intellectual traditions of the Old World and classified the United States as still primitive in its youth. As signs of the country's savagery, some cited the continuing persecution of its black folk and white Americans' marked susceptibility to their rhythms. "In America, there is deep rooted contempt for the Negroes," continues the Dutch reviewer. "But the Yankee's feeling is more primitive and they are already subdued, and now Europe is about to be conquered, via America and with the help of Americans, by this 'art' of these primitive peoples."[14] Just who (what) was American and who (what) was primitive it is hard to decipher.

Not all Europeans thought the presence of black artists was an infectious disease threatening the purity or health of the European peoples. Europeans' contact with black artists, and their quickly learned interpretations of black artistic practices offered a bolstering dose of vitality, an inoculation for the mentally and physically degenerative effects of the Great War and the bloody body count of advancing industrialization. Particularly for the French, the desire was for the youthful colonies to nourish the ailing empire. African Americans came from a particular kind of colony, traveling with the wind of ultra-modern prosperity behind them. They traveled the cities and provinces of Europe partly as representatives of the New World, of its expanding technological advances and cultural markets.

FLORENCE MILLS: "AN EXOTIC DONE IN BRASS"

Revisionist feminist histories, seeking redress for the masculinist blues man trope of black migration, have successfully restored women blues singers as key representatives of black constituencies. Alongside Ma Rainey and Bessie Smith we also need to recognize a host of black women from the variety stage. Chorus girls, comedians, songstresses, dancers, and artists such as Florence Mills also represented migrating black people and resituating black communities (see fig. 42). The set of qualities Mills brought to the stage resonated with a more optimistic perspective in the 1920s among African Americans toward the effects of mobility and urban migration on African American culture and society. Her reedy-toned, thin-legged persona affirmed the light-hearted right to an independent young womanhood that many black women in the cities were living for themselves. Mills's trilling voice and quick step suggested a joyful but sophisticated exuberance. She was the New Black Woman—urban, emancipated, cultivated, traveling abroad to represent the black cultural capital and the mobility of its people. One reason she remained a loved figure for black people in the United States is that she consistently asserted her race belonging. "I do not live in Park Avenue," she told a European interviewer. "I love being with my own people. I feel at home amongst them. We do not seek white people's society, and we are a happy family, although a large one. In America we have our own restaurants and cabarets and theatres, and your people come to see our shows. The white people say, 'let's go slumming.' They seek us out."[15] Mills left her heart in the neighborhood.

No film or musical recordings have ever been found of Mills. But European, British, and American reviews as well as her fellow performers' accounts describe her as a "lithe and nervous embodiment" of ineffable, contrasting qualities.[16] Small-boned and high-strung, with a plaintive bell-like voice and a delicate nimble form, she was compared and contrasted with Baker, described as a "rococo Creole" to Baker's "simian" animality.[17]

Mills was not sexualized as was Baker. Instead she is described as prepubescent and like a work of primitivist modern art. "This sensational little personality, slim, jaunty, strung on fine and tremulous wires, con-

42 Florence Mills,
    Dixie to Broadway.
    Beinecke Rare Book and
    Manuscript Library,
    Yale University.

tinues to tease the public's sense of the beautiful and odd," reads a review from a white newspaper, the *Evening Mail*. "There is an impudent fragility about her, a grace of grotesqueness, a humor of wrists, ankles, pitching hips and perky shoulders that are not to be resisted. She is an exotic done in brass."[18] These contrasting qualities were noted in her singing voice. For a reviewer in Liverpool, Mills "captured" audiences with her "amazing throat noises and screeches," which he describes as those of "disconsolate 'high brown' women."[19] Heywood Broun wrote, "She does not precisely sing, but she makes strange high noises which seem to fit in somehow with a rapid fire sort of sculpture. Sometimes the intent is the creation of the grotesque and then it fades into lines of amazing beauty. Now I have seen grace."[20] Broun's review builds on her angularity to describe her as a work of abstract primitivist art.

Her strange ability to combine grotesquery and grace is reminiscent of the black children performers from the turn of the century. Mills began performing as a child, and her stylistics were a conscious use of such eccentric techniques. "Do you know how the Charleston came to New York?" she asks an English reviewer. "It came on the feet of the coloured picaninnies."[21] Mills was raised and trained as a performer, winning a cakewalk contest at a Black Patti's Troubadours amateur night. "Baby Florence" was then added as a specialty to Williams's and Walker's comedy *Sons of Ham* in 1902. She sang "Miss Hannah from Savannah," a song associated with Ada Overton Walker. There is a long-standing legend that Overton Walker personally trained Florence for the song, but this is impossible as Overton Walker was in London at the time.[22] After working in the picaninny chorus of Pauline Hall, the "Cuban and African Midgets," Mills and her family moved to New York, where Florence and her sisters Olivia and Maude worked the variety circuits as the Mills Sisters. Hitting the TOBA time, Mills landed at Chicago's Panama Café, where she met and teamed up with Bricktop and Cora Green, performing as the Panama Girls until 1917. After working with her future husband, the tap dancer U. S. Thompson, in a troupe called the Tennessee Ten, she replaced Gertrude Saunders in *Shuffle Along* in 1921. It was her performance here, notably her rendition of Blake's song "I'm Craving for That Kind of Love" that brought her to wide public attention. She then took a contract with Lew Leslie as the lead act for his newly opening Plantation Club and as the lead in his first revue set for London. Her quick-fire success brought begrudging praise from the notoriously competitive Ethel Waters. "Florence was vivacious, a cutie, and a whirlwind when it came to selling a song," Waters recalled.[23] "I felt that Broadway and all downtown belonged to Florence," Waters remembers, at the prospect of filling in at the Plantation for Mills while she toured. White Manhattan may have been her territory (northeastern moneyed whites her captive audiences), but Mills still belonged to Harlem. It was Mills's frequent tours, her trips to Britain and France and her triumphant returns to New York that galvanized her in black cultural memory (see fig. 43).

In the summer of 1926 Mills went to Paris as the showcased star of Lew Leslie's first *Blackbirds* revue. After an eight-week run in Paris, the show moved to England, where Mills fell ill while on tour in the provinces. "I feel quite right on the stage," she told the English papers, "but the minute I come off, I simply collapse."[24] Recuperating from her collapse, Mills and Thompson stayed with Belle Davis at her home in London. The black English singer Mabel Mercer replaced Mills in Leslie's revue.

Mills's health was the consequence of overwork, but also of advanced pelvic tuberculosis. After visits to Baden Baden and other European

43 Florence Mills. Beinecke Rare
Book and Manuscript Library,
Yale University.

health centers, Mills decided to return to New York for treatment. But her
condition was too far advanced and she died in New York's Hospital for
Joint Diseases on November 1, 1927, a week after her operation.[25] A huge
public outpouring of grief followed her death. For the first two weeks in
November, the major New York newspapers as well as African American,
British, and French papers gave front-page coverage to her death and then
her funeral in Harlem.

Mills's final return to Harlem, to die among her people, resonated as
a narrative of continued race loyalty. This return sealed her even more
securely into the history of the U.S. black capital. Mills was perceived as
a product of Harlem, anthologized after her death in the *Negro Digest*.
"Harlem . . . was . . . proud of Florence Mills. . . . She was one of them,
dancing and laughing and living as they did; she was Harlem itself, and she
always loved Harlem and came home to Harlem, despite all those jewels
and motorcars and such, whenever she could," Ward Greene wrote.[26] Her
significance as a symbol of Harlem was in fact produced by her success
in England and France, as with the black soldiers of the 369th Regiment
returning from the war. Marching on Fifth Avenue up into Harlem, the
soldiers returned to the city and claimed it as home. Recognition from

abroad was leverage, legitimating black claims to full citizenship in the United States.

Florence Mills's funeral was the largest theatrical event in New York that season. Surrounded by over 150,000 mourners, Mills's hammered copper coffin wended its way through Harlem—down to 125th Street, over to Lenox Avenue, and north again to the Mother Zion A.M. E. church on 137th Street. The hearse and all of the cars in the cortege were heavily burdened with wreaths, sprays, and blankets of flowers. Mills's funeral procession was made up of an all-star cast. Behind thirty little girls in gray crepe de chine walked Mills's honorary pallbearers, Ethel Waters, Cora Green, Edith Wilson, Gertrude Saunders, Maude Russell, Ada Ward, Lena Wilson, and Evelyn Preer, also in gray crepe de chine and gray moire hats.[27] Carrying her coffin into the church were Will Vodery, Flournoy Miller, Aubrey Lyles, Charles Gilpin, and Hamtree Harrington. Inside Jesse Shipp read notes of condolence from around the world. Many musicians performed, including the spiritual singers Julius Bledsoe and Clarence Tisdale, and Hall Johnson directed the one hundred choral singers.

The streets were the stage for a performance of grief. Ten thousand people visited her body at Howell's Mortuary on 137th and Seventh Avenue while Mills's body lay in state the week before the funeral. Harlemites paid their respects, "headed by housewives and their children in arms" and "schoolchildren." Harlem's premier portrait artist, the photographer James VanDerZee, took a series of photographs of Mills as she lay in her open casket and included them in his collection of mortuary portraits, *Harlem Book of the Dead*. Like his other photographs in this collection, these photos of Mills read as poetic elegies, giving black Harlem a view onto its own life. The streets, doorways, and sidewalks were packed for blocks outside the church during the funeral, and "scores during the two hours the service lasted were overcome," including the cornet player Robert Brown, who fell dead of heart failure.[28]

Florence's cast mate Juanita Stinnette staged the funeral's punctuating moment of grief. While singing a song she and her stage partner Chappy Chappelle had composed for the funeral, Stinnette collapsed, sobbing and shrieking "Florence!" The flourishing touch to the funeral was the release of hundreds of blackbirds as the cortege reached 145th Street on the way to Woodlawn Cemetery in the Bronx. Mills's coffin was lowered into the ground, covered by six carloads of flowers.

Mills's funeral was a significant moment of self-recognition for black variety stage performers based in New York. The public lavishness of her funeral was also in honor of the previous decade's losses, the early and tragic deaths of its most public popular performers. Ernest Hogan had died of heart failure on May 20, 1909 at the age of forty-six. George Walker had gone next. Falling ill with symptoms of late syphilis early in 1909, he deteriorated over the next two years, dying in January 1911 at the age of thirty-eight. Bob Cole also fell ill with syphilis, and in August 1911 he committed suicide, drowning himself in a lake outside the sanatorium where he was being treated.[29] Their deaths curtailed a period of artistic momentum and collective productivity. More tragic deaths followed; Ada Overton Walker died of "kidney infection" in October 1914 at the age of thirty-four, and James Reese Europe was murdered by one of his drummers in 1919. Bert Williams died at the age of forty-six in March 1922 of pneumonia, heart problems, and anemia, his heavy drinking having weakened his body.[30] These deaths marked historically critical moments of black stage life. And now Mills had died, at the peak, or end, of a period of black stage successes and black female stage presence, which had begun the decade with *Shuffle Along*.

The deaths of these public figures had a wider resonance, as black stage performers were metaphorical extensions of a larger black public presence. James Reese Europe's funeral was the first public funeral ever allowed for a black person in New York City. Occurring only months after the triumphant return of the 369th Regiment from Europe, his funeral dramatized the betrayed hopes following the return of the black soldiers to their homeland. Mills's funeral eight years later marked a different set of successes and disappointments, but it hinged upon the same politics of race and place. Harlem had claimed both of them, and the representation of modern black subjecthood involved both voyages of discovery and the modernist project of return. Mills's final return punctuated the end of a period of optimism that believed public attention to the best and finest the race could produce would force white recognition and bring about lasting social improvement.

44 Josephine Baker, *Chocolate Dandies*. Billy T. Rose Theatre Collection, New York Public Library for the Performing Arts, Astor, Lenox, and Tilden Foundations.

UNE PETITE TONKINOISE

Like Florence Mills, Josephine Baker had performed as a young teenager. Like Mills, she remembered the eccentric dancing of black children performers in her routines. Their eye crossing and angular bodily poses were iconic, and Baker adopted them as her own (see figs. 44 and 45). In *Revue Nègre* Baker recycled eccentric dances. In "Darkey Impressions," her hyperbolic mimicry was a series of animal dances, bodily impressions against a shadowed screen. Baker would retain this act, repeating it in the 1932 film *Zou Zou*. A German reviewer found Josephine Baker's dances "without variation," as they were so similar to the scampering routines of the black children performers touring the European variety circuits. But he did notice her staged hyper-physicality and described her buttocks as "flexible as a chocolate coloured semolina pudding, her final Venus is of an unmistakably Callipygian nature."[31]

Baker's presence referenced the masculinist European fantasies of the female colonial subject imported to the city. As this generation's "Black Venus," Baker was the means by which the violence of gruesome pathological dissection was once again muffled under romantic reveries of male

45 Josephine Baker, *Chocolate Dandies*. Billy T. Rose Theatre Collection, New York Public Library for the Performing Arts, Astor, Lenox, and Tilden Foundations.

poetic lust. Possession of the primitive female was proof of the bohemian male's artistically questing spirit, abroad and at home. "The plastic sense of a race of sculptors came to life and the frenzy of the African Eros swept over the audience. It was no longer a grotesque dancing girl that stood before them, but the black Venus that haunted Baudelaire," the dance critic Andre Levinson wrote from Paris.[32]

All of Baker's French stage and screen appearances, including *Revue Nègre* in 1925, Folies Bergère in 1926, her first film, *Sirène des Tropiques* in 1927, *Zou Zou* in 1934, and *Princess Tam Tam* in 1935, were based in discourses of French colonial encounters in Southeast Asia and North Africa. She was the embodiment of the importation of the exotic products to the metropole and subsequent narratives of contact in popular romantic fiction. Readings of Baker, as a précis for French Negrophilia and primitivism, are plentiful. What is germane to my argument is that her multi-dispositioned body, alternately Haitian, Tunisian, Vietnamese, was staged in a mediating role during World War II, but only as she remained a celebration of the benevolence of French colonial regimes.

Her performance of loyalty to de Gaulle, especially in her eighteen-month tour across North Africa, was part of this celebration. What does it mean when an artistically expressive black body represents a national body that does not represent its subjects, that is, nations whose law and practice have been to subjugate particular populations? Her vision was to represent the universal ideals of brotherhood and equality. Her role as such was as a mediating figure between the nations and races. And perhaps she represented that for a time, for the African American soldiers stationed in Europe, as well as for the Francophone Caribbean soldiers fighting against Vichy France, such as Frantz Fanon, who watched Baker's films and saw her perform in North Africa. But this loyalty to a concept of universal brotherhood was actually based in a belief in a sovereignty that made false claims, as the young soldier Fanon and his fellow Martiniquans, stationed in France, realized.[33]

In the early 1930s, with France beginning to feel the effects of an economic depression, the colonies represented a very real sense of renewal, their riches in the form of labor, raw material, and luxury goods spelling hope for economic recovery and national prestige. The colonial exposition of 1931 represented this hoped-for regaining of economic and imperial power. Baker was not elected as the exposition's royal representative. Instead, replacing Mistinguett at the Casino de Paris, she reigned as queen of the colonies on the French dance hall stage. The exposition and the cabaret were two theaters for the enactment of the fantasy of French colonialism as the welcome absorption of new subjects into the French social body.

France prided itself on its model of assimilation for its colonial subjects. According to the former colonial administrator Hubert Deschamps, colonialist policies were made "on the basis of real evolution," allowing the natives to be educated in the ways of the civilized.[34] According to many others, such as Albert Saurraut, colonialism was the condition under which natives could be redeemed and welcomed into civilization. "It does not oppress, it liberates; it does not exhaust, it makes fertile; it does not exploit, it shares," wrote Saurraut in 1923; "In the shapeless clay of the primitive multitudes, it models the form of a new humanity."[35] Deschamps celebrated 1919 as marking the "end of the conquests" and opening "the era of peaceful achievements," for France brought peace to the warring savages. "It seemed that, taken as whole, the Africans, despite taxes and dependence, appreciated the cessation of domestic wars and the *razzias* (slave raids) and local tyrannies," he writes. "They were grateful for the enlarging of horizons, the opening of roadways, and a certain liberty for the individual."[36] On the streets of Paris, with her beloved pet leopard Chiquita, or strolling through the exposition, Baker was a combination of the infinitely metropolitan and the timelessly savage, the colonial subject produced inside the metropole. She represented the triumphant success of the French *mission civilisatrice* in bequeathing freedom and democracy to its colonial subjects.

While the colonial exposition went on, *Paris qui remue* at the Casino de Paris drew in huge crowds night after night. Baker's opening skit followed essentially the same plot as she performed for the Folies Bergère in 1926. In this piece she starred as "La Petite Tonkinoise," the mistress to a French colonial administrator in the French colony of Tonkin (Vietnam). In an additional skit, with much the same plot, she played Ouwana, the lover of a French colonial, this time in North Africa. Ouwana yearns to return to France with her love, but her tribe refuses her permission to go. For this skit, the show's composer, Vincent Scotto, wrote what was to be remembered as her signature tune, "J'ai Deux Amours."

All of Baker's French stage and screen appearances were based in discourses of French colonial encounters in Southeast Asia and North Africa, their plot lines those of nineteenth-century French romantic Orientalist fiction. Baker's vehicles (particularly *Princess Tam Tam*) mirror most closely such narratives as Gérard de Nerval's *Voyage en Orient*, a text remembered as the culmination of the genre. In his book, Nerval buys a young Javanese slave girl and teaches her to speak.[37] The voyages en Orient were male voyages of self-discovery and authorial restoration. On each voyage, rituals of contact with native women were central to the retooling of the author's pen, the explicit masculinization of authority/authorship forged out of sexual narrative. Artists traveled to countries boundaried as the Orient by religious and racial topographies in order to replenish their creativity and affirm their authorial powers, but also to launch criticisms of European civilization. "Writers asserted the primacy of oriental civilization in order to place themselves at odds with their own bourgeois culture," Miller writes. "The *Voyage en Orient* was not merely an escape from the ennui of Europe but also a pilgrimage designed to enrich one's artistic production."[38]

Baker remembers rehearsing the finale to her Casino de Paris show. "Again and again we rehearsed a flamboyant number about the French colonies, which included Algerian drums, Indian bells, tom-toms from Madagascar, coconuts from the Congo, cha-chas from Guadeloupe, a number laid in Martinique during which I distributed sugar cane to the audience, Indochinese gongs, Arab dances, and finally my appearance as the empress of jazz."[39] At the Casino de Paris Josephine wore what she remembers as her favorite costume, a tight body suit fitted with a huge pair of electrified butterfly wings. She was indeed *le papillon*, emerging from her native cocoon into a vision of urban splendor. The skit accompanying this costume, in which a band of hunters tore off the papillon's wings, was one of lost innocence and native freedoms, of the "rape fantasy so closely allied to the sexual fantasy of French colonialism."[40] Pleasure and violence were intertwined, and forms of possession were sexualized.

Possession works as a trope for the mimetic contact Europeans sought. It becomes a poetic refrain in the anthropological writings of discovery, of *l'art nègre*. Possession was a key concept for French ethnographers and artists during the surrealist period. To be possessed promised a reconnection with repressed aspects of the self; it promised a reunification of self, alienated by modern life. The unconscious was a deep well of repressed and primal urges. Primitives, island, and African peoples existed in coeval time, but within them these urges and animal instincts remained untamed. The meaning of the repressed differed for Sigmund Freud than for Andre Breton and his fellow surrealists. For the latter, this space within was premised "less on dark, primordial and perverse infantile contents a la Freud than on '*one original faculty* of which the eidic image gives us an idea of which one still finds a trace among primitives and children.'"[41] Speaking in gendered and sexualized terms, Michel Leiris writes of his desire for a kind of possession through a dual directed penetration. "I'd rather be possessed myself than study possessed people," he wrote. He writes of this lust for possession as "an ardent sensation of being at the edge of something whose depths I will never touch, lacking, among other things, an ability to let myself go as necessary, the result of factors very hard to define but among which figure prominently questions of race, of civilization, of language."[42]

The state of possession was not limited to a pre-industrial terrain; the urban space of the industrial West had its own facilities for accessing this state. One could be overstimulated by the sights, sounds, and rhythms of the city, this state both a desirable celebration and a thing to be feared.

The mechanization of modern life was an ambivalent source of power and pleasure. Its effects were hypnotic, seductive, potentially unmanning. Its pleasures were symbolized by jazz. "[Jazz] functioned magically, and its means of influence can be compared to a kind of possession," Michel Leiris writes.

> Swept along by violent bursts of tropical energy, jazz still had enough of a "dying civilization" about it, of humanity blindly submitting to The Machine, to express quite completely the state of mind of at least some of that generation: a more or less conscious demoralization born of war, a naive fascination with the comfort and the latest inventions of progress . . . an abandonment to the animal joy of experiencing the influence of modern rhythm.[43]

Leiris describes a state of pleasure created within and elicited by a compression of time and space. "Violent bursts of tropical energy" paradoxically expressed a modern urban condition. Leiris continues, "In jazz, too, came the first appearance of Negroes, the manifestation and the myth of black Edens which were to lead me to Africa and beyond Africa, to ethnography."[44] The shock of modern rhythms, channeled by the Negro, would overtake the Western body.

It was Baker's physical presence as the female primitive in the heart of the metropole that excited European desires; Baker's twirling and twisting body suggested the excitement of proximity to an alternative and anterior time and space. But Baker was also a figure of the ultra-modern, born and bred far away from "home"; she was a symbol of modern triumphs realized in the United States as well as the gifts of civilization with which the French bequeathed their colonies.

Baker followed her success in the Folies with an extended tour outside France under the management of her husband and agent, Pepito Abatino. Debates about sex and the racial sanctity of the national body raged around her dancing form during this tour. In Austria and Germany, her reception was shaped by long festering racist resentment following France's mobilization of troops from its colonies in the occupation of the Rhineland during World War I. Representing France, troops had come from Senegal, Morocco, Algiers, and Tunisia. The black soldiers were demonized in the popular press, which depicted them as savage rapists, threatening the innocent purity of Aryan women. Although generated out of Germany the reactionary backlash whipped throughout Europe, the United States, and South America. Eugenicists in the United States held a rally in Madison Square Garden in 1921 in which twelve thousand people demonstrated against what was described in the racist German press as the "Schwarze Schmach am Rhein" (the black horror/humiliation on the Rhine").[45] Baker was banned from making appearances in Munich because of this association with invading Senegalese troops, and she was met in Austria with "disastrous publicity."[46] Baker recalls, "The capital was flooded with leaflets denouncing me as the 'black devil. . . .' There was no way to ban me from Vienna, but it was made clear that I was the embodiment of moral decadence."[47] With economic crisis, Weimar Germany—decadent, modernist—was folding, and conservative political influences were taking over. Strains of racialized thinking were hardening into much more systematic reactionary politics; Adolph Hitler's *Mein Kampf*, published in 1925, was mustering troops. Galvanizing nationalist sentiment in Eastern European countries erased the memory of the many years in which black performers had toured through them.

As Baker toured Europe and South America over the next two years, protests and counterprotests gathered around her body—from the dubious support of *Nacktkultur* enthusiasts in Vienna to Catholic moral outrage from President Hipolito Irigoyan in Argentina.[48] Stern nationalistic calls for racial purity were coded as calls for moral sanctity, shaping around Baker the threat of seductive contamination and libertarian hedonism. The nativist and racially reactionary protests rising in the wake of Baker's tour were framed as moral objections to Baker's nude and scantily clad dancing. But her perceived nudity had little to do with the amount of clothing Baker actually wore. Masculinist trajectories of militarism, sex, and power inflected Baker's brown body as naked proof of the black rape of the Rhineland, which itself mirrored German desires for the genetic overthrow of Europe.

Baker's response was urged into a book by Pepito and published as *Mon Sang dans tes vienes* in which the black heroine saves her white lover's life with a blood transfusion. "However inept as fiction," this book was written as a response to the numerous "racist blood novels" being published in Germany during the 1930s.[49] After this tour, Baker was glad to return to France, where, at least in fantasy, the mixing of blood stood for the necessary rejuvenation of Western civilization.

With the Folies Bergère in 1926, Baker lay ensconced on her royal couch, which she had draped in the tri-color. This is the first of many snapshots of Baker adopting the colors of the French flag as the sheets of her boudoir. In this early version the tri-color belongs to the monarchial dictatorship of Napoleon. In later stagings the tri-color will represent the Free France of Charles de Gaulle. Baker's contract with Free France was a reciprocal intimacy, a romantic narrative of loyalty and patriotism. In 1941, her bedside in a Casablanca clinic would be the theater for staged patriotic sacrifice as fugitive resistance fighters exchanged information over her wounded body. Back in France in 1946 Baker lay wrapped in a robe of red and white as she received the Médaille de la Résistance from de Gaulle. These stagings served both Baker, in her self-creation as a figure of political freedom, and the de Gaullists, in their propagandist efforts, utilizing her public presence as a forum for their own self-construction.[50]

The politics of colonial belonging ran at the center of Baker's contract with France. Baker represented the peripheries of empire at the center of the free world, and she carried the heart of that free world into the wilds of the colonies. *Sirène des Tropiques*, filmed in 1927 (directed by Mario Malpas and Luis Buñuel), was Baker's first film appearance as the scampering Caribbean native girl (see fig. 46). The film was meant to take place in the Antilles but was actually filmed in the wooded French countryside of Fontainebleau outside Paris. *Princess Tam Tam* was filmed entirely on location in Tunisia. Baker loved this film. "It all seems so real, so true, that I sometimes think it's my own life being played out on the sets."[51] Back in North Africa five years later, the "real" Baker would stage her wartime heroism as a supporter of de Gaulle's resistance movement. From 1943 until the end of the war Baker toured throughout the Middle East, Egypt, and Algiers lifting the flagging spirits of the Allied troupes by evoking, in the desert, the rhythms of cosmopolitan Paris.

Baker's support of de Gaulle's movement reveals the complex relationship between freedom and colonial rule during the war. Baker committed to assisting the resistance movement despite the support of the United States for General Henri Giraud and, with the Cold War beginning, the desire of the United States to "free" the North African colonies from French rule. Baker relocated to Morocco in 1940 with her partner, the

46 Josephine Baker, *Sirène des Tropiques*. Beinecke Rare Book and Manuscript Library, Yale University.

military intelligence officer Jacques Abtey. She lived under the lavish care of Arab and Moroccan aristocracy, including the Paris-educated pasha of Marrakesh, Si Thami el Glaoui, and relations of the sultan, Moulay Larbi el Alaoui and Si Mohamed Menebhi. Disliked by Moroccan nationalists, El Glaoui was supported by French colonial power and invested in this support as it insured his feudal grip on the region.[52]

Baker posits her decision to fight as a patriot of the French resistance as inspired by her anger at the inequality she faced as a child growing up under racist conditions. But there is an obvious irony here. Baker's wartime loyalty to the French model of freedom involved the support of not only French rule, but the rule of her aristocratic friends in North Africa as well. From the Napoleonic tours in Egypt, the rhetoric of French universalism claimed that it had brought light to the dark continent, that French rule was one of inclusivity, an invitation to belong. "The nineteenth century . . . had come to admit the diversity of men and of their civilizations and to respect the latter while at the same time dominating them."[53] But in practice the terms of assimilation rested on France's primary access to raw resources, the perpetuation of colonial feudal systems, and the collusion of indigenous aristocratic classes in the extraction of exports. In

Morocco as elsewhere, different laws applied to the colonized subalterns than to the native ruling classes and the colonial administrators. Baker, then, was positioned as a model for French assimilationist policy, but she could only play this role as an outsider, a guest, an adopted daughter protected by the ruling class in the colonies.

In 1941 Baker's grave case of uterine peritonitis and septicemia would render her bedridden in Casablanca for nineteen months, from June 1941 until December 1942.[54] "Visits and exchanges" between members of de Gaulle's resistance movement, the well-placed North African aristocracy, and wealthy Americans took place in Baker's clinic room. "I couldn't wait to leave the sickroom. But Captain Abtey saw things differently. My sickroom was a perfect rendezvous spot."[55] Leaving the clinic, Baker had a relapse, sick again with paratyphoid. She went to recover at Si Menebhi's palace. While she was recovering, the African American director for Red Cross activities in North Africa, Sydney Williams, visited the palace. "It was strictly out of Arabian Nights," Williams recalled.[56]

Here the iconic significance of Baker rests on the trope of the nation as woman, the land as female. The politics of the resistance needed publicity and a theater; her body represented the suffering French nation, the condition of its people under the German boot. As she lay prone in her sickbed, her body was the site for meaningful exchanges between brave men as they planned the new governance of the land. The specific effect of the way in which Baker filled this role was the naturalization of France's relationship to its colonies, fending off the approaching rebellions in North Africa.

Williams had come to invite Baker to perform at the opening of a Red Cross center in Casablanca. In 1943 Baker performed at the opening of this facility, the Liberty Club. Despite its name, it was a segregated service club for black soldiers. "My program included two American songs— a Negro lullaby to prove I hadn't forgotten my origins and a Gershwin tune to show the poetry of the American soul—then 'J'ai Deux Amours' to emphasize that I was French now and that France was a land of liberty. For this reason she must be returned to her people."[57] The first *Josephine Baker Show*, following her Liberty Club appearance, was a French Red Cross benefit in Casablanca. For her number "J'ai Deux Amours," Baker was dressed in a "floating red and blue crepe gown."[58] For Baker's tour of North Africa and the Middle East in support of de Gaulle, the backdrop of her traveling stage was a gigantic French flag and the Croix de Lorraine. Baker traveled across North Africa on a grueling schedule, entertaining Allied troops until the liberation of Paris in 1944. Back in France, Baker was once again hospitalized. At a clinic in Neuilly, she was awarded the Medal of Resistance. De Gaulle himself sent a letter of thanks for her services.

Performing jazz, the compositions of Jewish and black artists, had become a signature expression for resistance to Nazi oppression and terror. It had become a metaphor for freedom. But for racialized subjects, freedom was never a politically self-evident condition. That U.S. segregation should reach into Allied territory on the African continent (the need for a black officer's club) was a resonating irony in this wider international context. For French colonial subjects, French rule on the African continent as in the Caribbean was a complex cipher for freedom. To claim allegiance to de Gaulle's resistance was to fight Vichy and Nazi oppression, but it also meant that colonial peoples had to pledge the nation of France as their homeland, the land of their origin.

While stationed in France, Frantz Fanon grew eager to leave. "It is a year since I left Fort-de-France," Fanon wrote to his parents in April 1945. "Why? I defend an obsolete ideal. . . . The false ideology that shields these secularists and the idiot politicians must not delude us any longer. *I was wrong!* . . . Nothing justifies my sudden decision to defend the interests of farmers who don't give a damn."[59] However sincere Baker's passionate support of de Gaulle, her voluntary alliance with France served to obscure real colonial relations. Returning France to "her people" was a particular type of assimilation, which "signified putting One and the Other under the sign of the Same."[60]

AND SO SAY THE JAZZ AFICIONADOS: ON THE POLITICS OF BLACK FEMINIST REMEMBRANCE

In December 1940, eight months into the Nazi occupation of Denmark, the jazz trumpeter Valaida Snow sat sipping coffee in the Hotel Sanders in Copenhagen, giving an interview to the provincial newspaper *Randers Amtsavis*. "The little black, temperamental lady Miss Valaida is currently delighting a high-swinging public at Norreriis with her intense jazz utterances," the article reads. "This is pure-bred jazz, fetched directly from the jungle. Away for a while from the stage and the swing-orgies, Miss Valaida is just as charming, but a stylish, dreamy and clever little lady. She is distinctly female."[61]

Snow had been in Denmark for over a year, entertaining in the Swedish and Danish provinces, as well as in Copenhagen and Stockholm. Her manager had already been deported.

The newspaper interview continued:

> "Do you speak Danish, Miss Valaida?"
>
> "Well, listen, I can say 'Yes,' 'No,' 'Thanks,' 'Thanks for tonight,' 'Old Carlsberg,' and I can sing a little Danish. This one song: "I'm so gla-a-ad when the sun shines." . . . I came to Denmark for two visits. On my last one, I've been here seven months. I'm here all by myself. My manager was able to slip away via Petsamo, but I'm gla-a-ad to be here."[62]

Snow would stay in occupied Denmark until May 1942, when a ship chartered by the United States was finally able to enter the waters controlled by the Axis powers. This ship, the S.S. *Gripsholm*, brought Snow and stranded U.S. embassy workers to New York.

Tall tales and rumors have swirled around the years Snow spent in Scandinavia, many stirred by Snow herself. "I Came Back from the Dead," she allegedly wrote upon her return, telling a story of internment in a Nazi concentration camp, of starvation, torture, and frequent whippings. According to the *Amsterdam News* on April 10, 1943, Snow was supposedly "the only colored woman entertainer on record to have been interned in a Nazi concentration camp. . . . The goose steppers grabbed her among their first victims, but didn't kill her because the U.S. and Hitlerland were at peace—then. But they did clap her into a concentration camp, fed her on potatoes and water, kicked, beat, and insulted her until our diplomatic service was able to get her out of Denmark and home last summer."[63] This article was designed to garner attention for her upcoming appearance, and Jack Carter, who managed her career for a while upon her return to the United States, may have had something to do with this spin.

Versions of her concentration camp experience have been reproduced in several biographical sources. They furnish the liner notes of Rosetta Reitz's 1982 rerelease of Snow's recordings as well as several other biographical sources. "What a foremother! What an inspiration!" read Reitz's notes.[64] This tale reads well, but it is a functional fiction. It is far easier to resurrect a heroine from such a tale than from the reports of Snow's drug use and petty thievery and Danish protection in the form of house arrest. That Snow and her second manager, Jack Carter, would produce a concentration camp tale upon her return to the United States makes sense. Considering the racial and legal climate of the United States, Snow's decision to keep silent about her own legal experiences in Denmark during the war was perhaps shaped by what had happened recently to other black women performers stateside. Bessie Smith had died in a car accident in 1937 while traveling down Route 61 from Memphis. This event generated its own fiction, that she died from excessive blood loss as the result of being denied access to an all-white hospital. While not true, it resonates with very real segregation policies in southern hospitals.[65] From the beginning of her career Billy Holiday had been hounded by the law and kept under surveillance. As treatment for her heroin addiction, Holiday was subjected to a form of hospitalized internment.[66] Although recordings of her voice circulated widely around the world, Holiday was repeatedly denied a passport and so did not tour outside the United States until the mid-1950s.

Sensitive attention to the lives of black women performers need not be a search for a stable, unified subject, or for one set of truths about them. To do justice to the complexities and ambiguities of their multi-valenced presences across the globe, the messiness of history must not be ironed out, even in the service of restoring them to the many histories from which they have been systematically excluded. Such "feminist" recuperation as Reitz's relies on clear-cut tales of heroism and resistance, which are threatened by the ambiguities of actual women's lives. These stories actually obscure the more complicated, and no less terrifying, politics of racial assignation black women face every day, as well as their strategies of survival.

Snow was notorious for creating stories about herself, and as Mark Miller points out the concentration camp story was just the final tale in a "long pattern of mythomania."[67] There are other ways to think about this tendency to dissemblance, apart from as a perverse personal trait, which it may well have been. Blatant lies and contradictory self-constructions appear as creative forms of resistance to the misrepresentative clusters of racialized and gendered codes that always already clung to her, clusters of meaning that were the product of long histories. The skin crawls with the sense of these ideologies actively reproducing themselves on one's own body. Why not create a false self, or selves, a shell to protect from what is already a surrounding web of lies?

Perhaps fictions are as telling as "truths"; perhaps the lines between them are not always easy to police. Perhaps the gaps are the most interesting spaces anyway. The mystery of Snow's life has invited fictional interpretation. The independent filmmaker St. Clair Bourne prepared a treatment and a script for a film about Snow, and Diana Ross had a brief interest in producing a biographical film. John Edgar Wideman wrote a short story about her and, most recently, Candace Allen has published a novel based on her life.[68] Historical gaps are the space for conjecture, for a kind of creative mourning. This mourning does not anticipate the recovery of a whole person, but is rather a permanent melancholia over what is irrecoverably lost and that which is continually lost over and over again as the result of limiting historical and analytical paradigms. Searching archives is a negotiation between this urge to detect the "true events" and the challenge to instead spread out a panoply of possibilities, a set of contextualizations for how to read Snow. What "really" happened will continue to change over time.

"DAT VAR NEGRESSEN WALAIDA SNOW"

Snow's first tour of Sweden was as the trumpet-playing star of Louis Douglas's show *Blackflowers Liza*. The large cast was composed of over thirty performers who had resettled in Europe and underwent frequent changes: Sonny Jones and Belle Davis were with the company when Valaida joined, as was Arabella Fields, an opera singer and veteran of the German stage, and Mabel Mercer, a jazz singer from the London cabaret circuit. Snow had joined the cast while she was working in Paris, in June 1930, as the revue came into town from a two-month tour of Egypt, Athens, Istanbul, Tirana, and Zagreb. Strange forms of identification suggest themselves, as these black artists living in Europe performed as U.S. subjects, representing the New World as they toured British and French colonial territories. Scandinavia was next, in July 1930. After playing Helsinki in July, the large troupe, now with Snow, went to Copenhagen in August and Stockholm in September.

In his private journal, the Swedish jazz percussionist Elis Egneby remembers the first time he and his band saw Valaida Snow, that September at the outdoor Circus Theatre on Djurgarden Island in Stockholm. The plot includes a wedding scene, with Snow as the bride. He and his friends expressed disbelief that a woman was capable of such horn playing as they heard that night. "At the Circus this summer there was a Negro revue, *Blackflowers Liza*, all evenings free. You went to look and listen, because in the finale, about a wedding, the bride took a trumpet and blew a very nice solo. We musicians talked about whether she was really playing, or if she just held it and someone in the orchestra played." He and his friends went to see the show again. Their astonishment was compounded, for now it was obvious that the small black lady was indeed responsible for the strong, rich, tones. "*Dat var negressen Walaida Snow*," the drummer wrote.[69]

As an instrumentalist who was particularly talented in brass, Snow faced a masculinist bias among musicians as well as within the developing transnational community of jazz aficionados. Few women horn players were given equal recording time or critical acknowledgment as "serious" jazz musicians, particularly in the United States. "Only God can make a tree . . . and only men can play good jazz," wrote the historian George Simon.[70] All of Snow's major recorded sessions were set to wax in London, Stockholm, and Copenhagen between 1935 and 1940. European audiences received Snow enthusiastically, but she still faced the sexist views of many male jazz buffs. "She seemed to be a nice little girl on stage," states one English jazz fan after he heard Snow perform in London in 1935. "I cannot say I was very interested in her . . . [as I] am somewhat repulsed at the idea of a woman playing the trumpet."[71] Even while her talents were favorably assessed, her style was described and evaluated in relation to her "tribal relatives," that is, African American male horn players."[72] The Swedish *Estrad* described her musical tone as having a "typically Negroid quality," and her phrasing as "reminiscent of her favorite and mentor Louis Armstrong."[73] Snow had given herself this moniker in 1934, and while in London with Lew Leslie's *Blackbirds* in 1935 the press continued to refer to her as Little Louie.[74] But she had not trained with Armstrong. In the United States she trained with her mother.

Like Mills, Baker, and so many other black performers, Valaida had started out as a child, performing in a troupe led by her mother on the variety circuit.[75] She may also have trained with the black female trumpet player and instructor Dyer Jones. The history of female musicians includes that of music instructors, as many female musicians were tracked straight into teaching positions. Those who wanted a stage career were encouraged to sing and dance, as instrumentalism was male territory.

Snow had musical talent. She played a number of instruments and as Sissle and Blake remember, she possessed perfect pitch.[76] But as a woman she had to develop a wily versatility in order to keep working. A Danish review from 1941 expressed surprise at her skill, strength, and stamina. "In the nightclubs, the fact that a woman was playing the trumpet was in itself enough to attract attention, since it requires a tremendous physique, even a man must have an extraordinary constitution to master this demanding instrument, and then [sic] a lady of 49 kilos and 146 kilometers. And added to that she plays well!"[77] It is notable that this male reviewer assumes that it took more strength to master the trumpet than to play and also successfully execute the demanding dance routines through an entire night of performances.

Rather than competing directly for inclusion in all-male orchestras, Snow established herself on the variety stage. A fellow musician recalls Snow's act while in Shanghai with Jack Carter's band. "She sang excellently, then played a solo on trumpet, on which instrument she could do all sorts of tricks and improvise tremendous breaks. After this she would give out with some more choruses of dancing . . . tap dancing too and finish her act by shoving herself on her knees through the audience for the last few bars!"[78] For most women musicians, finding regular orchestral work in the 1930s was quite difficult. Snow's tactic, combining her musicianship with dancing and singing, was a practical decision. She also played it safe with her repertoire, sticking to classics such as "St. Louis Blues" and to a handful of songs her public associated her with, including "I Can't Dance, I've Got Ants in My Pants" (a favorite in Scandinavia) and her own composition, "You Let Me Down."

Snow was also a conductor and a musical arranger. Coming back to the United States after her East Asia tour, Snow directed the thirty-member orchestra in Lew Leslie's show *Rhapsody in Black* in 1931 in New York before performing in her own segment. In 1933 she produced, arranged, and conducted a show at the Grand Terrace in Chicago with Earl Fatha Hines's orchestra. "She could dance and she could sing and she knew what to do," Hines remembers.

> She put that show together herself. She saved [manager Ed Fox] an awful lot
> of money too, because whenever a new show went on there had to be a lot

of new arrangements for it. She was so talented. She picked out numbers from the band's book that could be used, memorized them, and hummed or scatted them to the chorus. Then when we came in the rehearsals were very short because the girls already knew the band's routines.[79]

The lines between black stage performance and what would become known as "pure" jazz were not as strictly policed as they would become in later years, the result of the efforts of jazz purists, those aficionados developing approaches to the analysis of jazz during this period. Drawing these defining lines around "real" jazz involved dismissing as contaminated those forms of jazz performance that combined and blurred the lines between black variety stage techniques and pure music. Many women were singers; part of their marginalization from the jazz canon is due to this critical urge toward uncontaminated instrumentalism, which was and still is understood as the progeny of blessed unions between men.[80]

Women musicians took advantage of opportunities as they could; wartime loosened the bonds for many. During both wartime periods, all-female orchestras found work, "replacing" the men drafted into the war effort. Replacing her father, Sam Lucas, from 1916 to 1920, Marie Lucas headed the Lafayette Theatre band, which she named the Lafayette Ladies' Orchestra, and booked all-female groups for engagements at the theater. Snow's contemporary, the trumpeter Dolly Jones (Dyer Jones's daughter), toured with Ma Rainey in 1925, and then with Lil Hardin Armstrong's all-female group in the 1930s. Many of Snow's contemporaries headed all-girl orchestras, including the trumpeter Leora Meoux Henderson, the pianist Lil Hardin Armstrong, and Mary Lou Williams.[81] Several "all-girl" orchestras were formed during World War II, providing work for hundreds of women musicians. The largest of these "all-girl" orchestras, the International Sweethearts of Rhythm, toured extensively through the war.[82]

Snow did not work in the all-female orchestral circuit. She had begun on the variety stage, as there was more work for women singers and dancers in the internationally touring variety revues. Snow was billed in the *Blackbirds* revue of 1934 not as a musician but as its star turn, the blues-singing lead (see fig. 47). Like Adelaide Hall had been in the 1928 edition, Snow was booked as a replacement for the late Florence Mills. A critic from London's *Daily Telegraph* described Snow as

a dusky young woman with versatile talents but lacking the electrifying personality of her predecessor. Valaida has a fair singing voice, and she can

47 Program, *Blackbirds* revue, 1934, London Coliseum.

dash from the syncopated sob-stuff of "St. James' Infirmary" to "Walking the Chalkline," the latest thing in eccentric dance rhythms, in the course of a few minutes. When she is not singing she is playing the trumpet or dancing or conducting the magnificent "Blackbirds' Choir."[83]

As well as playing the trumpet, Snow arranged and conducted one number, Gershwin's "Rhapsody in Blue." She also danced a duo with her young husband, the tap dancer Ananais Berry.

Europe offered more chances for Snow to perform and record. Following her *Blackbirds* appearance, Snow began working with British and European all-male jazz orchestras, with whom she recorded several sessions in London between 1935 and 1937.[84] Traveling to Paris, Snow also made musical appearances in two films.[85] Her live appearances included a return to the East Asia circuit and Egypt in 1937 and an engagement in Vienna with Johnny Pillitz's Orchestra in 1938, a band Snow had recorded with in London the previous year.

The growing climate of racial terror touched this Vienna engagement. Snow and the orchestra were in Vienna when the Nazis annexed Austria. Johnny Pillitz's Orchestra was a mixed troupe; it included a German Jewish pianist named Gun Finlay (Gunther Freundlich) and the Spanish

TRANSLOCATIONS

48　Valaida Snow conducting the orchestra on the set of the show *Blackbirds* at the Coliseum in London, October 5, 1934. Photo by Sasha/Getty Images, Hulton Archive, Getty Images.

African bassist Louis Barriero. The *Anschluss* claimed them both. Nazi soldiers killed Finlay and handed Barriero over to the Spanish Falangists, who assassinated him.[86]

As the 1930s progressed, participation in the jazz scene in Europe was increasingly marked as a politicizing set of pleasures and musical practices. Jazz in Germany during the Weimar Republic was the "essence of the era's modernism, an influence toward greater equality and emancipation—in short, democracy for Germans. . . . To some it was the very incarnation of American vitalism."[87]

As nationalist conservative and racist forces grew, jazz was identified as the product of Jewish and black collusion. Many racist and nationally conservative German composers were members of the National Socialist Party before the ascension of Adolf Hitler to power in 1933. Along with the modernists, jazz and swing music were denounced as "degenerate art," and African American artists were banned from performing in Germany. Jazz disgusted the Nazi minister of propaganda, Joseph Goebbels. "Everyone knows, America's contribution to the music of the world consists merely of jazzed-up Nigger music, not worthy of a single mention,"

TIDSKRIFT FÖR DEN MODERNA DANSMUSIKEN

49 Valaida Snow, cover of *Estrad*, June
1939. Svenskt Visarkiv, Jazz Division.

he stated.[88] There was resistance to Nazi control of artistic production; in 1934, while Valaida Snow was heading the *Blackbirds* revue in London, the conductor Wilhelm Furtwängler resigned from the Berlin Philharmonic in support of the modern composer Paul Hindemith.[89] After the war began, jazz music in particular was clearly marked as protest music across Europe, a metaphor for resistance to the Nazis' program of hate and extermination. Swing music represented improvisation and collective composition, opposing the obsessive, rigid autocratic state decree. Swing and jazz were defined as inherently democratic, natural, a utopian call during a frightful time of terror. The "technical precision" of the art form was likened to the modernist works of painting, sculpture, and architecture classified as degenerate by the Nazis.[90] Circulated through records and music sheets, played by European and black musicians, jazz music reverberated underground throughout the city centers and provinces (see fig. 49).

While jazz was the clarion call of democracy, familiar primitivist fantasies also circulated, forming the basis for a strain of jazz enthusiasm. Various interpretations of the effects of black music, both as liberatory and as degenerate, would shape Snow's reception upon her return to Sweden in the spring of 1939; there political and cultural conservatives considered jazz as decadent and immoral, threatening to the moral fiber of the country, and a corrupting influence on Scandinavian youth.[91] Conservative resentment over the "loss" of cultural dominance was couched in racialist language. When Louis Armstrong performed in Sweden in 1933, a Swedish composer wrote a shockingly racist depiction of the artist:

> Mr. Jazz-king and cannibal offspring Louis Armstrong shows his clean-shaven hippopotamus physiognomy. . . . bares his teeth, snuffles, raises one of the original howls of his wild Negro-African ancestors, now and then alternating with a grave-hoarse gorilla roar from the bush. . . . One should not at all talk of music when it comes to Louis Armstrong and his hot Harlem band. . . . It is an irritating rhythmic throbbing, which in its grotesque ugliness and eccentricity can never be enjoyable and hardly even fun to hear.[92]

But despite the racist and defensive opinions of a reactionary elite, many European musicians welcomed the chance to learn jazz technique and to train and perform with visiting African American jazz musicians. Although participation in the jazz scene was an assertion of a more progressive politic, much of the Swedish enthusiasm and embrace of jazz music was framed by equally fantastic racial discourses. "Hot-Jazz American Negroes" brought with them the ineffable rhythms of both modern and primitive rejuvenation; in the words of Arthur Lundkvist, a member of the Royal Swedish Academy, they were "often fabulously musical, in an instinctive, originary way, not intellectually. It is racially tinted melodic, rich, sensual, substantial and of great immediacy. . . . It bears the stamp of the big city, technology, industrialism; it contains complications conflicts." Lundvist continues:

> But it also has a nature side, founded in elementary man. . . . This music from the subconscious is deliverance, confession, liberation; in this it may be likened to a dream. . . . Machine-song fuses with jungle cacaphony, cries of jungle birds: the intricate union of civilization and primitivity. . . . According to this argument, hot-jazz is humanly and socially revolutionary— though not in a doctrinary, constructivist but in a spontaneous, organic way.[93]

These frothy exaltations of primitive infusion, in conjunction with the growing use of jazz as a democratic protest, framed Snow's successful two-week engagement at the China-Varieten Theater in Stockholm in June 1939.

Her appearance met favorable and plentiful reviews, and in July, after a short trip to Switzerland, Snow returned for a tour of the provinces. Snow played the Swedish "folk parks," amusement parks organized by the Swedish Social Democratic Party in conjunction with the trade unions and the temperance movement. "There was . . . an agitprop movement among young communists and social democrats, inspired by German and Soviet models, using theatre and music for propaganda," the Swedish cultural critic Johan Fornas writes. "The 'Blue Blouses' utilized whatever music they found, including some jazz, to popularize political messages." Fornas qualifies the Swedish Left's political relationship to jazz music. "There remained quite a suspicion towards this new American musical genre among working-class activists, related to both race, class and generation gaps." The young political agitators were not involved with the radical jazz scene or its "left-wing intellectual fans," despite the use of jazz as an affirmation of democratic ideals meant to counter the growing fascist movements.[94]

After her tour of the Swedish provincial folk parks, Snow had a one-week engagement in August at the Saga Theatre in Oslo, Norway with the Danish violinist Svend Asmussen and His Orchestra. (Asmussen had played with Josephine Baker in 1938 on her Scandinavian tour.) "The Tropical Oslo," reads a review of Snow's appearance in Norway, which was advertised as a "Swingorgy."

> Half an hour of genuine swing music is usually enough for a white man. In the span of that time even eardrums of iron have been overheated by insistent rhythmic beats, and a non-African imagination has seen enough of the roaring interior of the jungle to make the nerves crave for escape. The entire display of tropical lifeforms comes together in sound and motion—the obscene belly-writhings of naked Negro women . . . and bundles of muscle, a jackal's scream from the jungle, the answering howl of an ape, the bass-purring of a lion . . . all this conjured up by a burst of sound and a suggestively frightening imagery by a handful of instruments up on the podium, from a penetrating voice that works directly on your senses. Here one has all of Africa and its music—a drum skin stretched over our own amplifying hollow.[95]

Snow was the only black musician performing that night. "There wasn't much of Africa left in Svend Asmussen," but when Valaida Snow arrived "tropical Oslo burst out in exotic flowering. It took a black artist to change our fellow countrymen so much that it was hard to recognize them."[96] The overactive imagination of this reviewer reveals the association of pleasure and terror, located as the often welcome foreign invasion of the white male body. Snow worked with Asmussen in Copenhagen through the early 1940s.

Despite the Nazi occupation, Copenhagen had some of the liveliest jazz clubs in Europe during the war. Asmussen was a prominent jazz musician on the Danish scene, in the face of Nazi disapproval. In 1943, after Snow was gone and after the Nazis had taken over governance of the city, Svend Asmussen and other prominent Danish jazzers were rounded up by the Gestapo and spent a month under Nazi detainment in Vestre Faengsel, a prison for political prisoners in the southeastern section of Copenhagen.[97]

Snow's activities just before the declaration of war in September 1939, and for the two years following as she survived in occupied Denmark, have been historically obscured. This is the result of both the willful desires of her supporters to control the way she would be remembered and the standard neglect of black women artists by jazz historians. For this reason, a detailed accounting of Snow's whereabouts needs to be recorded.

In August 1939, after her engagement in Norway, Snow returned to Stockholm, where she would record some of her best work on wax with Lulle Ellboy and His Orkester for the Swedish recording company Sonora. Before her trip to Copenhagen on September 15, her live appearances included a stint in Malmo. "The directors of the . . . arena made a lucky choice when they hired Valaida 'the queen of the trumpet' for performances on September 12, 13, and 14. Despite Emergency restrictions and the declining number of people in the audiences because of it, Valaida averaged about 1,200 people a night."[98] Snow opened at the National-Scala in Copenhagen on September 15, 1939. The show was an enormous success, and Snow decided to stay in Denmark after the show's end on November 1. Her decision to do so was despite the growing spread of violence across Europe following Hitler's invasion of Poland. She then played a small number of venues in Copenhagen until January 31, 1940.[99] After her stint of January 16–31 at Scala-Salen, Snow and her manager, Earl Sutcliff Jones, were advised the leave the country, as, according to Morton Clausen, they would not be allowed any more work permits in Denmark.

They chose to stay. After the Nazis occupied Norway and Denmark on April 9, 1940 it was impossible for them to leave, as they were dependent on the occupying powers for exit visas. Remaining in Copenhagen, Snow was unemployed until June 1, when she was allowed by Danish authorities to work a number of small shows. On July 26, she recorded four titles with Winstrup Oleson's Swingband for the Danish Tono Company.

Snow and her manager were presented with another chance to leave; the American embassy told the Danish police that an American transport ship would be leaving Petsamo in northern Finland in mid-August. Snow, again, refused to leave. She had already booked an engagement in Aarhus, Denmark to run the whole of August. Her manager, Earl Sutcliff Jones, however, was forced to leave Denmark, expelled on drug charges and for various "unfortunate episodes."[100] Returning to New York, Jones told friends and fellow musicians versions of his deportation as escape, perhaps to cover up the rather tame truth of his own expulsion.

Jones's story was perhaps an easier explanation to people back home than the complicated and messy terms of the racial war going on overseas. African Americans were not the stated focus of the genocidal project run by legal decree and bureaucratic order, the "administrative massacres" of the Third Reich. The experiences and treatment of black people in Germany in the years before the war, as well as in occupied countries during and after the war, were far from ordered and consistent, as the Nazis' initial and most consuming concern was with the extermination of Jews and other "*European* undesirables." Nazis had been deporting, containing, and exterminating non-Aryans and sexual, political, and genetic "deviants" with increasing intensity since 1933; but Nazi policies of racial extermination were still being developed and not yet efficiently applied. The Final Solution was only made official in September 1941. The inconsistent treatment of black people by the Nazis occurred because Nazis considered black people to be subhuman, below the surveillance range of the Nazi gunsight. The African American painter Josef Nassy was captured and survived his camp experiences. Camp officials allowed him to paint his impressions of the camp.[101] Black people were subnational rather than "supra-national" and so did not threaten the same type of "extra-territorial" ambivalence as did the Jewish people.[102]

But the children of the French colonial soldiers, the so-called Rhineland Bastards, were within the visual range of the Nazis. Hitler incorporated into his program of hate the earlier fury over the power black soldiers had held in Germany's humiliation of the First World War. In 1937, the Nazis began a program of forced sterilization for black men, following the Nuremberg Blood Laws of 1935. Berliners of African descent became the practice subjects in the Nazis' development of medical extermination.[103] Among the Africans living in and born in Germany during the time, some were interned, but some managed to stay living in Berlin. Pockets of seeming indulgent permissiveness from the Nazis, despite Goebbels's concern over the degenerate effect of jazz, remained.[104]

After the departure of her manager, Valaida Snow played in Aarhus and then toured the Danish provinces, returning to Copenhagen in September for engagements through December 16, 1940. Toward the end of September, Snow recorded six sides with Tono, accompanied by a band called Matadorerne. From December 16 to December 31, she played again in Aarhus. Back in Copenhagen, Snow had two engagements in 1941; at Den Kvikke Kanin (the Fast Rabbit) from January 16 through January 31 and then at Prater from February 1 through February 15. It was in the month of February that Snow's own drug use created a legal problem.

At the end of February, a young actress named Henny Melander, then living with Snow, was found dead from an overdose of the prescription drug Eukodal, a liquid stomach medication derived from morphine. The court soon found out that Snow had been acquiring large amounts of Eukodal without a prescription from a pharmacy, the Hjorteapoteket, in Stockholm. Most likely she had begun taking this as a painkiller for a sprained arm. Snow's work permit was revoked.[105] Because of the occupation, American ships could not enter Danish ports, and no Danish ships could leave for an Allied country. Snow was unable to leave Scandinavia until May 28, 1942, when she traveled back to New York from Gothenburg, Sweden on the S.S. *Gripsholm*, which had been chartered by the U.S. government to bring U.S. diplomats home.

In the fifteen months or so before she returned to the United States, from February 1941 to March 1942, Snow was not in a concentration camp. Her activities from February 1941 to October 1941 are sketchy. She worked a few months back in Sweden; in July 1941 she did a show in Stockholm at the Nojesfaltet.[106] She was also booked to do a jam session at the Bal Palais on October 13, but was denied a permanent work permit.[107]

Snow was not legally detained in Denmark, but she lived under some kind of official surveillance in Copenhagen from October 1941 until March 12, 1942, when the Danes detained her in Vestre Fængsel. The Germans had not taken over Denmark's judicial and penal systems yet, as they had by the time Svend Asmussen and his colleagues were held there in 1943.

The end of Snow's time in Copenhagen was hard. She was staying in a rough section of town, full of one-room occupancy apartments in the center of a black-market area and nearby a slaughterhouse. She was required to check in with Danish officials but was most likely not doing so, which may account for her detainment at Vestre Fængsel, though this detainment was not on criminal charges. I suspect that this detainment was a way for the Danes to treat Snow's drug addiction as well as protect her until they could insure her passage out.

Snow's period of detention has been a mystery, but for an interesting reason. Snow was moved from Vestre Fængsel to the psychiatric ward of University Hospital on March 18, to treat her drug addiction. This was unknown because the records from the hospital were sealed to protect the Danish political prisoners who had been hidden there. By relocating prisoners from Vestre Fængsel to the hospital, the Danes had managed to protect a number of their political prisoners and resisters.[108] Snow was returned to Vestre Fængsel on April 14, where she stayed until May 23. Although the *Gripsholm* was originally scheduled to depart on May 24, a stowaway was discovered on board and the ship's departure from Gothenburg was delayed until May 28. Escorted to Sweden by two Danish police officers, Snow was detained for these last six days in a jail at Spannmalsgatan, Gothenburg.

Snow "was forbidden to perform and for six months she has been living in a small hostel where she has given lessons in order to earn money," the Swedish paper *Aftonbladet* of March 15, 1942 reports.[109] News of her earlier "criminal activities" was not released until the proceedings at Vestre Fængsel that March. "Negro Star Arrested in Copenhagen," read the headline in *Aftonbladet*:

> The American Negro star, Miss Valaida who has, among other things, been involved in two scandals, one concerning the death of a young girl following drug abuse, the other concerning the purchase of narcotics at a pharmacy without a prescription at a cost of several thousand crowns, has been arrested by the Copenhagen police. . . . The police want to be sure that she is at their disposal.[110]

Reporters had managed to find out more about Snow's so-called criminal activities. "The dark-skinned swing director, obviously gifted with a black soul," had now been "exposed as a major thief" for stealing silverware from Swedish and Danish restaurants, and from aboard the Swedish passenger railway.

> Investigating her luggage, the police determined that she has high-handedly stolen knives, forks, and spoons from various restaurants in Sweden and Denmark. In Sweden she has especially collected silverware from the Swedish dining cars. No less than 120 knives, forks, and spoons carry the stamp of sj. Miss Valaida has confessed that she had stolen them in dining cars and from the restaurant at Central Station in Stockholm.[111]

The charges of a jazz musician's drug abuse and petty thievery made good print. But Snow's Danish supporters were protective, and the Swedish papers soon tempered their earlier tabloid versions of Snow's predicament. On May 24, a report in *Aftonbladet* described the conditions of Snow's detainment as the caring legal protection of Danish officials, who took pains to exonerate Snow of all accusations of theft. "Miss Valaida not as black as people would like to believe," reads the *Aftonbladet* headline. "The black queen of jazz Miss Valaida has been a guest of the police in Gothenburg since Saturday afternoon, waiting for the Gripsholm to take her back to America on Thursday. She longs for her trumpet and spends her time reading *Gone with the Wind* in English." This detail regarding Snow's activities in her cell is a deliberate and pointed one and would probably not have been lost on readers. Goebbels had greatly admired the filmed version of Margaret Mitchell's grand epic of U.S. racial drama, even though he had banned it.[112] Reports give the sense of Snow as a representative of resistance to Nazi occupation, a primitivist erotic fantasy, and a damsel in distress needing protection. "Yesterday, Officer Brant at the headquarters had a pleasant meeting with the famous lady, who was mildly flirtatious in the loneliness of her cell. She smiled broadly and was quite simply charming said the officer, who added with enthusiasm: 'I actually felt like taking her in my arms.'" This *Aftonbladet* report reveals the relationship between Snow and her European detainees to be quite different from the descriptions Snow herself gave upon her return to the United States. Her detention awaiting deportation was described as fatherly protection. "When Miss Valaida wants to go out in the city and get some air she can do so, and the Danes come along as polite gentlemen.

They enjoy their job." In fact, Officers Oxvard and Krause take pains to diffuse the "scent of scandal surrounding Valaida." They "defend her against all the ugly rumors and evil gossiping. They explain that Miss Valaida has done nothing wrong. She has been a victim of disgusting circumstances." Snow did not steal the silverware from Aarhus, the officers explain, nor did she steal the silver and glassware from the Swedish dining cars found in her trunk. These were "given to her by more or less dizzy admirers. . . . Valaida is not banished from Denmark . . . she is not a prisoner. . . . You might say she is a guest of the Gothenburg police."[113]

In this climate of surveillance and fear, the Danes had protected Snow. The Danish police and officials had had every opportunity to arrest, imprison, and deport her since the Nazi occupation, but hadn't until it was a useful way of smuggling her out of the country. Danish officials had probably suppressed the police reports taken in February 1941 and had not used them as a means to deport her. Most likely, they did not release them until they could be sure Snow would get safely to the United States. By keeping Snow under surveillance, the local Danish officials shielded her from what would possibly have been a worse fate in the hands and camps of the Nazis. This is the most likely version of events, considering the Danish protection of Jewish people, both refugees from the Third Reich as well as Danish Jews, during the occupation.[114] Snow was brought out just in time, while the Danes still had control of their government. One year later the Gestapo had control of Vestre Fængsel.

Snow herself was aware of Danish resistance, commenting on the daily morning ride of the Danish king through Copenhagen to her interviewer from *Randers Amtsavis*. This daily ride was an act of resistance in itself to German occupation. It is not clear why she could not bring the experience of Danish kindness home with her; perhaps intra-European politics were not understood well enough stateside to counter the process of criminalization she would have faced there for her legal transgressions.

After returning to the United States Snow began to perform again, initially taking up her career with the aid of Jack Carter. The *Amsterdam News* article reporting her camp internment credits "Jack Carter . . . the man with the big heart" for booking a week with Frank Schiffman at the Apollo, "her first 'week' at home in five years."[115] In this article Carter helped spin the tale of her concentration camp internment. This tale, as well as obscuring the more despairing version of low-grade addiction and poverty, made much more exciting postwar press.

Returning to the United States bred ambivalence for most African American artists. It was home, but after living outside of U.S. segregation, who wanted to return for good? And most of the women who returned met a stage culture that was very different from the one that they left, for stage culture underwent a sea change following the war. Snow still performed and recorded a few tracks in the 1940s and 1950s, but not to the same kind of reception she had enjoyed in Europe. Snow married her last manager, Earl Edwards, in the fall of 1943 and moved to California. She died in New York's King's County Hospital in 1956 of a cerebral hemorrhage.

In 1908 Ada Overton Walker acknowledged how difficult it was for women to develop their artistic talents. She expressed frustration over the ways that, for black women, "the greatest of all gifts is negated or suppressed," and at the ways that "intelligent women were not allowed to follow their artistic yearnings."[116] To be historically remembered as an artist, not just as someone's wife (as with Stella Wiley) or as the interesting exception to the rule (as with Josephine Baker or Valaida Snow) seems an even more remarkable feat. Many of the voices that we can trace are often mislabeled or incorrectly catalogued, buried deep in the bowels of various archives. And without knowing something about these women, how can we really "know" about black jazz in Europe?

But then we ask, if the official record does recall a few of such voices, on what terms do they offer inclusion? Forms of invisibility, sometimes rendered by the most ardent forms of glaring light, are the product of systemic and stubborn aporias that can send all of our careful work down the vortex once again, even as the hegemonies they are a part of absorb it. As we examine the margins of the archival records, what governs our own need to know, to redress? What are the terms of our remembrance? Is it simply an obscurantist urge to collect, to construct a huge scrapbook of memorabilia to flip through for its own sake? What kind of loyalty do we hold to Overton Walker, or can we even really understand what she herself was asking for in the name of recognition? I would love to claim my own investment in this work as a useful form of creative mourning, guided by some version of black feminist politics, and as a productive contribution to conversations out of which new ways to think about history, performance, gender, and the body can arise.

The nature of musical and theatrical performance changed during the war, and Valaida Snow's return to the United States marks the end of an era in black variety stage culture. With the development of communication technologies, much of the cultural work that had taken place on the variety stages now happened on the radio, records, and film. This was the end of an era for black variety chorus girls in particular (see fig. 50). "One day . . . it was the late 40s . . . something happened and the well went dry," explains Marion Cole, Cleo Hayes, and Elaine Ellis of the Apollo Rockets. "There were no more sixteen chorus girls working the theaters in New York and Washington and Philadelphia and Baltimore. All of a sudden it just stopped . . . many [theaters] started having music . . . and they didn't use chorus girls anymore."[1] Many of the black women who had traveled to Europe with the black revues had settled there. Adelaide Hall was in London, Josephine Baker was in the French woods with her Rainbow Tribe of adopted children. A new generation of African American dancers, musicians, visual artists, intellectuals, and writers also moved out of the United States, claimed expatriate status, and set up communities abroad. With this choice and in their art they made their protests of U.S. racist policies explicit.

After the war black women artists became increasingly political with what they created. Katherine Dunham and Pearl Primus developed combinations of dance cultures from Africa, the West

50   The champion Charleston dancer Gwendlyn Graham with the chorus of the
      Blackbirds revue taking part in their first rehearsal on the roof of the Pavilion Theater
      in London in 1928. Photo by General Photographic Agency/Getty Images, Hulton
      Archive, Getty Images.

Indies, and the United States as consciousness-building affirmations of black diasporic mobility. The pianist Nina Simone became a symbol of black female political resistance, refusing to move back to the United States from her home in the south of France.

The jazz singers Billie Holiday, Ella Fitzgerald, and Dinah Washington brought a new level of technical skill and expressivity to the form, but the stage techniques of the earlier generations of black women variety performers also profoundly shaped subsequent eras in black expressive arts. We see them remembered on the Motown stage in the vocal techniques and dance routines of female singing groups, including The Supremes and The Marvelettes, working out of Detroit during the 1960s and 1970s. We can link up earlier black traveling variety stage practices, "under the kinetoscope," to the fantastic voyages of 1970s and 1980s funk bands, including LaBelle as well as Funkadelic, Cameo, and early Grandmaster Flash and the Furious Five. We can easily recognize the importance of black social dance techniques under the glitzy baroque shine of the 1970s disco ball and the house club smoke machines of the 1990s. Recent dance scholars continue to produce articulate analyses of more contemporary dance techniques from break dancing and double dutch to later hip hop forms.[2] Rather than focusing on the connections between these later movements and the earlier movements I have analyzed here, I have tried to provide a cultural prehistory to these later movements, marking a significant cultural shift after World War II. I emphasize the crucial importance of reading these dances very specifically as articulations from within particular historical conjunctures rather than marveling at what look like timeless retentions. I seek instead to find ways of affirming self-conscious communal expressivity within changing modalities.

Linkages are still important to understand, not as retentions but as developments. Partly, recognition of artists and forms from this era and links to present forms (except for male tap dancers) have been obscured as the collateral in the process of black cultural classification, decisions made about what forms were acceptable and which were race betrayals. The black arts movement yelled at many of the artists in this study, and their techniques were permanently coated with an unforgivable shame, emblematic of self-hate, denigration. Theirs was an era to get over, the dark ages before we discovered ourselves.

More recently, scholars have begun letting the forbidden histories of early black performance out of the vault, and not always in the form of restorative hagiography, though recognizing that these artists' techniques often retained the power of critique through satire and the politics of the comedic. The chuckle of the absurd is free of fear of obliteration, as it slides under and around regimes of power.[3] Many new studies of earlier performance periods are productive theoretical examinations that limn the complexity of performance techniques and recognize the multi-signification behind the masks and springing from the box. Daphne Brooks's *Bodies in Dissent* brilliantly recognizes the performative powers of dissemblance and transformative manipulations of self in the works of activists and performers, including Henry Box Brown, Adah Isaacs Menken, and Ada Overton Walker. In her study of Menken, Brooks contends that Menken and other performers used their bodies "not as evidence of some incontrovertible proof, but as an instrument of ontological deception." My work joins in with this assertion as well as her poignantly phrased claim that "racially marked women used their bodies in dissent of the social, political, and juridical categories assigned to them."[4] My project began with a desire to resituate away from a perspective centered on the United States. New performance scholarship is addressing the conceptualization of diaspora in committed ways. In her study of Araci Cortes, Judith Williams creates new analytic space to think about the "intra-diasporic gaze of recognition" between racialized women performers.[5]

The implication of such work is a deeper awareness of how expressive artistry brings into view the staged nature of racialization and the performed nature of defiant responses to racial discursive claims. This way of thinking about vernacular forms frees us from proscriptive narratives of authenticity, of regimes of racial truth, and challenges us to find alternate ways of retaining critiques of physio-socio-political inequality, even as we keep a wary eye on the rearticulation of techniques of domination designed specifically for racialized subjects. More work suggests itself regarding how relations of power are performed and how contest and critique operate in the realms of the body. But it is important to retain a sense of what is at stake in our studies, not just a freedom from but a freedom to. I argue for the "protean capabilities of the human bond through music and the very body that was supposedly possessed by another" to affirm the continual presence of a utopian impulse in music, dance, and the practical everyday.[6] Robin Kelley reminds us that it is "dreams of the marvelous" at the heart of rebellion and revolution, that our work can bear witness to the ways in which our dissenting movement has been and continues to be governed by beauteous wished-for possibility.[7]

Writing this book has brought me to new and divergent grounds of inquiry, most of which is an expansion of what remains nascent in this book. The first grouping of questions that have developed for me since beginning this project ten years ago have to do with ways to think about the body, its expressive vocabularies, and its spaces of performance and circulation. In this era of the "posthuman," race disappears and then reappears in the interpretation of the evidence. In what forms do scientific regimes of knowledge continue to render bodies, even as they disarticulate them? I believe we can continue to explore the creative nature of physicality and the force of expressive arts within and against these developing regimes.

Diasporic creative, social, and political bodies continue to be created across geographic boundaries. New medias and technologies suggest expanding forms of circulation that move with the speed of light from continent to continent. These bodies of music and performance transcend boundaries, earthly and otherwise, but they also stay tethered to specific performance sites, particular bodies in physical contact. I am interested in this articulation between remote and local realms. But as we consider new modes of mobility and migration, as we decenter identities and no longer hold them along national lines, our working concepts of diaspora must shift. They must be read in specific historical contexts, for paradigms of diaspora continue to change over time. So-called overlapping diasporas are heterogeneous places where distinctions are hard to maintain and artistic production is consciously multifarious.

Performing women are still at the center of these questions. I think immediately of the collaboration between Erykah Badu and Zap Mama/ Marie Daulne, who joined Badu on her European tour in 2003. I think of Daulne, Badu, and Caron Wheeler singing together on stage and aboard Badu's tour bus, producing "Bump It," one of Badu's best songs from her *Worldwide Underground* album. Another moment strikes me, again out of the friendship between Dualne and Badu, as they co-composed "Bandy Bandy" for Zap Mama's *Ancestry in Progress* album. The song is beautifully illustrated in a partly animated music video. The video opens with Daulne and Badu, clad in matching pilot's hats, aboard a lovely animated version of Captain Nemo's Nautilus, at once a submarine and a spaceship. They are floating down a tributary in the midst of tall buildings, a river view that combines Brussels and Manhattan. It is at once organic—around them are trees, animals, flying fish—but the tributary never leaves the urban land- scape; it is its median. The video is composed of split scenes, between the animated mise-en-scène and a pristine, heavenly white stage set. Daulne is wearing an Orientalist kimono dress, hair up in Afro-Asian hair twists. Badu wears a hot leather studded suit consisting of tight pants and bus- tier reminiscent of 1970s interplanetary costumes. Singing to and with each other, their sisterly phonic interchange (notably free of competition) creates a vibrating force field of encompassing purple light. The aural is the physical, and the call of the song, the "Bandy Bandy," to "wave your body," is about refreshing your body and senses through movement. The ship floats in and above Manhattan, above the band shell in Central Park, where they alight momentarily to perform before rising again into the clouds. We end as we began, aboard a ship as it sets sail, on the water and into the sky.

INTRODUCTION

1 See Desmond, ed., *Meaning in Motion*; McCarren, *Dancing Machines.* Books on dance published since 1995 include Burt, *Alien Bodies*; Franko, *The Work of Dance*; Koritz, *Gendering Bodies / Performing Art*; Lepecki, ed., *Of the Presence of the Body*; Tomko, *Dancing Class.* Recent books of theater history include George, *The Royalty of Negro Vaudeville*; Krasner, *A Beautiful Pageant*; Elam and Krasner, *African American Performance and Theater History.* Work on theories of the body includes Brooks, "'The Deeds Done in My Body,'" and her *Bodies in Dissent*; Gatens, *Imaginary Bodies*; Grosz, *Volatile Bodies.*
2 Here I am referring to Lott, *Love and Theft*; Lhamon, *Raising Cain*; Roediger, *The Wages of Whiteness.*
3 Nenno, "Femininity, the Primitive and Modern Urban Space," 149.
4 Phelan, *Unmarked.*
5 Bakhtin, *Rabelais and His World*, 59–144.
6 De Certeau, *The Practice of Everyday Life*, 37.
7 Carlson, *Performance*, 173.
8 Brody, *Impossible Purities*, 53.
9 Lhamon, *Raising Cain*, 15.
10 Unidentified clipping, n.p., Williams and Walker file, Locke Collection, BR, LC, NYPL.
11 Clifford, *Routes*, 267.
12 Ibid., 7.
13 "'Good' travel (heroic, educational, scientific, adventurous, ennobling) is something men (should) do. Women are impeded from serious travel. Some of them go distant places, but largely as companions or as 'exceptions.'" Ibid., 6.
14 Ibid., 32.
15 Peterson, *"Doers of the Word,"* 98.
16 Prince, *The Narrative of Nancy Prince*, 1–88.
17 Seacole, *Wonderful Adventures of Mrs. Seacole in Many Lands.* For secondary reading, see Terborg-Penn, "Free Women Entrepreneurs from the 1820s and 1850s," 159–75.
18 Jacobs, *Incidents in the Life of a Slave Girl.*

19 J. Harrison, *My Great Wide Beautiful World*. Subsequent references to Harrison's work are cited parenthetically hereafter in the chapter. Harrison's narrative was published, in unedited form, in the *Atlantic Monthly* at the behest of one of Harrison's former employers. However invested in some primitivist concept of black female curiosity the editors may have been, their decision to leave Harrison's spelling and grammatical configurations as they were does not manage to squelch the power of Harrison's message.

20 Antoine, *Achievement*, 259.

21 Clifford, *Routes*, 3.

22 Desmond, "Embodying Difference," 30.

23 Bryson, "Cultural Studies and Dance History," 72.

24 Mumford, *Interzones*, chapter 2.

25 I draw on Frantz Fanon's concept of this doubled perception of the self, as developed in his first book, *Black Skin, White Masks*, as well as on Susan Buck-Morss's readings of Walter Benjamin's explorations of seeing and being seen on the city streets from her essay "The Flaneur, the Sandwichman and the Whore," 128.

26 Walter Benjamin, "Über einige Motive bei Baudelaire," *Gesammelte Schriften* vol. 1 pt. 2 ed. Teidemann and Schweppenhauser (Frankfurt am Main: Suhrkamp, 1974) 630. Quoted in translation by Petro, "Perceptions of Difference: Women as Spectator and Spectacle," 53.

27 Here I am using the "final prayer" with which Frantz Fanon concludes *Black Skin, White Masks*: "Oh my body, make of me always a man who questions!" Fanon, *Black Skin, White Masks*, 232.

CHAPTER ONE "LITTLE BLACK ME"

1 *The Referee*, June 9, 1901, 6. Quoted in Lotz, *Black People*, 68.

2 Lotz, *Black People*, 299.

3 Egan, *Florence Mills*, 270.

4 Spillers, "Changing the Letter," 545.

5 Stampp, *The Peculiar Institution*, 250.

6 McLaughlin, *Jefferson and Monticello*, 7.

7 Agamben, *Homo Sacer*, 4.

8 Melville, *Moby Dick or the Whale*, 188. Pip appears primarily in chapters 40, 93, 99, and 129.

9 Ibid., 193.

10 Ibid., 453.

11 Ibid., 580.

12 De Frantz, "The Black Beat Made Visible," 70–71.

13 Dickens, *American Notes for General Circulation*, 139. Hereafter cited parenthetically in the text.

14 James Cook's descriptions of beautiful dancing island women, from his travel-

ogue *A Voyage to the Pacific Ocean* of 1784, is quoted in St. Johnson, *A History of Dancing*, 69. Johnson opens chapter 5, "Allegorical Dances Among Primitive Peoples," by quoting David Livingstone from his *Travels*, in which the colonist gives his impressions of African dance practices from his initial encounters with the tribes of Central Africa (61–63).

15 Blakely, *Russia and the Negro*, chapters 1–3; Blakely, *Blacks in the Dutch World*.

16 The history of Badin, an African slave raised in the Swedish court, is well worth recovering. As a child, Badin was given as a gift to the Swedish royal family. Influenced by the recent theories of Rousseau, the family raised Badin as an experiment; he received no formal schooling and was given free reign of the castle at Gripsholm. In his early life he became a renowned court spy working for the queen mother. He lived a long and prosperous life and left behind two key documents: a journal and a biographical fragment. Two novels have been written based on these documents, neither of which is available in English. They are Larsmo, *Maroonberget*; and Eggehorn, *En Av Dessa Timmar*. For histories of blacks in Britain, see Gerzina, *Blacks in London*; and Okokon, *Black Londoners, 1880–1990*.

17 Prince, *The Narrative of Nancy Prince*.

18 Juba stayed in London until his death three years later in 1851. Thorpe, *Black Dance*, 42–44.

19 Marshall and Stock, *Ira Aldridge*, 275.

20 Emery, *Black Dance*, 89.

21 Stearns and Stearns, *Jazz Dance*, 250.

22 Ida Hubbard Forsyne, interview by Cassandra Willis, audiotape, 1972, JHCB.

23 Ibid.

24 Ida Forsyne, interview by Marshall Stearns, February 6, 1960, artist's file, IJS.

25 Ida Forsyne, interview by Cassandra Willis, 1972.

26 Louis Douglas, undated Cairo press cutting from *The 1930's Douglas Scrap Book*, trans. Ali Al-Iriani, quoted in Lotz, *Black People*, 297.

27 Lotz, *Black People*, 299.

28 Tanner, *Dusky Maidens*, 62.

29 Ida Forsyne, interview by Marshall Stearns, February 6, 1960.

30 *Darktown Frolics* program, January 6, 1901, Crescent Theatre, New Orleans, SNT.

31 Stearns and Stearns, *Jazz Dance*, 78, from an unspecified phone interview with Ida Forsyne.

32 *The Referee*, January 7, 1906, 4, in Lotz, *Black People*, 75.

33 Palace Theatre Files, 1904–7, TML.

34 *The Era*, December 15, 1906, 21.

35 *The Sketch* 52, no. 673 (December 20, 1905). Palace Theatre playbills file, TML.

36 Ida Forsyne, interview by Marshall Stearns, July 29, 1964; artist file, IJS.

37 *The Referee,* July 1, 1906, 4, in Lotz, *Black People,* 75.

38 For the history of the Whitman Sisters, see Stearns and Stearns, *Jazz Dance,* 84–91; and George, *The Royalty of Negro Vaudeville.*

39 Essie Whitman, from the transcript of an interview with the Whitman Sisters by Marshall Stearns and Jean Stearns, January 26, 1962; artist file, IJS.

40 Albertson, *Bessie Smith,* 27.

41 Stearns and Stearns, *Jazz Dance,* 90.

42 Ibid., 87. From Marshall Stearns's numerous interviews with Aaron Palmer, 1962–63.

43 Ida Forsyne, interview by Cassandra Willis, 1972.

44 Antoine, *Achievement: The Life of Laura Bowman,* 206.

45 Quoted in Hartman, *Scenes of Subjection,* 151.

46 Hobsbawm, *The Age of Empire, 1875–1914.*

47 Kolchin, *Unfree Labor.*

48 Marshall and Stock, *Ira Aldridge,* 222.

49 *Der Artist* 1022 (September 11, 1904), in Lotz, *Black People,* 73.

50 *Das Organ* 44 (September 25, 1909), 13, in Lotz, *Black People,* 79.

51 *Der Artist* 997 (March 20, 1904), in Lotz, *Black People,* 72.

52 *Der Artist* 1129 (September 30, 1906), in Lotz, *Black People,* 76.

53 Ida Forsyne, interview by Cassandra Willis, 1972.

54 Taussig, *Mimesis and Alterity,* 21.

55 Kislan, *Hoofing on Broadway,* 43.

56 *The Encore,* June 28, 1917, in Lotz, *Black People,* 85.

57 *Chicago Defender,* October 21, 1916, 5.

58 "Louis Douglas is dancing at the London Pavilion, and is engaged for a new revue. He's going into the third season at the above house," reports Smith in 1916.

59 I am referring to Siegfried Kracauer's later analysis of chorus girls in industrialized Europe and America in his essay "Mass Ornament." The line reads, "The hands in the factory correspond to the legs of the Tiller Girls." Kracauer, *Mass Ornament,* 79. I stretch his analogy again in chapter 3.

60 Blackett gives as examples the Bristol and Clifton Ladies Anti Slavery Society, and the Ladies Emancipation Societies in Edinburgh and Glasgow. Blackett, *Building an Antislavery Wall,* 122–23.

61 Ibid., 5.

62 Cunliffe, *Chattel Slavery and Wage Slavery,* 11.

63 Carey, *The Slave Trade, Domestic and Foreign,* quoted in Cunliffe, *Chattel Slavery and Wage Slavery,* 50.

64 Ibid., 18.

65 Blackett, *Building an Antislavery Wall,* 201.

66 Ibid., 23.

67 *The Glory and Shame of England,* 1:viii, quoted in Cunliffe, *Chattel Slavery and Wage Slavery,* 70.

68 *Hampshire Independent*, February 5, 1853, quoted in Blackett, *Building an Antislavery Wall*, 198–99.

69 Yellin, *Women and Sisters*, 9.   HQ1423 Y.45 1989

70 Nardinelli, *Child Labor and the Industrial Revolution*, 126.

71 Cruickshank, *Children and Industry*, 2, 97.

72 FN Report of the Proceedings at a Public Meeting of the Edinburgh Ladies Emancipation Society Held at Queen's Hall, Friday, December 28, 1849, quoted in Blackett, *Building an Antislavery Wall*, 31.

73 Cohen, "Thomas Jefferson and the Problem of Slavery," quoted in King, *Stolen Childhood*, 2.

74 *Sheffield and Rotterdam Independent*, April 3, 1847, quoted in Blackett, *Building an Antislavery Wall*, 202.

75 Trollope, *The Life and Adventures of Michael Armstrong, the Factory Boy*.

76 Berte Coote, an actor and the manager of over one hundred children, spoke out prominently in these debates in the pages of *The Era*. In an interview after the bill was passed, Coote says, "The time fixed is prohibitive. It absolutely bars the performance on the stage of any 'child' under the age of fourteen, and this, though we have the greatest sympathy for the proper upbringing and education of children, is downright cruelty for those youngsters and parents who depend upon the theatre for their bread and butter." "Children on Stage," *The Era*, April 11, 1904, 13.

77 White, *Aren't I a Woman?*, 94.

78 Douglass, *My Bondage and My Freedom*, 206.

79 Cartwright, "Diseases and Peculiarities of the Negro Race," 392.

80 Laurie, Jr., *Vaudeville*, 56, 203.

81 Trollope, 17.

82 A.J.G. Perkins, Theresa Wolfson, Frances Wright, *Free Inquirer: The Study of a Temperament* (New York: Harper & Row, 1939).

83 Wells, *Southern Horrors and Other Writings*, 80.

84 Laurie, Jr., *Vaudeville*, 56, 203.

85 *Variety*, June 26, 1914, Williams and Walker clipping file, BR, LC, NYPL.

86 Brody, *Impossible Purities*, 53.

87 Trollope, *Domestic Manners of the Americans*, 168.

88 Ibid., 16.

89 Jacobs, *Incidents in the Life of a Slave Girl*.

90 Picquet, *Louisa Picquet, Octoroon Slave and Concubine*, 21.

91 The narratives of women are much more often questioned than those written by men, whose own work, I argue, while it may be self-penned, was also mediated in anticipation of their white audiences.

92 It was in 1773, right before working on his draft of the Declaration of Independence, that Jefferson inherited Betty Hemings and ten of her children from Wayles.

93 Trollope, *Domestic Manners of the Americans*, 57.

94 Ibid., 157.

95 H. Stowe, *Uncle Tom's Cabin*, 136.

CHAPTER TWO   LETTING THE FLESH FLY

1 *The Era*, December 9, 1905, 20.

2 Grosz, *Volatile Bodies*, 9.

3 Ibid., 57.

4 Ibid., 12.

5 E. Patrick Johnson, cited by Brooks, "'The Deeds Done in My Body,'" 65.

6 Ida Forsyne, interview by Marshall Stearns, June 27, 1964, artist file, IJS.

7 Hartman, *Scenes of Subjection*, 23.

8 Stearns and Stearns, *Jazz Dance*, 253, my emphasis.

9 Stowe, *Uncle Tom's Cabin*, 204.

10 Lhamon, *Raising Cain*, 97.

11 After successfully staging a version of his show at the small theater the Howard family managed in Troy, New York, the show opened in 1852 at the National Theatre in New York City. Aiken played George Harris, George Howard played St. Clare, the Howard's small daughter Cordelia played Eva, and Caroline played Topsy. Harry Birdoff, *The World's Greatest Hit*, 49.

12 Fletcher, *100 Years of the Negro in Show Business*, 7.

13 *New York Dramatic Mirror*, December 6, 1890, 5.

14 Fletcher, *100 Years of the Negro in Show Business*, 7.

15 William Foster, "History of a Negro Showman, from an overheard conversation between Sam Lucas the old comedian and Horace Western the great Alabama banjo player," SNT. Birdoff, *The World's Greatest Hit*, 241.

16 Fletcher, *100 Years of the Negro in Show Business*, 71.

17 Birdoff, *The World's Greatest Hit*, 270.

18 Thomas Riis cites a review from the *Folio* (January 1877) in which a black woman performed as Topsy in blackface; see Riis, "The Music and Musicians in Nineteenth-Century Productions of *Uncle Tom's Cabin*," 274.

19 Wood, *Blind Memory*, 146.

20 Birdoff, *The World's Greatest Hit*, 153.

21 Wood, *Blind Memory*, 191.

22 *Punch*, April 21, 1894. Reprinted in Carter and Harlow, *Imperialism and Orientalism*, 258.

23 MJE Book Listings/Enid Blyton.www.foxall.com.au/users/mje/Blyton.htm.

24 Website, *Sterling Times*, "the virtual scrapbook of British Nostalgia." www.sterlingtimes.co.uk. "SaveOurGollywoggs!" www.sterlingtimes.co.uk/golliwog.htm.

25 www.tourisminternet.com.au/chilt.htm. In a segment that has since been taken down, this site described a wildlife preserve where Gollywogs live in Chiltern, 280 kilometers west of Melbourne. Gollywogs are still listed at this

website as one of the products made in Chiltern. "These two naughty Gollywogs have wandered in from the Dark, Dark Woods," it reads, next to a photo of two dolls. "You can see them and their friends at Duffa's Dinkum Den d'Arts, a shop where nearly everything is made in Chiltern." www.tourism internet.com.au/chshop2.htm.

26 Stowe, *Uncle Tom's Cabin*, 207.
27 Lhamon, *Raising Cain*, 143.
28 Williams, "Uncle Tom's Women," 24. Williams's essay was the first and only source I have found that adequately addresses this historical phenomenon.
29 Birdoff, *The World's Greatest Hit*, 49. Other white women Topsy delineators described in Birdoff's book are Mrs. Harry Chapman (197), Alice Kingsbury, Helen Dauvray, and Charlotte Crabtree (220–21).
30 Directed by William Daly, distributed by World Film Corporation. *Moving Picture World*, n.d., 1077, Michelle Wallace file. I respectfully disagree with Wallace's positive analysis in my assessment of Mona Ray's performance.
31 John Sullivan, "Topsy and Eva Play Vaudeville," www.iath.virginia.edu/utc/interpret/exhibits/sullivan/sullivanf.html. TOBA stands for Theater Owners' Booking Association, a circuit of theaters in the South where black acts performed. It was also known as the "chitlin' circuit" and was referred to by black performers as "Tough on Black Asses" for its rough conditions and racist climate.
32 Desmond, "Dancing Out the Difference"; Koritz, "Dancing for the Orient."
33 Hartman, *Scenes of Subjection*, 29.
34 Elizabeth Chandler, "Mental Metempsychosis," *The Genius*, 3rd ser., 1 (February 1831): 171, quoted in Yellin, *Women and Sisters*, 13.
35 Gregory, "The Drama of Negro Life," 155.
36 Bakhtin, *Rabelais and His World*, 11.
37 Gregory, "The Drama of Negro Life," 155.
38 Ibid., 159.
39 Hartman, *Scenes of Subjection*, 26.
40 Young, *Colonial Desire*, 92.
41 Horsman, *Race and Manifest Destiny*, 58.
42 George Combe, *A System of Phrenology*, 5th ed., 2 vol. (Edinburgh, 1843) II, 328. Quoted in Horsman, 58.
43 Cartwright, "Diseases and Peculiarities of the Negro Race," 390–94.
44 Stowe, *A Key to Uncle Tom's Cabin*, 27.
45 Weld, *American Slavery as It Is*, 62.
46 Ibid., 21.
47 Ibid., 62.
48 Prince, *The Narrative of Nancy Prince*, 66.
49 Ibid., 73.
50 Thanks to Dwight McBride for rightly acknowledging the importance of considering Mary Prince's narrative. D. McBride, *Impossible Witnesses*.

51 See, for instance, Lucy A. Delany's physical resistance to her mistress's whip in Delany, *From the Darkness Cometh the Light, or Struggles for Freedom*, 43–64.

52 Prince, *The Narrative of Nancy Prince*, 72.

53 Wood, *Blind Memory*, 246–50.

54 King, *Stolen Childhood*, 166.

55 Stowe, *A Key to Uncle Tom's Cabin*, 16.

56 Stowe, *Uncle Tom's Cabin*, 215.

57 Ibid., 214.

58 George Cunnabell Howard, "Oh! I'se So Wicked" (New York: Horace Waters, 1854), in American Memory Collection, Library of Congress.

59 Eliza Cook and Asa B. Hutchinson, "Little Topsy's Song" (Boston: Oliver Ditson, 1863), in American Memory Collection, Library of Congress. This version, which Asa B. Hutchinson "composed" for "and dedicated" to "his mother," was "sung at the concerts of the Hutchinson Family."

60 Stowe, *Uncle Tom's Cabin*, 217.

61 Ibid.

62 Hartman, *Scenes of Subjection*, 23.

63 Ibid., 17.

64 Ibid., 21.

65 Scarry, *The Body in Pain*, 5.

66 Ibid., 4.

67 Stowe, *Uncle Tom's Cabin*, 141.

68 Ibid., 207, 208; Aiken, *Uncle Tom's Cabin*, 91.

69 Stowe, *Uncle Tom's Cabin*, 209–10.

70 Fabian, *Time and the Other*.

71 Ibid., 24.

72 Ibid., 17, 40, and 45.

73 Ibid., 216.

74 M. Smith, *Mastered by the Clock*, 5.

75 Ibid., 4.

76 Ibid., 12.

77 Ibid., 7.

78 Ibid., 152.

79 Gilroy, *The Black Atlantic*, 40.

80 Hartman, *Scenes of Subjection*, 37.

81 *The Referee*, from advertisements in December 24, 1916; December 31, 1916; and January 7, 1917, in Lotz, *Black People*, 305.

82 *The Era*, July 5, 1916, 18, in Lotz, *Black People*, 305.

83 February 16, 1938, cited in Stearns, *Jazz Dance*, 231.

84 Charles Honi Coles, interview by Marshall Stearns, Philadelphia, 1963; Stearns and Stearns, *Jazz Dance*, 232.

85 Ida Forsyne, interview by Marshall Stearns, July 29, 1964, artist file, IJS.

86 Beecher, *Treatise on Domestic Economy*, in B. Davis, *Antebellum American Culture*, 15.

87 Stowe, *Uncle Tom's Cabin*, 216.

88 Waters, *His Eye Is on the Sparrow*, 68.

CHAPTER THREE "EGYPTIAN BEAUTIES"
AND "CREOLE QUEENS"

1 As cast members changed frequently, I concentrate on the women who appeared consistently in the cast listings of Sam T. Jack's *Creole Burlesque*, documented in the *New York Dramatic Mirror* between 1890 and 1895, LC.

2 J. Johnson, *Black Manhattan*, 95.

3 William Foster, "History of a Negro Showman," SNT.

4 Hughes and Meltzer, *Black Magic*, 48.

5 J. Johnson, *Black Manhattan*, 95.

6 Unidentified review in Sampson, *The Ghost Walks*, 92.

7 Scheiner, *Negro Mecca*, 8.

8 Tour listings, *New York Dramatic Mirror*, 1891–95, LC.

9 Blanco, "A Case of Hip(g)nosis," 35.

10 Clinton-Baddeley, *The Burlesque Tradition in the English Theatre after 1660*, 110.

11 *Indianapolis Freeman*, September 20, 1890, n.p.

12 *Haverhill Evening Gazette*, August 4, 1890, cited in Riis, *Just Before Jazz*, 13. Riis cites this write-up as the show's first advertisement.

13 Washington *Morning Times*, November 14, 1896, cited in Sampson, *The Ghost Walks*, 113–14.

14 Stanley Green describes the cast as a "Parisian ballet troupe" in his *Broadway Musicals, Show by Show*, 3. Robert Allen is probably more accurate, citing them as "David Costa's ballet troupe" from London, in his *Horrible Prettiness*, 109.

15 Allen, *Horrible Prettiness*, 141–42.

16 Sobel, *A Pictorial History of Burlesque*, 48.

17 Indian women dancers touring America also influenced white women's dance conventions during this period. See Priya.

18 Samuel P. Langley and G. Browne Goode to Secretary of the Treasury, March 12, 1890, cited in Rydell, *All the World's a Fair*, 56.

19 Rydell, *All the World's a Fair*, 46.

20 Ibid., 44.

21 Hubert Howe Bancroft, quoted in ibid., 60.

22 Sobel, *A Pictorial History of Burlesque*, 55–57.

23 Ibid., 60.

24 Koritz, "Dancing for the Orient."

25 Uncited entry, dated August 11, 1894, in Sampson, *The Ghost Walks*, 98.

26 Unidentified review, dated January 12, 1895, in Sampson, *The Ghost Walks*, 104.

27 Eliminated by the local Law and Order League from a show in Bridgeport, Connecticut, the dance was performed at a special matinee given for the press. *New York Dramatic Mirror*, March 17, 1894, 9.

28 For more on the political history of American imperialism, sugar plantation economies, and their impact on Asia, see Chan, *Asian Americans*.

29 "The hands in the factory correspond to the legs of the Tiller Girls." Kracauer, *Mass Ornament*, 79. See, in particular, chapter 1, p. 27, n. 59.

30 Lili'uokalani, *Hawai'i's Story by Hawai'i's Queen*.

31 Washington *Morning Times*, November 14, 1896, cited in Sampson, *The Ghost Walks*, 113–14.

32 Scheiner, *Negro Mecca*, 22.

33 Carby, *Reconstructing Womanhood*; Higginbotham, *Righteous Discontent*; Deborah White, *Too Heavy a Load*; Hine and Thompson, *A Shining Thread of Hope*.

34 Carby, "On the Threshold of the Woman's Era," 263–77.

35 Carby, *Reconstructing Womanhood*.

36 Brody, *Impossible Purities*, 52. One literary character perhaps recoverable with this in mind is Harriet Beecher Stowe's character Cassie, who disappears in staged versions of the play. Cassie is unrepentant in her desire for revenge and haunts the evil Simon Legree to his own self-destruction.

37 Brody, *Impossible Purities*, 21.

38 Ibid., 53.

39 Ibid., 50.

40 Blanco, "A Case of Hip(g)nosis."

41 Roach, *Cities of the Dead*. Roach analyzes the performance of fancy girl trade auctions in New Orleans, pp. 211–33.

42 Ibid., 214.

43 Sarah Wheelock gives an excellent social and cultural history of Storyville and the mulatto Madame Lulu White in "A Question of Color," the first chapter of her dissertation. See Wheelock, "Octoroon Madams and White Slavery."

44 Private collection of Joseph Roach. Thanks to Professor Roach for sharing this with me.

45 Blair, "Private Parts in Public Spaces," 205.

46 In 1881, the showman Toni Pastor opened a show on the fringes of the theater district. Advertising his show as "respectable" and keeping the prices reasonable, he broke the all-male rule associated with concert saloons, successfully re-drawing audience composition to include white (European immigrant and Anglo Saxon) women and children and the middle classes. His efforts spelled the birth of vaudeville. African American audiences, however, remained segregated in the upper tiers of the theater. In 1883, the circus man

Benjamin Franklin Keith opened dozens of similar popular-priced theaters. Keith booked only the most famous African American acts and would book no more than one in a show (a typical show ran nine acts). For more history of vaudeville, see Snyder, *The Voice of the City*. For more on the relationship between the white middle class and white-collar workers of the city and the growth of mass amusement, see Nasaw, *Going Out*. While Nasaw argues that African Americans were excluded from participating in mass cultural amusements, he still describes the rise of such amusements as a process of "democratization." He does not sufficiently interrogate this flagrant contradiction or the centrality of re-versioned African American dance and song within this white idea of democratic amusements.

47 The case of Sylvester Stay and his wife, who were refused admission to general seating at a minstrel show, is an ironic illustration of these policies.

> Sylvester Stay, colored, janitor of the Cornell Steamboat company's buildings in Rondout, bought two reserved seat tickets for a minstrel entertainment at the Kingston, New York Opera House. . . . When he presented the tickets . . . he was refused admission to the body of the house but was told he could go in the gallery. Stay brought suit against [the house's manager] Dubois under the Civil Rights Act, placing his damages at $1,000. On the trial of the case he was non-suited, the defense being that the minstrel company had hired to the Opera House, and that the refusal to admit Stay and his wife was the act of the minstrel management and not that of the local manager. The general term of the Supreme Court has just reversed this decision and ordered a new trial. (*New York Dramatic Mirror*, December 16, 1893, 16)

48 G. S. Rousseau and Roy Porter use this phrase to describe the attitudes of early British explorers in the Tahitian islands. Porter, *Exoticism in the Enlightenment*, 2.

49 Mumford, *Interzones*, chapter 2.

50 For an insightful study of the development of this black artistic community in New York City, see Brooks, "Your Negro Melodies."

51 Mumford, *Interzones*, 7.

52 Ottley and Weatherby, *The Negro in New York*, 145.

53 Bederman, *Manliness and Civilization*, chapter 1.

54 *New York Times*, August 16, 1900; J. Johnson, *Black Manhattan*, 127.

55 J. Johnson, *Along This Way*, 177.

56 Walker, "The Real Coon on the American Stage," 225.

57 This scrapbook can be found in the Scrapbook of the Negro in Theater in the Beinecke Library, Yale University. It is not labeled as Stella Wiley's compilation, but as James Weldon Johnson's.

58 J. Johnson, *Black Manhattan*, 104.

59 *Providence News*, undated clipping of review from show at the Olympic Theatre, J W J, Scrapbooks, box 1, book 2, page 3.

60 *Providence News*, undated clipping of review from show at the Olympic Theatre, SNT.

61 *Providence Telegram*, Music and Drama section, probably 1900, SNT.

62 Unidentified clipping from a show at the Brooklyn Music Hall, probably 1900, SNT.

63 Willard Gatewood, "*Smoked Yankees*," 5.

64 Brooks, "Your Negro Melodies," chapter 3 explores the anti-imperialist critique of Bob Cole and James Weldon Johnson as articulated in their play *Tolosa*.

65 Letter dated November 1899, reprinted in Willard Gatewood, "*Smoked Yankees*," 257.

66 Quoted in the Richmond *Planet*, November 11, 1899, reprinted in Willard Gatewood, "*Smoked Yankees*," 258–59.

67 For a description of the Sam Hose case, from the *Atlanta Constitution*, see Wells's pamphlet "Mob Rule in New Orleans" in Wells, *Southern Horrors and Other Writings*, 204–5.

68 Allen and Als et al., *Without Sanctuary*.

69 Osofsky, *Harlem*, 13, 45.

70 Bederman, *Manliness and Civilization*; Hoganson, *Fighting for American Manhood*.

71 Mumford, *Interzones*, chapter 3.

72 J. Johnson, *Black Manhattan*, 97.

73 Washington, D.C. *Morning Times*, November 14, 1896.

74 *Indianapolis Freeman*, September 25, 1897, n.p. To track their tour through Britain, see the weekly music hall listings in *The Era*, April 1897–98, WNP. The show appeared in various places, including the northern cities and towns of Liverpool, Sheffield, Walsall, Wolverhampton, Burnley, and Rhyl.

75 Review from Rhyl, *The Era*, August 28, 1897, 24.

76 Review from Wolverhampton, *The Era*, August 7, 1897, 7.

77 "Amusements in Liverpool," *The Era*, May 1, 1897, 22.

78 *The Era*, April 10, 1897, 11. In March and April *The Bicycle Girl* played in Nottingham and Sheffield, and in April *A Trip to Chinatown* opened at the Prince Theatre in Manchester. *The Lady Cyclist, or the Bicycle Belle* played the Luton Town Hall in May. *The Era*, May 1, 1897, 13.

79 Unidentified clipping, review from Washington, D.C. show, SNT.

80 Ibid.

81 Unidentified clipping, review of a show Sunday afternoon at the Bijou, SNT.

82 "The Black Patti's Troubadours at the Grand Opera House," unidentified clipping, review of Washington, D.C. show, SNT.

83 Stansell, *City of Women*; Peiss, *Cheap Amusements*.

84 Unidentified review from a show at the Holiday Theatre, Baltimore, SNT.

85 Riis, *Just before Jazz*, 34.

86 Washington, D.C. *Morning Times*, November 14, 1896, in Sampson, *The Ghost Walks*, 114.

87 Greeson, "The Mysteries and Miseries of North Carolina."

88 Mumford, *Interzones*, 43.

89 "Black Patti and Her Troubadours," undated review from Proctor's Pleasure Palace, *New York Journal*, SNT.

90 Review of Black Patti's Troubadours at the Empire Theatre, *Indianapolis Freeman*, December 19, 1896, cited in Sampson, *The Ghost Walks*, 116.

91 Riis, *Just before Jazz*, 77–78.

92 Ibid.

93 Unidentified clipping, SNT, quoted by J. Johnson, *Black Manhattan*, 101. For a biographical history of Bob Cole, see Riis, "Bob Cole.

94 Gilbert, *American Vaudeville*, 60–68; Snyder, *The Voice of the City*, chapter 3.

95 Snyder, *The Voice of the City*, 111.

96 Morrison, *Playing in the Dark*, 35.

97 John Beddoe, *The Races of Britain*, 11, quoted in Young, *Colonial Desire*, 71.

98 Horsman, *Race and Manifest Destiny*, 74.

99 De Certeau, *The Practice of Everyday Life*, 37.

100 Hartman, *Scenes of Subjection*, 151.

101 "Bouquet Causes Trouble," clipping, SNT.

102 "Flowers for Another Cause Trouble between a Husband and a Wife," clipping, SNT.

103 Ibid.

104 Clipping, Utica, New York, SNT.

105 *New York Times*, September 11, 1903, SNT.

106 Unidentified clipping, SNT.

CHAPTER FOUR   THE CAKEWALK BUSINESS

1 Foucault, "Space, Power and Knowledge," 140.

2 Erenburg, *Steppin' Out*.

3 Peiss, *Cheap Amusements*.

4 Sherrie Tucker argues eloquently that we consider carefully the ways individual white women negotiated segregation in her essay, "'They Got Corns for My Country.'"

5 For discussion of these transitions in gender ideals, see Bederman, *Manliness and Civilization*. For focus on the transformation of middle-class black manhood and masculinity, see Martin Summers's careful and illuminating history, *Manliness and Its Discontents*.

6 Bederman, *Manliness and Civilization*, chapters 1 and 5.

7 Tomko, *Dancing Class*.

8 Goldman, *Living My Life*, 56.

9 *The London Tatler*, July 1, 1903, 13.

10 "Amusements in Liverpool," *The Era*, May 1, 1897, 22.

11 Ida Forsyne, interview by Marshall Stearns, July 29, 1964, artist's file, IJS.

12 Huggins, *Harlem Renaissance*, 274.

13 Carby, *Race Men*, 37.

14 Ade, "Stories of Benevolent Assimilation," *Chicago Record* (July 9–October 18, 1899). Online at http://boondocksnet.com/adelsba07.html.

15 Nasaw, *Going Out*, 172.

16 Ida Forsyne, interview by Marshall Stearns, July 29, 1964, artist's file, IJS.

17 Ida Forsyne, interview, Cassandra Willis, 1972.

18 African American Sheet Music, Brown Collection, American Memory, Library of Congress. http://memory.loc.gov/ammem/award97/rpbhtml/aasmhome .html.

19 Fletcher, *100 Years of the Negro in Show Business*, 91.

20 Unidentified advertisement for *Black America*, in ibid., 93.

21 Ibid., 94.

22 Sundquist, *To Wake the Nations*, 287.

23 Brooks, "'Journey to a Land of Cotton,'" 16.

24 *Boston Transcript*, July 1895, quoted in Brooks, "'Journey to a Land of Cotton,'" 13.

25 Ida Forsyne, interview by Cassandra Willis, 1972, JHCB.

26 Bederman, *Manliness and Civilization*, 8.

27 Fletcher, *100 Years of the Negro in Show Business*, 106.

28 Ibid., 107.

29 S. Davis, "Cakewalk," 33.

30 Lindsay Patterson, ed., *Anthology of the American Negro in the Theatre: A Critical Approach* (New York: Publisher's Company, 1968), 53.

31 Riis, *Just before Jazz*, 80.

32 Cook, *Anthology of the American Negro in Theater*.

33 Hughes and Meltzer, *Black Magic*, 123.

34 Riis, *Just before Jazz*, 52. Riis's assessment of the musical composed for black comedies, and of coon songs as both denigrating but also satirical and multi-signifying, is quite useful.

35 Janet Brown, "The Coon Singer and the Coon Song"; Dormon, "Shaping the Popular Image of Post Reconstruction Blacks." Neither Brown nor Dormon account for black women coon singers, but these are useful secondary sources from which to start.

36 Walker, "The Real Coon on the American Stage," 224–26.

37 E. Smith, *Bert Williams*, 30–31; Charters, *Nobody*, 36; J. Johnson, *Black Manhattan*, 105. All of these texts cite in full the famous missive from Williams and the Walkers to William Vanderbilt.

38 *New York Journal*, Sunday, August 22, 1897, SNT.

39 Fletcher, *100 Years of the Negro in Show Business*, 112.

40 *New York Times*, September 11, 1903, SNT.

41 *Variety*, June 28, 1914, 27.

42 *New York Age*, May 7, 1908, 6.

43 Unidentified review dated December 11, 1908. Williams and Walker clipping file, Robinson Locke Collection, BR.

44 Review from Dean's last week at the American Theatre, *Variety*, February 5, 1915.

45 *The Era*, April 5, 1906, 21.

46 Fletcher, *100 Years of the Negro in Show Business*, 112.

47 Garelick, "Electric Salome," 86.

CHAPTER FIVE   EVERYBODY'S DOING IT

1 "*Darktown Follies* in Negro Theatre Is New York's Newest Stage Success," *The World*, November 9, 1913, SNT.

2 The *World* reviewer identifies the well-dressed working-class black audience as "the wealthier class of negro," and upper Seventh Avenue as "now the high class black belt of New York." Most likely the reviewer had never seen so many of the city's porters, deliverymen, janitors, laundresses, and cleaning women looking so good.

3 Ethel Williams, interview with Marshall Stearns, December 1961. Artist's file, IJS. Williams gives her date of birth as 1897. Although unverified, this date is quite plausible.

4 Stearns and Stearns, *Jazz Dance*, 128.

5 Waters, *His Eye Is on the Sparrow*. Waters talks about her relationship with Williams in chapters 9 through 12.

6 Kraut, "Recovering Hurston, Reconsidering the Choreographer," 74.

7 "Opportunities the Stage Offers Intelligent and Talented Women," *New York Age*, December 24, 1908, 1. See also "Colored Men and Women on the Stage," 571–75.

8 Ellis, "The Dance of Life," 495.

9 Desmond, "Embodying Difference," 35–37.

10 The boll weevil reached Louisiana in 1903 and devastated crops there from 1906 through 1910, Mississippi after 1913, and Alabama after 1916. Grossman, *Land of Hope*, 28–30.

11 J. Johnson, *Black Manhattan*, 174.

12 Stearns and Stearns, *Jazz Dance*, 125.

13 Leonore Emery, *Black Dance in the United States from 1619–1970*, 132–33, 164–71.

14 *Variety*, June 5, 1914, 14.

15 Ethel Williams, interview by Marshall Stearns, December 1961, artist's file, IJS.

16 Stearns and Stearns, *Jazz Dance*, 130.

17 Nobel Sissle, from interviews by Marshall Stearns, 1952–66, in ibid., 129.

18 Ida Forsyne, interview by Marshall Stearns, July 21, 1964, artist's file, IJS.

19 Stearns and Stearns, *Jazz Dance*, 130.

20 See McCarren, *Dancing Machines*; Burt, *Alien Bodies*, chapter 4; Franko, *The Work of Dance*, chapter 1.

21 Parker and Parker, *The Natural History of the Chorus Girl*, 102.

22 Ibid., 103.

23 Kislan, *Hoofing on Broadway*, 45. Subsequent consecutive citations to this work are cited parenthetically in the text.

24 Ibid.

25 Kracauer, *The Mass Ornament*, 76.

26 Ibid., 81.

27 Ibid., 66–67. Ramsay Burt gives a descriptive analysis of Kracauer's essays on mass ornament in his book *Alien Bodies*, 84–100. He does not talk about the phenomenon in relation to race.

28 Kracauer, *The Mass Ornament*, 67.

29 Petro, "Perceptions of Difference," 41. For example, Petro cites an article by the journalist Harold Nicholson, in which major cities in Europe and America take on female forms. He describes London as "an old lady in black lace," while Paris is "a woman in the prime of her life," and Berlin is "a girl in a pull-over, not much powder on her face." In the poetic reveries of another male writer, "Berlin was a highly desirable woman . . . all wanted to have her . . . she enticed all" (42–43).

30 Erenburg, *Steppin' Out*, 210.

31 Kislan, *Hoofing on Broadway*, 60.

32 Ibid., 57.

33 *Variety*, December 5, 1913, 21.

34 *Variety*, December 19, 1913, 5.

35 Stearns and Stearns, *Jazz Dance*, 96.

36 Ethel Williams, interview by Marshall Stearns, December 1961, artists file, IJS.

37 Undated clipping, *Dancing Times*, Irene and Vernon Castle scrapbooks, DC, quoted in Erenburg, *Steppin' Out*, 164.

38 S. Cook, "Passionless Dancing and Passionate Reform," 134.

39 Erenburg, *Steppin' Out*, 166.

40 Mr. W. C. Wilkinson, "The Dance of Modern Society," quoted in Faulkner, *The Immorality of Modern Dances*, 29. Chapter 4 is entitled "The Sinful Pose of Round Dances."

41 Faulkner, *The Lure of the Dance*, 10.

42 Ibid., 29–30.

43 *New York Age*, January 8, 1914, 1.

44 Transcript from New York City Club Committee on Public Amusements and Morals, Irene and Vernon Castle scrapbooks, DC, quoted in Badger, *A Life in Ragtime*, 100.

45 Castle, *Modern Dancing*, 175.

46 Ibid.

47 Badger, *A Life in Ragtime*, 102.

48 Koritz, *Gendering Bodies / Performing Art* and "Dancing for the Orient"; Desmond, "Dancing out the Difference."
49 Kermode, "Poet and Dancer Before Diaghilev," 149–50, 152, 154, 156, 160.
50 Garelick, "Electric Salome," 93.
51 Kendall, *Where She Danced*, 21.
52 Ibid., 24.
53 For more on François Delsarte and his influence on American expressive culture, see Shawn, *Every Little Moment*; and Ruyter, *The Cultivation of Mind and Body in Nineteenth Century American Delsartism*.
54 *Indianapolis Freeman*, December 12, 1896.
55 Kendall, *Where She Danced*, 50.
56 Ibid., 54.
57 Ibid., 75.
58 Ibid., 77.
59 Cherniavsky, *The Salome Dancer*, 142.
60 Bade, *La Femme Fatale*, 16; also quoted in Cherniavsky, *The Salome Dancer*, 184.
61 Koritz, "Dancing for the Orient," 133.
62 See the Palace Theatre playbill in Cherniavsky, *The Salome Dancer*, 94.
63 *Times Literary Supplement*, March 25, 1908, 102.
64 Koritz, "Dancing for the Orient," 133.
65 "All dances in *Abyssinia* were created and arranged as well as rehearsed by her." *Pittsburgh Leader*, May 11, 1906, Williams and Walker file, BR; Krasner, *A Beautiful Pageant*, 55.
66 Duncan, *My Life*, 244.
67 *Variety*, July 17, 1909, Williams and Walker file, BR.
68 *Cleveland Plain Dealer*, July 31, 1912, Williams and Walker file, BR.
69 *Vanity Fair*, August 3, 1912, Williams and Walker file, BR.
70 Williams and Walker file, BR, n.d.
71 Ibid.
72 "Victoria Show Pleases Crowds," *New York Telegraph*, August 19, 1912, Williams and Walker file, BR.
73 D. Brooks, *Bodies in Dissent*, 328.
74 Paul Laurence Dunbar and E. P. Moran, "Evah Dahkey Is a King," sheet music, Brown University's African American Sheet Music Collection, on line at the Library of Congress, American Memory Collection. http://memory.loc.gov/ammem/collections/sheetmusic/brown.
75 Walker, "The Real Coon on the American Stage," 224–26.
76 "Colored Men and Women on the Stage," 571.
77 "A Creator of Dances," in *Pittsburgh Leader*, May 11, 1906, Williams and Walker file, BR.
78 "Opportunities the Stage Offers Intelligent and Talented Women," *New York Age*, December 24, 1908, 1.

1 McDonald, *Been Rich All My Life*.
2 Ibid.
3 Wall, *Hurston*, 842.
4 William Houghton, "Color Notes," March 18, 1927, SNT.
5 Kimball and Bolcom, *Reminiscing with Sissle and Blake*, 144.
6 Hughes, *The Big Sea*, 223–24.
7 *Variety*, May 27, 1921.
8 Kimball and Bolcom, *Reminiscing with Sissle and Blake*, 88.
9 Ibid.
10 Ibid.
11 Baker and Bouillon, *Josephine*, 33–34.
12 Lilly Yuen, interview by Jean-Claude Baker, in Baker and Chase, *Josephine*, 76.
13 McDonald, *Been Rich All My Life*.
14 Ibid.
15 Adelaide Hall, interview with June Knox-Mawer, Radio 4 series "Sweet Adelaide," Part 2, April 20, 1992, BLMC.
16 Ibid.
17 Adelaide Hall, interview with June Knox-Mawer, Radio 4 series "Sweet Adelaide," Part 1, April 13, 1992, BLMC.
18 Adelaide Hall, interview with June Knox-Mower, Radio 4 series "Sweet Adelaide," Part 3, April 27, 1992, BLMC.
19 Adelaide Hall, interview, John Dunne Show, Radio 2, June 28, 1985, BLMC.
20 Ibid.
21 Adelaide Hall obituary, *London Times*, November 8, 1993, artist file, TML. See also the interview with Adelaide Hall in the Vivian Perlis Oral History Collection, Music Library, Yale University. See also the documentary *Sophisticated Lady*, Channel Four Films, spring 1989.
22 Woll, *Black Musical Theatre*, 77.
23 *Variety*, June 23, 1922, 15.
24 Lafayette Theatre playbill, in Hughes and Meltzer, *Black Magic*, 123. David Levering Lewis mentions the production but not the involvement of the Lafayette Players; Lewis, *When Harlem Was in Vogue*, 92.
25 Waters, *His Eye Is on the Sparrow*, 153.
26 "The Colonial is but a block from the 63rd street (now called Daly's) adjacent to the West Side colored section known as 'San Juan Hill,' and also to the subway lines which tap Harlem's colored belt." *Variety*, November 1, 1923, SNT.
27 *Daily News*, November 1, 1923, SNT.
28 An early title for the Sissle and Blake show was *George White's Black Scandals*, but this was discarded, as Sissle and Blake didn't want their show confused with White's yearly white chorus girl revue, *Scandals*. Woll, *Black Musical Theatre*, 85. White's longest running edition of *Scandals*—his eighth, open-

ing in 1926—offered a "musical debate between the blues and the classics, featured George Gershwin's 'Rhapsody in Blue,' Handy's 'St. Louis Blues,' and introduced the Black Bottom to the theatre-going audience." Green, *Broadway Musicals, Show by Show*, 52.

29 "The dances were staged by Lyda Webb [*sic*], a girl director being something of a novelty and the numbers were well paced." *Variety*, November 1, 1923.

30 J. Johnson, *Black Manhattan*, 190.

31 "'Chocolate Dandies,' Colored Show, Better Than 'Shuffle Along,'" *New York Tribune*, September 2, 1924. In Kimball and Bolcom, *Reminiscing with Sissle and Blake*, 172.

32 Baker and Bouillon, *Josephine*, 34.

33 Ibid., 26.

34 Ida Forsyne, interview with Marshall Stearns, 21 July 1964, artist file, IJS.

35 "[Lew Leslie] Prefers to Stage All-Negro Shows. Lew Leslie Declares no White Girls Work So Hard as Do the Harlem Belles," quoted in Woll, *Black Musical Theatre*, 97.

36 Waters, *His Eye Is on the Sparrow*, 183.

37 U. S. Thompson, quoted in Baker and Chris, *Josephine*, 82.

38 For three days in 1924, Baker sang as the replacement for an ill Ethel Waters. Waters, *His Eye Is on the Sparrow*, 185.

39 Baker and Buillone, *Josephine*, 36.

40 Hughes and Meltzer, *Black Magic*, 103.

41 Florence Mills obituary, *New York Amsterdam News*, November 2, 1927.

42 *Blackbirds of 1934* program from London Coliseum, October 27, 1934, TML.

43 "Wildest of Dancing but Slow Comedy. All Coloured Revue at Coliseum," by George W. Bishop, *London Daily Telegraph*, August 27, 1934 n.p., TML.

44 *London Daily Telegraph*, November 24, 1934, n.p., TML.

45 "'A Caribbean,'" *Chicago Defender*, December 15, 1934, 8.

46 *Variety*, Broadway Reviews, August 11, 1922, 16.

47 Telegram, dated June 15, 1923 from Piccadilly, Helen Armistead Johnson Collection, Florence Mills File, SCB.

48 "Irene Castle in Cork at Fancy Dress Ball," *Variety*, July 4, 1923, 2.

49 Letter from Irene Castle to Florence Mills, Helen Armistead Johnson Collection, Florence Mills File, SCB.

50 Tucker, *Some of These Days*, 159.

51 Waters, *His Eye Is on the Sparrow*, 138.

52 Wall, *Hurston*, 635–65.

53 Ida Forsyne, interview by Marshall Stearns, July 29, 1964, artist file, IJS.

54 Ibid.

55 Tucker, *Some of These Days*, 62.

56 Ibid., 63.

57 *Chicago Defender*, November 21, 1931, 5, cited in D. Harrison, *Black Pearls*, 246.

58 Ashton Stevens, *Chicago Herald*, March 31, 1924.

59 *Variety*, August 26, 1921, 17.

60 Horsman, *Race and Manifest Destiny*; Higham, *Strangers in the Land.*

61 *Variety*, August 26, 1921, 17.

62 Wolf, *Europe and the People without History.*

63 William Houghton, "Color Notes," March 18, 1927, SNT.

64 Ibid.

65 Ibid.

66 Percy Hammond, *New York Herald Tribune*, October 30, 1924, SNT.

67 Heywood Broun, *The World*, October 30, 1924, SNT.

68 Zora Neale Hurston coined the term. Lewis, *When Harlem Was in Vogue*, 98.

69 Alexander Woollcott, *The Sun*, October 30, 1924, SNT.

70 Percy Hammond, *New York Herald Tribune*, October 30, 1924, SNT.

71 Ibid.

72 *Variety*, August 26, 1921, 17.

73 *Evening Mail*, October 30, 1924, SNT.

74 Gilman, "Black Bodies, White Bodies," 213.

75 Scheibinger, *Nature's Body*, 169.

76 Ibid., 95.

77 Long, *History of Jamaica*, 2:383, quoted in Young, *Colonial Desire*, 50–51.

78 Scheibinger, *Nature's Body*, 98.

79 Ibid., 95.

80 William Bolitho, "Blackbirds," *The World*, January 19, 1929, SNT.

81 Poulantzas, *State, Power, Socialism*, 114, quoted in Bennett, *The Birth of the Museum*, 141.

82 William Bolitho, "Blackbirds," *The World*, January 19, 1929, SNT.

83 Collomb, introduction, 1026, cited in Edwards, *The Practice of Diaspora*, 164.

84 Edwards, *The Practice of Diaspora*, 167.

85 Levinson, "The Negro Dance," 74. The Russian intellectual émigré to Paris has been credited as the first dance critic.

86 Baker and Buillone, *Josephine*, 55.

87 Gilman, "Black Bodies, White Bodies," 204–41; Willis and Williams, *The Black Female Body*, 59–63.

88 "France Returns Old Remains to Homeland," *New York Times*, May 5, 2002, A28.

89 Rampersad, *The Life of Langston Hughes*, 1:71; Lewis, *When Harlem Was in Vogue*, 81, 85.

90 Barnes, "Negro Art in America," 21.

91 In his essay "The New Negro," Alain Locke thought that Harlem had "the same role to play for the New Negro as Dublin has had for the New Ireland or Prague for the New Czechoslovakia." See Locke, *The New Negro*, 7.

92 Rogers, "Jazz at Home."

93 *Cleveland Plain Dealer*, SNT.

94 Rogers, "Jazz at Home," 224.

95 Wall, *Hurston*, 635–65.

96 The dance scholar Anthea Kraut brilliantly reveals and analyzes Hurston's work in dance. See Kraut, "Recovering Hurston, Reconsidering the Choreographer," 70.

97 Ellis, "The Art of Dancing," 478.

98 Hughes, *The Weary Blues*, 25.

99 Hughes, *Selected Poems of Langston Hughes*, 7.

100 Langston Hughes, "Danse Africaine," in *Selected Poems of Langston Hughes* (New York: Vintage, 1959), 7.

101 Hughes, *The Weary Blues*, 35.

102 Ethel M. Caution, "Last Night," *Crisis* (February 1929), quoted in Honey, *Shadowed Dreams*, 155.

103 Marjorie Marshall, "To a Dark Dancer," *Crisis* (January 1928), quoted in Honey, *Shadowed Dreams*, 140.

104 Zora Neale Hurston, "How It Feels to Be Colored Me," *Memoirs and Other Writings*, ed. Cheryl Hall (New York: Library of America, 1995), 828.

105 McKay, *Home to Harlem*, 29.

106 Ibid., 197.

107 Jayna Brown, "Drifting with the Occidental: Black Male Play Space in Claude McKay's *Banjo*."

108 McKay, *Selected Poems of Claude McKay*, 60.

109 Ibid., 61.

110 S. Brown, *Southern Road*, 59.

111 Ibid., 105.

112 Ibid., 62.

113 Brown, "Cabaret (1927, Black & Tan Chicago)," *Southern Road*, 117. All further quotations from "Cabaret" are from *Southern Road*, 115–18.

114 *Opportunity*, January 1931; S. Brown, *Negro Poetry and Drama and the Negro in American Fiction*, 119–20.

115 Rex Ingram played "De Lawd" and Ida Forsyne made a cameo appearance as Mrs. Noah.

116 This is from the film. "Nobody can squirm like those Babylon girls!" is how it reads in the working script for Connelly's play. Helen Armistead Johnson collection, scb.

117 McDonald, *Been Rich All My Life*.

118 Ibid.

119 Ibid.

CHAPTER SEVEN   TRANSLOCATIONS

1 Fletcher, *100 Years of the Negro in Show Business*, 266, 268.

2 Baker and Chase, *Josephine*, 92.

3 Allard J. Moller, "A Jazz Odyssey: Jack Carter's Orchestra," *Storyville* 63 (February–March 1976), Valaida Snow artist file, ijs.

4   Howard Rye, "The Blackbirds and Their Orchestras," Visiting Firemen 9, *Storyville* (April–May 1984), Valaida Snow artist file, IJS.

5   Dorothy White, *Black Africa and de Gaulle*, 37.

6   Bricktop and Haskins, *Bricktop*, 83.

7   Tyler Stovall tends to this kind of celebration in *Paris Noir*.

8   Bauman, *A Life in Fragments*, 192–206. Although Adorno and Horkheimer were not considering black people as the agents of history involved in the dialectical drama of civilization's progress, their essays in their *Dialectic of Enlightenment* encapsulate the inseparability of progress, terror, and oppression forming in and out of the Enlightenment project.

9   Bricktop and Haskins, *Bricktop*, 203–4.

10 Howard Rye, liner notes, *Valaida*, vol. 1, 1935–1937 (London: Harlequin, 1992). Rye draws on Theo Zwicky's research; see minutes to presentation given by Theo Zwicky, October 30, 1963, "Miss Show Biz. alias Queen of the Trumpet alias Valaida Snow," in "Dig It," *Bulletin of the New Jazz Club* (Zurich) 5, no. 3 (1964): 133, SVJD. The liner notes by Rye that accompany vol. 1 and Morton Clausen's liner notes to *Valaida*, vol. 2, 1935–1940 (London: Harlequin, 1992) are the most accurate and reliable biographical sources of Snow's activities during her time in Scandinavia.

11 "De Negerrevue Black People Te Berlijn—Een Bijdrage Over Het Thema 'Der Untergang des Abendlandes,'" *Het Vaderland*, July 16, 1926, evening edition B., trans. H. Bergemeier, quoted in Lotz, *Black People*, 324.

12 Ibid.

13 Ibid., 325.

14 Ibid., 324.

15 Swaffer, "Two Women But One Public," 21, quoted in Egan, *Florence Mills*, 271.

16 E. W. Osborn in *The Evening World*, October 30, 1924, SNT.

17 Ibid.

18 *Evening Mail*, October 30, 1924, SNT.

19 "A Coloured Star's Death," *Liverpool Echo*, November 2, 1927, SNT.

20 Heywood Broun in *The World*, October 30, 1924, SNT.

21 "Magic Moon That Brought Me Money," undated clipping, 1926, HAJC, Schomburg Institute. In Egan, *Florence Mills*, 270.

22 James Weldon Johnson calls Mills's stint with *Sons of Ham* her first professional appearance and cites a *Washington Star* review; see J. Johnson, *Black Manhattan*, 197–98. Henry T. Sampson claims that Ada Overton Walker trained her; see Sampson, *Blacks in Blackface*, 402.

23 Waters, *His Eye Is on the Sparrow*, 183.

24 "Bye Bye to a Blackbird," *Liverpool Evening Express*, August 3, 1927.

25 *New York Herald Tribune*, November 2, 1927, 20; *New York Times*, November 2, 1927, 27.

26 Greene, introduction, 31.

27 *New York Herald Tribune*, November 7, 1927, 5. The list of pallbearers in the

New York Times differs slightly. It includes Ada Walsh, Lottie Gee, and Elizabeth Walsh and not Ada Ward (probably the same as Ada Walsh), Maude Russell, or Evelyn Preer. *New York Times*, November 7, 1927, 25.

28 "Scores Collapse at Mills Funeral," *New York Times*, November 7, 1927, 25.

29 Unidentified Bob Cole obituary, SNT.

30 E. Smith, *Bert Williams*, 225.

31 "Revue Nègre," *Der Querschnitt*, Lotz, 318.

32 Levinson, "The Negro Dance," 74.

33 Macey, *Frantz Fanon*, 104.

34 Hubert Deschamps, "French Colonial Policy in Tropical Africa between the Two World Wars," in *France and Britain in Africa: Imperial Rivalry and Colonial Rule*, ed. Gifford and Louis (New Haven: Yale University Press, 1971), 561.

35 Albert Saurraut, "La Mise en Valeur des Colonies Françaises" (Paris: Payout, 1923), quoted in Deschamps, "French Colonial Policy," 553.

36 Deschamps, "French Colonial Policy," 549.

37 Miller, "Orientalism, Colonialism," 702.

38 Ibid., 701.

39 Baker and Buillone, *Josephine*, 84.

40 P. Rose, *Jazz Cleopatra*, 47.

41 Foster, *Compulsive Beauty*, 4, citing Breton, "Le message automatique," trans. as Breton, "The Automatic Message," 105, 109.

42 Leiris, *L'Afrique fantôme*, 324, trans. in Clifford, "Negrophilia," 905.

43 Leiris, *L'Afrique fantôme*, 42.

44 Leiris, *Manhood*, 109.

45 Nenno, "Femininity, the Primitive and Modern Urban Space," 150–52.

46 P. Rose, *Jazz Cleopatra*, 133.

47 Baker and Buillone, *Josephine*, 74.

48 P. Rose, *Jazz Cleopatra*, 130.

49 Ibid., 138.

50 Abtey, *La Guerre secrète de Josephine Baker*.

51 P. Rose, *Jazz Cleopatra*, 163.

52 Haney, *Naked at the Feast*, 224.

53 Deschamps, "French Colonial Policy," 545.

54 For accounts of Baker's illness, see Baker and Buillone, *Josephine*, 126–27; Baker and Chase, *Josephine*, 243–44; P. Rose, *Jazz Cleopatra*, 196–97; Haney, *Naked at the Feast*, 224–25. Haney does not hesitate to attribute Baker's infection to a stillborn pregnancy, but Jean-Claude Baker's interview with Dr. Georges Barou (Baker and Chase, *Josephine*, 243–44) and Josephine's own accounts do not support this.

55 Baker, *Josephine*, 127.

56 Kenneth Crawford, "Josephine Baker in North Africa," PM, April 1, 1943, Josephine Baker artist file, JWJ.

57 Baker and Buillone, *Josephine*, 130.

58 Ibid., 132.

59 Frantz Fanon quoted in Macey, *Frantz Fanon*, 104. From *Mémorial International Frantz Fanon*.

60 Sibony, *Écrits sur le racisme*, 118, trans. in Verges, *Monsters and Revolutionaries*, 135.

61 *Randers Amtsavis*, December 4, 1940, trans. "D. M.," Valaida Snow artist file, IJS.

62 Ibid.

63 *New York Star / Amsterdam News*, April 10, 1943, 13. Thanks to Mark Miller for sharing some of his research and pointing this article out to me. His forthcoming biography of Valaida Snow will offer much new information about her early life as well as her life in the United States after the war.

64 Rosetta Reitz, liner notes, *Hot Snow: Queen of the Trumpet Sings and Swings*, Women's Heritage Series, Foremothers, vol. 2 (Rosetta Records, 1982). Not all U. S. sources are as undependable as Rosetta Reitz's liner notes. The encyclopedia entry for Snow in J. Smith, *Notable Black Women*, 1056; and Claghorn's entry in his *Biographical Dictionary of Jazz*, 276, are more accurate. Chilton, *Who's Who in Jazz*, 383, retains the concentration camp story. Among the contributionist histories of women musicians that have included Snow, Placksin, *American Women in Jazz, 1900 to the Present*, 94, quotes Harrison Smith's account of Valaida, "hauled into Wester Feangle concentration stockade." Linda Dahl's coverage in *Stormy Weather*, 81–84, while not exhaustive, at least reports the difficulty of finding out the "true" events of Snow's time in Scandinavia.

65 Albertson, *Bessie Smith*, 215–26.

66 Holiday and Dufty, *Lady Sings the Blues*.

67 Mark Miller, personal correspondence, November 9, 2006.

68 John Edgar Wideman, "Valaida"; Wideman, *The Stories of John Edgar Wideman*; and C. Allen, *Valaida*.

69 I am indebted to Elis Egneby's son, Bjorn Egneby, who not only shared his personal file on Valaida Snow, but translated this section from his father's unpublished journal for me.

70 Simon, *The Big Bands*, 261, quoted in Tucker, *Swing Shift*, 12.

71 "Miss Show Biz. alias Queen of the Trumpet alias Valaida Snow," minutes to presentation given by Theo Zwicky, October 30, 1963, in "Dig It," *Bulletin of the New Jazz Club* (Zurich) 5, no. 3 (1964): 128, SVJD.

72 "Valaida Was Great," *Orkesterjournalen*, July 1939, 8, trans. Moa Matthis.

73 "A Magnificent Artist," *Estrad*, July 1939, 4, trans. Moa Matthis.

74 See an article by Snow in *Melody Maker*, September 15, 1934, 8. Thanks to Mark Miller for this source.

75 See Mark Miller's forthcoming biography of Valaida Snow. Antoinette Handy asserts that Snow's mother trained at Howard University. See A. Handy, *Black Women in American Bands and Orchestras*, 131, but in light of Miller's current scholarship this seems unlikely.

76 Kimball and Bolcom, *Reminiscing with Sissle and Blake*, 178.

77 Henrik Rechendorff, "Dette der Valaida," *Berlingske Ti Dene*, February 12, 1941. Erik Wiedemann cites this article as a primary source for information on Valaida Snow. See Wiedemann, *Jazz i Danmark*, 1:434. Looking at bound copies of *Berlingske Ti Dene* in the Kungligen Bibliotek in Stockholm, I could not find the article under this date. I found a translated copy by "D.M.," Valaida Snow artist file, IJS.

78 Allard J. Moller, "A Jazz Odyssey: Jack Carter's Orchestra," *Storyville* 63 (February–March 1976), 101, Valaida Snow artist file, IJS.

79 Dance, *The World of Earl Hines*, 64.

80 See the chapter on Miles Davis in Carby, *Race Men*.

81 Dahl, *Stormy Weather*.

82 In *Swing Shift*, Sherrie Tucker offers a well-researched history of the International Sweethearts and other female jazz musicians working together in the United States during and after World War II.

83 George W. Bishop, "All Colored Revue at Coliseum," *Daily Telegraph*, August 27, 1934, theater file, TML.

84 In 1935 Snow recorded with Billy Mason and His Orchestra, in 1936 with Scott Wood and His Six Swingers, and in 1937 with Johnny Pillitz's Orchestra. See the recording *Valaida*, vol. 1, 1935–37 (Harlequin).

85 In 1936 she played alto saxophone in Pierre Chenal's *L'Alibi* and in early 1939 she appeared in the nightclub sequences of Robert Siodmak's film *Pieges*. Snow appeared in other films. In the mid-1930s she may have appeared in two U.S. films, possibly titled *Take It from Me* and *Irresistible You*. In 1946, back from Europe after the war, she made two films with the Ali Baba Trio: *Patience and Fortitude* and *If You Only Knew*, directed by Dave Gould.

86 Howard Rye, liner notes, *Valaida*, vol. 1. Rye cites Theo Zwicky as the source of this information, which also appears in "Miss Show Biz. alias Queen of the Trumpet alias Valaida Snow," minutes to presentation given by Theo Zwicky, October 30, 1963, in "Dig It," *Bulletin of the New Jazz Club* (Zurich) 5, no. 3 (1964): 128, SVJD.

87 Kater, *A Different Drummer*, 17.

88 Ibid., 30.

89 *London Daily Telegraph*, December 7, 1934, 6.

90 Kater, *A Different Drummer*, 17.

91 *Social Demokraten*, August 17, 1939.

92 The composer Gösta Nystroem in *Handels—och Sjofartstidning*, November 1, 1933, quoted in translation in Fornas, "Yodeling Negroes and Swinging Lapps," 8. I am grateful to Johan Fornas for sharing his work on the Scandinavian reception of jazz.

93 Gunnar Eriksson and Arthur Lundkvist, *Karavan*, 1935, quoted in translation by Fornas, "Yodeling Negroes and Swinging Lapps," 9. Arthur Lundkvist was credited with bringing African American literature to Scandinavia.

94 Fornas, "Yodeling Negroes and Swinging Lapps," 8.

95 "Det Tropiske Olso," unidentified Norwegian newspaper, trans. "D.M.," Snow artist file, IJS.

96 Ibid.

97 Kater cites the year of their detainment as 1941, in Kater, *A Different Drummer*, 146. But his detainment was actually in 1943. Candace Allen met with Svend Asmussen, who related to her that he was detained briefly in 1943. Private communication, May 1, 2006. See also the Danish film website, http://www.danskefilm.dk/index2.html.

98 "Valaida gor succeˆ i Malmo," *Orkester Journalen*, October 1939, 10, trans. Moa Matthis.

99 For detailed coverage of Snow's performances in Denmark during this time, see Wiedemann, *Jazz i Danmark*, 150, 159, 187, 252, 266, 287, 289. I am indebted to the jazz archivist Ingemar Olsson for translating segments of Wiedemann's book for me.

100 Morton Clausen, liner notes to *Valaida*, vol. 2, 1935–1940 (London: Harlequin, 1992).

101 Gilroy, *Between Camps*, 324.

102 Baumann, *Modernity and the Holocaust*, 52, 51.

103 *Hitler's Forgotten Victims*, dir. David Okuefuna, Afro-Wisdom Productions, 1997.

104 Zwerin, *La Tristesse de Saint Louis*.

105 See proceeds of this trial in *Politiken*, January 1942, trans. "Tor," Snow artist file, IJS. It seems the report of these proceedings was not released until a year later, while Snow was detained at Vestre Faengsel.

106 Snow's performance back in Sweden is announced in an unidentified clipping, SVJD. It is also reported in *Estrad*, August 1941. I had a conversation with the reporter Rolf Dahlgren, who saw Snow perform in May but remembers it being an outdoor appearance at the Tivoli.

107 Announcement in *Estrad*, October 1941.

108 I am grateful to Candace Allen for her scholarly and intellectual generosity. We shared work in a series of exchanges in May and June 2002, as she was writing her novel on *Valaida*.

109 *Aftonbladet*, March 15, 1942, trans. Lena Ahlin.

110 Ibid.

111 *Aftonbladet*, May [?24], 1942, trans. Moa Matthis.

112 Gilroy, *Between Camps*, 298. Gilroy cites Ruth, *Goebbels*, 194.

113 *Aftonbladet*, probably May 24, 1942, SVJD. Snow was deported on May 28, which the article says was a Thursday. If she had been in Gothenburg "since Saturday" (May 23) this report was probably from the paper on Sunday, May 24.

114 Unlike in any other occupied country, the people of Denmark protected their Jewish population, using the policy of declaring Jews stateless as an asset. If they were stateless, Danish officials told the Germans, then the Germans had

no right to deport them without Danish approval. Arendt, *Eichmann in Jerusalem*, 175.

115 *New York Star / Amsterdam News*, April 10, 1943, 13.

116 "Opportunities the Stage Offers Intelligent and Talented Women," *New York Age*, December 24, 1908, 1.

CONCLUSION

1 McDonald, *Been Rich all My Life*.

2 Gaunt, *The Games Girls Play*.

3 Watkins, *Stepin Fetchit*; Watts, *Hattie McDaniel* are popular biographies motivated by this revisionist possibility.

4 Brooks, *Bodies in Dissent*, 162.

5 Williams, "Uma Mulata Sim!," 7.

6 Mbembe, "Necropolitics," 22.

7 Kelley, *Freedom Dreams*, 158.

NEWSPAPERS AND PERIODICALS

Aftonbladet
Amsterdam News
Chicago Defender
Chicago Herald
Colored American Magazine
Crisis
Daghens Nyheter
Era
Estrad
Indianapolis Freeman
Jazz Podium
London Herald
London Tatler

London Telegraph
London Times
Melody Maker
Metronome
Negro Digest
New York Age
New York Dramatic Mirror
New York Times
Opportunity
Orkester Journalen
Stage
Variety

BOOKS, ARTICLES, AND DOCUMENTARIES

Abtey, Jacques. *La Guerre secrète de Josephine Baker*. Paris: Sibney, 1948.

Ade, George. *Stories of Benevolent Assimilation*. Ed. Perry Gianakos. Quezon City: New Day, 1985.

Adorno, Theodor. "On the Fetish Character of Music and the Regression of Listening." In *The Essential Frankfurt Reader*, ed. Andrew Arato and Eike Gebhardy, 270–99. New York: Continuum, 1998.

Adorno, Theodor W., and Max Horkheimer. *Dialectic of Enlightenment*. New York: Continuum, 1995.

Agamben, Giorgio. *Homo Sacer: Sovereign Power and Bare Life*. Stanford, Calif.: Stanford University Press, 1998.

Aiken, George. *Uncle Tom's Cabin*. 1853. In *American Melodrama*, ed. Daniel Gerould, 75–133. New York: Performing Arts Journal Publications, 1983.

Albertson, Chris. *Bessie Smith: Empress of the Blues*. New York: Schirmer, 1975.

Allen, Candace. *Valaida*. London: Virago, 2004.

Allen, James, and Hilton Als, eds. *Without Sanctuary: Lynching Photography in America*. Santa Fe: Twin Palms, 2000.

Allen, Robert. *Horrible Prettiness: Burlesque and American Culture*. Chapel Hill: University of North Carolina Press, 1991.

Anderson, Benedict. *Imagined Communities: Reflections on the Origin and Spread of Nationalism*. London: Verso, 1983.

Antoine, Le Roi. *Achievement: The Life of Laura Bowman*. New York: Pageant, 1961.

Arendt, Hannah. *Eichmann in Jerusalem: A Report on the Banality of Evil*. 1963. Reprint, New York: Penguin, 1992.

———. *The Human Condition*. Chicago: University of Chicago Press, 1958.

———. *On Violence*. New York: Harvest, 1969.

Bade, Peter. *La Femme Fatale*. New York: Mayflower, 1979.

Badger, Reid. *A Life in Ragtime: A Biography of James Reese Europe*. New York: Oxford University Press, 1995.

Baker, Jean-Claude, and Chris Chase. *Josephine: The Hungry Heart*. New York: Random House, 1993.

Baker, Josephine, and Jo Buillone. *Josephine*. Trans. Mariana Fitzpatrick. New York: Marlowe, 1988.

Bakhtin, Mikhail. *Rabelais and His World*. Trans. Helene Iswolsky. Bloomington: Indiana University Press, 1984.

Balibar, Etienne, and Immanuel Wallerstein. *Race, Nation, Class*. London: Verso, 1991.

Baral, Robert. *Revue: The Great Broadway Period*. New York: Fleet, 1962.

Barlow, William, and Thomas Morgan. *From Cakewalks to Concert Halls: An Illustrated History of African American Popular Music, 1895–1930*. Washington: Elliot and Clark, 1992.

Barnes, Albert C. "Negro Art in America." In *The New Negro: Voices of the Harlem Renaissance*, ed. Alain Locke, 19–28. New York: A. and C. Boni, 1925. Reprint, New York: Simon and Schuster, 1997.

Baudelaire, Charles. "The Painter of Modern Life." In *The Painter of Modern Life and Other Essays*, ed. and trans. Jonathan Mayne, 1–40. New York: Garland, 1978.

Bauman, Zygmunt. *A Life in Fragments: Essays in Postmodern Morality*. London: Blackwell, 1995.

———. *Modernity and Ambivalence*. Oxford: Polity, 1991.

———. *Modernity and the Holocaust*. Ithaca, N.Y.: Cornell University Press, 1989.

Bechet, Sidney. *Treat It Gentle*. New York: Hill and Wang, 1960.

Beddoe, John. *The Races of Britain: A Contribution to the Anthropology of Western Europe*. Bristol: Arrowsmith, 1885.

Bederman, Gail. *Manliness and Civilization: A Cultural History of Gender and Race in the United States, 1880–1917*. Chicago: University of Chicago Press, 1995.

Beecher, Catherine. *A Treatise on Domestic Economy.* Boston: T. H. Webb, 1842.

Behn, Aphra. *Oroonoko and Other Writings.* New York: Penguin, 1994.

Benhabib, Sayla, Judith Butler, Drucilla Cornell, and Nancy Fraser. *Feminist Contentions.* New York: Routledge, 1995.

Benjamin, Walter. *Charles Baudelaire: A Lyric Poet in the Era of High-Capitalism.* London: New Left, 1973.

———. *Illuminations.* Trans. Harry Zohn. Ed. Hannah Arendt. New York: Schocken, 1969.

———. *Reflections.* Trans E. Jephcott. Ed. Peter Demetz. New York: Harcourt Brace, 1978.

———. "Über einige Motive bei Baudelaire." In *Gesammelte Schriften,* vol. 1, pt. 2, ed. Teidemann and Schweppenhauser. Frankfurt am Main: Suhrkamp, 1974.

Bennett, Tony. *The Birth of the Museum: History, Theory, Politics.* London: Routledge, 1995.

Berenger, Jean. *A History of the Habsburg Empire, 1700–1918.* Trans. C. A. Simpson. London: Longman, 1997.

Bergreen, Laurence. *Louis Armstrong: An Extravagant Life.* New York: Broadway, 1997.

Berman, Marshall. *All That Is Solid Melts into Air: The Experience of Modernity.* New York: Penguin, 1988.

Birdoff, Harry. *The World's Greatest Hit.* New York: S. F. Vanni, 1947.

Blackburn, Robin. *The Making of New World Slavery: From the Baroque to the Modern, 1492–1800.* London: Verso, 1999.

———. *The Overthrow of Colonial Slavery, 1776–1848.* London: Verso, 1988.

Blackett, R. J. M. *Building an Antislavery Wall: Black Americans in the Atlantic Abolitionist Movement, 1830–1860.* Baton Rouge: Louisiana State University Press, 1983.

Blair, Juliet. "Private Parts in Public Spaces: The Case of Actresses." In *Women and Space: Ground Rules and Social Maps,* ed. Shirley Ardener, 205–28. London: Croom-Helm, 1981.

Blakely, Allison. *Blacks in the Dutch World: The Evolution of Racial Imagery in a Modern Society.* Bloomington: Indiana University Press, 1993.

———. *Russia and the Negro: Blacks in Russian History and Thought.* Washington: Howard University Press, 1989.

Blanco, Melissa. "A Case of Hip(g)nosis: An Epistemology of the Mulata Body and Her Revolutionary Hips." Ph.D. diss., University of California, Riverside, 2006.

Breton, André. "Le message automatique." *Minotaure* 3–4 (December 14, 1933). Trans. in André Breton, *What Is Surrealism? Selected Writings,* ed. Franklin Rosemount. New York: Pathfinder, 1978.

Bricktop, and James Haskins. *Bricktop.* New York: Atheneum, 1983.

Brody, Jennifer DeVere. *Impossible Purities: Blackness, Femininity, and Victorian Culture.* Durham: Duke University Press, 1998.

Brooks, Daphne. *Bodies in Dissent: Spectacular Performances of Race and Freedom, 1850–1910.* Durham: Duke University Press, 2006.

———. "'The Deeds Done in My Body': Black Feminist Theory, Performance, and the Truth about Adah Isaacs Mencken." In *Recovering the Black Female Body: Self Representations by African American Women*, ed. Michael Bennett and Vanessa Dickerson, 41–70. New Brunswick, N.J.: Rutgers University Press, 2000.

Brooks, Lori. "'Journey to a Land of Cotton': Black America, Urban Nostalgia and Race Tourism." Unpublished paper, 2002.

———. "Negro in the new World: The Cultural Politics of Race, Nation and Empire." Ph.D. diss., Yale University, 2002.

Brown, Janet. "The Coon Singer and the Coon Song: A Case Study of the Performer-Character Relationship." *Journal of American Culture* 7 (spring–summer 1984): 1–8.

Brown, Jayna. "Drifting with the Occidental: Black Male Play Space in Claude McKay's *Banjo*." Unpublished essay, 1995.

Brown, Jayna, and Tavia Nyong'o, eds. *Recall and Response: Black Women Performers and the Mapping of Memory*. Special issue, *Women and Performance: A Journal of Feminist Theory* 16, no. 1 (March 2006).

Brown, Sterling. *Negro Poetry and Drama and the Negro in American Fiction*. 1937. Reprint, New York: Atheneum, 1969.

———. *Southern Road*. New York: Harper and Row, 1980.

Brown, William Wells. *Clotel, or the President's Daughter*. Bedford Cultural Edition, ed. Robert S. Levine. Boston: Bedford / St. Martin's, 2000.

Bryson, Norman. "Cultural Studies and Dance History." In *Meaning in Motion: New Cultural Studies in Dance*, ed. Jane Desmond, 55–77. Durham: Duke University Press, 1997.

Buck-Morss, Susan. "Aesthetics and Anaesthetics: Walter Benjamin's Artwork Essay Reconsidered." *October* 62 (autumn 1992): 3–41.

———. *The Dialectics of Seeing: Walter Benjamin and the Arcades Project*. Cambridge: MIT Press, 1993.

———. "The Flaneur, the Sandwichman and the Whore: The Politics of Loitering." *New German Critique* 39 (1986): 99–140.

Burt, Ramsay. *Alien Bodies: Representations of Modernity, "Race" and Nation in Early Modern Dance*. London: Routledge, 1998.

Butler, Judith. *Bodies That Matter*. New York: Routledge, 1993.

———. *Gender Trouble: Feminism and the Subversion of Identity*. New York: Routledge, 1990.

Carby, Hazel V. *Cultures in Babylon*. London: Verso, 1999.

———. "'On the Threshold of the Woman's Era': Lynching, Empire and Sexuality in Black Feminist Theory." *Critical Inquiry* 12 (autumn 1985): 263–77.

———. *Race Men*. Cambridge: Harvard University Press, 1998.

———. *Reconstructing Womanhood: The Emergence of the Afro-American Woman Novelist*. New York: Oxford University Press, 1987.

———. "White Women, Listen! Black Feminism and the Boundaries of Sisterhood." In *Empire Strikes Back: Race and Racism in '70's Britain*, 212–35. London: Routledge, 1992.

Carlson, Marvin. *Performance: A Critical Introduction*. New York: Routledge, 1996.

Carretta, Vincent, ed. *Unchained Voices: An Anthology of Black Authors in the English-Speaking World of the 18th Century*. Lexington: University Press of Kentucky, 1996.

Carter, Mia, and Barbara Harlow, eds. *Imperialism and Orientalism: A Documentary Sourcebook*. London: Blackwell, 1999.

Cartwright, Samuel A. "Diseases and Peculiarities of the Negro Race." In *Clotel, or the President's Daughter, a Narrative of Slave Life in the United States*. Bedford St. Martin's Cultural Edition, ed. Robert S. Levine. New York: Bedford / St. Martin's, 2000.

Castle, Mr. and Mrs. Vernon. *Modern Dancing*. New York: World Syndicate, 1914.

Chan, Sucheng. *Asian Americans: An Interpretive History*. Boston: Twayne, 1991.

Chandler, Elizabeth. "Mental Metempsychosis." *The Genius*, 3rd ser., 1 (February 1831).

Charters, Ann. *Nobody: The Story of Bert Williams*. London: Macmillan, 1970.

Cherniavsky, Felix. *The Salome Dancer: The Life and Times of Maud Allen*. Toronto: McLellan and Stewart, 1991.

Cheshire, David F. *Music Hall in Britain*. Newton Abbott: David and Charles, 1974.

Chilton, John. *Who's Who in Jazz: Storyville to Swing Street*. London: Bloomsbury, 1970.

Claghorn, Charles Eugene. *Biographical Dictionary of Jazz*. Englewood Cliffs, N.J.: Prentice-Hall, 1982.

Clifford, James. "Negrophilia." In *New Histories of French Literature*, ed. Denis Hollier, 900–25. Cambridge: Harvard University Press, 1989.

———. *The Predicament of Culture*. Cambridge: Harvard University Press, 1993.

———. *Routes: Travel and Translation in the Late Twentieth Century*. Cambridge: Harvard University Press, 1997.

Clinton-Baddeley, V. C. *The Burlesque Tradition in the English Theatre after 1660*. London: Methuen, 1952.

Cohen, William. "Thomas Jefferson and the Problem of Slavery." *Journal of American History* 56 (December 1969): 518.

Collier, John Lincoln. *The Making of Jazz: A Comprehensive History*. New York: Dell, 1987.

Collomb, Michel. Introduction to *Nouvelle Complete*, vol. 1, by Paul Morand. Paris: Gallimard, 1992.

"Colored Men and Women on the Stage." *Colored American Magazine*, October 1905, 571–75.

Combe, George. *A System of Phrenology*. 5th ed. Edinburgh, 1843.

Cook, Will Marion. *Anthology of the American Negro in the Theatre: A Critical Approach*. Ed. Lindsay Patterson. New York: Publishers Company, 1968.

Cook, Susan C. "Passionless Dancing and Passionate Reform: Respectability, Modernism, and the Social Dancing of Irene and Vernon Castle." In *The Passion of Music and Dance: Body, Gender, and Sexuality*, ed. William Washabaugh, 133–50. London: Oxford University Press, 1998.

Coombes, Annie E. *Reinventing Africa: Museums, Material Culture and Popular Imagination in Late Victorian and Edwardian England*. New Haven: Yale University Press, 1994.

Copeland, Roger, and Marshall Cohen, eds. *What Is Dance? Readings in Theory and Criticism*. New York: Oxford University Press, 1983.

Cressey, Paul. *Taxi Dance Halls: A Sociological Study in Commercialized Recreation and City Life*. Chicago: University of Chicago Press, 1932.

Cruickshank, Marjorie. *Children and Industry: Child Health and Welfare in North-West Textile Towns During the Nineteenth Century*. Manchester: Manchester University Press, 1981.

Cuguano, Quobna Ottobah. *Thoughts and Sentiments on the Evil of Slavery*. New York: Penguin, 1999.

Cunard, Nancy. *Negro: An Anthology*. London: Wishart, 1934.

Cunliffe, Marcus. *Chattel Slavery and Wage Slavery: The Anglo-American Context, 1830–1860*. Athens: University of Georgia Press, 1979.

Curtain, Philip D. *The Rise and Fall of the Plantation Complex*. Cambridge: Cambridge University Press, 1998.

Dahl, Linda. *Stormy Weather: The Music and Lives of a Century of Jazz Women*. New York: Pantheon, 1984.

Dance, Stanley. *The World of Earl Hines*. New York: Da Capo, 1977.

Daughtry, Willa Estelle. "Sissieretta Jones: A Study of the Negro's Contribution to Nineteenth Century American Concert and Theatrical Life." Ph.D. diss., Syracuse University, 1968.

Davis, Angela. "Black Women and Music: A Historical Legacy of Struggle." In *Wild Women in the Whirlwind*, ed. Joanne Braxton and Andree Nicola McLaughlin, 3–21. New Brunswick, N.J.: Rutgers University Press, 1990.

———. *Blues Legacies and Black Feminism: Gertrude "Ma" Rainey, Bessie Smith, and Billie Holiday*. New York: Pantheon, 1998.

Davis, Brion David. *Antebellum American Culture: An Interpretive Anthology*. Lexington, Mass.: D. C. Heath, 1979.

Davis, Mike. *City of Quartz: Excavating the Future of Los Angeles*. New York: Vintage, 1990.

———. *Dead Cities and Other Tales*. New York: New Press, 2002.

Davis, Sheila Marion. "Cakewalk." Master's thesis, New York University, 1989.

Davis, Thadious M. *Nella Larsen, Novelist of the Harlem Renaissance: A Woman's Life Unveiled*. Baton Rouge: Louisiana State University Press, 1994.

de Certeau, Michel. *The Practice of Everyday Life*. Berkeley: University of California Press, 1984.

de Frantz, Thomas. "The Black Beat Made Visible: Hip Hop Dance and Body Power." In *Of the Presence of the Body: Essays on Dance and Performance Theory*, ed. Andre Lepecki, 64–81. Middletown: Wesleyan University Press, 2004.

Delany, Lucy A. *From the Darkness Cometh the Light, or Struggles for Freedom*. Circa 1891. Reprinted in *Six Women's Slave Narratives*, ed. Henru Louis Gates Jr., 43–64. New York: Oxford University Press, 1988.

Denning, Michael. *The Culture Front: The Laboring of American Culture in the Twentieth Century*. London: Verso, 1997.

Desmond, Jane "Dancing Out the Difference: Cultural Imperialism and Ruth St. Denis's *Rahda* of 1906." *Signs* 17, no. 1 (autumn 1991): 28–49.

———. "Embodying Difference: Issues in Dance and Cultural Studies." In *Meaning in Motion: New Cultural Studies in Dance*, ed. Jane Desmond, 29–54. Durham: Duke University Press, 1997.

———, ed. *Meaning in Motion: New Cultural Studies in Dance*. Durham: Duke University Press, 1997.

Dickens, Charles. *American Notes for General Circulation*. 1842. Reprint, London: Penguin, 1985.

Dijkstra, Bram. *Evil Sisters: The Threat of Female Sexuality and the Cult of Manhood*. New York: Alfred A. Knopf, 1996.

———. *Idols of Perversity: Fantasies of Feminine Evil in Fin-de-Siècle Culture*. New York: Oxford University Press, 1986.

Dodge, Roger Pryor. *Hot Jazz and Jazz Dance: Collected Writings 1929–1964*. New York: Oxford University Press, 1995.

Dormon, James. "Shaping the Popular Image of Post Reconstruction Blacks: The Coon Song Phenomenon of the Gilded Age." *American Quarterly* 40, no. 4 (1988): 450–71.

Douglas, Ann. *Terrible Honesty: Mongrel Manhattan in the 1920's*. New York: Farrar, Straus and Giroux, 1995.

Douglass, Frederick. *My Bondage and My Freedom*. New York: Dover, 1969.

Duberman, Martin Bauml. *Paul Robeson*. New York: Alfred A. Knopf, 1989.

Du Bois, W. E. B. *The Philadelphia Negro*. New York: Benjamin Bloom, 1899.

Dudden, Faye E. *Women in the American Theatre: Actresses and Audiences, 1790–1870*. New Haven: Yale University Press, 1994.

Duncan, Isadora. *My Life*. London: Sphere, 1968.

Durkheim, Emile, and Marcel Mauss. *Primitive Classification*. Trans. Rodney Needham. London: Cohen and West, 1963.

Edwards, Brent. *The Practice of Diaspora: Literature, Translation, and the Rise of Black Internationalism*. Cambridge: Harvard University Press, 2003.

Egan, Bill. *Florence Mills: Harlem Jazz Queen*. Lanham, Md.: Scarecrow, 2004.

Eggehorn, Ylva. *En Av Dessa Timmar*. Stockholm: Bonniers, 1996.

Elam, Harry, and Kennel Jackson, eds. *Black Cultural Traffic: Crossroads in Global Performance and Popular Culture*. Ann Arbor: University of Michigan Press, 2005.

Elam, Harry, and David Krasner, eds. *African American Performance and Theater History*. New York: Oxford University Press, 2001.

Ellis, Havelock. "The Art of Dancing." From *the Dance of* Life. Boston: Houghton Mifflin, 1923. Reprinted in *What Is Dance? Readings in Theory and Criticism*, ed. Roger Copeland and Marshall Cohen. New York: Oxford University Press, 1983.

Emery, Lynne Fauley. *Black Dance: From 1619 to Today*. London: Dance Books, 1988.

Engelstein, Laura. *The Keys to Happiness: Sex and the Search for Modernity in Fin-de-Siècle Russia*. Ithaca, N.Y.: Cornell University Press, 1992.

Engle, Gary D., ed. *This Grotesque Essence: Plays from the Minstrel Stage*. Baton Rouge: Louisiana State University Press, 1978.

Equiano, Olaudah. *The Interesting Narrative of the Life of Olaudah Equiano: Written by Himself*. New York: Bedford / St. Martin's, 1995.

Erenburg, Lewis. *Steppin' Out: New York Nightlife and the Transformation of American Culture, 1890–1930*. Chicago: University of Chicago Press, 1981.

Eze, Emanuel Chukwudi, ed. *Race and the Enlightenment*. Oxford: Blackwell, 1997.

Fabian, Johannes. *Time and the Other: How Anthropology Makes Its Object*. New York: Columbia University Press, 1983.

Fanon, Frantz. *Black Skin, White Masks*. Trans. Charles Lam Markmann. New York: Grove Weidenfeld, 1967.

Faulkner, Thomas. *The Immorality of Modern Dances*. Ed. Beryl and Associates. New York: Everitt and Francis, 1904.

———. *The Lure of the Dance*. Los Angeles: T. A. Faulkner, 1916.

Felski, Rita. *The Gender of Modernity*. Cambridge: Harvard University Press, 1995.

Flaubert, Gustave. *Flaubert in Egypt: A Sensibility on Tour*. Trans. Francis Steegmuller. London: Michael Hag, 1983.

Fletcher, Thomas. *100 Years of the Negro in Show Business*. New York: Da Capo, 1984.

Floyd, Samuel, ed. *Music and the Harlem Renaissance*. Knoxville: University of Tennessee Press, 1990.

Fornas, Johan. "Yodeling Negroes and Swinging Lapps: Others Encountered in Early Swedish Jazz Discourses." Paper presented at the international conference Crossroads in Cultural Studies, Tampere, Finland, August 1–4, 1996.

Foster, Hal. *Compulsive Beauty*. Cambridge: MIT Press, 1995.

Foucault, Michel. *The History of Sexuality*. Vol. 1. Trans. Robert Hurley. New York: Vintage, 1990.

———. *The Order of Things: An Archeology of the Body*. New York: Vintage, 1994.

———. *Power/Knowledge: Selected Interviews*. Ed. Colin Gordon. New York: Pantheon, 1972.

———. "Space, Power and Knowledge." Interview with Paul Rabinow in *The Cultural Studies Reader*, ed. Simon During, 161–69. London: Routledge, 1993.

Franko, Mark. *The Work of Dance: Labor, Movement, and Identity in the 1930s*. Middletown: Wesleyan University Press, 2002.

Freeman, Arnold. *Boy Life and Labour: The Manufacture of Inefficiency*. London: King and Son, 1914.

Fyfe, Alec. *Child Labour*. London: Polity, 1989.

Gainor, J. Ellen, ed. *Imperialism and Theatre: Essays on World Theatre, Drama and Performance*. London: Routledge, 1995.

Gallagher, Catherine, and Thomas Lacquer, eds. *The Making of the Modern Body: Sexuality and Society in the Nineteenth Century*. Berkeley: University of California Press, 1987.

Garelick, Rhonda. "Electric Salome." In *Imperialism and Theatre: Essays on World Theatre, Drama and Performance*, ed. J. Ellen Gainor, 85–103. London: Routledge, 1995.

Gatens, Moira. *Imaginary Bodies: Ethics, Power and Corporeality*. London: Routledge, 1996.

Gatewood, Willard B., Jr. *"Smoked Yankees" and the Struggle for Empire: Letters from negro Soldiers, 1898–1902*. Urbana: University of Illinois, 1971.

Gatewood, William. *Aristocrats of Color*. Bloomington: Indiana University Press, 1990.

Gaunt, Kyra, *The Games Girls Play: Learning the Ropes from Double Dutch to Hip Hop*. New York: New York University Press, 2006.

Geertz, Clifford. *The Interpretation of Cultures*. New York: Basic Books, 1973.

George, Nadine. *The Royalty of Negro Vaudeville: The Whitman Sisters and the Negotiation of Race, Gender and Class in African American Theatre, 1900–1940*. New York: St. Martin's, 2000.

Gerzina, Gretchen. *Blacks in London: Life before Emancipation*. Newark, N.J.: Rutgers University Press, 1997.

Giddings, Paula. *Where and When I Enter: The Impact of Black Women on Race and Sex in America*. New York: William Morrow, 1984.

Gifford, Prosser, and William Roger Louis, eds. *France and Britain in Africa: Imperial Rivalry and Colonial Rule*. New Haven: Yale University Press, 1971.

Gilbert, Douglas. *American Vaudeville: Its Life and Times*. New York: Dover, 1940.

Gilman, Sander L. "Black Bodies, White Bodies: Toward an Iconography of Female Sexuality in Late Nineteenth-Century Art, Medicine and Literature." *Critical Inquiry* 12 (autumn 1985): 204–41.

Gilroy, Paul. *Between Camps: Nations, Cultures and the Allure of Race*. London: Penguin, 2000.

———. *The Black Atlantic: Modernity and Double Consciousness*. Cambridge: Harvard University Press, 1993.

———. *Small Acts: Thoughts on the Politics of Black Cultures*. London: Serpent's Tail, 1993.

———. *There Ain't No Black in the Union Jack: The Cultural Politics of Race and Nation*. Chicago: University of Chicago Press, 1987.

Goldberg, David Theo. *The Racial State*. London: Blackwell, 2002.

Goldman, Emma. *Living My Life*. New York: Alfred A. Knopf, 1934.

Gordon, Taylor. *Born to Be*. Lincoln: University of Nebraska Press, 1995.

Gottlieb, Robert. *Reading Jazz: A Gathering of Autobiography, Reportage and Criticism from 1919 to Now*. New York: Pantheon, 1996.

Gottschild, Brenda Dixon. *The Black Dancing Body: A Geography from Coon to Cool*. New York: Palgrave, 2003.

———. *Digging the Africanist Presence in American Performance: Dance and Other Contexts*. Westport: Greenwood, 1996.

Green, Stanley. *Broadway Musicals, Show by Show*. Milwaukee: Hal Leonard, 1985.

Greene, Ward. Introduction to "Bye Bye Blackbird" by W. A. McDonald. *Negro Digest*, March 1949, 30–37.

Greeson, Jennifer. "The Mysteries and Miseries of North Carolina: New York City, Urban Gothic Fiction, and Incidents in the Life of a Slave Girl." *American Literature* 73, no. 2 (2001): 277–309.

Gregory, Montgomery. "The Drama of Negro Life." In *The New Negro: Voices of the Harlem Renaissance*, ed. Alain Locke. New York: A. and C. Boni, 1925. Reprint, New York: Simon and Schuster, 1997.

Grossman, James B. *Land of Hope: Chicago, Black Southerners and the Great Migration*. Chicago: University of Chicago Press, 1989.

Grosz, Elizabeth. *Volatile Bodies: Toward a Corporeal Feminism*. Bloomington: Indiana University Press, 1994.

Gubar, Susan. *Race Changes: White Skin, Black Face in American Culture*. New York: Oxford University Press, 1997.

Habermas, Jürgen. *The Philosophical Discourse of Modernity*. Trans. Fredrick G. Lawrence. Cambridge: MIT Press, 1995.

Hadju, David. *Lush Life*. New York: Farrar, Straus and Giroux, 1996.

Hall, Stuart. "Gramsci's Relevance for the Study of Race and Ethnicity." In *Stuart Hall: Critical Dialogues in Cultural Studies*, ed. D. Morley and K. H. Chen, 411–40. London: Routledge, 1996.

———. "New Ethnicities." In *Stuart Hall: Critical Dialogues in Cultural Studies*, ed. D. Morley and K. H. Chen, 441–49. London: Routledge, 1996.

———. "Race, Articulation and Societies Structured in Dominance." *Sociological Theories: Race and Colonialism*. Paris: UNESCO, 1980.

Handy, Antoinette. *Black Women in American Bands and Orchestras*. New York: Scarecrow Press, 1981.

Handy, W. C. *Father of the Blues*. New York: Da Capo, 1969.

Haney, Lynn. *Naked at the Feast: The Biography of Josephine Baker*. London: Robson Books, 1981.

Harper, Kenn. *Give Me My Father's Body: The Life of Minik, the New York Eskimo*. New York: Washington Square Press, 2000.

Harrison, Daphne Duvall. *Black Pearls: Blues Queens of the 1920's*. New Brunswick, N.J.: Rutgers University Press, 1988.

Harrison, Juanita. *My Great Wide Beautiful World*. New York: G. K. Hall, 1996.

Hartman, Saidiya. *Scenes of Subjection: Terror, Slavery and Self-Making in Nineteenth Century America*. New York: Oxford University Press, 1997.

Haskins, James. *Mabel Mercer*. New York: Da Capo, 1977.

Hegel, Georg Wilhelm Friedrich. "The Geographical Basis of History." In *The Philosophy of History*, trans. J. Sibree, 79–103. New York: Dover, 1956.

Hekman, Susan. *Gender and Knowledge*. London: Polity, 1990.

Higginbotham, Evelyn. *Righteous Discontent: The Women's Movement in the Black Baptist Church, 1880–1920*. Cambridge: Harvard University Press, 1993.

Higham, John. *Strangers in the Land: Patterns of American Nativism, 1860–1925*. New Brunswick, N.J.: Rutgers University Press, 1992.

Hine, Darlene Clark, and Jacqueline McLeod. *Crossing Boundaries: Comparative History of Black People in Diaspora*. Bloomington: Indiana University Press, 1999.

Hine, Darlene Clark, and Kathleen Thompson. *A Shining Thread of Hope: The History of Black Women in America*. New York: Broadway, 1998.

Hobsbawm, Eric. *The Age of Empire, 1875–1914*. New York: Vintage, 1987.

Hoganson, Kristin L. *Fighting for American Manhood: How Gender Politics Provoked the Spanish-American War and Philippine-American Wars*. New Haven: Yale University Press, 1998.

Holiday, Billie, and William Dufty. *Lady Sings the Blues*. New York: Penguin, 1956.

Hollier, Denis, ed. *New History of French Literature*. Cambridge: Harvard University Press, 1989.

Honey, Maureen, ed. *Shadowed Dreams: Women's Poetry of the Harlem Renaissance*. New Brunswick, N.J.: Rutgers University Press, 1996.

Horsman, Reginald. *Race and Manifest Destiny: The Origins of American Racial Anglo-Saxonism*. Cambridge: Harvard University Press, 1981.

Huggins, Nathan Irvin. *Harlem Renaissance*. New York: Oxford University Press, 1971.

Hughes, Langston. *The Big Sea: An Autobiography*. New York: Thunder's Mouth, 1986.

———. *Selected Poems of Langston Hughes*. New York: Vintage, 1990.

———. *The Weary Blues*. New York: Alfred A. Knopf, 1926.

Hughes, Langston, and Milton Meltzer. *Black Magic: A Pictorial History of the Negro in American Entertainment*. Englewood Cliffs, N.J.: Prentice-Hall, 1968.

Huhndorf, Shari. *Going Native: Indians in the American Imagination*. Ithaca, N.Y.: Cornell University Press, 2001.

Hulme, Peter. *Colonial Encounters: Europe and the Native Caribbean, 1492–1797*. London: Routledge, 1996.

Jacobs, Harriet. *Incidents in the Life of a Slave Girl*. 1861. Reprint, Cambridge: Harvard University Press, 1987.

James, C. L. R. *American Civilization*. Cambridge: Blackwell, 1993.

Jameson, Fredric. *Archaeologies of the Future: The Desire Called Utopia and Other Science Fictions*. London: Verso, 2005.

———. *Postmodernism or, the Cultural Logic of Late Capitalism*. Durham: Duke University Press, 1991.

Johnson, E. Patrick. *Appropriating Blackness: Performance and the Politics of Authenticity*. Durham: Duke University Press, 2003.

Johnson, James Weldon. *Along This Way: The Autobiography of James Weldon Johnson*. New York: Penguin, 1990.

———. *Autobiography of an Ex-Coloured Man*. London: Alfred A. Knopf, 1927.

———. *Black Manhattan*. New York: Atheneum, 1968.

Jones, Jacqueline. *Labor of Love, Labor of Sorrow: Black Women, Work, and the Family from Slavery to the Present*. New York: Basic Books, 1985.

Jones, LeRoi. *Blues People: The Negro Experience and the Music That Developed from It*. New York: Morrow Quill, 1973.

Kaplan, Amy, and Donald Pease, eds. *Cultures of United States Imperialism*. Durham: Duke University Press, 1993.

Kater, Michael H. *A Different Drummer: Jazz in the Culture of Nazi Germany*. New York: Oxford University Press, 1992.

Kelley, Robin. *Freedom Dreams: The Black Radical Imagination*. Boston: Beacon, 2002.

———. *Race Rebels: Culture, Politics, and the Black Working Class*. New York: Free Press, 1994.

Kendall, Elizabeth. *Where She Danced*. New York: Alfred A. Knopf, 1979.

Kermode, Frank. "Poet and Dancer before Diaghilev." In *What Is Dance? Readings in Theory and Criticism*, ed. Roger Copeland and Marshall Cohen. New York: Oxford University Press, 1983.

Kimball, Robert, and William Bolcom. *Reminiscing with Sissle and Blake*. New York: Viking, 1973.

King, Wilma. *Stolen Childhood: Slave Youth in Nineteenth-Century America*. Bloomington: Indiana University Press, 1995.

Kislan, Richard. *Hoofing on Broadway: A History of Show Dancing*. New York: Prentice Hall, 1987.

Kolchin, Peter. *Unfree Labor: American Slavery and Russian Serfdom*. Cambridge: Harvard University Press, 1987.

Koritz, Amy. "Dancing for the Orient: Maud Allen's 'The Vision of Salome.'" In *Meaning in Motion: New Cultural Studies in Dance*, ed. Jane Desmond, 133–52. Durham: Duke University Press, 1997.

———. *Gendering Bodies/Performing Arts: Dance and Literature in Early Twentieth-Century British Culture*. Ann Arbor: University of Michigan Press, 1995.

Kracauer, Siegfried. *Mass Ornament: The Weimar Essays*. Cambridge: Harvard University Press, 1995.

Krasner, David. *A Beautiful Pageant: African American Theatre, Drama and Performance in the Harlem Renaissance, 1910–1927*. New York: Palgrave, 2004.

————. *Resistance, Parody and Double Consciousness in African American Theatre, 1895–1910*. New York: St. Martin's, 1997.

————. "Rewriting the Body: Aida Overton Walker and the Social Formation of Cakewalking." *Theatre Survey* 37, no. 2 (November 1996): 66–92.

Krauss, Rosalind. *The Optical Unconscious*. Cambridge: MIT Press, 1993.

Kraut, Anthea. "Between Primitivism and Diaspora: The Dance Performances of Josephine Baker, Zora Neale Hurston, and Katherine Dunham." *Theatre Journal* 55 (2003): 434–50.

————. "Recovering Hurston, Reconsidering the Choreographer." In *Recall and Response: Black Women Performers and the Mapping of Memory*, ed. Jayna Brown, and Tavia Nyong'o. Special issue, *Women and Performance: A Journal of Feminist Theory* 16, no. 1 (March 2006): 71–90.

Larsen, Nella. *Quicksand*. New York: Negro Universities Press, 1969.

Larsmo, Ola. *Maroonberget*. Stockholm: Bonniers, 1996.

Laurie, Joe, Jr. *Vaudeville: From the Honky-Tonks to the Palace*. New York: Henry Holt, 1953.

Lefebvre, Henri. *The Production of Space*. Trans. Donald Nicholson-Smith. London: Blackwell, 1991.

Leib, Sandra. *Mother of the Blues: A Study of Ma Rainey*. Amherst: University of Massachusetts Press, 1981.

Leiris, Michel. *L'afrique fantôme*. Paris: Gallimard, 1951.

————. *Manhood: A Journey from Childhood into the Fierce Order of Virility*. Trans. Richard Howard. New York: Grossman, 1963.

Lemann, Nicolas. *The Promised Land: The Great Black Migration and How It Changed America*. New York: Alfred A. Knopf, 1991.

Lepecki, Andre, ed. *Of the Presence of the Body: Essays on Dance and Performance Theory*. Middletown: Wesleyan University Press, 2004.

Levi, Primo. *The Drowned and the Saved*. New York: Vintage, 1996.

Levine, Laurence. *Black Culture and Black Consciousness: African American Folk Thought from Slavery to Freedom*. New York: Oxford University Press, 1977.

Levinson, Andre. "The Negro Dance: Under European Eyes." In *Andre Levinson on Dance: Writings from Paris in the Twenties*, ed. Joan Acocella and Lynn Garafola. Middletown: Wesleyan University Press, 1991.

Lewis, David Levering. *When Harlem Was in Vogue*. New York: Oxford University Press, 1981.

Leyda, Si-lan Chen. *Footnote to History*. New York: Dance Horizons, 1984.

Lhamon, W. T. *Raising Cain: Blackface Performance from Jim Crow to Hip Hop*. Cambridge: Harvard University Press, 1998.

Lili'uokalani. *Hawai'i's Story by Hawai'i's Queen*. 1897. Reprint, New York: Mutual, 1991.

Lipsitz, George. *Dangerous Crossroads: Popular Music, Postmodernism and the Poetics of Place*. London: Verso, 1994.

Locke, Alain, ed. *The New Negro: Voices of the Harlem Renaissance*. New York: A. and C. Boni, 1925. Reprint, New York: Simon and Schuster, 1997.

Lott, Eric. *Love and Theft: Black Face Minstrelsy and the Making of the American Working Class*. New York: Oxford University Press, 1993.

Lotz, Rainer E. *Black People: Entertainers of African Descent in Germany, and Europe*. Berlin: Birgit Lotz, 1998.

Macey, David. *Frantz Fanon*. New York: Picador, 2000.

Malone, Jacqui. "'Keep to the Rhythm and You'll Keep to Life': Meaning and Style in African American Vernacular Dance." In *The Routledge Dance Studies Reader*, ed. Alexandra Carter, 230–36. London: Routledge, 1998.

Marion, Sheila. "Cakewalk." Master's thesis, New York University, 1989. James Hatch and Camille Billops Collection.

Marks, Carol. *Farewell—We're Good and Gone: The Great Black Migration*. Bloomington: Indiana University Press, 1989.

Marshall, Herbert, and Mildred Stock. *Ira Aldridge: The Negro Tragedian*. Washington: Howard University Press, 1993.

Martin, Carol. *Dance Marathons: Performing American Culture of the 1920's and 1930's*. Jackson: University Press of Mississippi, 1994.

McBride, Bunny. *Molly Spotted Elk: A Penobscot in Paris*. Norman: University of Oklahoma Press, 1995.

McBride, Dwight. *Impossible Witnesses: Truth, Abolitionism, and Slave Testimony*. New York: New York University Press, 2001.

McCarren, Felicia. *Dancing Machines: Choreographies of the Age of Mechanical Reproduction*. Stanford: Stanford University Press, 2003.

McClintock, Ann. *Imperial Leather: Race, Gender and Sexuality in the Colonial Contest*. London: Routledge, 1995.

McDonald, Heather Lyn, dir. *Been Rich All My Life*. Toots Crackin, 2004.

McDougald, Elise Johnson. "The Task of Negro Womanhood." In *The New Negro: Voices of the Harlem Renaissance*, ed. Alain Locke, 369–84. New York: A. and C. Boni, 1925. Reprint, New York: Simon and Schuster, 1997.

McKay, Claude. *Banjo*. New York: Harcourt Brace and Jovanovich, 1957.

———. *Home to Harlem*. Boston: Northeastern University Press, 1987.

———. *A Long Way from Home*. New York: Arno, 1969.

———. *Selected Poems of Claude McKay*. New York: Harcourt Brace and World, 1953.

McLaughlin, Jack. *Jefferson and Monticello: The Biography of a Builder*. New York: Henry Holt, 1988.

Meeker, David. *Jazz in the Movies*. New York: Da Capo, 1981.

Meltzer, David, ed. *Reading Jazz*. San Francisco: Mercury House, 1993.

Melville, Herman. *Moby Dick or the Whale*. 1851. Reprint, New York: Penguin, 1992.

Membe, Achille. "Necropolitics." Trans. Libby Meintjes. *Public Culture* 15, no. 1 (2003): 1–40.

Mémorial international Frantz Fanon: 31 mars–3 avril 1992. Paris: Présence africaine, 1994.

Miller, Christopher. "Orientalism, Colonialism." In *New History of French Litera-ture*, ed. Denis Hollier, 698–705. Cambridge: Harvard University Press, 1989.

Montesquieu. *Persian Letters*. New York: Penguin, 1982.

Morrison, Toni. *Playing in the Dark: Whiteness and the Literary Imagination*. Cambridge: Harvard University Press, 1992.

Moss, George. *Nationalism and Sexuality: Respectability and Abnormal Sexuality in Modern Europe*. New York: Howard Fertig, 1985.

Moten, Fred. *In the Break: The Aesthetics of the Black Radical Tradition*. Minne-apolis: University of Minnesota Press, 2003.

Mumford, Kevin J. *Interzones: Black and White Sex Districts in Chicago and New York in the Early Twentieth Century*. New York: Columbia University Press, 1997.

Nardinelli, Clark. *Child Labor and the Industrial Revolution*. Bloomington: Indi-ana University Press, 1990.

Nasaw, David. *Going Out: The Rise and Fall of Public Amusements*. New York: Basic Books, 1993.

Nenno, Nancy. "Femininity, the Primitive and Modern Urban Space." In *Women in the Metropolis: Gender and Modernity in Weimar Germany*, ed. Katherina Von Ankum (Berkeley: University of California Press, 1997), 145–61.

Nicholson, Stuart. *Ella Fitzgerald, 1917–1996*. London: Indigo, 1996.

Noble, Peter. *The Negro in Films*. New York: Arno, 1970.

Norindr, Panivong. *Phantasmatic Indochina: French Colonial Ideology in Archi-tecture, Film, and Literature*. Durham: Duke University Press, 1997.

Okokon, Susan. *Black Londoners, 1880–1990*. Sutton: Stroud, 1998.

Oliver, Paul. *Songsters and Saints: Vocal Traditions on Race Records*. Cambridge: Harvard University Press, 1984.

Osofsky, Gilbert. *Harlem: The Making of a Ghetto*. New York: Harper and Row, 1966.

Ottely, Roi, and William Weatherby, eds. *The Negro in New York: An Informal So-cial History*. Dobbs Ferry, N.Y.: Oceana, 1967.

Parker, Derek, and Julia Parker. *The Natural History of the Chorus Girl*. Newton Abbott: David and Charles, 1975.

Peiss, Kathy. *Cheap Amusements: Working Class Women and Leisure in Turn-of-the Century New York*. Philadelphia: Temple University Press, 1986.

Perkins, A. J. G., Theresa Wolfson, and Frances Wright. *Free Inquirer: The Study of a Temperament*. New York: Harper and Row, 1939.

Peterson, Carla. *"Doers of the Word": African American Women Speakers and Writers in the North (1830–1880)*. New York: Oxford University Press, 1995.

Petro, Patrice. "Perceptions of Difference: Women as Spectator and Spectacle." In *Women in the Metropolis: Gender and Modernity in Weimar Germany*, ed. Katherina Von Ankum (Berkeley: University of California Press, 1997), 41–66.

Phelan, Peggy. *Unmarked: The Politics of Performance*. New York: Routledge, 1993.

Picquet, Louisa. *Louisa Picquet, Octoroon Slave and Concubine.* In *Collected Black Women's Narratives,* ed. Anthony G. Barthelemy, 90–150. New York: Oxford University Press, 1988.

Placksin, Sally. *American Women in Jazz, 1900 to the Present: Their Words, Lives and Music.* New York: Wideview, 1982.

Poulantzas, Nico. *State, Power, Socialism.* London: Verso, 1980.

Porter, Roy, and G. S. Rousseau, eds. *Exoticism in the Enlightenment.* Manchester: Manchester University Press, 1989.

Pratt, Mary Louise. *Imperial Eyes: Travel Writing and Transculturation.* London: Routledge, 1997.

Prince, Nancy. *The Narrative of Nancy Prince.* 1851. Reprinted in *Collected Black Women's Narratives,* ed. Anthony G. Barthelemy, 1–88. New York: Oxford University Press, 1988.

Rampersad, Arnold. *The Life of Langston Hughes.* Vols. 1 and 2. London: Oxford University Press, 1988.

Reinelt, Janelle, and Joseph Roach, eds. *Critical Theory and Performance.* Ann Arbor: University of Michigan Press, 1992.

Riis, Thomas. "Bob Cole: His Life and His Legacy to Black Musical Theatre." *Black Perspectives in Music* 13, no. 2 (spring 1985): 135–50.

———. *Just before Jazz: Black Musical Theater in New York, 1890–1915.* Washington: Smithsonian Institution Press, 1989.

———. "The Music and Musicians in Nineteenth-Century Productions of *Uncle Tom's Cabin.*" *American Music* 4, no. 3 (autumn 1986): 268–86.

Roach, Joseph. *Cities of the Dead: Circum-Atlantic Performance.* New York: Columbia University Press, 1996.

Rodriguez, Dylan. *Forced Passages.* Durham: Duke University Press, 2005.

Roediger, David. *The Wages of Whiteness: Race and the Making of the American Working Class.* London: Verso, 1991.

Rogers, J. A. "Jazz at Home." In *The New Negro: Voices of the Harlem Renaissance,* ed. Alain Locke, 268–86. New York: A. and C. Boni, 1925. Reprint, New York: Simon and Schuster, 1997.

Rose, Al. *Eubie Blake.* New York: Schirmer, 1978.

Rose, Margaret A. *Parody: Ancient, Modern and Post-Modern.* Cambridge: Cambridge University Press, 1993.

Rose, Phyliss. *Jazz Cleopatra: Josephine Baker in Her Time.* New York: Doubleday, 1989.

Ross, Marlon B. *Manning the Race: Reforming Black Men in the Jim Crow Era.* New York: New York University Press, 2004.

Ruth, Ralf George. *Goebbels.* Trans. Krishna Winston. New York: Harcourt Brace, 1993.

Rydell, Robert W. *All the World's a Fair: Visions of Empire at American International Expositions, 1876–1916.* Chicago: University of Chicago Press, 1984.

Ruyter, Nancy Lee Chalta. *The Cultivation of Mind and Body in Nineteenth Century American Delsartism.* Westport: Greenwood, 1999.

Said, Edward. *Culture and Imperialism*. New York: Alfred A. Knopf, 1993.
———. *Orientalism*. New York: Vintage, 1979.
Sampson, Henry T. *Blacks in Blackface*. Metuchen, N.J.: Scarecrow, 1980.
———. *The Ghost Walks: A Chronological History of Blacks in Show Business, 1865–1910*. Metuchen, N.J.: Scarecrow, 1988.
Savigliano, Marta E. *Tango and the Political Economy of Passion*. Boulder: Westview, 1995.
Scarry, Elaine. *The Body in Pain: The Making and Unmaking of the World*. New York: Oxford University Press, 1985.
Scheibinger, Londa. *Nature's Body*. Boston: Beacon, 1993.
Scheiner, Seth M. *Negro Mecca: A History of the Negro in New York City, 1865–1920*. New York: New York University Press, 1965.
Schuler, Catherine. *Women in Russian Theatre: The Russian Actress in the Silver Age*. London: Routledge, 1996.
Scott, Joan. *Gender and the Politics of History*. New York: Columbia University Press, 1988.
Seacole, Mary. *Wonderful Adventures of Mrs. Seacole in Many Lands*. 1857. Reprint, New York: Oxford University Press, 1988.
Shawn, Ted. *Every Little Moment: A Book about François Delsarte*. Brooklyn: Dance Horizons, 1968.
Sibony, Daniel. *Écrits sur le racisme*. Paris: Christiane Bourgeois, 1987.
Simon, George. *The Big Bands*. London: Macmillan, 1967.
Smith, Eric Ledell. *Bert Williams: A Biography of the Pioneer Black Comedian*. London: McFarland, 1992.
Smith, Jess Carney, ed. *Notable Black Women*. Detroit: Gale Research, 1992.
Smith, Mark M. *Mastered by the Clock: Time, Slavery and Freedom in the American South*. Chapel Hill: University of North Carolina Press, 1997.
Snyder, Robert. *The Voice of the City: Vaudeville and Popular Culture in New York*. New York: Oxford University Press, 1989.
Sobel, Bernard. *A Pictorial History of Burlesque*. New York: G. Putnam and Sons, 1956.
Southern, Eileen. *The Music of Black Americans*. New York: W. W. Norton, 1983.
Spillers, Hortense. "Changing the Letter: The Yokes, the Jokes of Discourse, or, Mrs. Stowe, Mr. Reed." *Uncle Tom's Cabin*, Norton Critical Edition, ed. Elizabeth Ammons, 542–68. New York: W. W. Norton, 1994.
Spivak, Gayatri. "Can the Subaltern Speak?" In *Marxism and the Interpretation of Culture*, ed. Cary Nelson and Lawrence Grossberg, 271–315. Urbana: University of Illinois Press, 1988.
———. *A Critique of Postcolonial Reason: Toward a History of the Vanishing Present*. Cambridge: Harvard University Press, 1999.
Stallybrass, Peter, and Allon White. *The Politics and Poetics of Transgression*. Ithaca, N.Y.: Cornell University Press, 1986.
Stampp, Kenneth M. *Peculiar Institution*. New York: Alfred A. Knopf, 1956.

Stansell, Christine. *City of Women: Sex and Class in New York, 1789–1860.* Chicago: University of Illinois Press, 1987.

Starr, S. Frederick. *Red and Hot: The Fate of Jazz in the Soviet Union, 1917–1980.* New York: Oxford University Press, 1983.

Stearns, Marshall, and Jean Stearns. *Jazz Dance: The Story of American Vernacular Dance.* New York: Macmillan, 1968.

Stocking, George. *Race, Culture and Evolution: Essays in the History of Anthropology.* Chicago: University of Chicago Press, 1968.

Stoler, Ann Laura. *Race and the Education of Desire: Foucault's History of Sexuality and the Colonial Order of Things.* Durham: Duke University Press, 1995.

Stovall, Tyler. *Paris Noir: African Americans in the City of Light.* Boston: Houghton Mifflin, 1996.

Stowe, David. *Swing Changes: Big Band Jazz in New Deal America.* Cambridge: Harvard University Press, 1994.

Stowe, Harriet Beecher. *A Key to Uncle Tom's Cabin: Presenting the Original Facts and Documents upon Which the Story Is Founded, Together with Corroborative Statements Verifying the Truth of the Work.* Boston: H. P. Jewett, 1853. Reprint, New York: Arno, 1968.

———. *Uncle Tom's Cabin, or Life among the Lowly.* Boston: John P. Hewett, 1852. Reprint, Norton Critical Edition, ed. Elizabeth Ammons, New York: W. W. Norton, 1994.

Stowe, Mr. Reed. *Uncle Tom's Cabin.* Norton Critical Edition. Ed. Elizabeth Ammons. New York: W. W. Norton, 1994.

St. Johnson, Reginald. *A History of Dancing.* London: Simpkin, Marshall, Hamilton, Kent, 1906.

Suleiman, Susan. *The Female Body in Western Culture: Contemporary Perspectives.* Cambridge: Harvard University Press, 1986.

Summers, Martin. *Manliness and Its Discontents: The Black Middle Class and the Transformation of Masculinity, 1900–1930.* Chapel Hill: University of North Carolina Press, 2004.

Sundvist, Eric. *To Wake the Nations.* Cambridge: Harvard University Press, 1994.

Swaffer, Hannen. "Two Women but One Public." *Bandwagon* 8, no. 3 (March 1949).

Tanner, Jo A. *Dusky Maidens: The Odyssey of the Early Black Dramatic Actress.* Westport: Greenwood, 1992.

Taussig, Michael. *Mimesis and Alterity: A Particular History of the Senses.* New York: Routledge, 1993.

———. *Shamanism, Colonialism and the Wildman: A Study in Terror and Healing.* Chicago: University of Chicago Press, 1987.

Taylor, Charles. *Sources of the Self: The Making of Modern Identity.* Cambridge: Harvard University Press, 1989.

Taylor, Frederick Winslow. *The Principles of Scientific Management.* New York: Harper and Row, 1911.

Terborg-Penn, Rosalyn. "Free Women Entrepreneurs from the 1820s and 1850s:

Nancy Prince and Mary Seacole." In *Crossing Boundaries: Comparative History of Black People in Diaspora*, ed. Darlene Clark Hine and Jacqueline McLeod, 159–75. Bloomington: Indiana University Press, 1999.

Tester, Keith, ed. *The Flaneur*. London: Routledge, 1994.

Theweleit, Klaus. *Male Fantasies*. Trans. Stephen Conway, Erica Carter, and Chris Turner. New York: Polity, 1987, 1989.

Thomas, Helen. *Dance Modernity and Culture: Explorations in the Sociology of Dance*. London: Routledge, 1995.

Thorpe, Edward. *Black Dance*. London: Chatto and Windus, 1989.

Todorov, Tzvetan. *On Human Diversity: Nationalism, Racism, and Exoticism in French Thought*. Trans. Catherine Porter. Cambridge: Harvard University Press, 1993.

Toll, Robert C. *Blacking Up: The Minstrel Show in Nineteenth Century America*. New York: Oxford University Press, 1974.

Tomko, Linda J. *Dancing Class: Gender, Ethnicity, and Social Divides in American Dance, 1890–1920*. Bloomington: Indiana University Press, 1999.

Torgovnick, Marianna. *Gone Primitive: Savage Intellects, Modern Lives*. Chicago: University of Chicago Press, 1990.

Trollope, Frances. *The Life and Adventures of Michael Armstrong, the Factory Boy*. 1840.

———. *Domestic Manners of the Americans*. London: Penguin, 1997.

Tucker, Sherrie. *Swingshift: "All-Girl" Bands of the 1940's*. Durham: Duke University Press, 2000.

———. "'They Got Corns for My Country': Hollywood Canteen Hostesses as Subjects and Objects of Freedom." Paper for the American Studies Association, Atlanta, 2004.

Tucker, Sophie. *Some of These Days*. Garden City, N.Y.: Garden City Publishing, 1946.

Turner, Victor. *Dramas, Fields, and Metaphors: Symbolic Action in Human Society*. Ithaca, N.Y.: Cornell University Press, 1974.

Verges, Françoise. *Monsters and Revolutionaries: Colonial Family Romance and Metissage*. Durham: Duke University Press, 1999.

Von Ankum, Katherina, ed. *Women in the Metropolis: Gender and Modernity in Weimar Germany*. Berkeley: University of California Press, 1997.

Walker, George. "The Real Coon on the American Stage." *Theatre Journal* 6, no. 65 (July 1906): 224–26.

Wall, Cheryl A., ed. *Hurston: Memoirs and Other Writings*. New York: Library of America, 1995.

Waters, Ethel, with Charles Samuel. *His Eye Is on the Sparrow*. New York: Da Capo, 1992.

Watkins, Mel. *Stepin Fetchit: The Life and Times of Lincoln Perry*. New York: Pantheon, 2005.

Watts, Jill. *Hattie McDaniel: Black Ambition, White Hollywood*. New York: Amistad, 2005.

Weld, Theodore Dwight. *American Slavery as It Is: Testimony of a Thousand Witnesses*. 1839. Reprint, New York: Arno, 1968.

Wells, Ida B. *Southern Horrors and Other Writings: The Anti-Lynching Campaign of Ida B. Wells, 1892–1900*, ed. Jacqueline Jones Royster. New York: Bedford, 1997.

West, Mae. *Goodness Had Nothing to Do with It*. Englewood Cliffs, N.J.: Prentice-Hall, 1959.

Wheelock, Sarah. "Octoroon Madams and White Slavery: Sexual Slavery in the American Imagination, 1890–1930." Unfinished Ph.D. diss., Yale University.

White, Deborah Gray. *Ar'n't I a Woman? Female Slaves in the Plantation South*. New York: W. W. Norton, 1985.

——. *Too Heavy a Load: Black Women in Defense of Themselves, 1894–1994*. New York: W. W. Norton, 1999.

White, Dorothy Shipley. *Black Africa and de Gaulle: From the French Empire to Independence*. University Park: Pennsylvania State University Press, 1979.

Wideman, John Edgar. *The Stories of John Edgar Wideman*. New York: Pantheon, 1992.

——. "Valaida." In *Fever: Twelve Stories by John Edgar Wideman*. New York: Henry Holt, 1989.

Wiedemann, Eric. *Jazz i Danmark: I Tyverne, Trediverne, og Fyrverne*. Copenhagen: Gyldendalske Boghandel, 1982.

Wiegman, Robyn. *American Anatomies: Theorizing Race and Gender*. Durham: Duke University Press, 1995.

Williams, Judith. "Uma Mulata Sim! Arci Cortes, the 'Mulatta' of the Teatro de Revista." *Women and Performance* 16, no. 1 (March 2006): 7–26.

Willis, Deborah, and Carla Williams. *The Black Female Body: A Photographic History*. Philadelphia: Temple University Press, 2002.

Wittke, Carl. *Tambo and Bones: A History of the American Minstrel Stage*. Durham: Duke University Press, 1930.

Wolf, Eric R. *Europe and the People without History*. Berkeley: University of California Press, 1982.

Wolin, Richard. *Walter Benjamin: An Aesthetic of Redemption*. New York: Columbia University Press, 1982.

Woll, Allen. *Black Musical Theater: From Coontown to Dreamgirls*. New York: Da Capo, 1989.

Wood, Marcus. *Blind Memory: Visual Representations of Slavery in England and America, 1780–1865*. London: Routledge, 2000.

Yellin, Jean Fagin. *Women and Sisters: The Antislavery Feminists in American Culture*. New Haven: Yale University Press, 1989.

Young, Robert. *Colonial Desire: Hybridity in Theory, Culture and Race*. London: Routledge, 1995.

Zwerin, Mike. *La Tristesse de Saint Louis: Jazz under the Nazis*. New York: William Morrow, 1985.

body (*continued*)
women and, 2, 6–7; captive, 84; as
contested site, 59; distortion of, 89;
expressivity of black body, 79; fragmentary, 16; market value of sexu-
ality and, 233; in motion, 60–61;
racialized, 58, 60; racist hegemony
and, 61; science and, 59, 77; Topsy
and, 58–59; violence and inscription
of ownership, 80; working-class
cultures of male body, 131; working
women's, 7, 99
Bolitho, William, 224–26
Boucicault, Dion, 106
Bowman, Laura, 13, 37
Brandow, Russell, 126–27
Bricktop, 241–43
Brody, Jennifer, 106
Brooks, Daphne, 282
Brooks, Lori, 140
Broun, Heywood, 219–20, 246
Brown, Sterling, 234–36
Brown, William Wells, 43–44
Buffalo Bill's Wild Wild West Show,
100, 138–41
burlesque: black, 95–97; blackface
minstrelsy and, 98; class and, 104–
5; female minstrelsy and, 57, 92;
minstrel shows as models for, 99;
mulatto and mixed-race women in,
102, 105; prostitution and, 108; style
and, 99; variety shows prefigured by,
117–18. *See also Creole Show, The*
Bush, Anita, 160

cakewalk, 110, 128–29, 132–37, 140,
143–44, 150–55; civic body and, 136;
class and, 134; counterhegemonic,
130; as critique of black bourgeoisie,
146–47; plantation origin of, 130; as
system of multiplicities, 145
Carby, Hazel, 135
Cartwright, Samuel, 48, 79

Castle, Irene, 2, 157, 170–71, 173–74,
211–12
Castle, Vernon, 170–71, 173–74
Caution, Ethel, 232
Chandler, Elizabeth, 72–73
Charleston, 3, 170, 198, 204
Chicago World's Fair, 100–101, 140
children, 22, 24–27, 30–35, 77; as
laborers, 41–42, 45–47; mimicry
and, 40; transnational worldviews
of, 21. *See also* Gollywog; picaninny;
picaninny chorus
Chocolate Dandies, 204–5
circle dance, 161–63
Clarke, Lewis, 44, 82
class, 38; gender and, 130–32
Clifford, James, 9–10, 13
*Clorindy, or the Origins of the Cake-
walk* (Cook), 146–49
Cole, Bob, 111–12, 115, 117–20, 122–26,
186, 229
colonialism: African American subjects and, 26; anthropology and,
87, 103; black subjugation and, 35;
black urban migration and, 103;
city and colony under, 93, 101; consent and, 103; European primitivisms and, 2; missionary programs
and, 65; Monticello and, 24; national belonging and, 240; nativism
and, 217; New Woman and, 175;
nostalgia and, 66; orientalism and,
96, 117, 176; picaninnies and, 30,
47; plantation and colonial lore, 55,
58, 65
Combe, George, 78
concubinage, 11, 53–54, 95, 103. *See
also* Hemings, Sally; orientalism
Connelly, Marc, 236–37
Cook, James, 29, 287n14
Cook, Will Marion, 118–19, 146–48
coon song, 148–49
Coote, Berte, 289n76

cosmopolitanism, 93
Costello, Julian, 210
Cotton Club, 201–2
Crabtree, Charlotte, 68–71, 74
Creole Show, The, 2, 19, 50, 92–97, 100, 102, 105. *See also* burlesque
Cunard, Nancy, 211
Cunliffe, Marcus, 42

dance, 13–16, 61–62; bodily contact and, 172; centrality in black culture of, 58–59; as critique of ownership, 85; as folk transmission, 230; kinetic vocabularies of, 38; mobility and, 13; orientalism and, 157; post-emancipation mobility and, 82; racialized female movement and, 102; Topsy and, 59. *See also* cakewalk; Charleston; circle dance
Darktown Follies, 2, 156–57, 160–64, 170
Darktown Frolic, A, 118
Darktown Frolics (Forsyne), 33
"Danse Africaine" (Hughes), 231–32
Daulne, Marie, 284
Davis, Belle, 19–20, 30–40, 46–47, 50, 118, 148–49
Dean, Dora, 50, 134, 152–54
de Certeau, Michel, 125
de Gaulle, Charles, 258–61
Delsarte, François, 177
de Nerval, Gerard, 254
Deschamps, Hubert, 253–54
Desmond, Jane, 14, 69
de Tocqueville, Alexis, 90
Dickens, Charles, 27–30
Dixie to Broadway (Leslie), 219–21
Domestic Manners of the Americans (Trollope), 29–30
double consciousness, 135; black women's experience of, 17
Douglas, Louis, 32, 40–41, 89, 239
Douglass, Frederick, 47, 81

Du Bois, W. E. B. 116–17, 135
Dunbar, Paul Laurence, 146–48
Duncan, Isadora, 181
Duncan Sisters, 69, 76

Edwards, Brent Hayes, 225–26
Egneby, Elis, 264–65
Ellis, Havelock, 158–59, 230–31
Employment of Children Act, 46
Erenburg, Lewis, 168–69, 171
ethnicity, 124–25
Europe, James Reese, 250

Fabian, Johannes, 87
farce, 5, 76–77, 97, 112, 124–25
Faulkner, Thomas, 172
Felix, Seymour, 170
Filipino insurrection, 115
Fletcher, Thomas, 64, 143–44
Fornas, Johan, 272
Forsyne, Ida, 7, 22, 31–33, 37, 39, 62, 89–90, 163, 213–14; cakewalk, 142; as Topsy, 34, 55–56, 61
Foucault, Michel, 129
Frohman, Charles, 64
Fugitive Slave Law, 42
Fuller, Loie, 176

Garelick, Rhonda, 176
Garland, Judy, 69
Georgia Picaninnies, 32
gestural technique, 61, 62, 157
gestural vocabulary, 130, 213
Gilroy, Paul, 88
Gliddon, George, 78
Goldman, Emma, 132
Golliwog, 65–66, 291n25
Gray, Gilda, 212–13
Great White Way, 2, 210
Green, Cora, 192
Green, Nancy, 66
Green Pastures (Connelly), 236–37
Gregory, Montgomery, 75–76
Grosz, Elizabeth, 59–60

Lucas, Sam, 64, 92
Lundkvist, Arthur, 271

Madison Square Garden, 26, 142–44
Marshall, Marjorie, 232–33
Mason, Patrick, 115–16
Mastered by the Clock (Smith), 87
Mattison, Hiram, 54
McClain, Billy, 138–39, 141
McKay, Claude, 229–30, 233
Meltzer, Milton, 92–93, 148
Melville, Herman, 26
Michael Armstrong (Trollope), 46
Micheaux, Oscar, 192–93
military, 114–17
Mills, Florence, 20, 207–8, 211–12,
    240, 245–50
minstrelsy: absorption of, 73; chorus
    line dancers and, 57; racialized
    gestural techniques and, 157; white
    female, 99–100; whiteness and, 74.
    See also blackface; whiteface
miscegenation, 219, 223–25
Mississippi River flood (1927), 234–36
Mitchell, Abbie, 22, 33, 56, 148
mobility, 11–12, 227; black people and,
    9–10; black urban migration as, 103,
    245; black vernacular dance and, 13
Moby Dick (Melville), 26–27
Modern Dancing (Castle), 173
Morton, Samuel, 77–78
Mumford, Kevin, 17, 117
My Great Wide Beautiful World
    (Harrison), 11–12, 286n19

nativism, 217–18
Nazis, 242–43; Austria annexed by,
    268; black men forcibly sterilized
    by, 275; black people viewed by, 274;
    Danish jazzers detained by, 273; jazz
    viewed by, 269–70
Negro Renaissance, 75
Nenno, Nancy, 4
Noddy (Blyton), 65
Nott, Josiah, 78

Octoroon (Boucicault), 106
Octoroons, The (Isham), 112–13
Oh Joy!, 203–4
Oriental America, 103, 117–18, 133
Orientalism, 69, 101–4, 122, 154, 175,
    178–79, 181–82, 254; burlesque and,
    95–96; modern dance and, 157; in
    Uncle Tom's Cabin, 78, 85–86. *See
    also* Salome craze
Origin of Species, The (Darwin), 78
Our Gang, 66–67
Overton, Aida, 9, 133, 150, 158, 180–88,
    279

Palace Theatre, 33–35, 55–56
Palmer, Aaron, 35–36
Pastor, Tony, 294n46
Petro, Patrice, 168
phrenology, 78
picaninny, 25–26, 65–67, 89; as colo-
    nial subject, 30; female, 71; *pica-
    yune*, 23–24; as representative of
    "childlike races," 55
picaninny chorus, 23, 26, 48–50, 89;
    Belle Davis and Her Picaninnies,
    19–20, 30–35, 38–40, 46–47; Geor-
    gia Picaninnies, 32; racial and sexual
    politics and, 2, 21–22; slavery and,
    41
Picquet, Louisa, 54
plantation, 23, 38, 41–48, 54–55, 58;
    children and, 24; *Darktown Follies*
    and "inheritance" of, 161; as family,
    25; plantation staging, 26, 139–40,
    142–43, 207–8; time and, 88; as
    transnational site, 85. *See also* pica-
    ninny
Plantation Club, 207
Plessy v. Ferguson, 135
possession, 255
Powell, Adam Clayton, 173
primitivism, 2, 9, 30, 47–48, 86–87,
    221; Harlem and, 228; modernism
    and, 191. *See also* time

JAYNA BROWN is an assistant professor of ethnic studies at the University of
California, Riverside.

Library of Congress Cataloging-in-Publication Data

Brown, Jayna, 1966–
Babylon girls : black women performers and the shaping of the modern /
Jayna Brown.
p. cm.
Includes bibliographical references and index.
ISBN 978-0-8223-4133-8 (cloth : alk. paper) —
ISBN 978-0-8223-4157-4 (pbk. : alk. paper)
1. African American women entertainers—Biography. I. Title.
PN2286.B76 2008
791.092′396073—dc22
[B]
2008011050

Amy Bieber
Dan Mueller